PandoraHearts

Jun Mochizuki

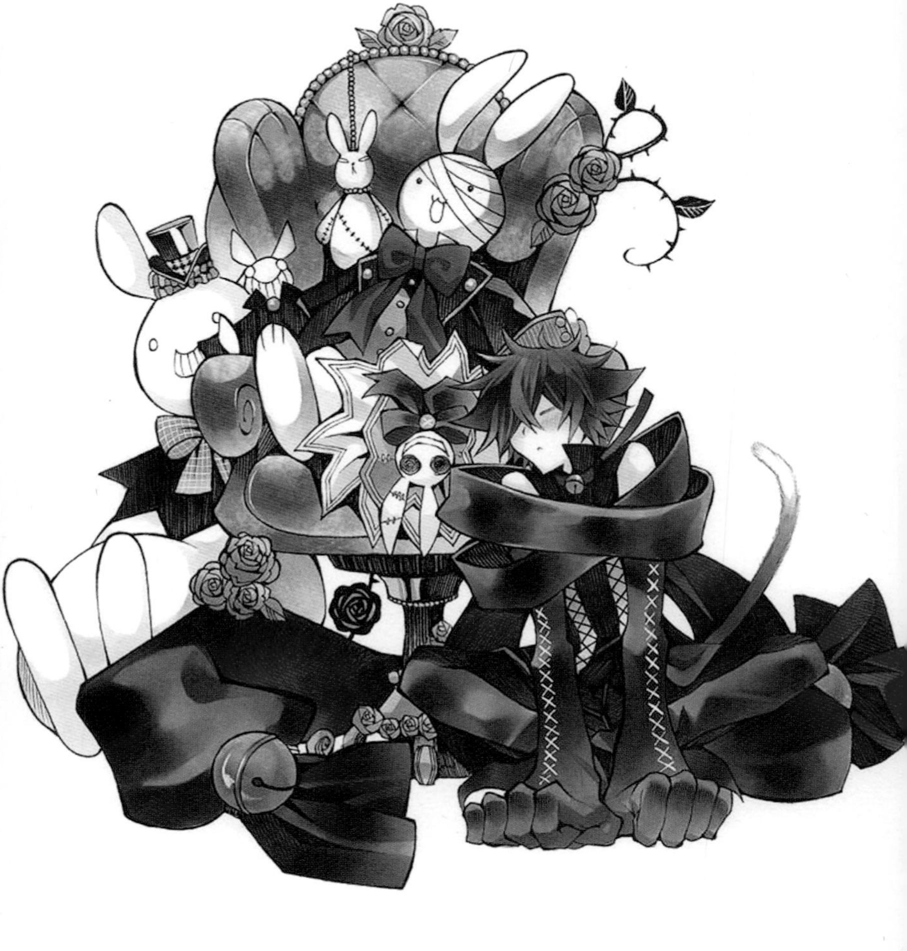

CONTENTS

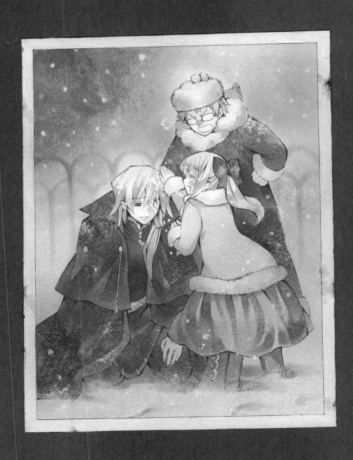

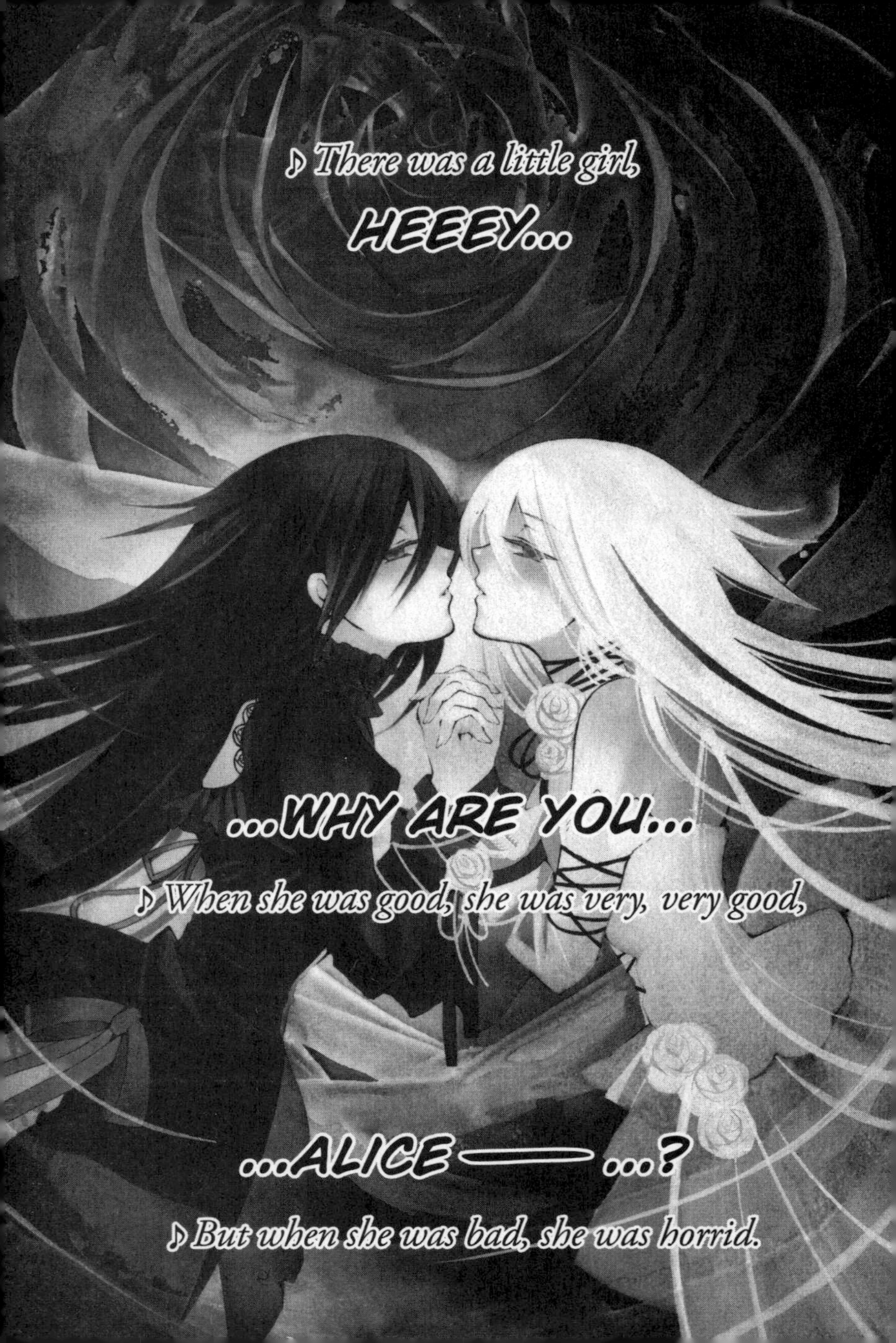
♪ There was a little girl,
HEEEY...
...WHY ARE YOU...
♪ When she was good, she was very, very good,
...ALICE——...?
♪ But when she was bad, she was horrid.

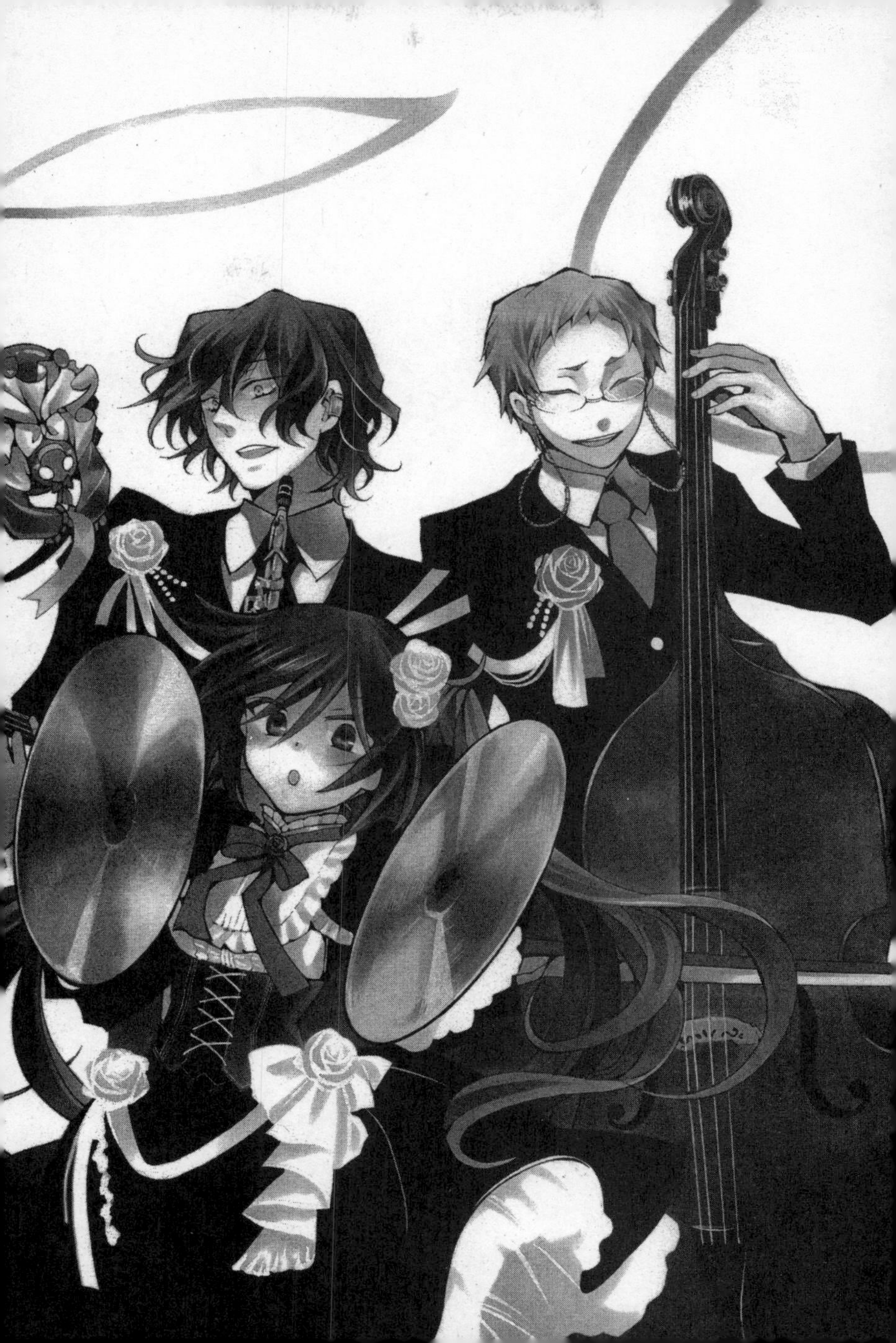

Retrace:XXXI
Countervalue of loss

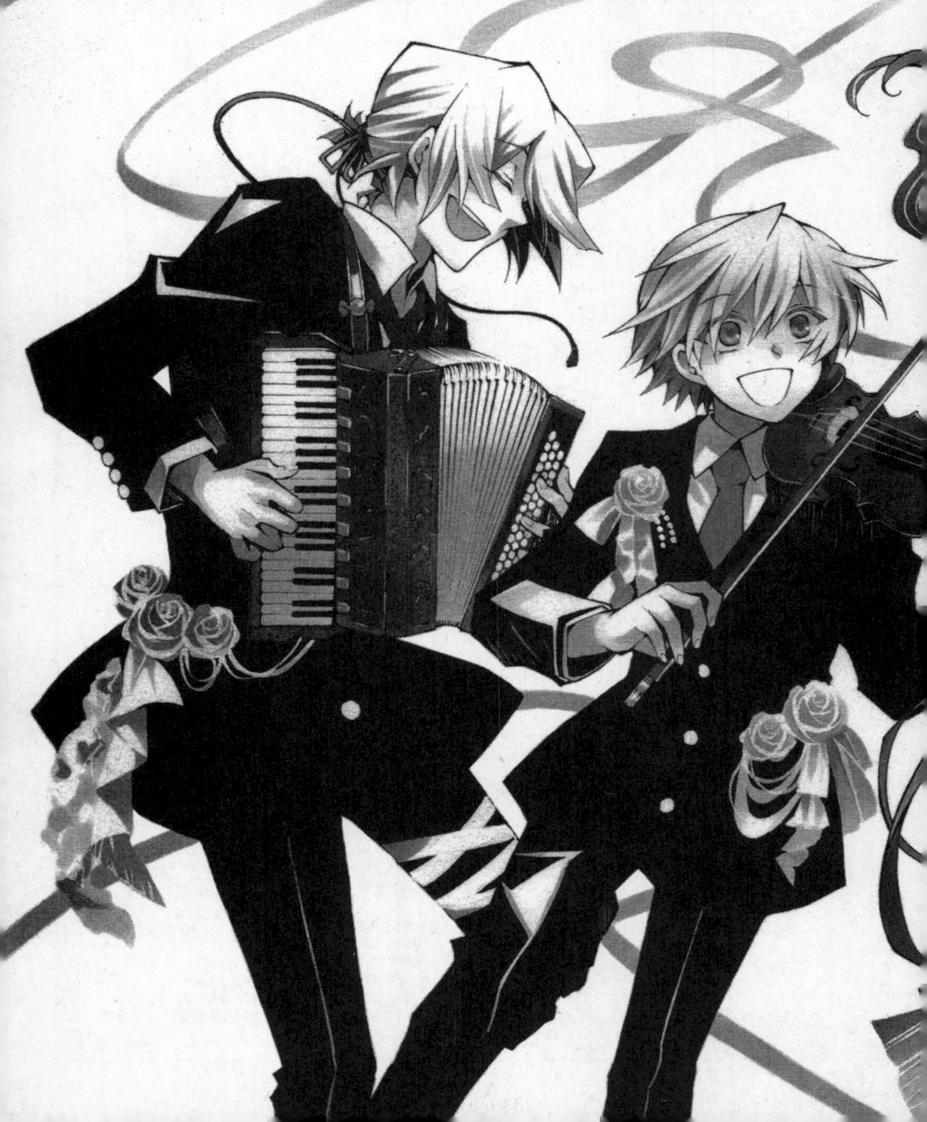

BONUS: "GO FOR IT!! LITTLE REIM-SAN!" ①

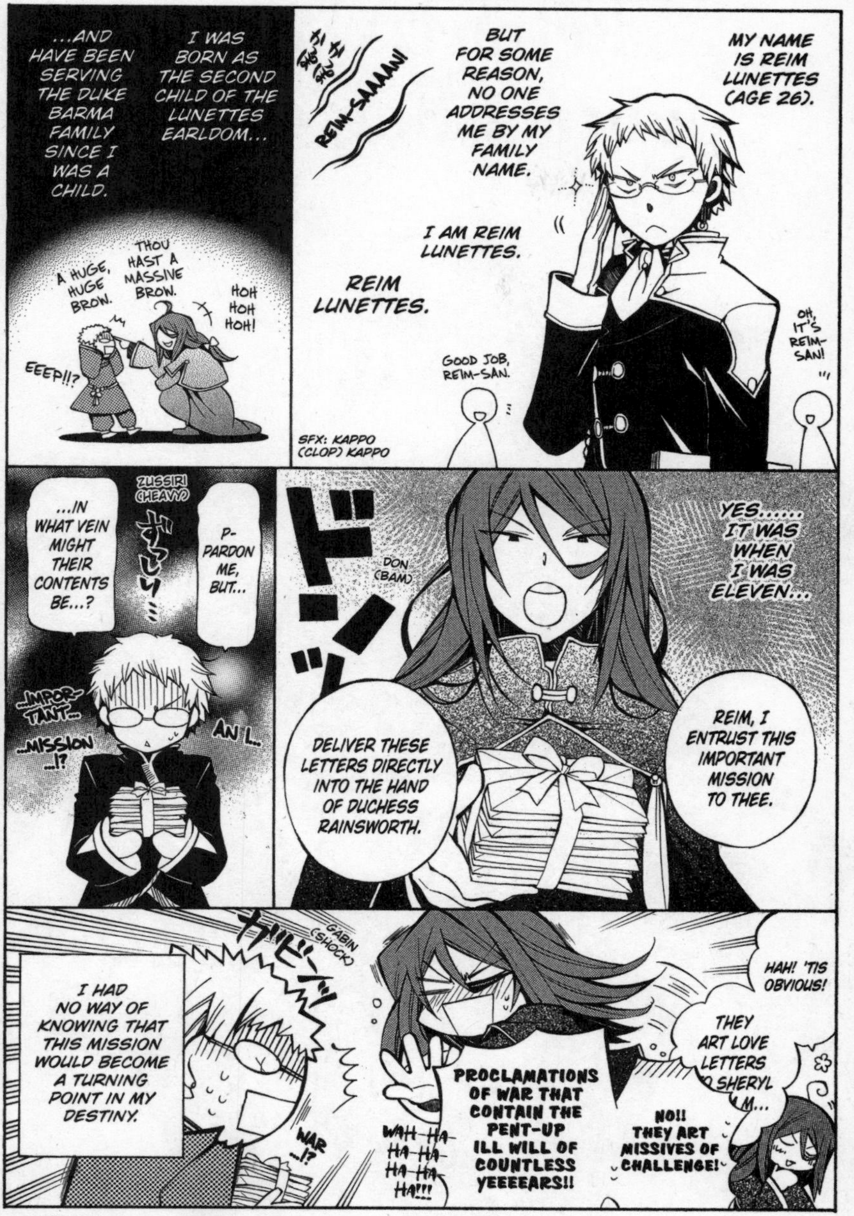
MY NAME IS REIM LUNETTES (AGE 26).
BUT FOR SOME REASON, NO ONE ADDRESSES ME BY MY FAMILY NAME.
REIM-SAAAAN!
I AM REIM LUNETTES.
REIM LUNETTES.
OH, IT'S REIM-SAN!
GOOD JOB, REIM-SAN.
SFX: KAPPO (CLOP) KAPPO
I WAS BORN AS THE SECOND CHILD OF THE LUNETTES EARLDOM...
...AND HAVE BEEN SERVING THE DUKE BARMA FAMILY SINCE I WAS A CHILD.
HOH HOH HOH!
THOU HAST A MASSIVE BROW.
A HUGE, HUGE BROW.
EEEP!!?
YES...... IT WAS WHEN I WAS ELEVEN...
REIM, I ENTRUST THIS IMPORTANT MISSION TO THEE.
DON (BAM)
DELIVER THESE LETTERS DIRECTLY INTO THE HAND OF DUCHESS RAINSWORTH.
P-PARDON ME, BUT...
ZUSSIRI (HEAVY)
...IN WHAT VEIN MIGHT THEIR CONTENTS BE...?
...IMPOR-TANT...
...MISSION ...!?
HAH! 'TIS OBVIOUS!
THEY ART LOVE LETTERS
NO!! THEY ART MISSIVES OF CHALLENGE!
PROCLAMATIONS OF WAR THAT CONTAIN THE PENT-UP ILL WILL OF COUNTLESS YEEEEARS!!
WAH-HA-HA-HA-HA-HA!!!
GABIN (SHOCK)
WAR ...!?
I HAD NO WAY OF KNOWING THAT THIS MISSION WOULD BECOME A TURNING POINT IN MY DESTINY.

CONT'D.

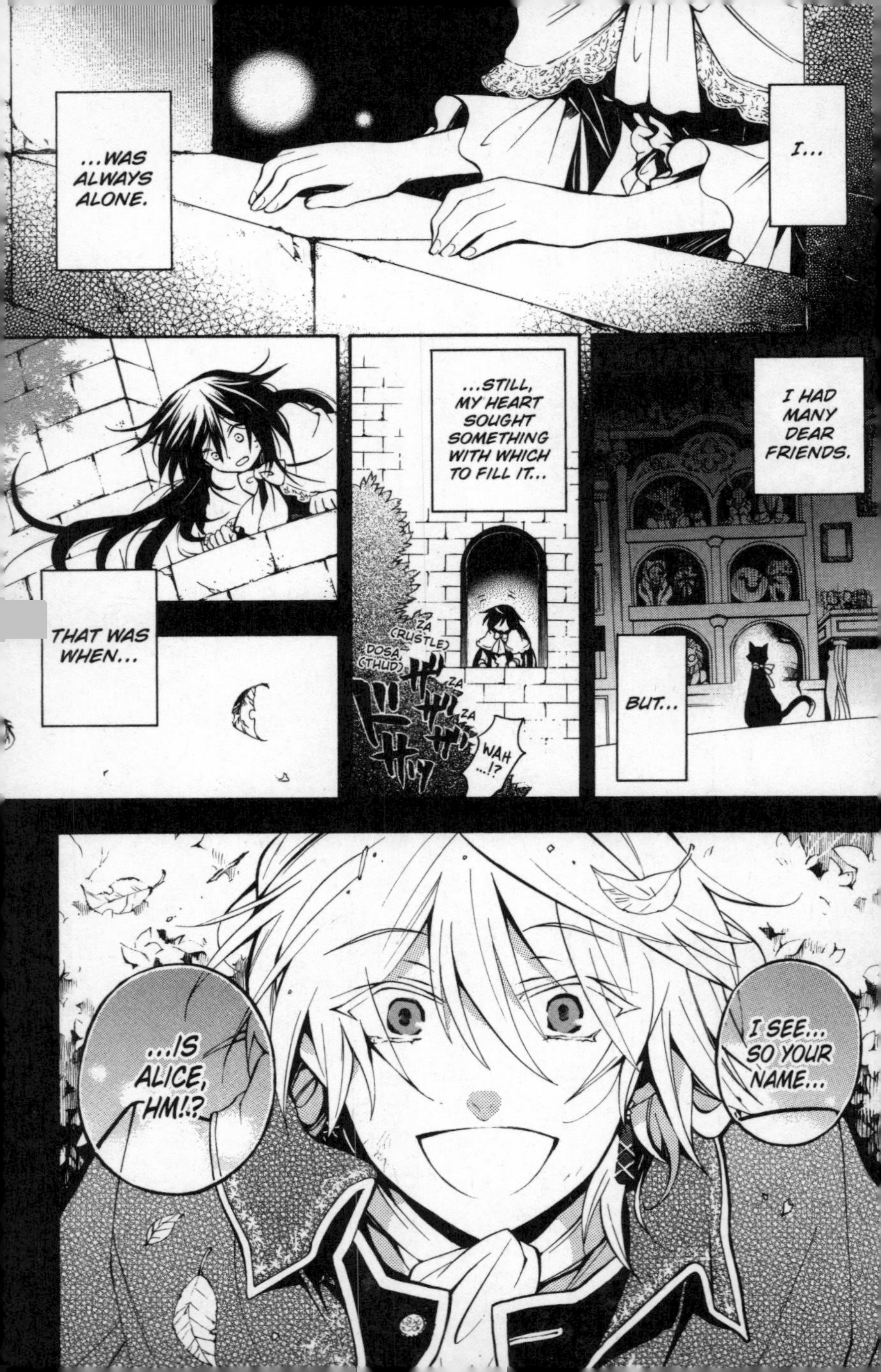
I...
...WAS ALWAYS ALONE.
I HAD MANY DEAR FRIENDS.
BUT...
...STILL, MY HEART SOUGHT SOMETHING WITH WHICH TO FILL IT...
ZA (RUSTLE)
DOSA (THUD)
ZA
ZA
WAH ...!?
THAT WAS WHEN...
I SEE... SO YOUR NAME...
...IS ALICE, HM!?

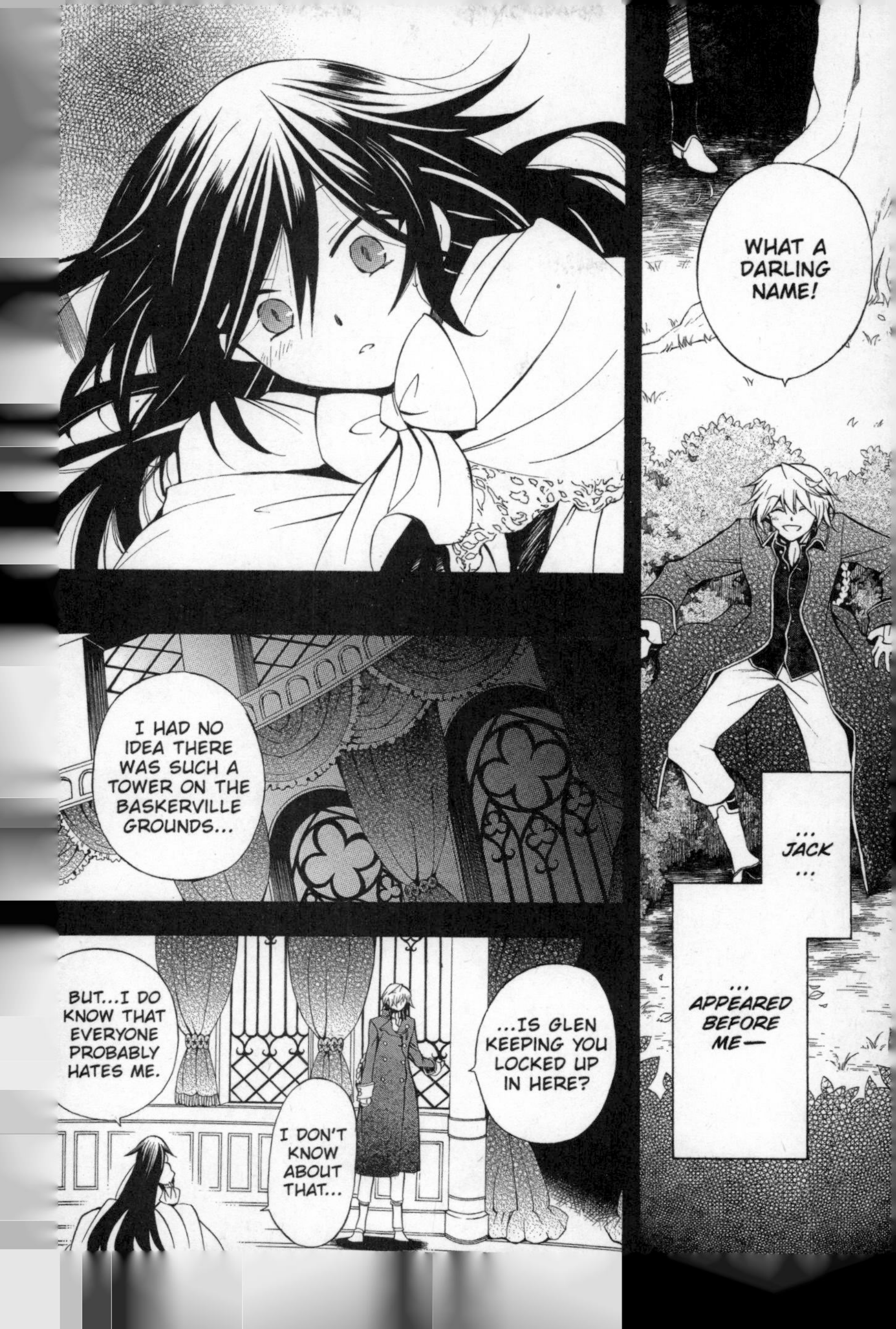
WHAT A DARLING NAME!
...JACK...
...APPEARED BEFORE ME—
I HAD NO IDEA THERE WAS SUCH A TOWER ON THE BASKERVILLE GROUNDS...
...IS GLEN KEEPING YOU LOCKED UP IN HERE?
I DON'T KNOW ABOUT THAT...
BUT...I DO KNOW THAT EVERYONE PROBABLY HATES ME.

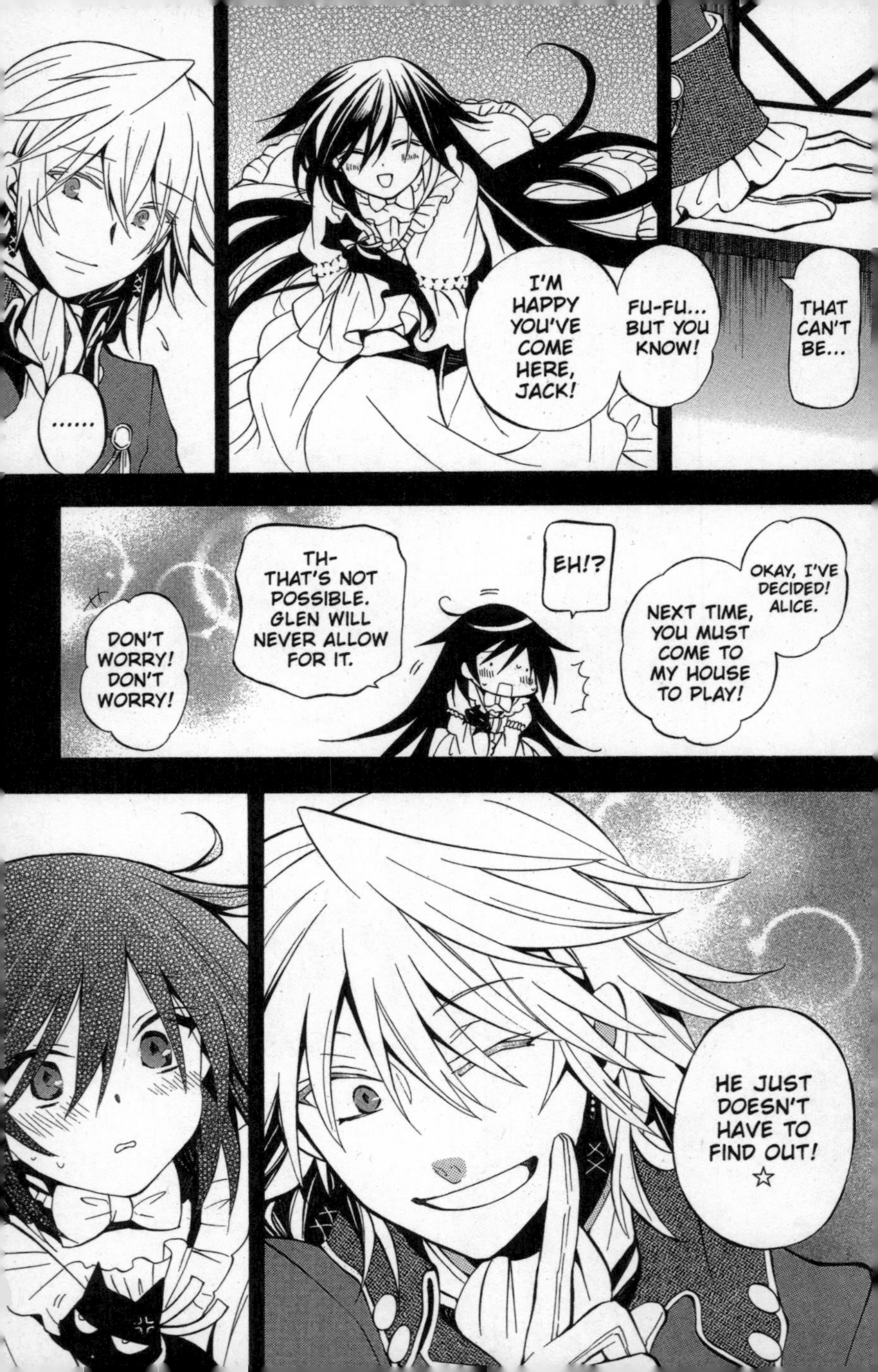
THAT CAN'T BE...
FU-FU... BUT YOU KNOW!
I'M HAPPY YOU'VE COME HERE, JACK!
......
OKAY, I'VE DECIDED! ALICE.
NEXT TIME, YOU MUST COME TO MY HOUSE TO PLAY!
EH!?
TH- THAT'S NOT POSSIBLE. GLEN WILL NEVER ALLOW FOR IT.
DON'T WORRY! DON'T WORRY!
HE JUST DOESN'T HAVE TO FIND OUT! ☆

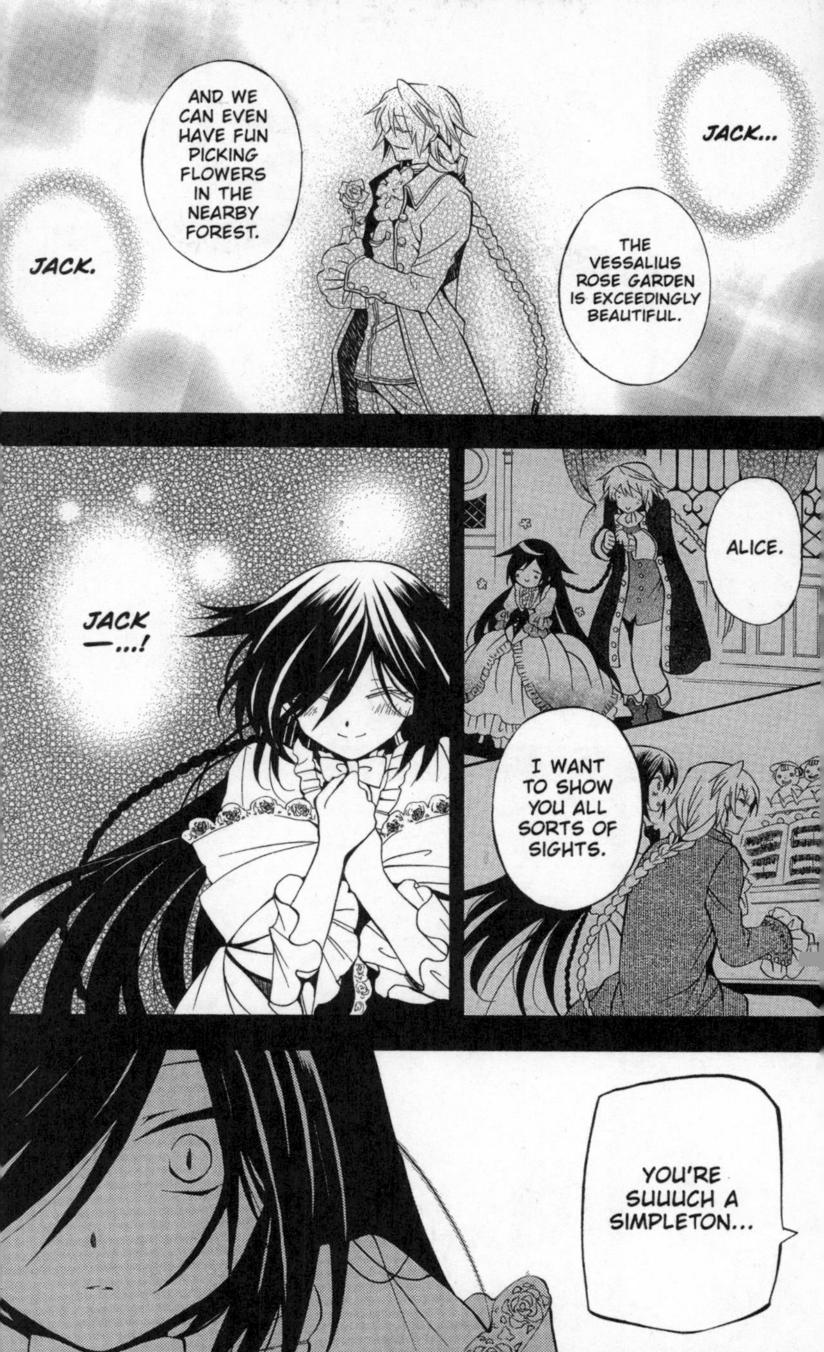
JACK...
THE VESSALIUS ROSE GARDEN IS EXCEEDINGLY BEAUTIFUL.
AND WE CAN EVEN HAVE FUN PICKING FLOWERS IN THE NEARBY FOREST.
JACK.
ALICE.
I WANT TO SHOW YOU ALL SORTS OF SIGHTS.
JACK —...!
YOU'RE SUUUCH A SIMPLETON...

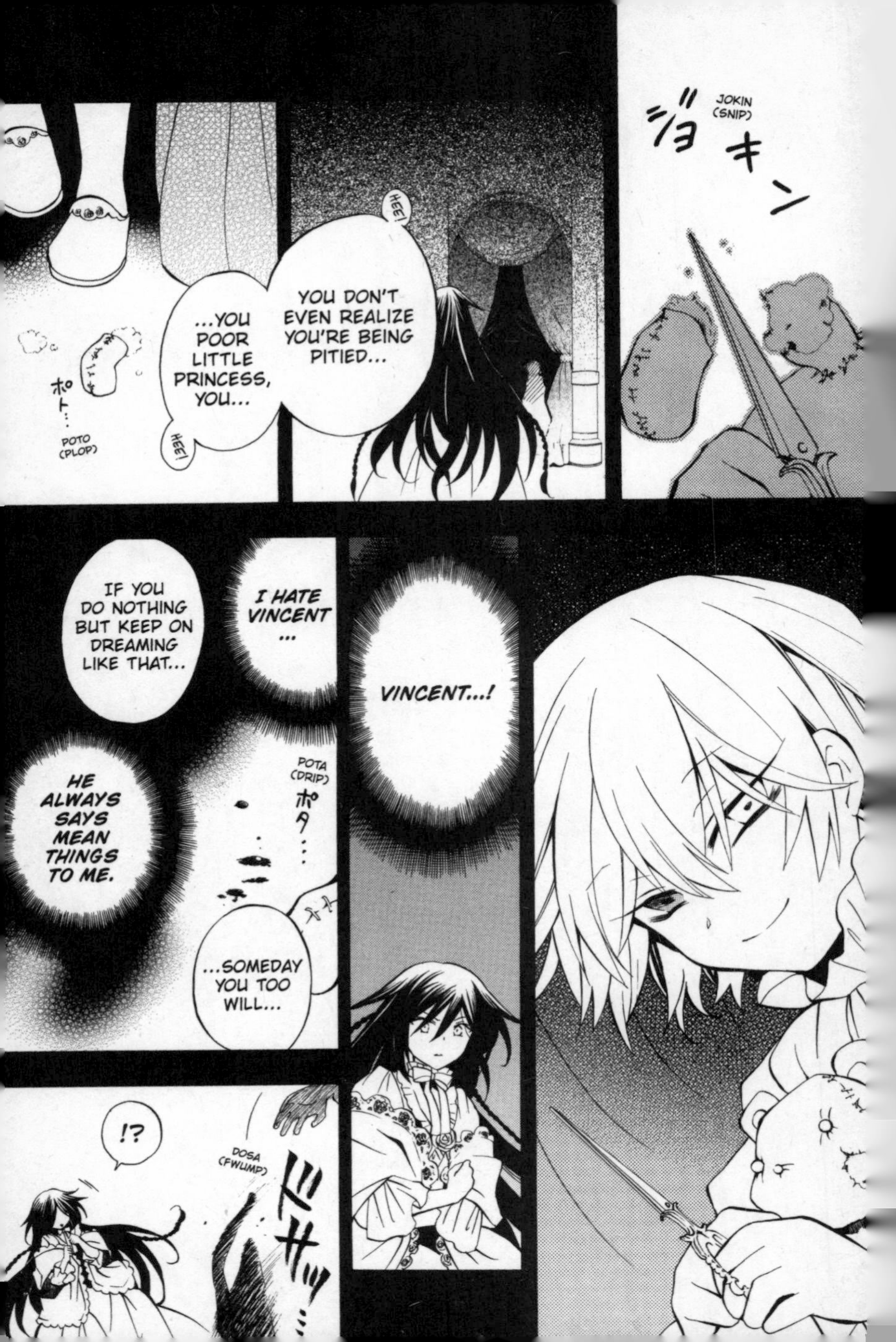
JOKIN (SNIP)
ジョキン
HEE!
YOU DON'T EVEN REALIZE YOU'RE BEING PITIED...
...YOU POOR LITTLE PRINCESS, YOU...
HEE!
ポト…
POTO (PLOP)
VINCENT...!
I HATE VINCENT ...
IF YOU DO NOTHING BUT KEEP ON DREAMING LIKE THAT...
HE ALWAYS SAYS MEAN THINGS TO ME.
POTA (DRIP)
ポタ…
...SOMEDAY YOU TOO WILL...
DOSA (FWUMP)
ドサッ
!?

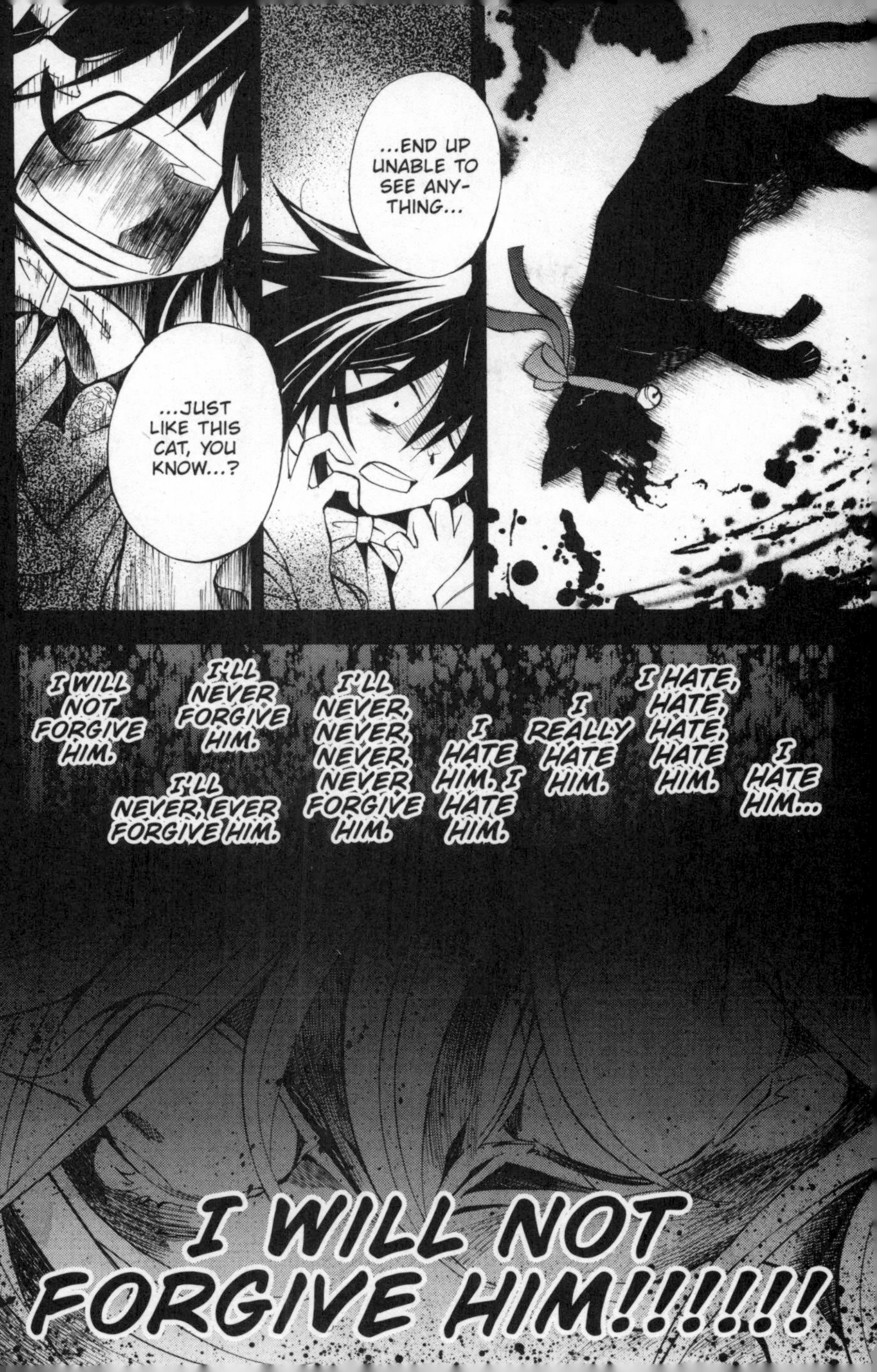
...END UP UNABLE TO SEE ANYTHING...
...JUST LIKE THIS CAT, YOU KNOW...?
I HATE HIM...
I HATE, HATE, HATE, HATE HIM.
I REALLY HATE HIM.
I HATE HIM. I HATE HIM.
I'LL NEVER, NEVER, NEVER, NEVER FORGIVE HIM.
I'LL NEVER FORGIVE HIM.
I'LL NEVER, EVER FORGIVE HIM.
I WILL NOT FORGIVE HIM.
I WILL NOT FORGIVE HIM!!!!!!

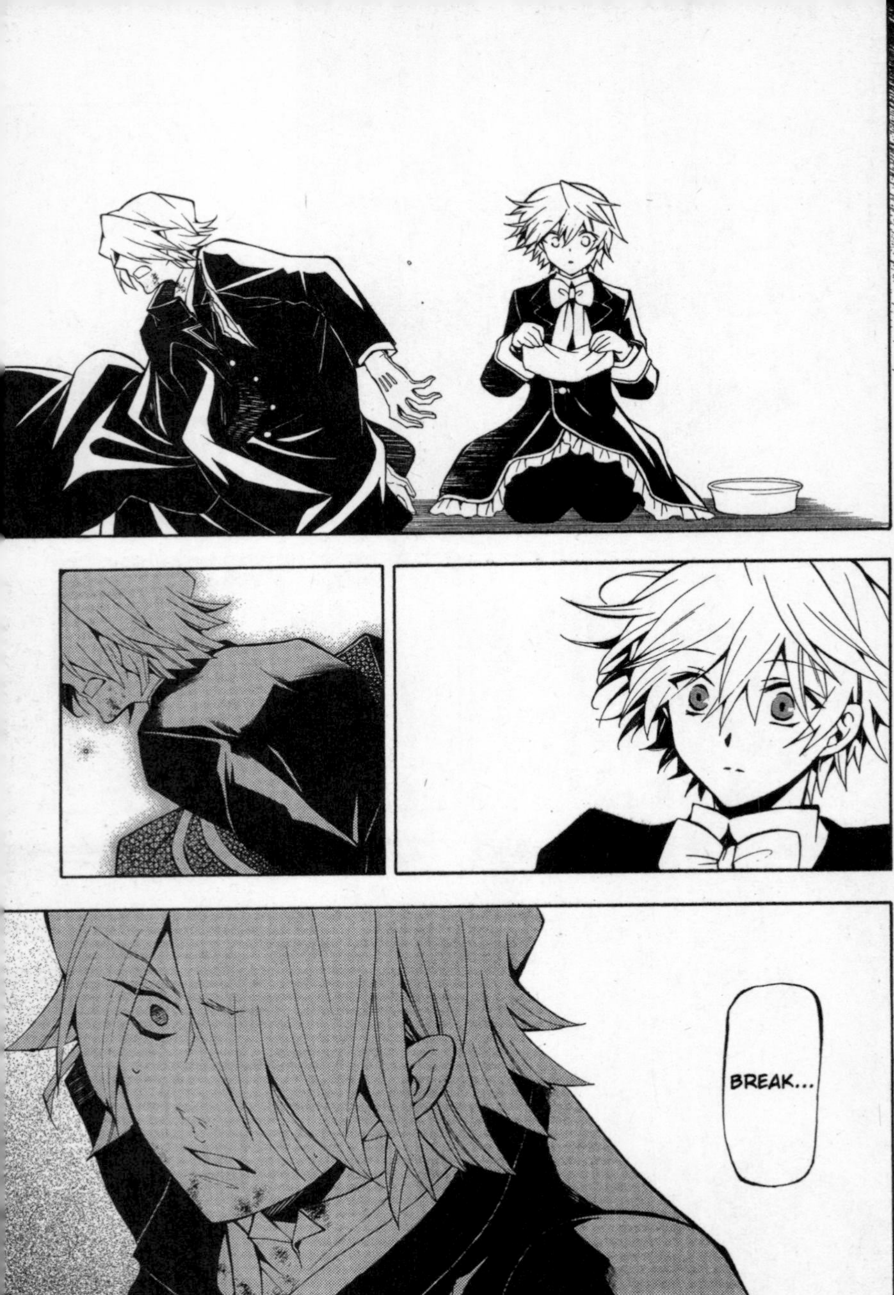
BREAK...

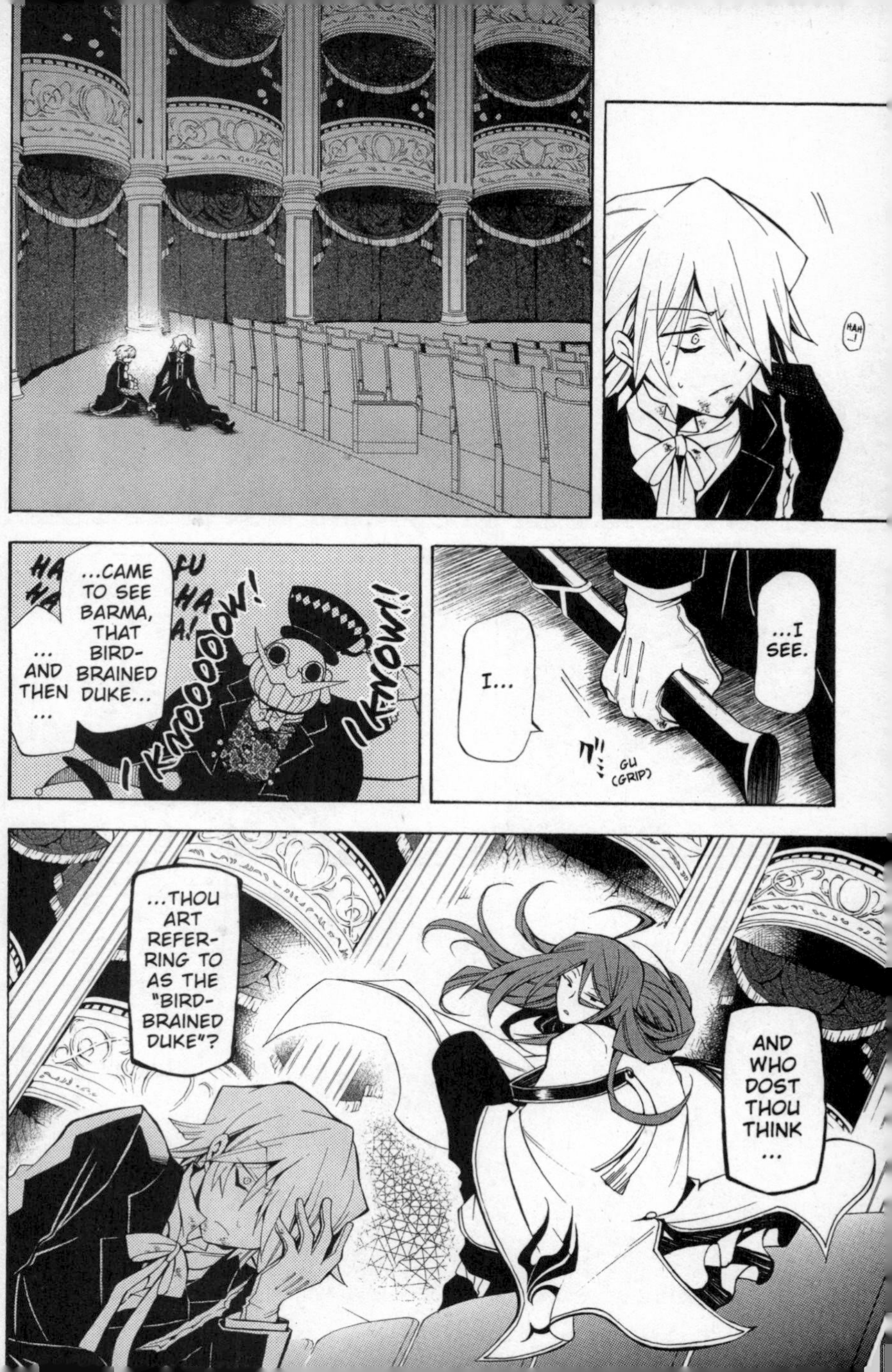
HAH ...!
...I SEE.
I...
GU (GRIP)
I KNOW!!
...CAME TO SEE BARMA, THAT BIRD-BRAINED DUKE...
... AND THEN ...
I KNOOOOOW!
AND WHO DOST THOU THINK ...
...THOU ART REFERRING TO AS THE "BIRD-BRAINED DUKE"?

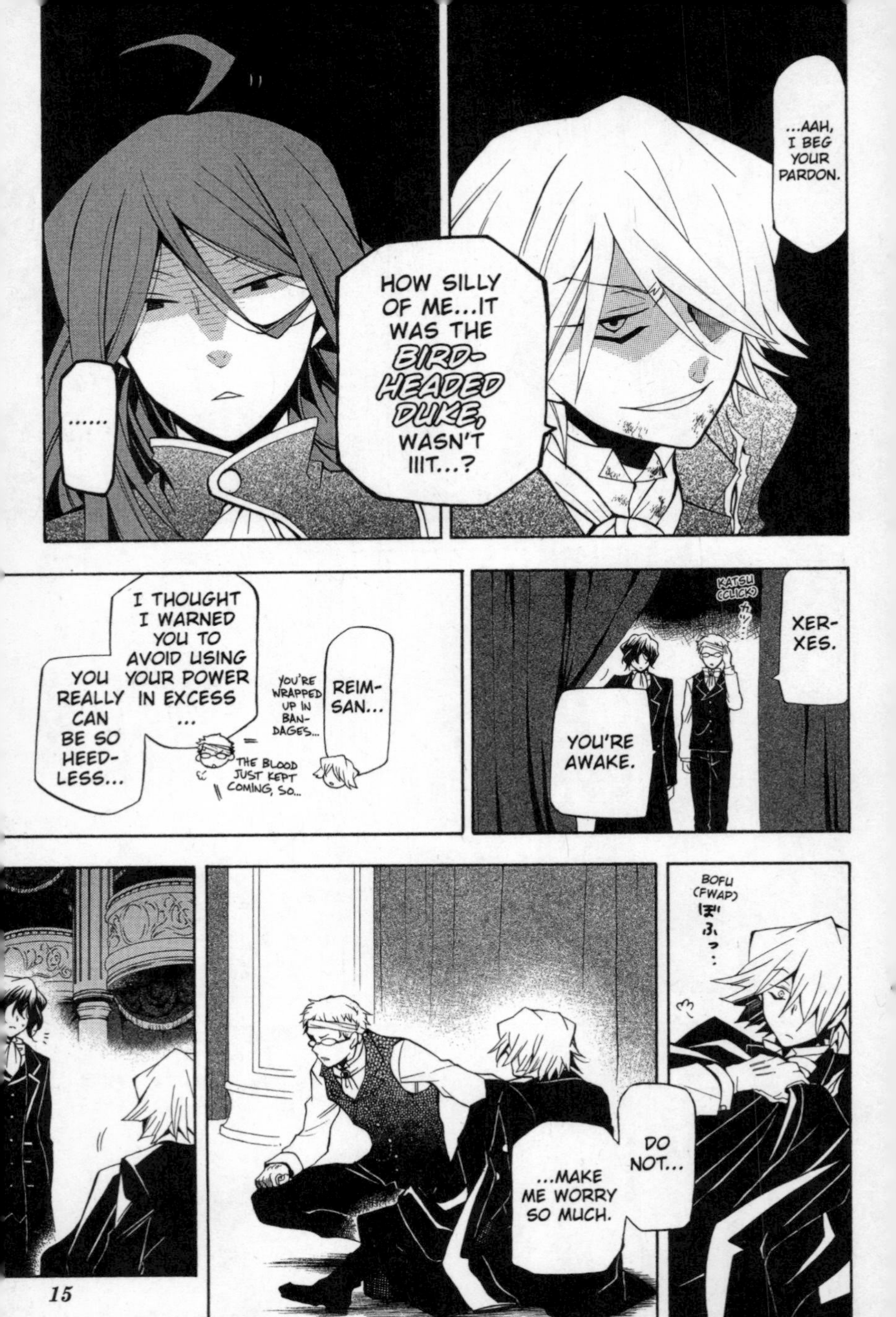
...AAH, I BEG YOUR PARDON.
HOW SILLY OF ME...IT WAS THE BIRD-HEADED DUKE, WASN'T IIIT...?
......
KATSU (CLICK)
カッ
XER-XES.
YOU'RE AWAKE.
REIM-SAN...
YOU'RE WRAPPED UP IN BAN-DAGES...
THE BLOOD JUST KEPT COMING, SO...
I THOUGHT I WARNED YOU TO AVOID USING YOUR POWER IN EXCESS...
YOU REALLY CAN BE SO HEED-LESS...
BOFU (FWAP)
ぼふっ
DO NOT...
...MAKE ME WORRY SO MUCH.

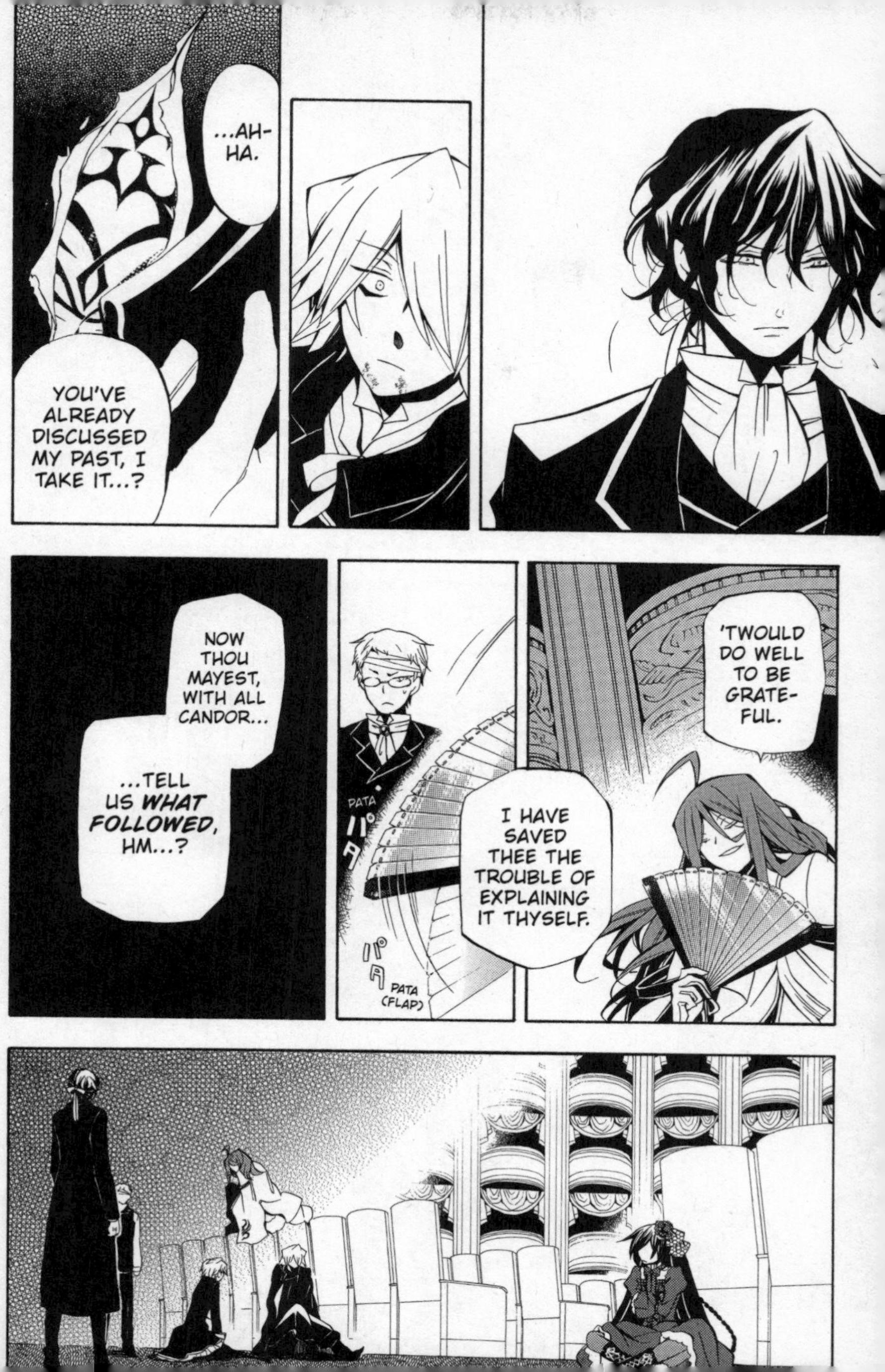
...AH-HA.
YOU'VE ALREADY DISCUSSED MY PAST, I TAKE IT...?
'TWOULD DO WELL TO BE GRATE-FUL.
I HAVE SAVED THEE THE TROUBLE OF EXPLAINING IT THYSELF.
PATA
PATA (FLAP)
NOW THOU MAYEST, WITH ALL CANDOR...
...TELL US *WHAT FOLLOWED*, HM...?

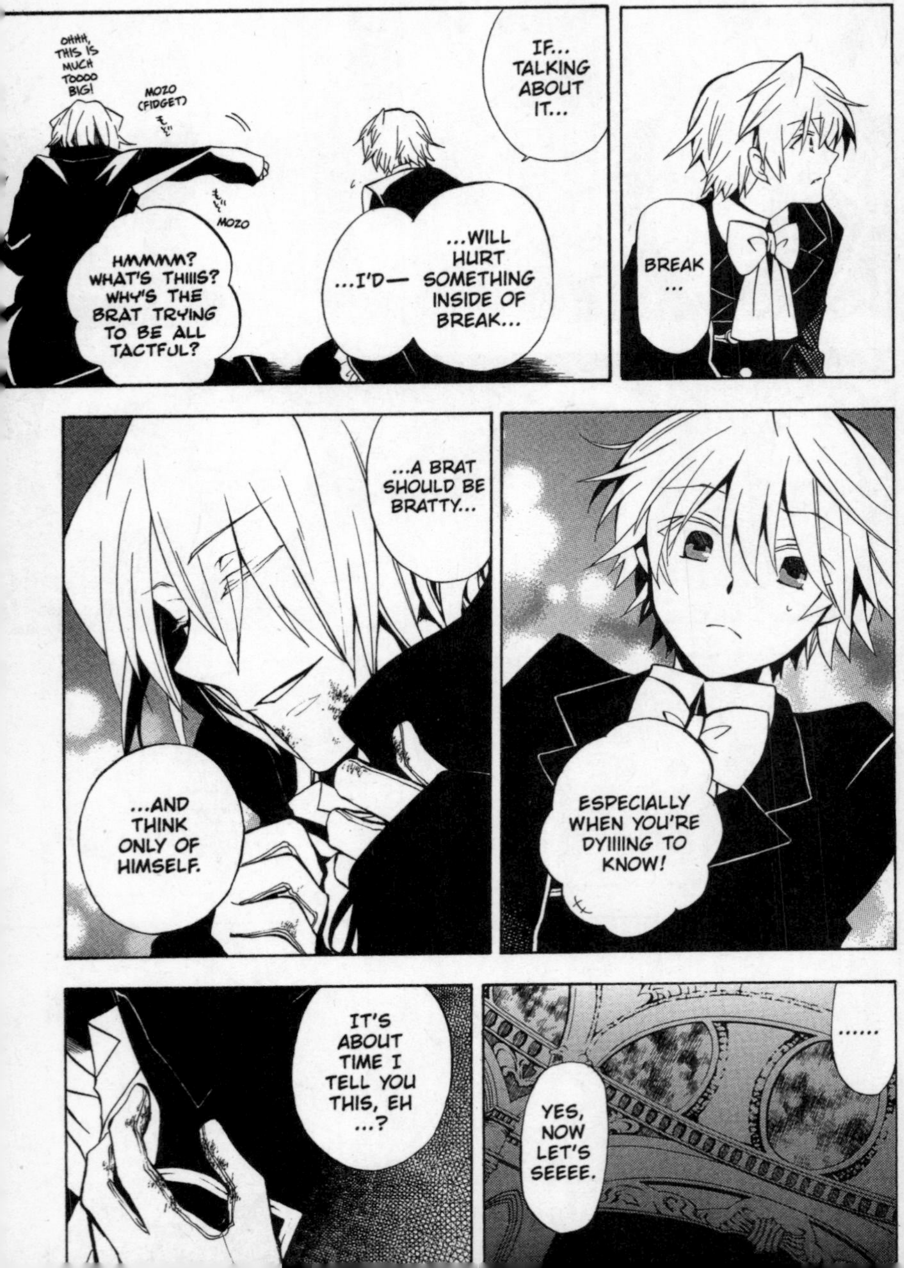
BREAK ...
IF... TALKING ABOUT IT...
...WILL HURT SOMETHING INSIDE OF BREAK...
...I'D—
OHHH, THIS IS MUCH TOOOO BIG!
MOZO (FIDGET)
MOZO
HMMMM? WHAT'S THIIIS? WHY'S THE BRAT TRYING TO BE ALL TACTFUL?
ESPECIALLY WHEN YOU'RE DYIIIING TO KNOW!
...A BRAT SHOULD BE BRATTY...
...AND THINK ONLY OF HIMSELF.
......
YES, NOW LET'S SEEEE.
IT'S ABOUT TIME I TELL YOU THIS, EH ...?

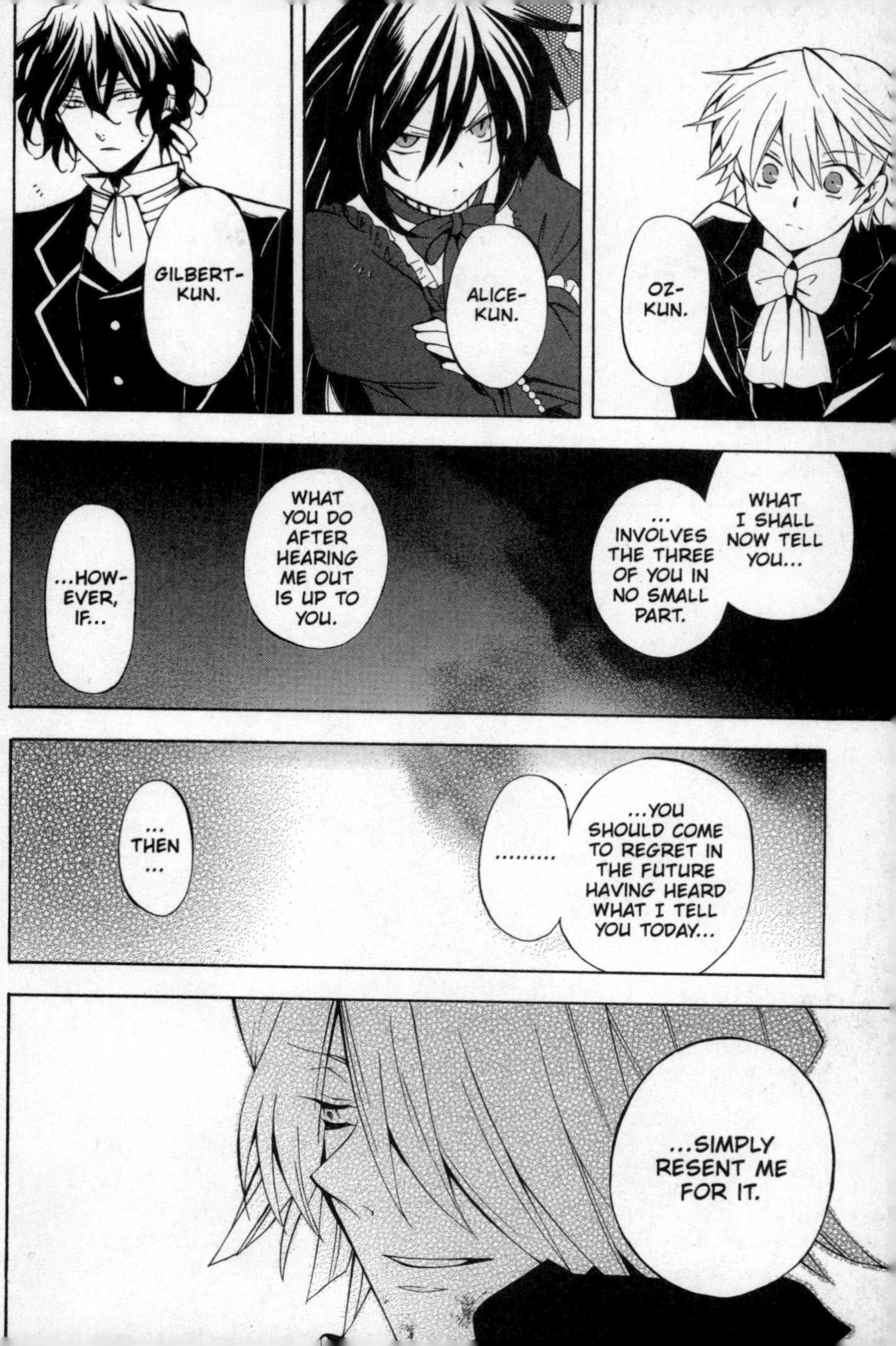
OZ-KUN.
ALICE-KUN.
GILBERT-KUN.
WHAT I SHALL NOW TELL YOU...
...INVOLVES THE THREE OF YOU IN NO SMALL PART.
WHAT YOU DO AFTER HEARING ME OUT IS UP TO YOU.
...HOWEVER, IF...
...YOU SHOULD COME TO REGRET IN THE FUTURE HAVING HEARD WHAT I TELL YOU TODAY...
....
...THEN...
...SIMPLY RESENT ME FOR IT.

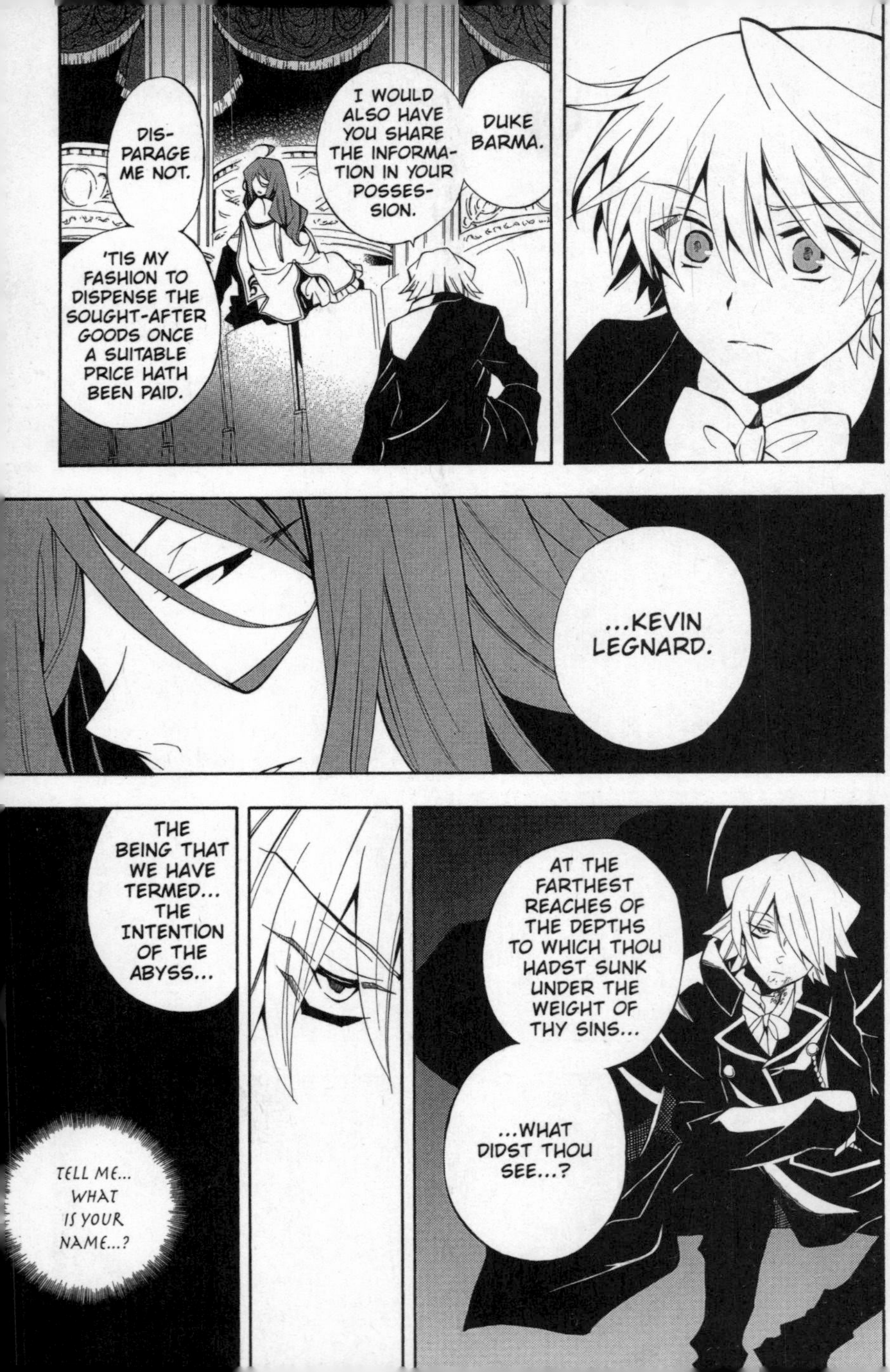
DUKE BARMA.
I WOULD ALSO HAVE YOU SHARE THE INFORMATION IN YOUR POSSESSION.
DISPARAGE ME NOT.
'TIS MY FASHION TO DISPENSE THE SOUGHT-AFTER GOODS ONCE A SUITABLE PRICE HATH BEEN PAID.
...KEVIN LEGNARD.
AT THE FARTHEST REACHES OF THE DEPTHS TO WHICH THOU HADST SUNK UNDER THE WEIGHT OF THY SINS...
...WHAT DIDST THOU SEE...?
THE BEING THAT WE HAVE TERMED... THE INTENTION OF THE ABYSS...
TELL ME... WHAT IS YOUR NAME...?

A TORN-OUT LEFT EYE.

THE FOOT-FALLS OF DEATH.

AND —...

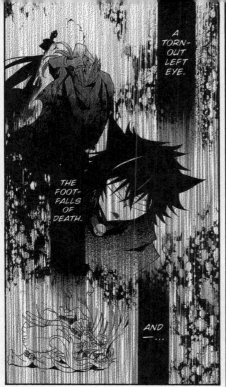

KATSU
CCLICK
+...

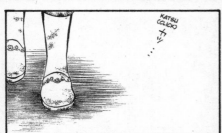

MY NAME...

...IS ALICE.

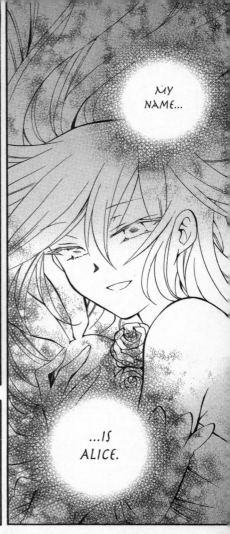

...HELLO THERE, ALICE.

WHY...

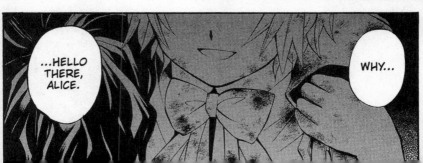

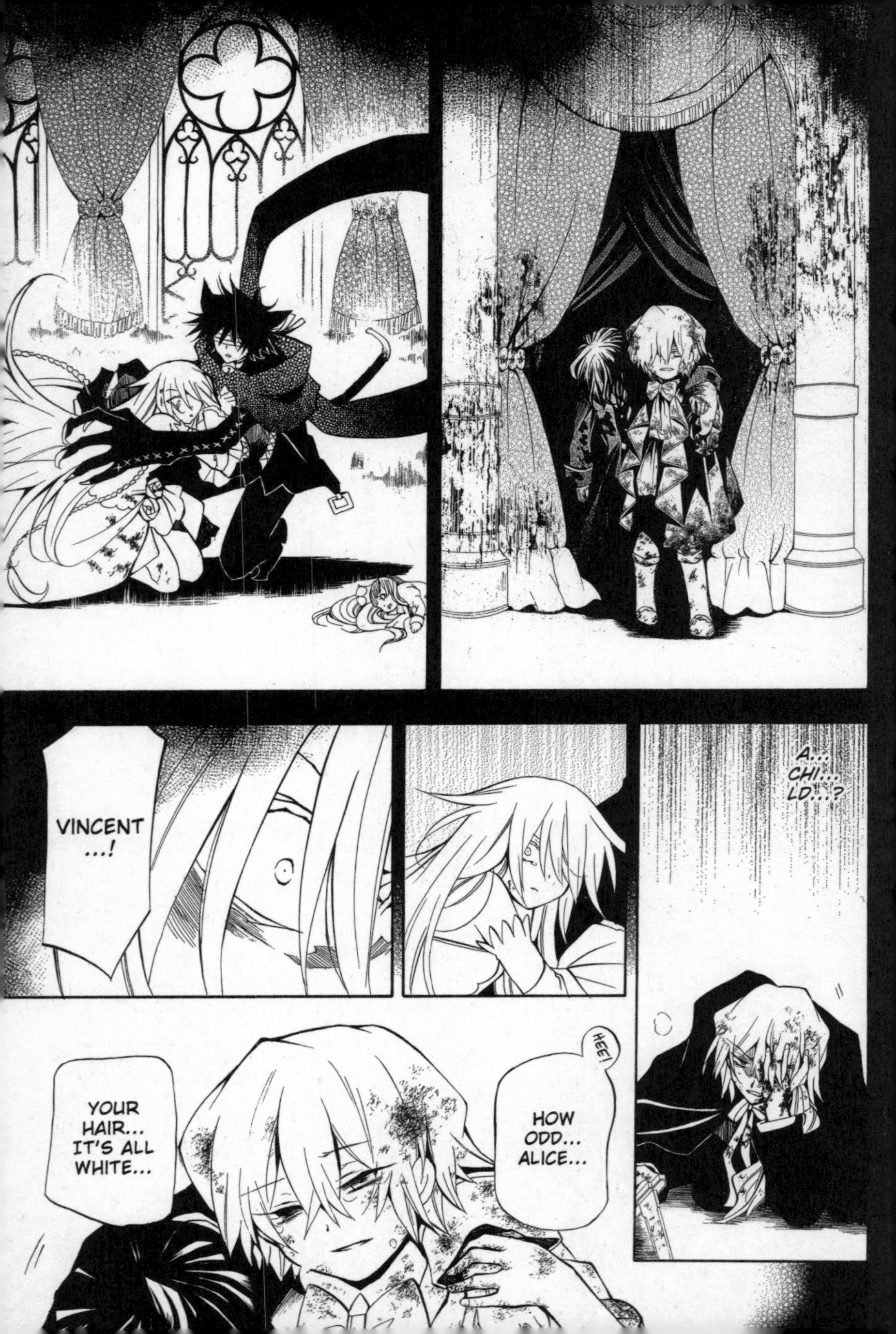
A... CHI... LD...?
VINCENT ...!
HEE!
HOW ODD... ALICE...
YOUR HAIR... IT'S ALL WHITE...

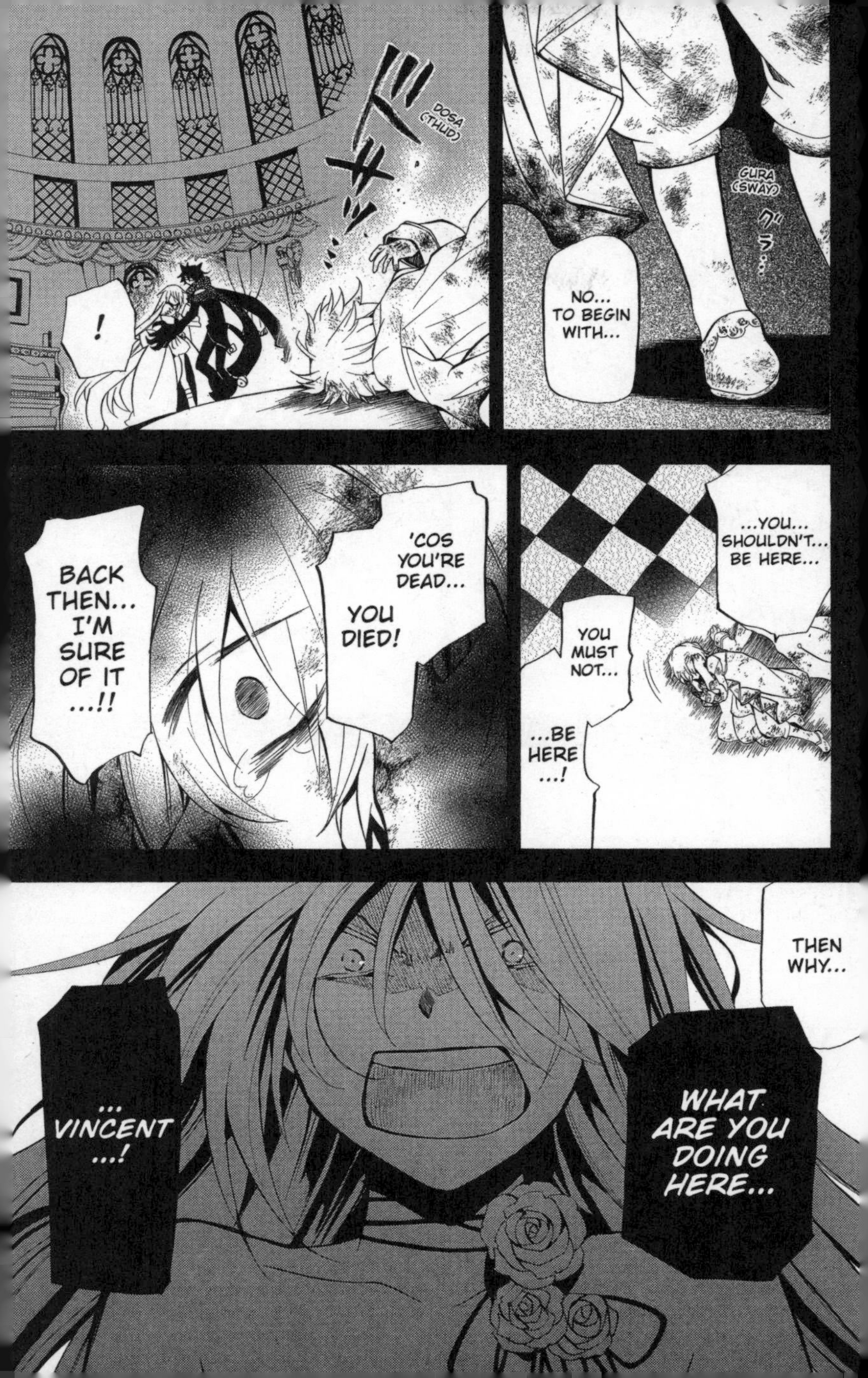
GURA (SWAY)
グラ…
NO... TO BEGIN WITH...
DOSA (THUD)
ドサッ
!
...YOU... SHOULDN'T... BE HERE...
YOU MUST NOT...
...BE HERE ...!
'COS YOU'RE DEAD...
YOU DIED!
BACK THEN... I'M SURE OF IT ...!!
THEN WHY...
WHAT ARE YOU DOING HERE...
... VINCENT ...!

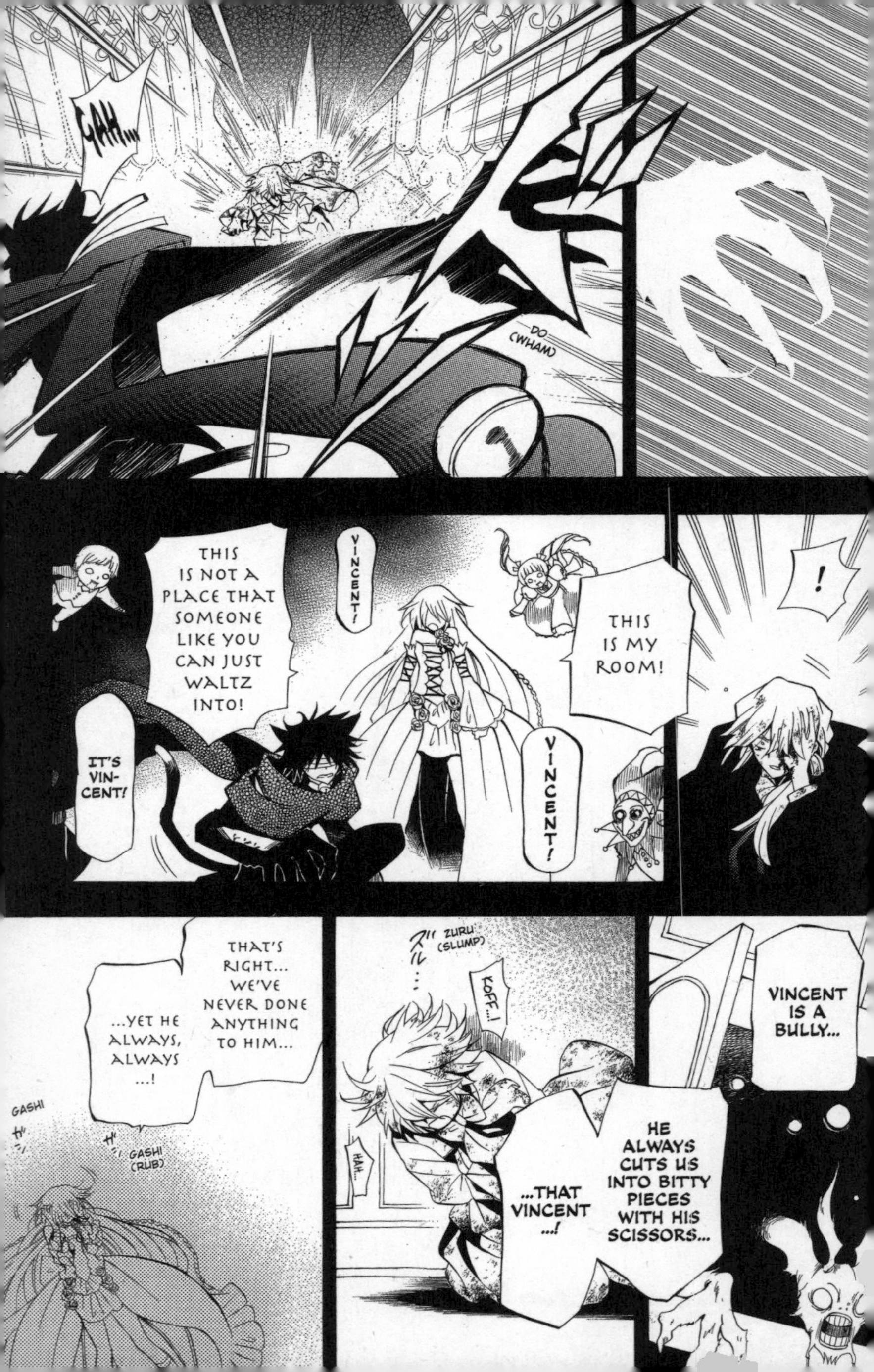
GAH...
DO (WHAM)
!
THIS IS MY ROOM!
VINCENT!
THIS IS NOT A PLACE THAT SOMEONE LIKE YOU CAN JUST WALTZ INTO!
VINCENT!
IT'S VIN-CENT!
VINCENT IS A BULLY...
HE ALWAYS CUTS US INTO BITTY PIECES WITH HIS SCISSORS...
...THAT VINCENT ...!
ZURU (SLUMP)
KOFF...!
HAA...
THAT'S RIGHT... WE'VE NEVER DONE ANYTHING TO HIM...
...YET HE ALWAYS, ALWAYS ...!
GASHI
GASHI (RUB)

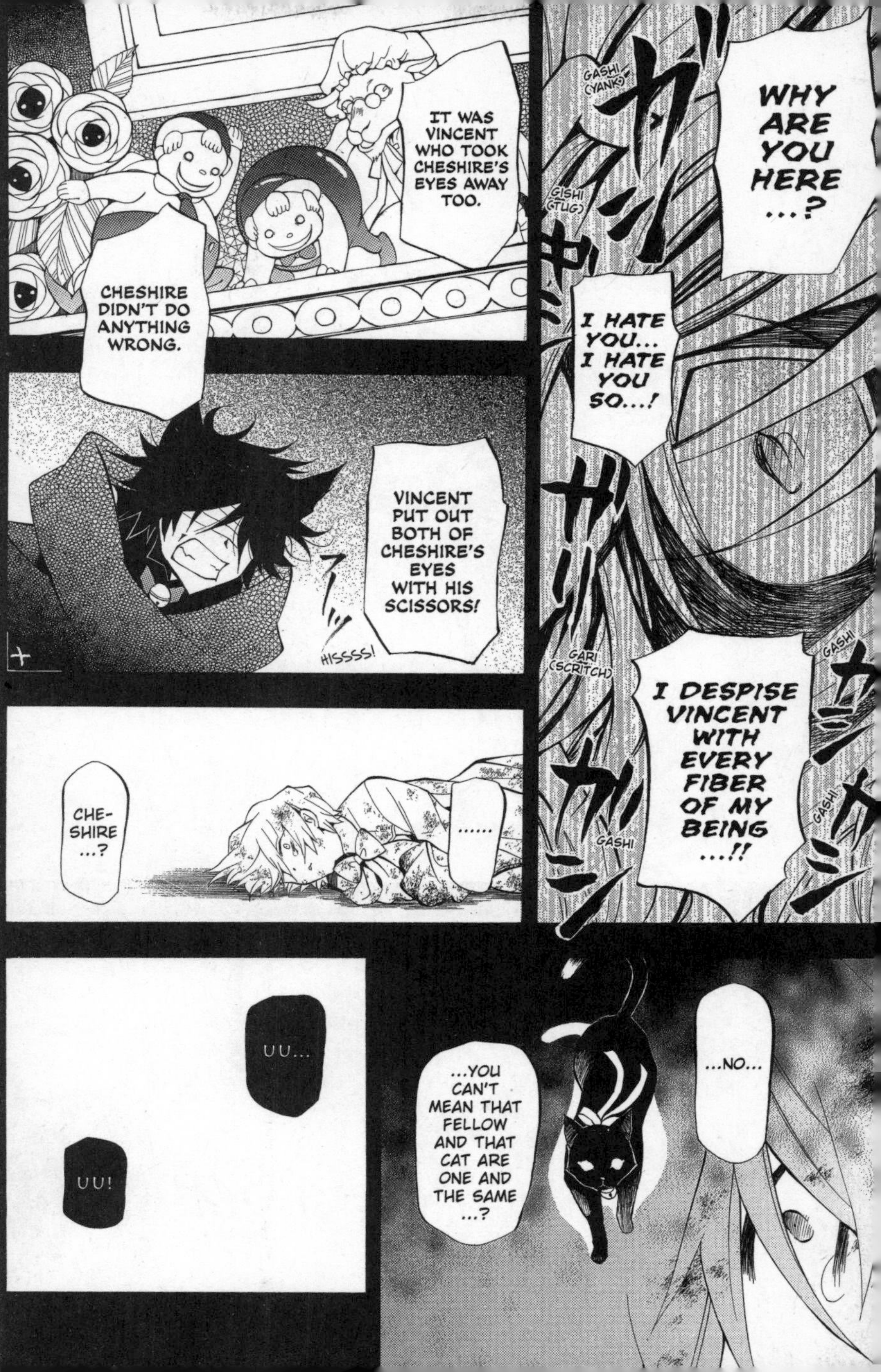
GASHI (YANK)
WHY ARE YOU HERE ...?
GISHI (TUG)
I HATE YOU... I HATE YOU SO...!
GARI (SCRITCH)
GASHI
I DESPISE VINCENT WITH EVERY FIBER OF MY BEING ...!!
GASHI
GASHI
IT WAS VINCENT WHO TOOK CHESHIRE'S EYES AWAY TOO.
CHESHIRE DIDN'T DO ANYTHING WRONG.
VINCENT PUT OUT BOTH OF CHESHIRE'S EYES WITH HIS SCISSORS!
HISSSS!
......
CHE-SHIRE ...?
...NO...
...YOU CAN'T MEAN THAT FELLOW AND THAT CAT ARE ONE AND THE SAME ...?
UU...
UU!

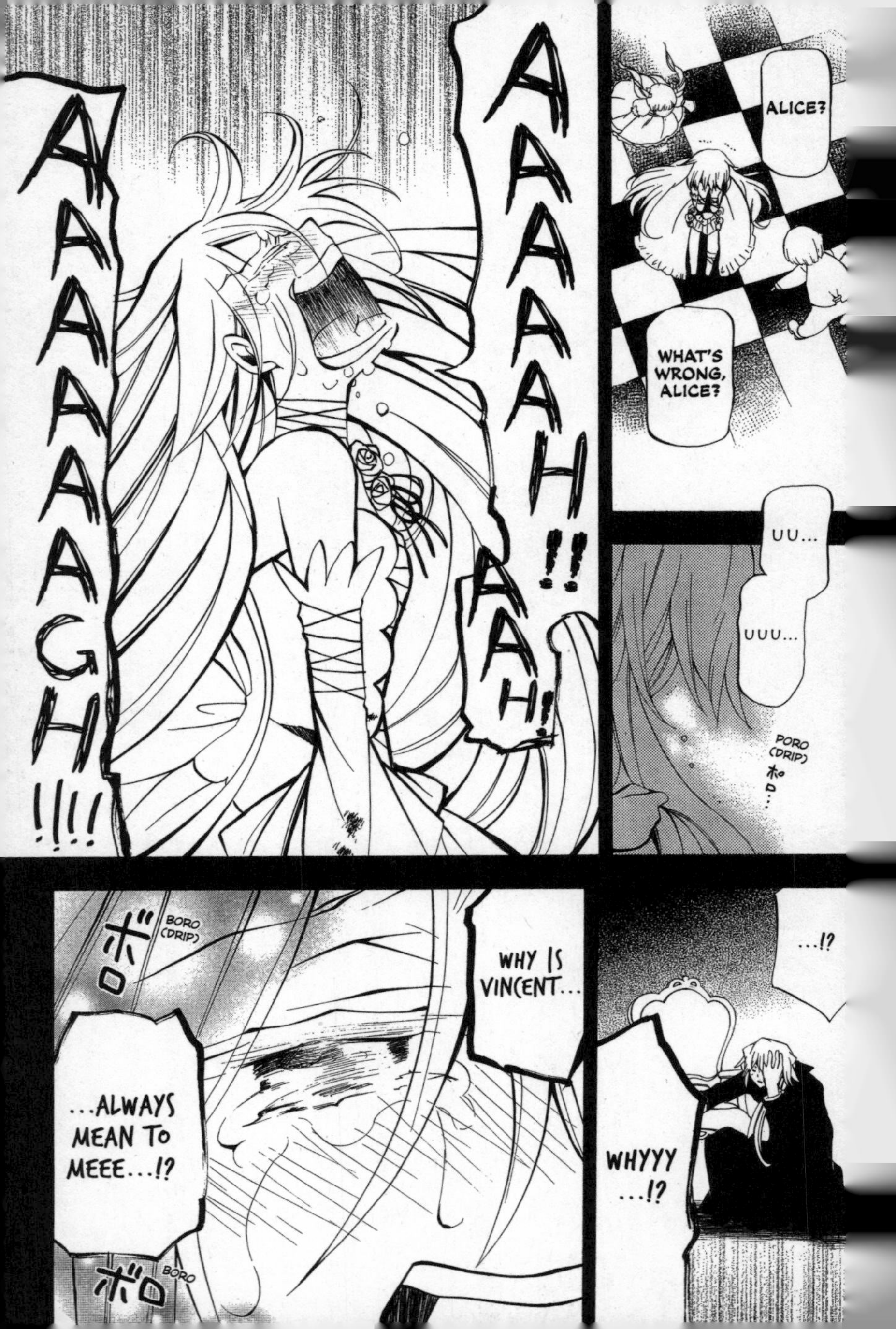
ALICE?
.....
WHAT'S WRONG, ALICE?
UU...
UUU...
PORO (DRIP)
ポロ...
AAAAAH!!
AAH!
AAAAAAAAGH!!!!
...!?
WHYYY ...!?
WHY IS VINCENT...
ボロ
BORO (DRIP)
...ALWAYS MEAN TO MEEE...!?
ボロ
BORO

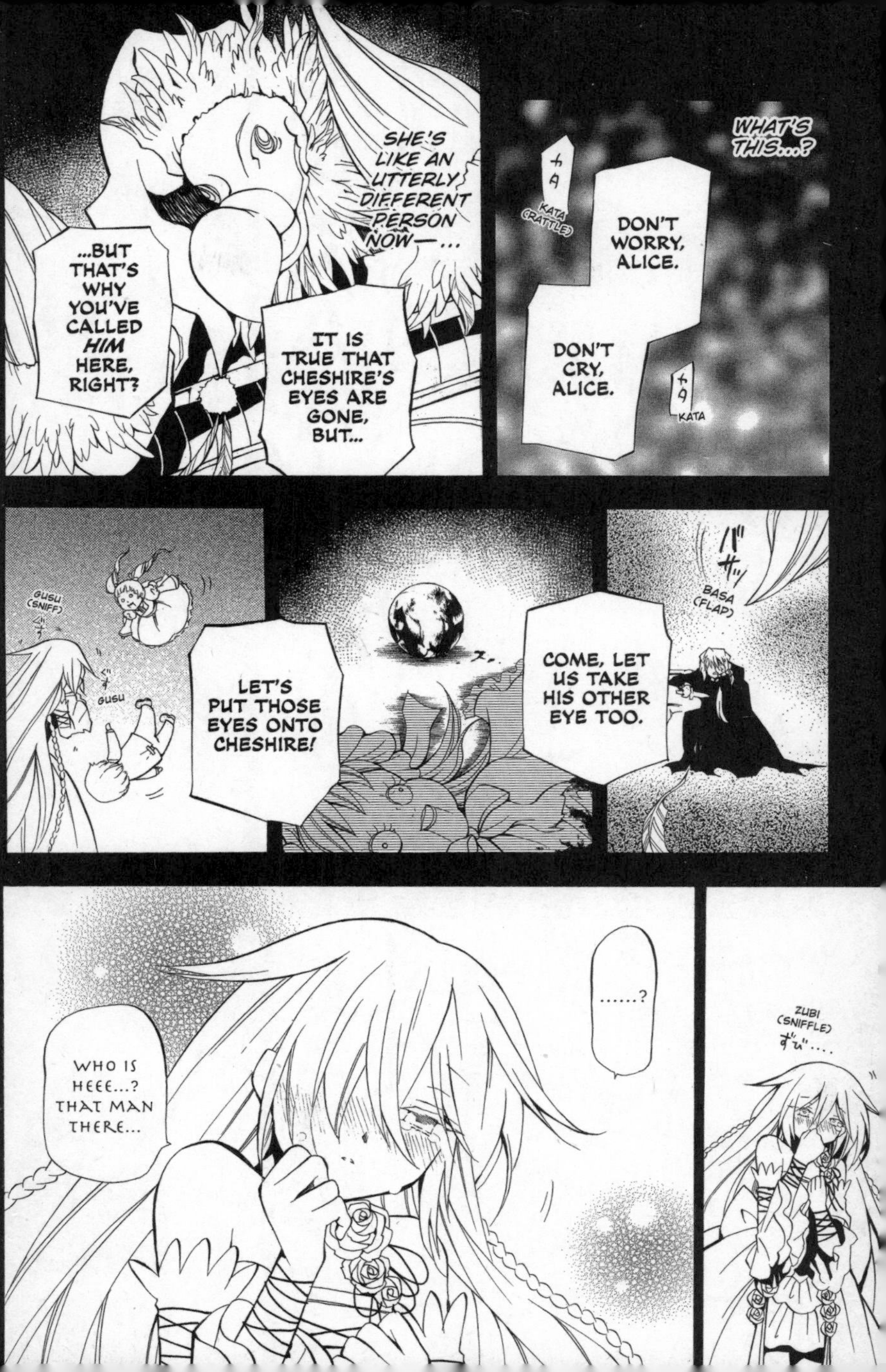
WHAT'S THIS...?
カタ
KATA (RATTLE)
DON'T WORRY, ALICE.
DON'T CRY, ALICE.
カタ
KATA
SHE'S LIKE AN UTTERLY DIFFERENT PERSON NOW—...
IT IS TRUE THAT CHESHIRE'S EYES ARE GONE, BUT...
...BUT THAT'S WHY YOU'VE CALLED *HIM* HERE, RIGHT?
バサッ
BASA (FLAP)
COME, LET US TAKE HIS OTHER EYE TOO.
LET'S PUT THOSE EYES ONTO CHESHIRE!
GUSU (SNIFF)
ぐす
ぐす
GUSU
ZUBI (SNIFFLE)
ずび....
......?
WHO IS HEEE...? THAT MAN THERE...

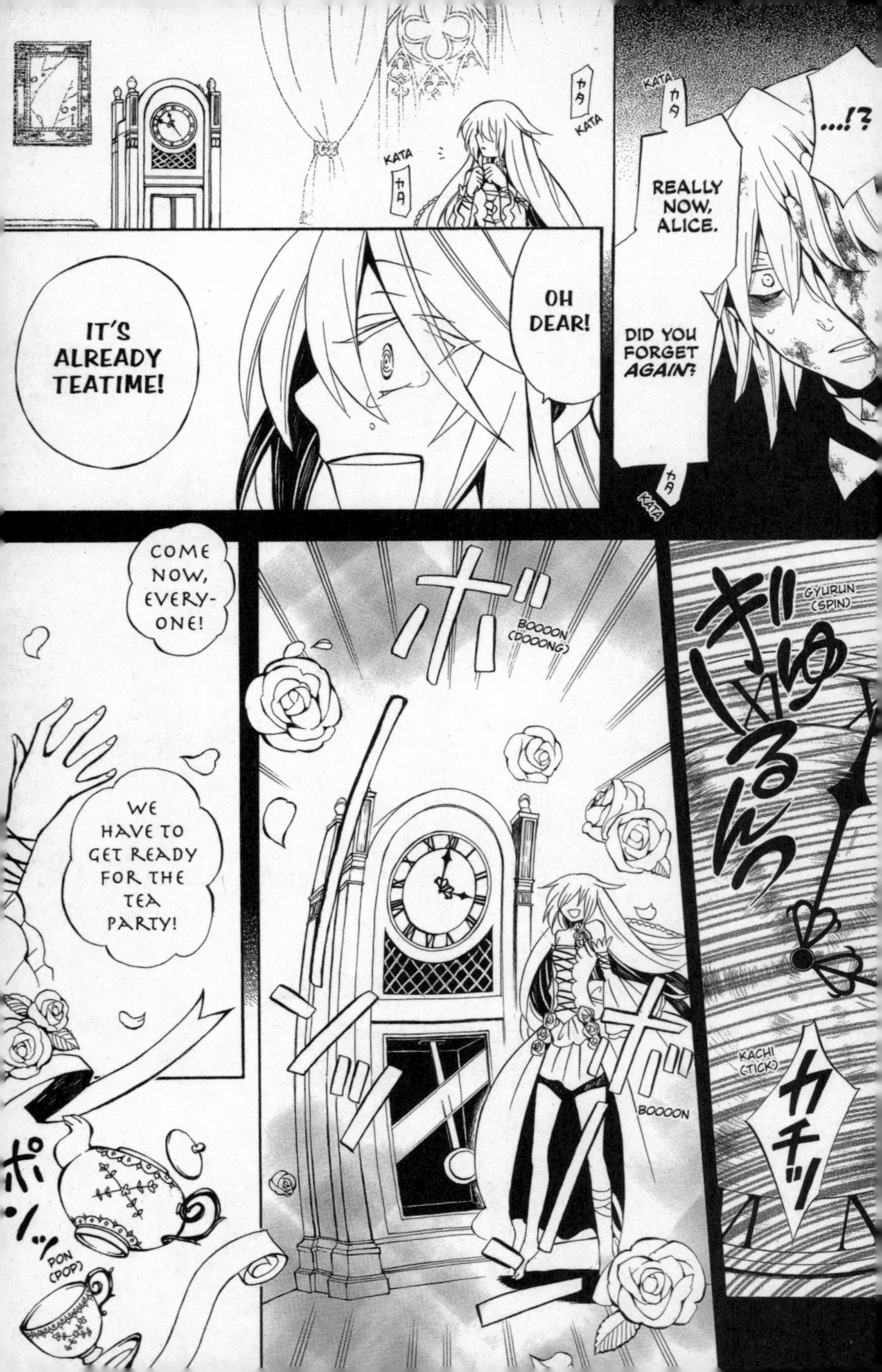
KATA
カタ
...!?
REALLY NOW, ALICE.
DID YOU FORGET *AGAIN*?
カタ
KATA
カタ
KATA
KATA
カタ
OH DEAR!
IT'S ALREADY TEATIME!
ぎゅるんっ
GYURUN (SPIN)
カチッ
KACHI (TICK)
ボーン
BOOOON (DOOONG)
ボーン
BOOOON
COME NOW, EVERY-ONE!
WE HAVE TO GET READY FOR THE TEA PARTY!
ポンッ
PON (POP)

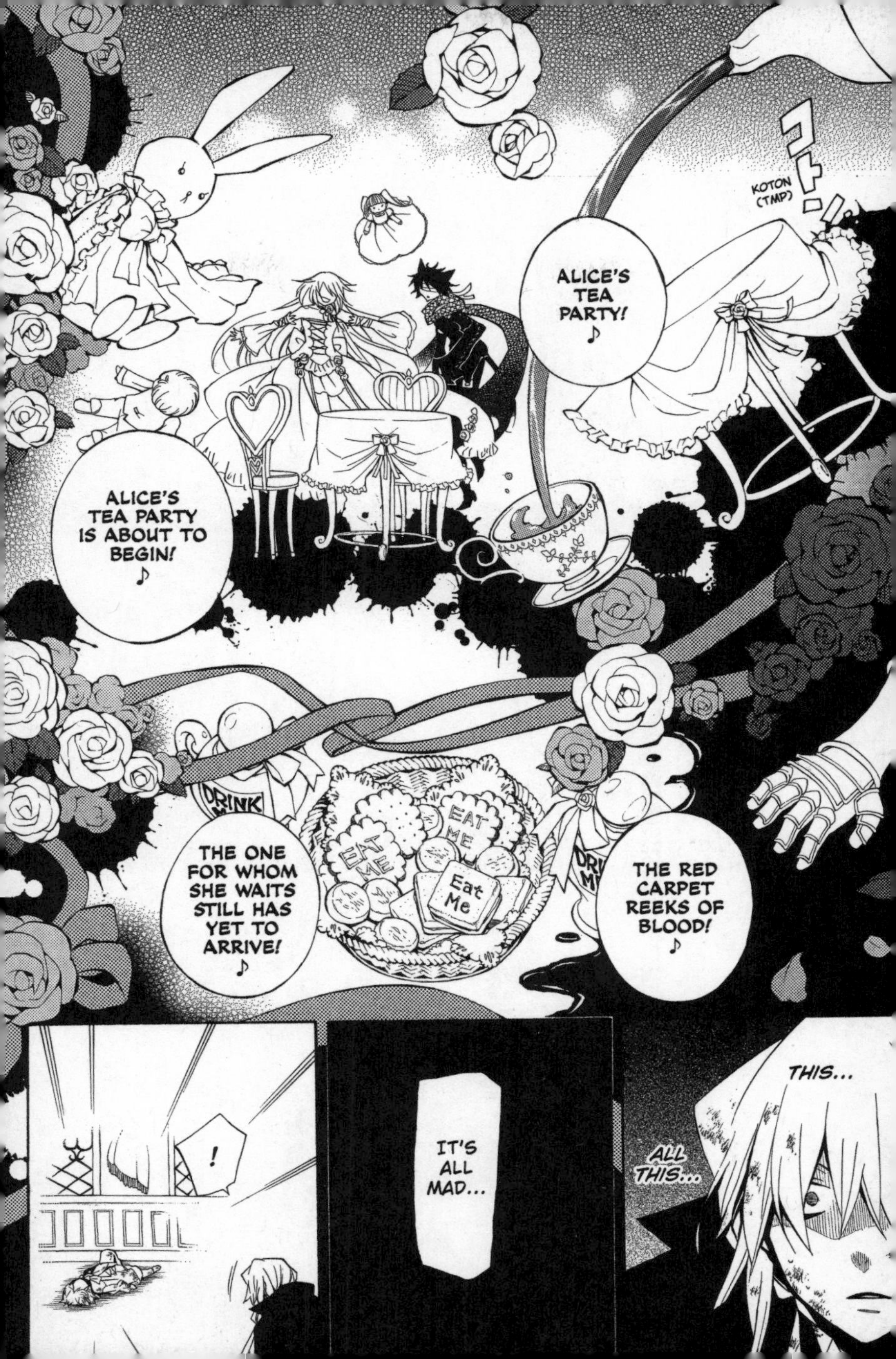

KOTON (TMP)
ALICE'S TEA PARTY! ♪
ALICE'S TEA PARTY IS ABOUT TO BEGIN! ♪
THE RED CARPET REEKS OF BLOOD! ♪
EAT ME
Eat Me
EAT ME
THE ONE FOR WHOM SHE WAITS STILL HAS YET TO ARRIVE! ♪
THIS...
ALL THIS...
IT'S ALL MAD...
!

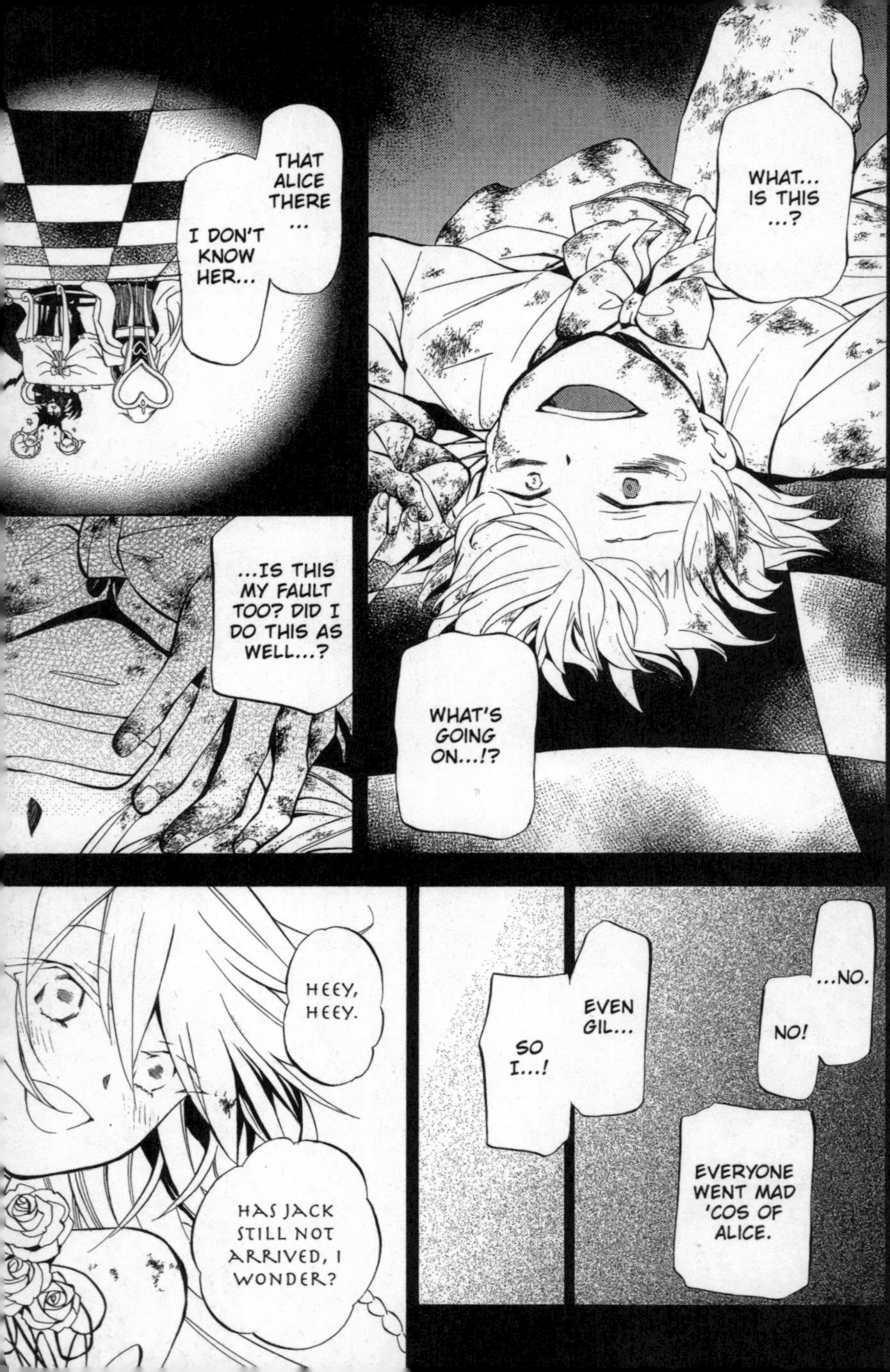
WHAT... IS THIS ...?
WHAT'S GOING ON...!?
THAT ALICE THERE ...
I DON'T KNOW HER...
...IS THIS MY FAULT TOO? DID I DO THIS AS WELL...?
...NO.
NO!
EVERYONE WENT MAD 'COS OF ALICE.
EVEN GIL...
SO I...!
HEEY, HEEY.
HAS JACK STILL NOT ARRIVED, I WONDER?

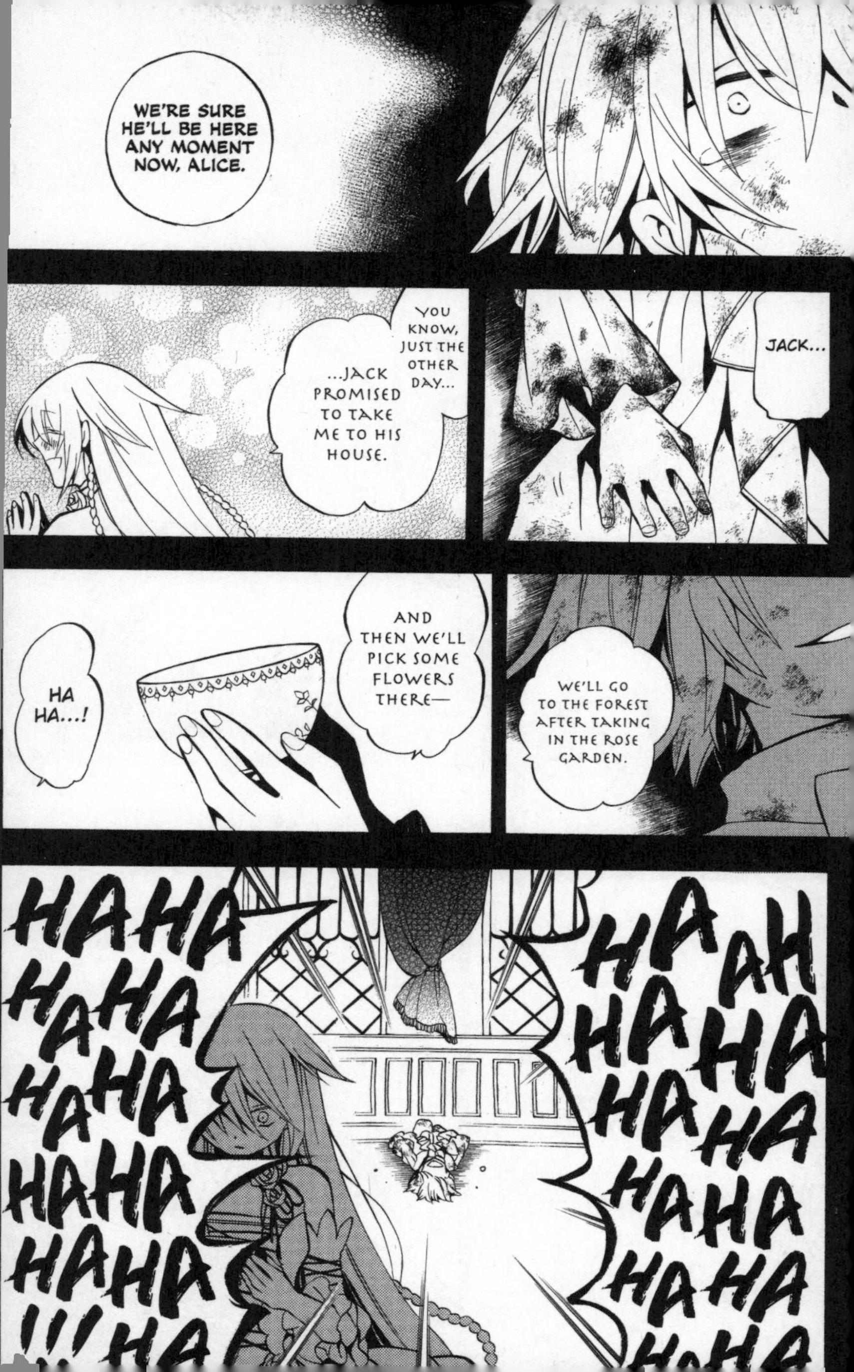
WE'RE SURE HE'LL BE HERE ANY MOMENT NOW, ALICE.
JACK...
YOU KNOW, JUST THE OTHER DAY...
...JACK PROMISED TO TAKE ME TO HIS HOUSE.
WE'LL GO TO THE FOREST AFTER TAKING IN THE ROSE GARDEN.
AND THEN WE'LL PICK SOME FLOWERS THERE—
HA HA...!
HAAH HAHA HAHA HAHA HAHA HAHA HAHA HAHA
HAHA HAHA HAHA HAHA HAHA HAHA HAHA HAHA !!! HA

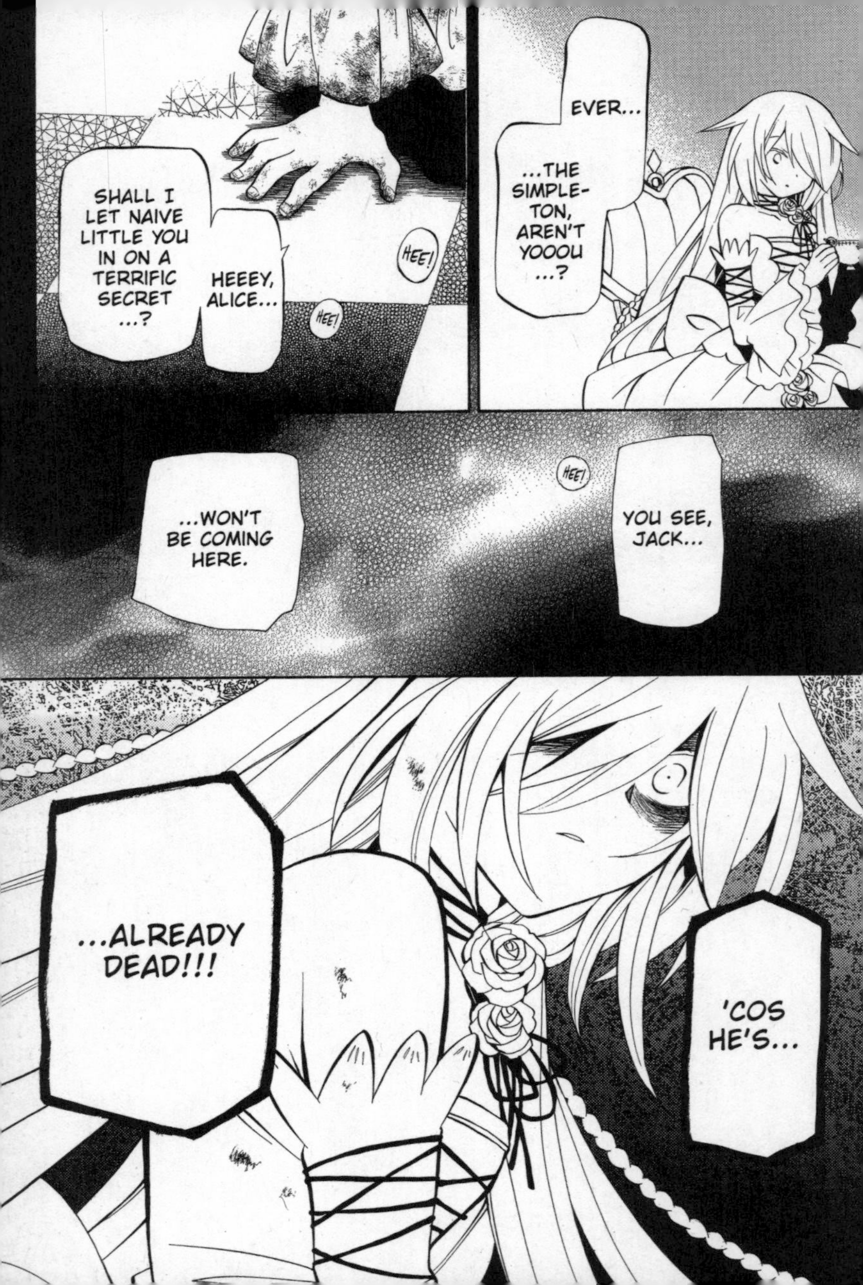
EVER...
...THE SIMPLE-TON, AREN'T YOOOU ...?
HEE!
HEEEY, ALICE...
SHALL I LET NAIVE LITTLE YOU IN ON A TERRIFIC SECRET ...?
HEE!
HEE!
YOU SEE, JACK...
...WON'T BE COMING HERE.
'COS HE'S...
...ALREADY DEAD!!!

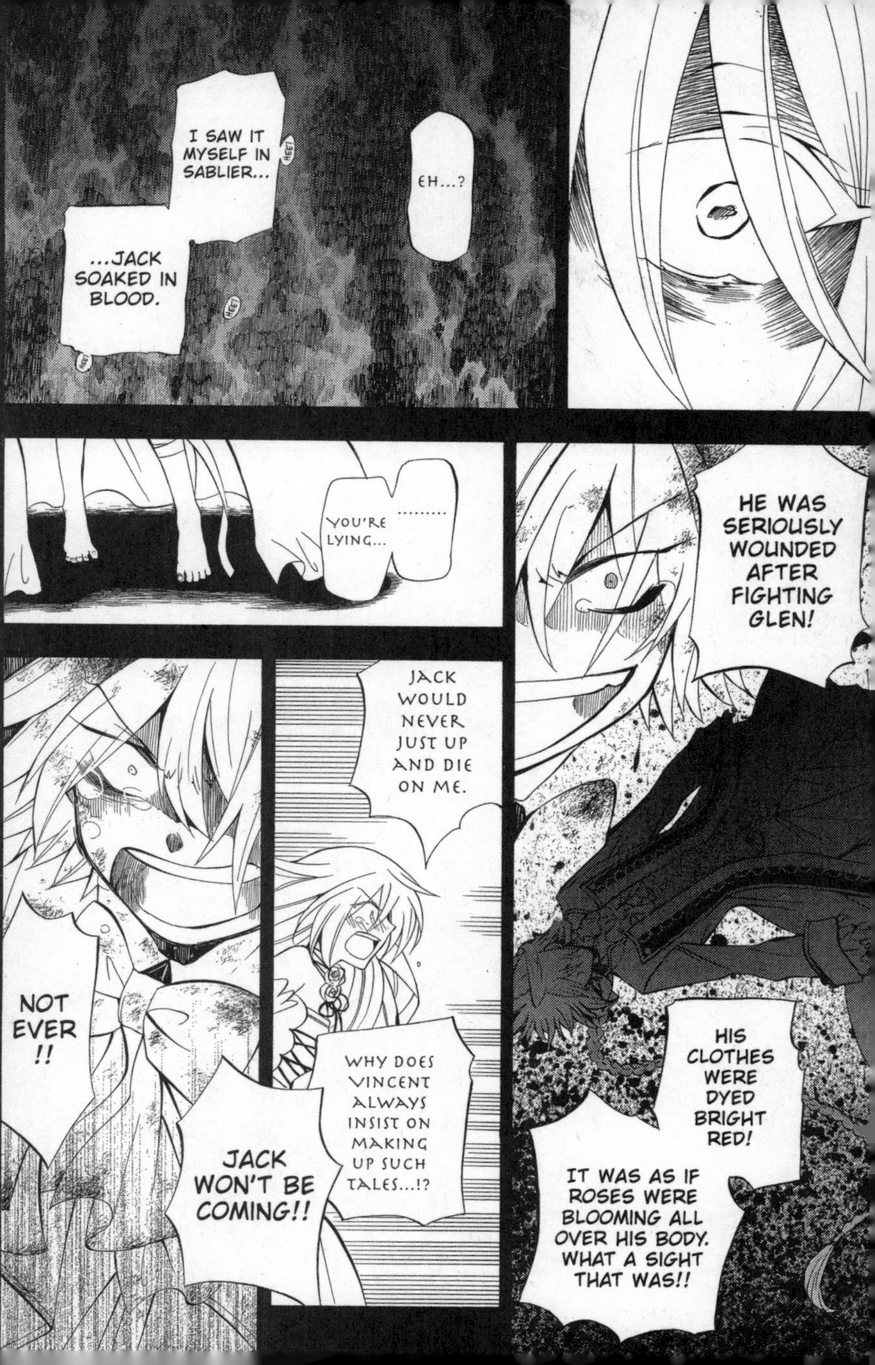
EH...?
I SAW IT MYSELF IN SABLIER...
HEE!
...JACK SOAKED IN BLOOD.
HEE!
HEE!
HE WAS SERIOUSLY WOUNDED AFTER FIGHTING GLEN!
HIS CLOTHES WERE DYED BRIGHT RED!
IT WAS AS IF ROSES WERE BLOOMING ALL OVER HIS BODY. WHAT A SIGHT THAT WAS!!
....
YOU'RE LYING...
JACK WOULD NEVER JUST UP AND DIE ON ME.
WHY DOES VINCENT ALWAYS INSIST ON MAKING UP SUCH TALES...!?
NOT EVER!!
JACK WON'T BE COMING!!

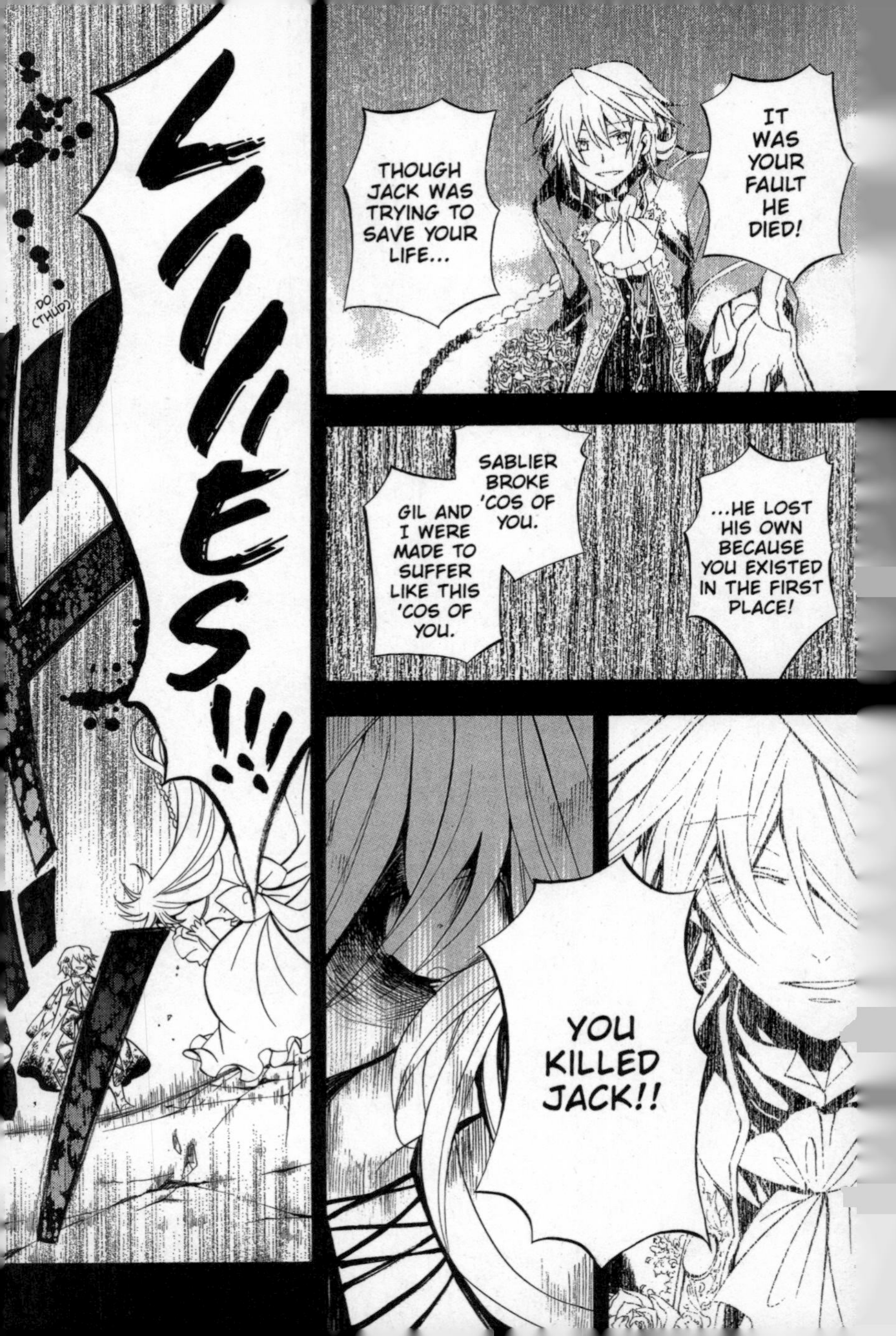
IT WAS YOUR FAULT HE DIED!
THOUGH JACK WAS TRYING TO SAVE YOUR LIFE...
...HE LOST HIS OWN BECAUSE YOU EXISTED IN THE FIRST PLACE!
SABLIER BROKE 'COS OF YOU.
GIL AND I WERE MADE TO SUFFER LIKE THIS 'COS OF YOU.
YOU KILLED JACK!!
DO (THUD)

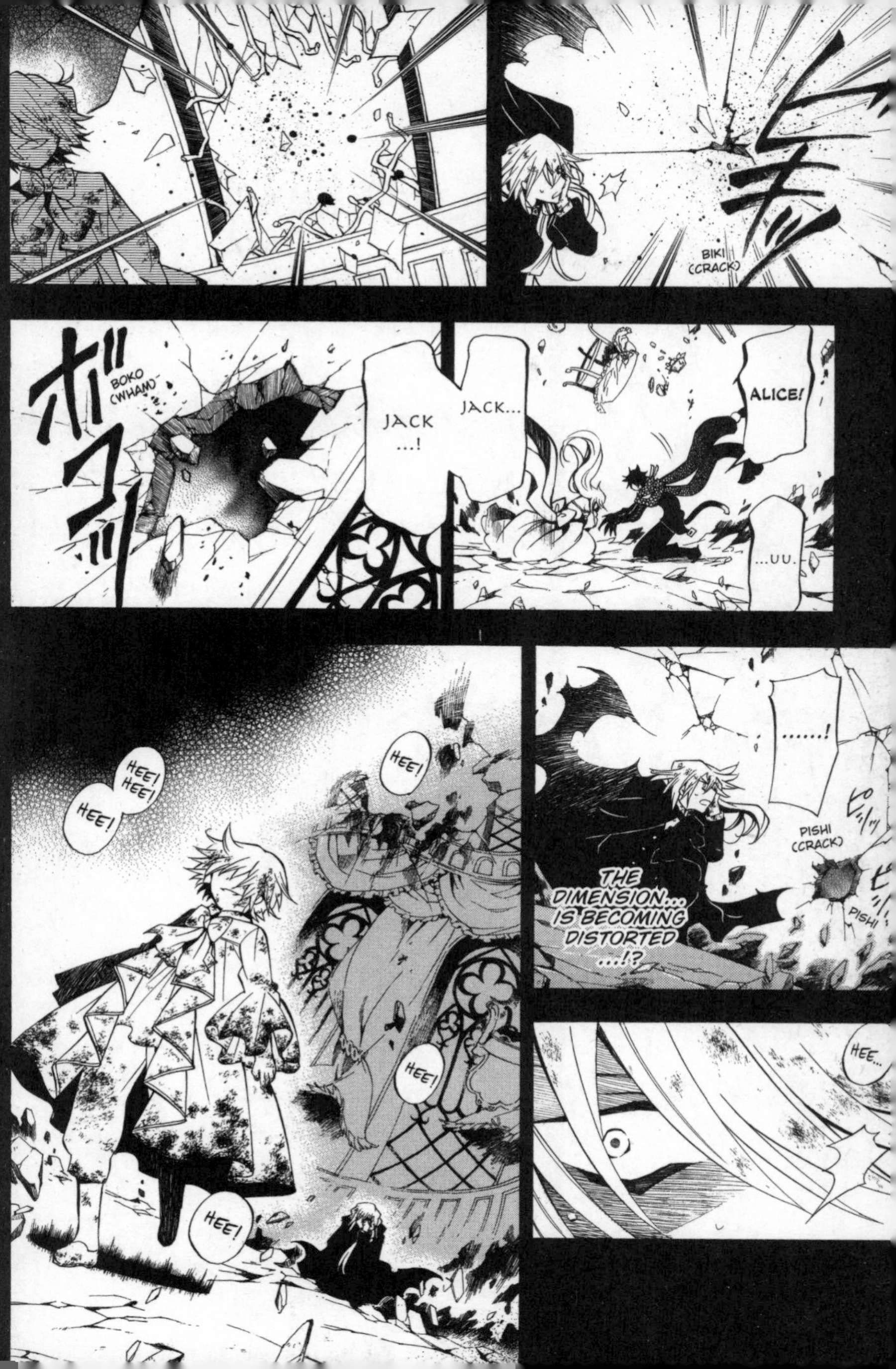

BIKI (CRACK)
ALICE!
...UU.
JACK...
JACK ...!
BOKO (WHAM)
......!
PISHI (CRACK)
PISHI
THE DIMENSION... IS BECOMING DISTORTED ...!?
HEE...
HEE!
HEE! HEE!
HEE!
HEE!
HEE!

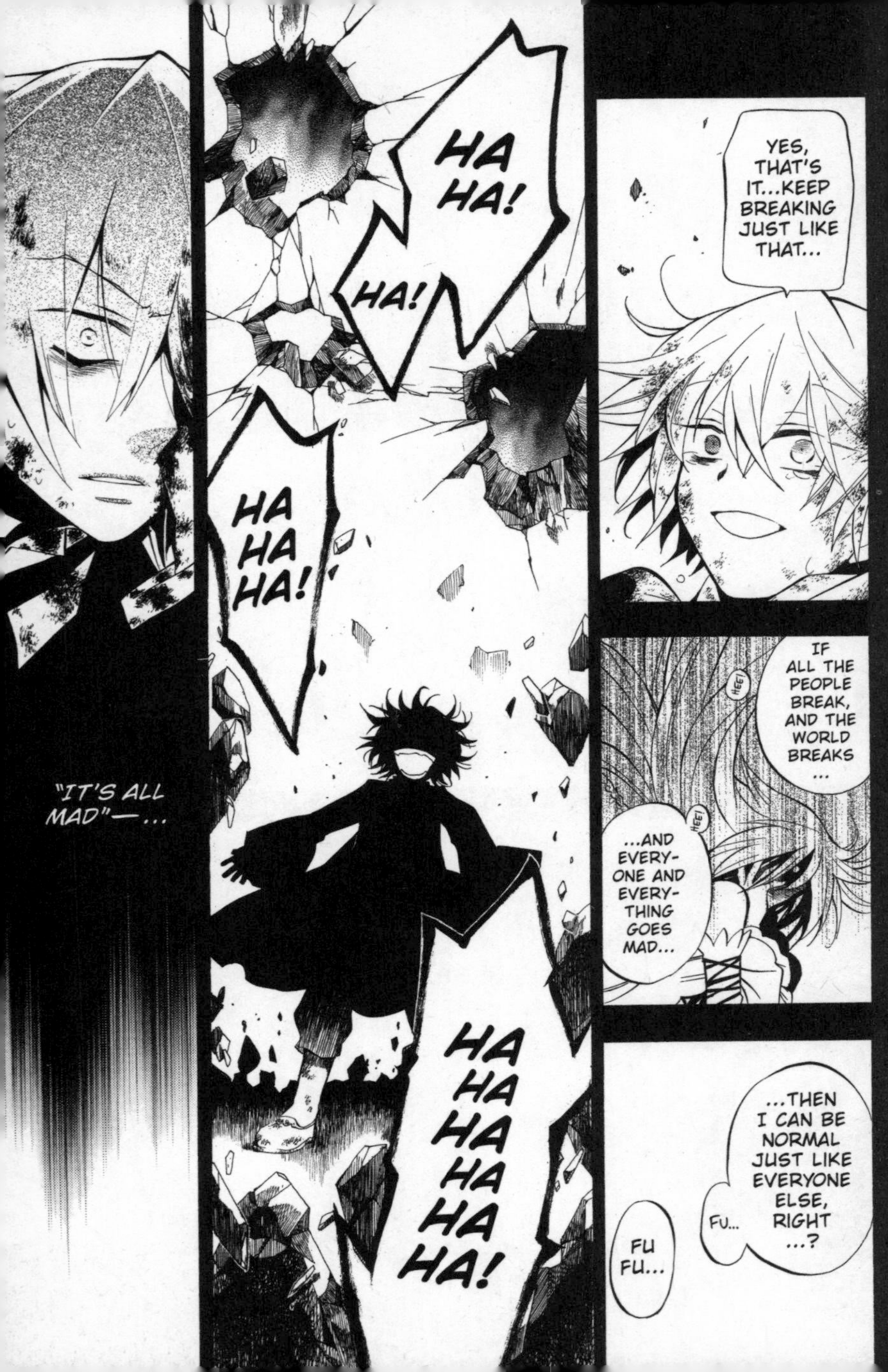
YES, THAT'S IT...KEEP BREAKING JUST LIKE THAT...
IF ALL THE PEOPLE BREAK, AND THE WORLD BREAKS...
HEE!
...AND EVERY-ONE AND EVERY-THING GOES MAD...
HEE!
...THEN I CAN BE NORMAL JUST LIKE EVERYONE ELSE, RIGHT...?
FU...
FU FU...
HA HA!
HA!
HA HA HA!
HA HA HA HA HA HA!
"IT'S ALL MAD"—...

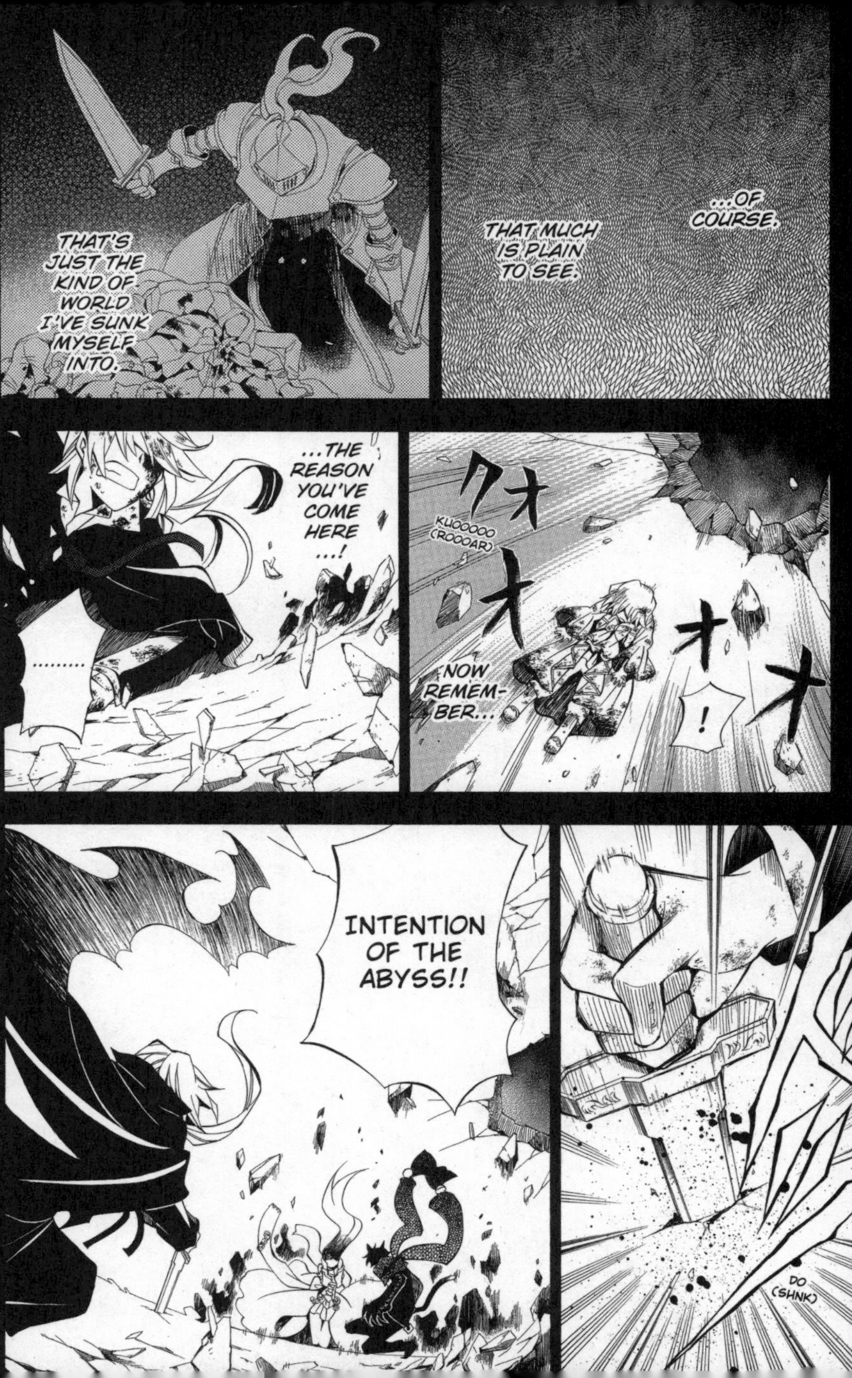
...OF COURSE.
THAT MUCH IS PLAIN TO SEE.
THAT'S JUST THE KIND OF WORLD I'VE SUNK MYSELF INTO.
クオオオオ
KUOOOOO (ROOOAR)
!
NOW REMEMBER...
...THE REASON YOU'VE COME HERE...!
....
DO (SHNK)
INTENTION OF THE ABYSS!!

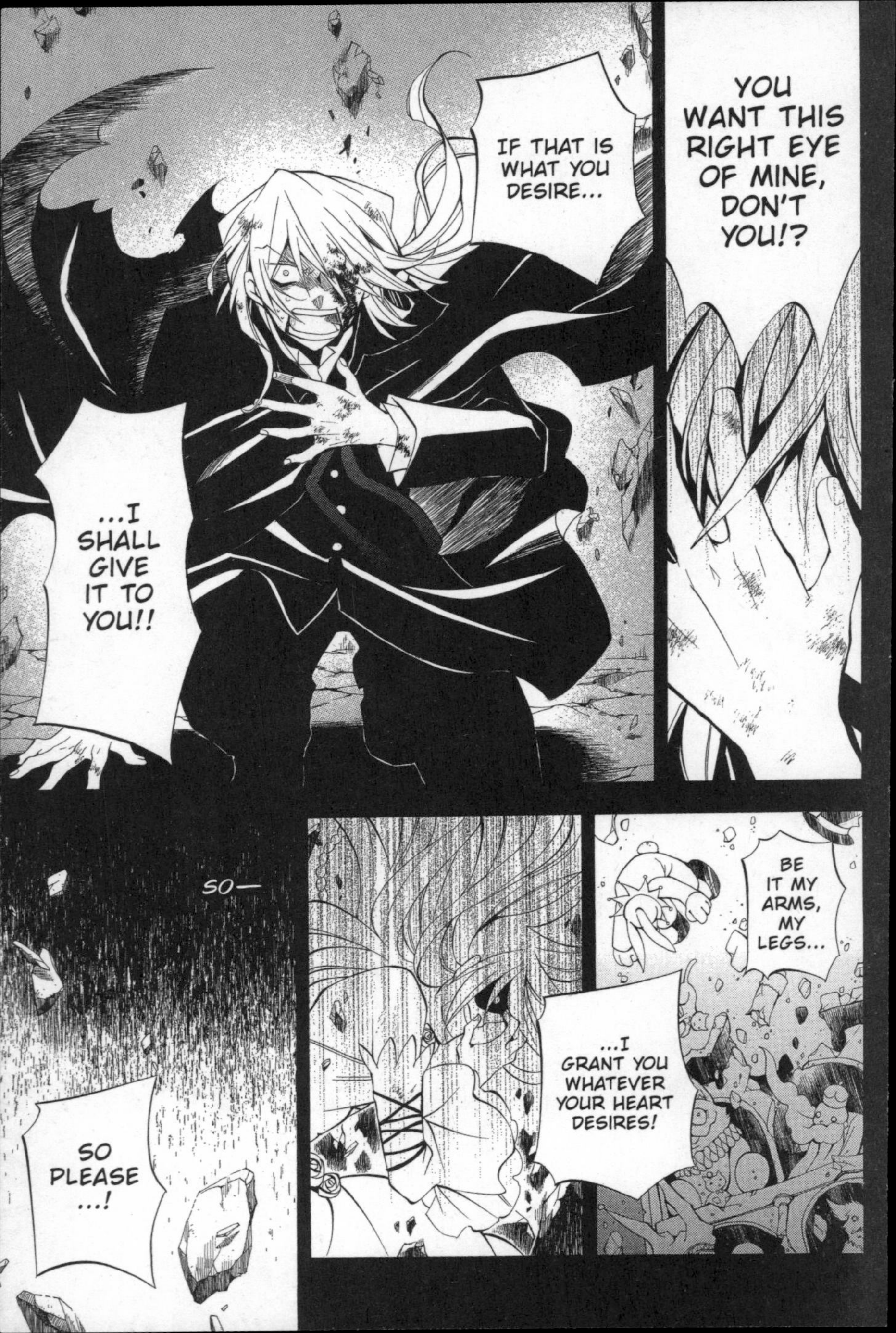
YOU WANT THIS RIGHT EYE OF MINE, DON'T YOU!?
IF THAT IS WHAT YOU DESIRE...
...I SHALL GIVE IT TO YOU!!
BE IT MY ARMS, MY LEGS...
...I GRANT YOU WHATEVER YOUR HEART DESIRES!
SO—
SO PLEASE ...!

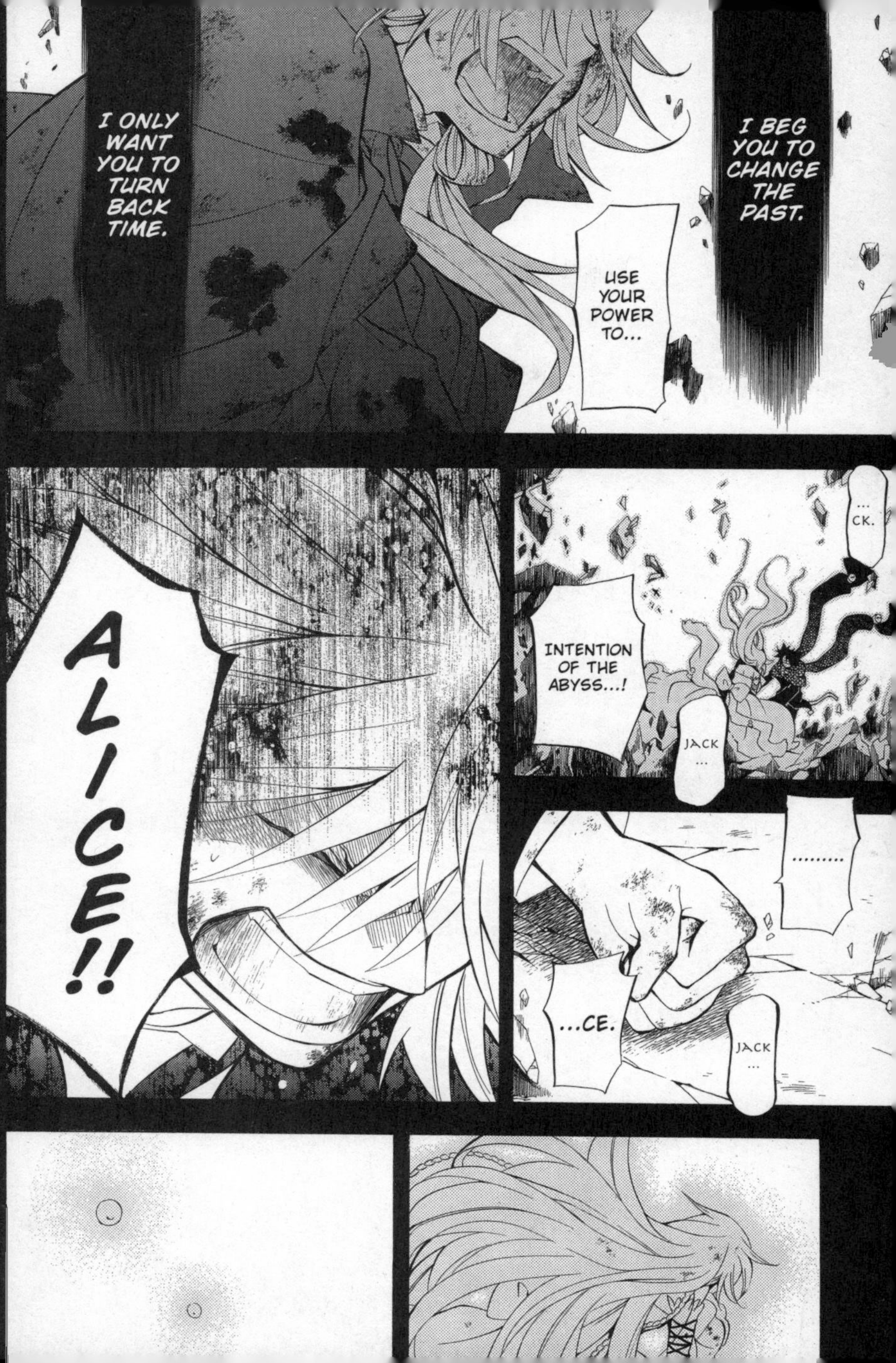
I BEG YOU TO CHANGE THE PAST.
USE YOUR POWER TO...
I ONLY WANT YOU TO TURN BACK TIME.
...CK.
INTENTION OF THE ABYSS...!
JACK...
....
...CE.
JACK...
ALICE!!

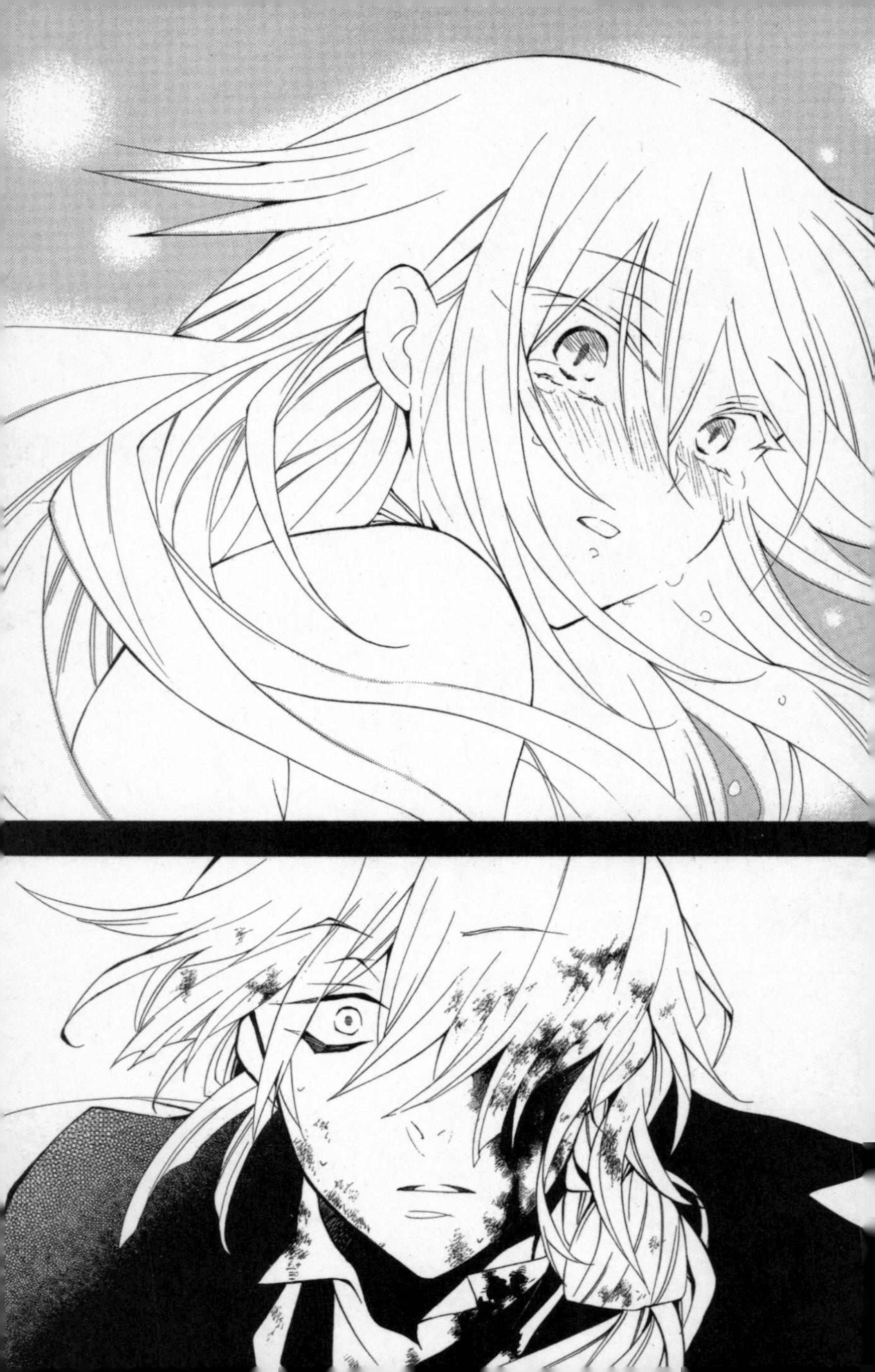

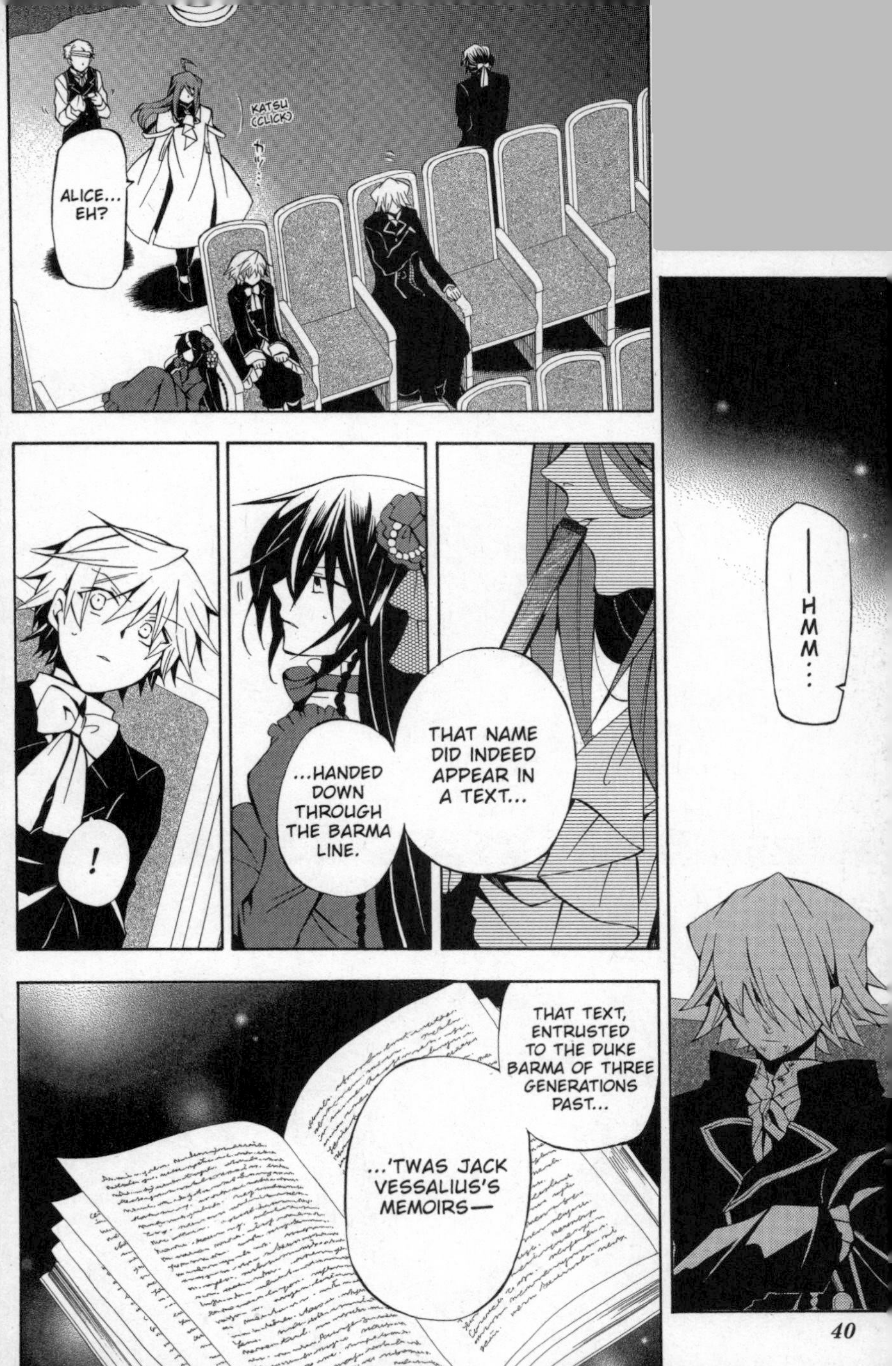

KATSU (CLICK)
カツ…
ALICE… EH?
—HMM…
THAT NAME DID INDEED APPEAR IN A TEXT…
…HANDED DOWN THROUGH THE BARMA LINE.
!
THAT TEXT, ENTRUSTED TO THE DUKE BARMA OF THREE GENERATIONS PAST…
…'TWAS JACK VESSALIUS'S MEMOIRS—

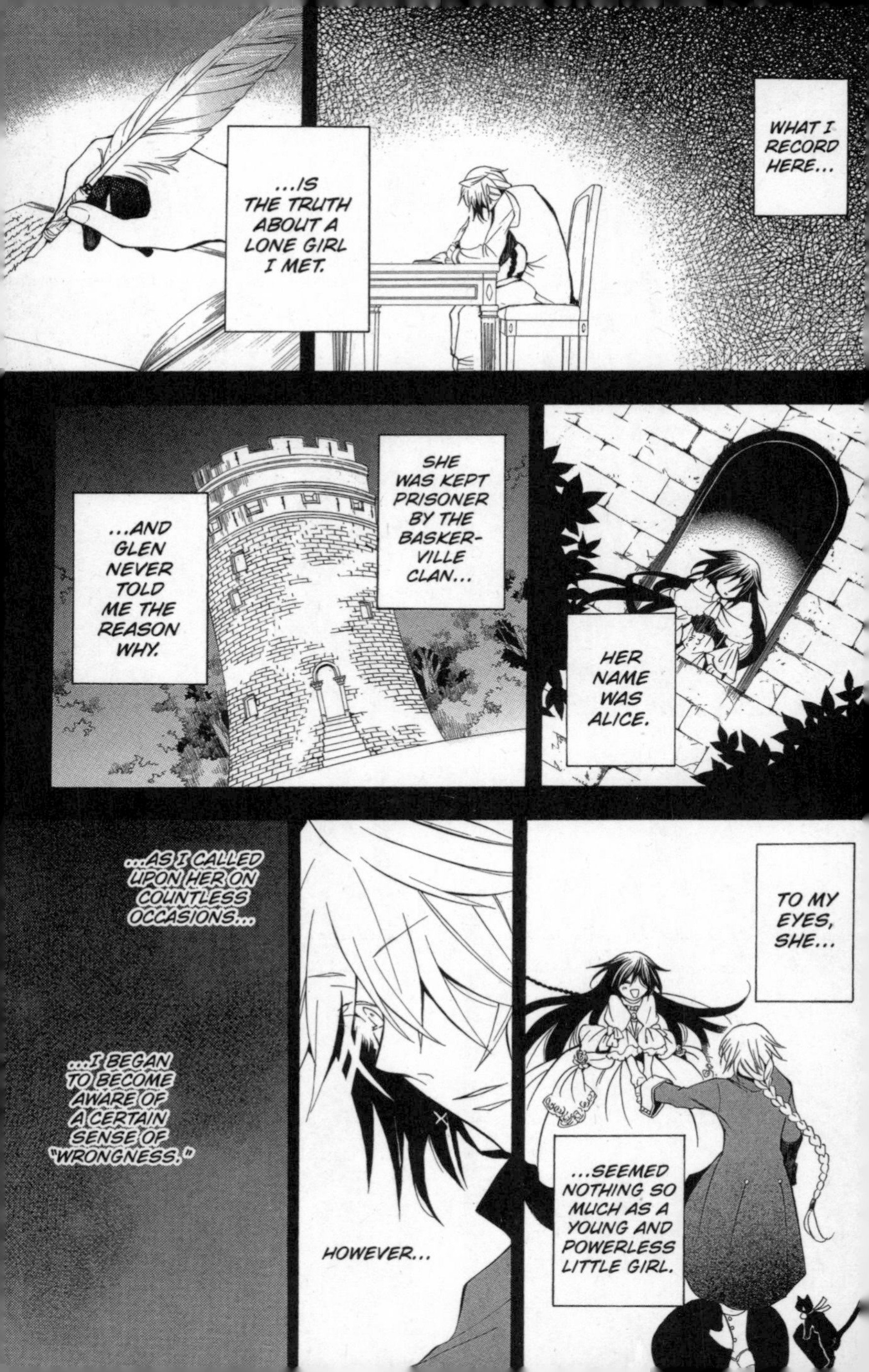
WHAT I RECORD HERE...
...IS THE TRUTH ABOUT A LONE GIRL I MET.
HER NAME WAS ALICE.
SHE WAS KEPT PRISONER BY THE BASKER-VILLE CLAN...
...AND GLEN NEVER TOLD ME THE REASON WHY.
TO MY EYES, SHE...
...SEEMED NOTHING SO MUCH AS A YOUNG AND POWERLESS LITTLE GIRL.
HOWEVER...
...AS I CALLED UPON HER ON COUNTLESS OCCASIONS...
...I BEGAN TO BECOME AWARE OF A CERTAIN SENSE OF "WRONGNESS."

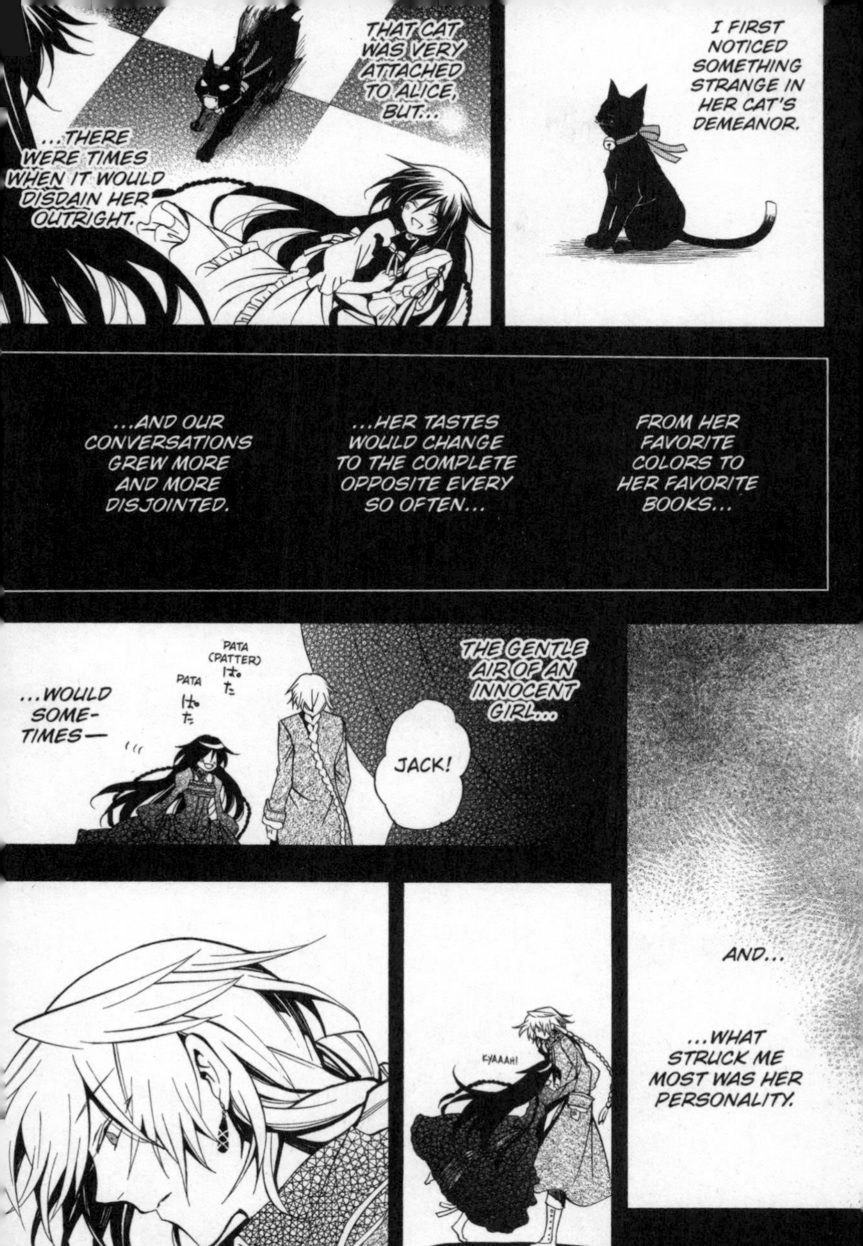
I FIRST NOTICED SOMETHING STRANGE IN HER CAT'S DEMEANOR.
THAT CAT WAS VERY ATTACHED TO ALICE, BUT...
...THERE WERE TIMES WHEN IT WOULD DISDAIN HER OUTRIGHT.
FROM HER FAVORITE COLORS TO HER FAVORITE BOOKS...
...HER TASTES WOULD CHANGE TO THE COMPLETE OPPOSITE EVERY SO OFTEN...
...AND OUR CONVERSATIONS GREW MORE AND MORE DISJOINTED.
AND...
...WHAT STRUCK ME MOST WAS HER PERSONALITY.
THE GENTLE AIR OF AN INNOCENT GIRL...
JACK!
PATA (PATTER) ぱた
PATA ぱた
...WOULD SOMETIMES—
KYAAAH!

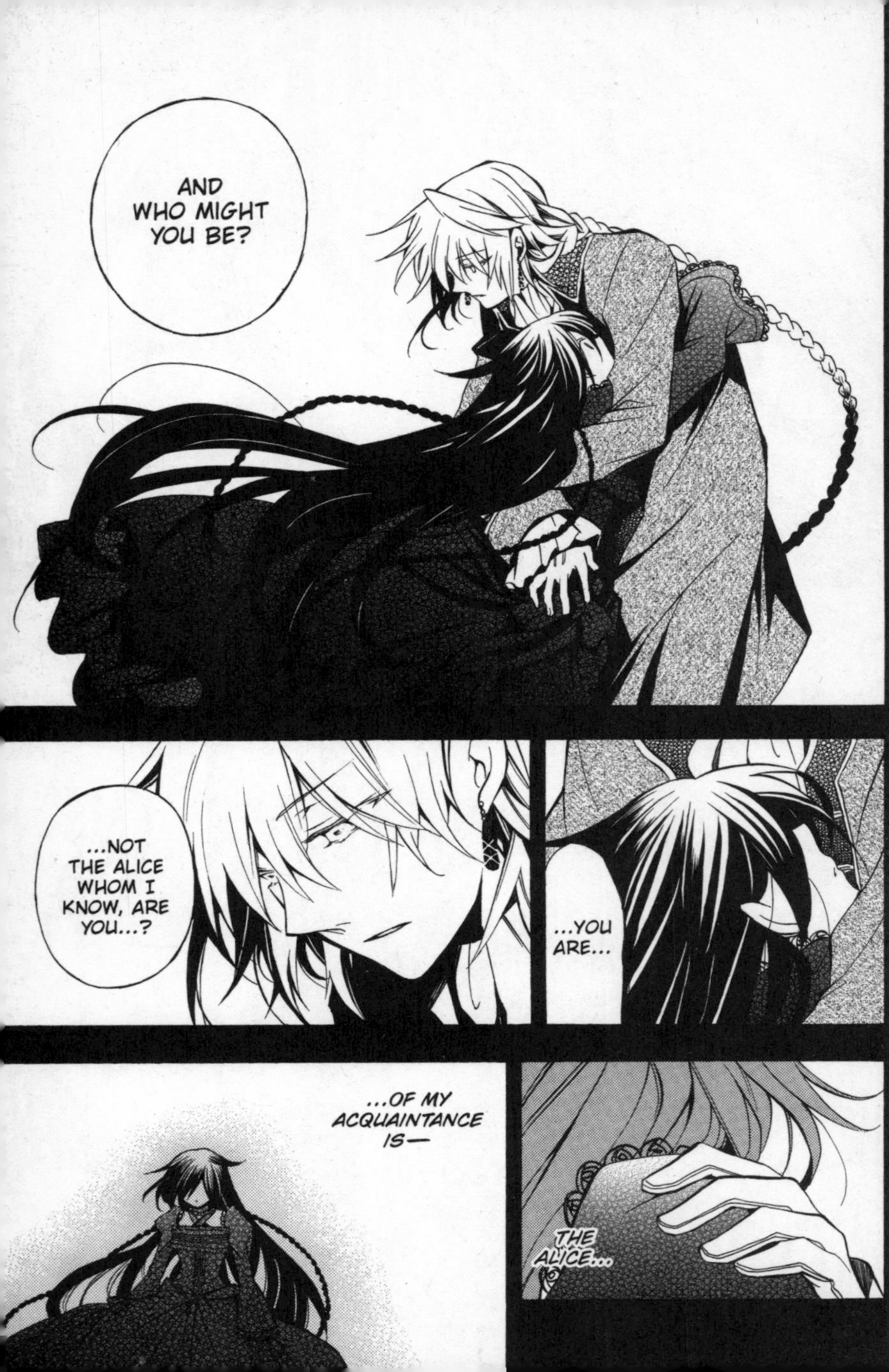
AND WHO MIGHT YOU BE?
...YOU ARE...
...NOT THE ALICE WHOM I KNOW, ARE YOU...?
THE ALICE...
...OF MY ACQUAINTANCE IS—

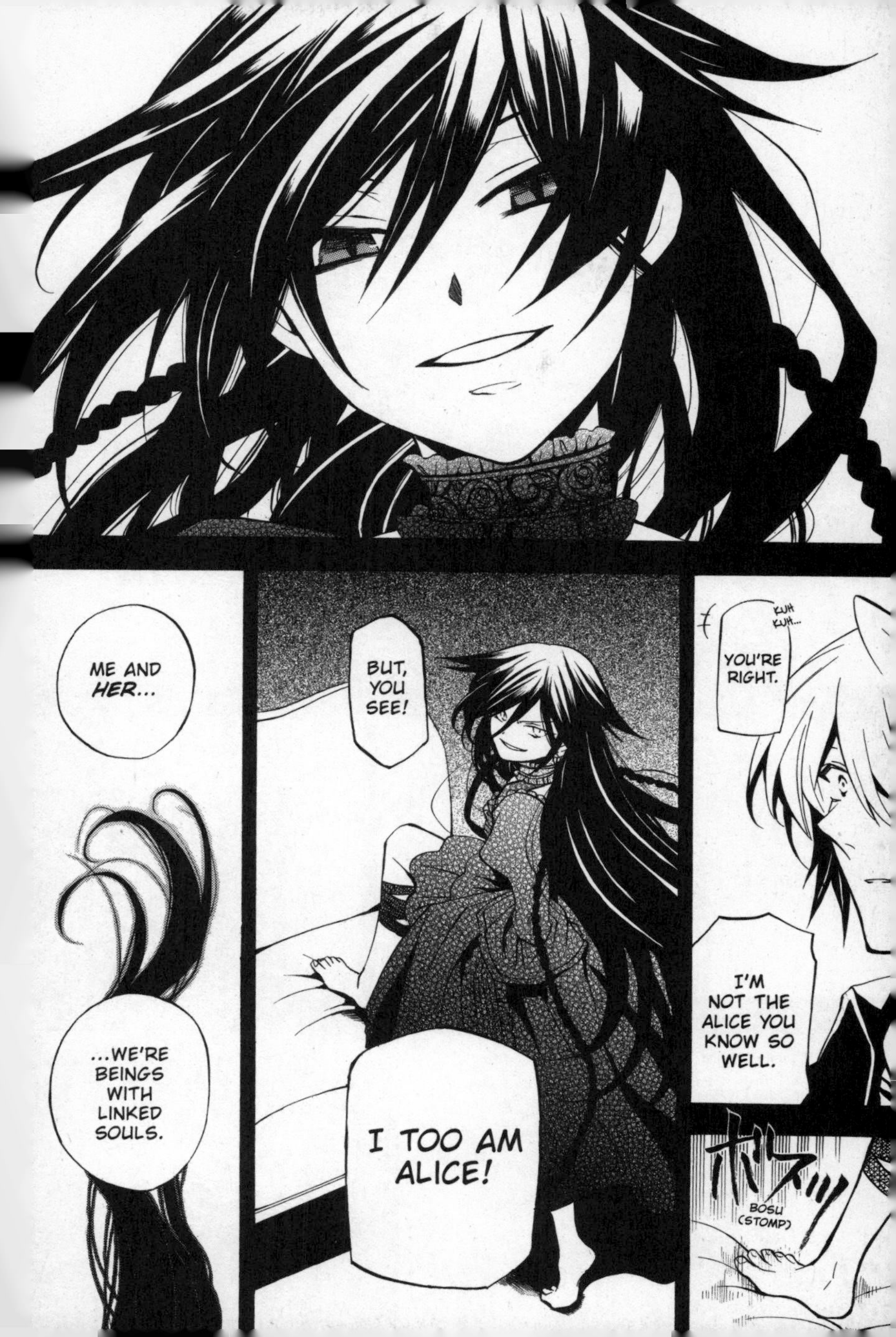
KUH KUH...
YOU'RE RIGHT.
I'M NOT THE ALICE YOU KNOW SO WELL.
BOSU (STOMP)
BUT, YOU SEE!
I TOO AM ALICE!
ME AND HER...
...WE'RE BEINGS WITH LINKED SOULS.

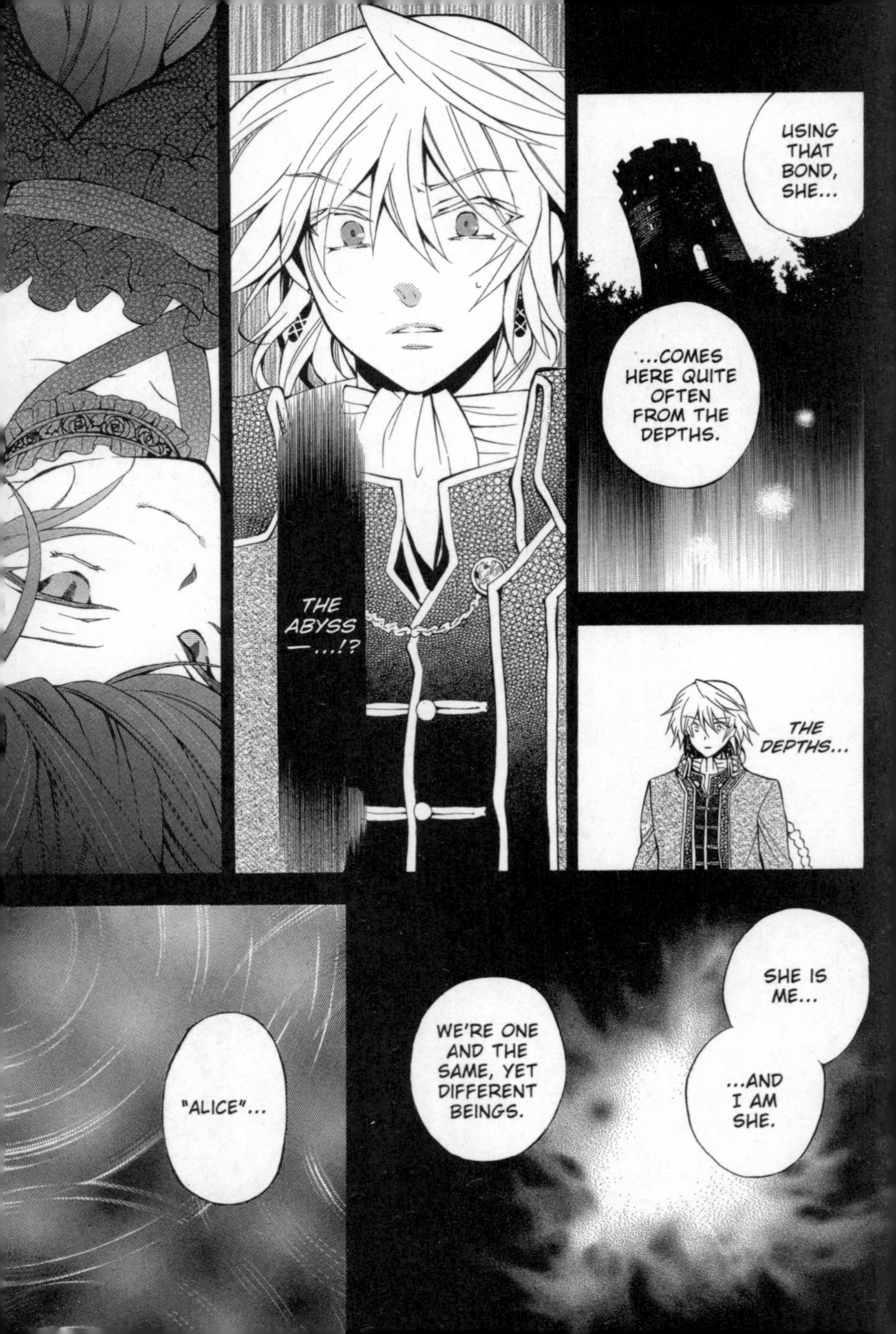
USING THAT BOND, SHE...
...COMES HERE QUITE OFTEN FROM THE DEPTHS.
THE DEPTHS...
THE ABYSS—...!?
SHE IS ME...
...AND I AM SHE.
WE'RE ONE AND THE SAME, YET DIFFERENT BEINGS.
"ALICE"...

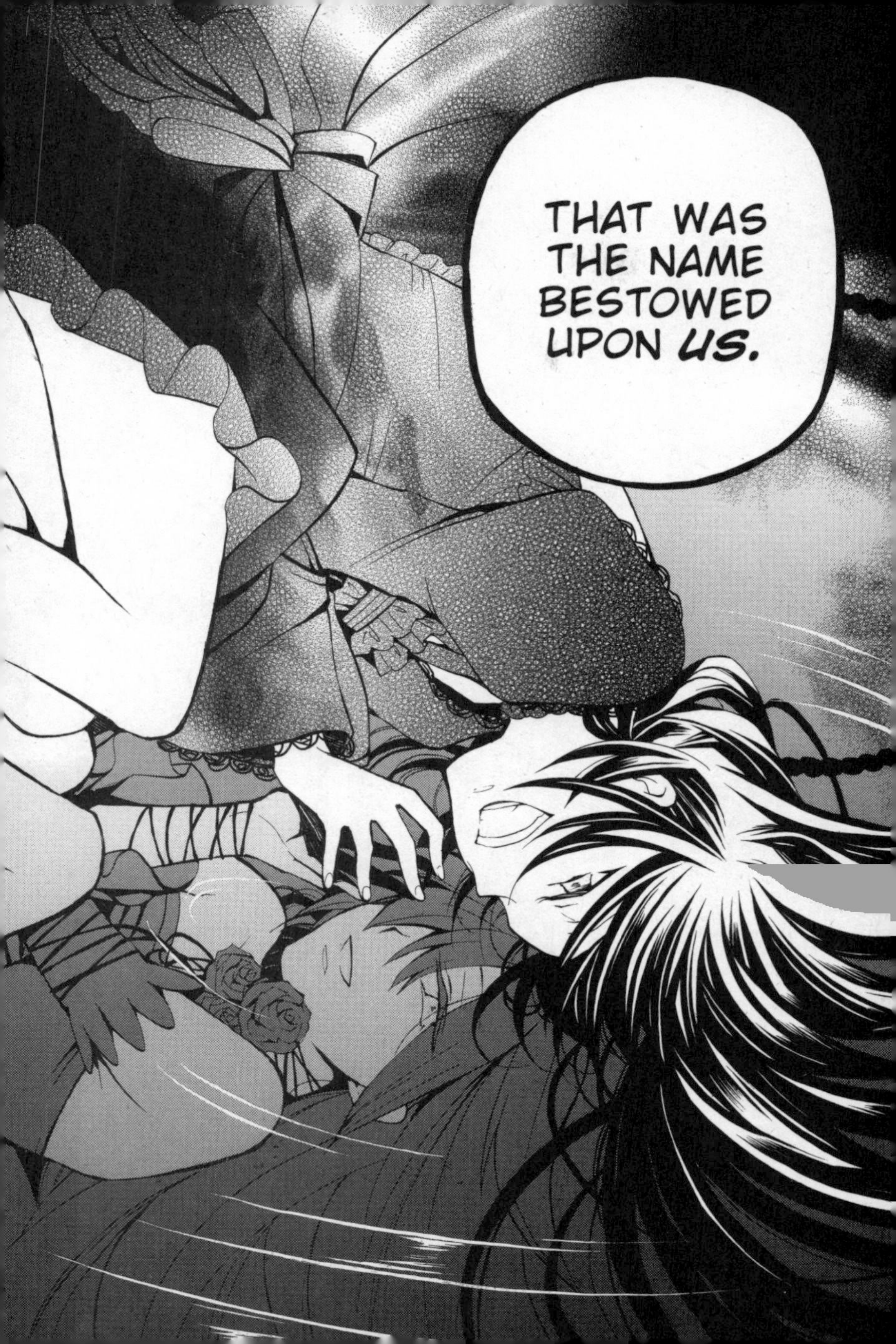
THAT WAS THE NAME BESTOWED UPON US.

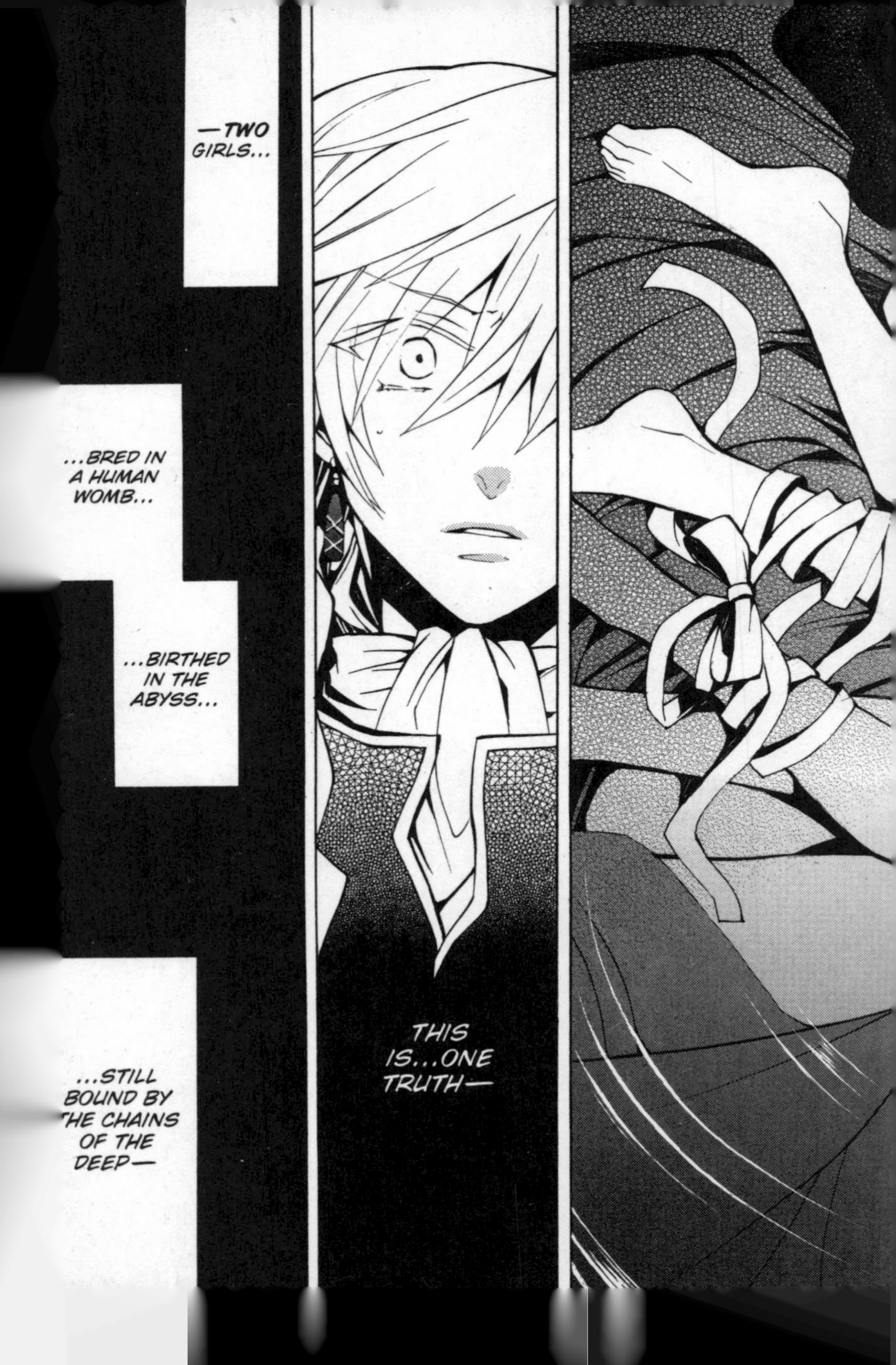
—TWO GIRLS...
...BRED IN A HUMAN WOMB...
...BIRTHED IN THE ABYSS...
...STILL BOUND BY THE CHAINS OF THE DEEP—
THIS IS...ONE TRUTH—

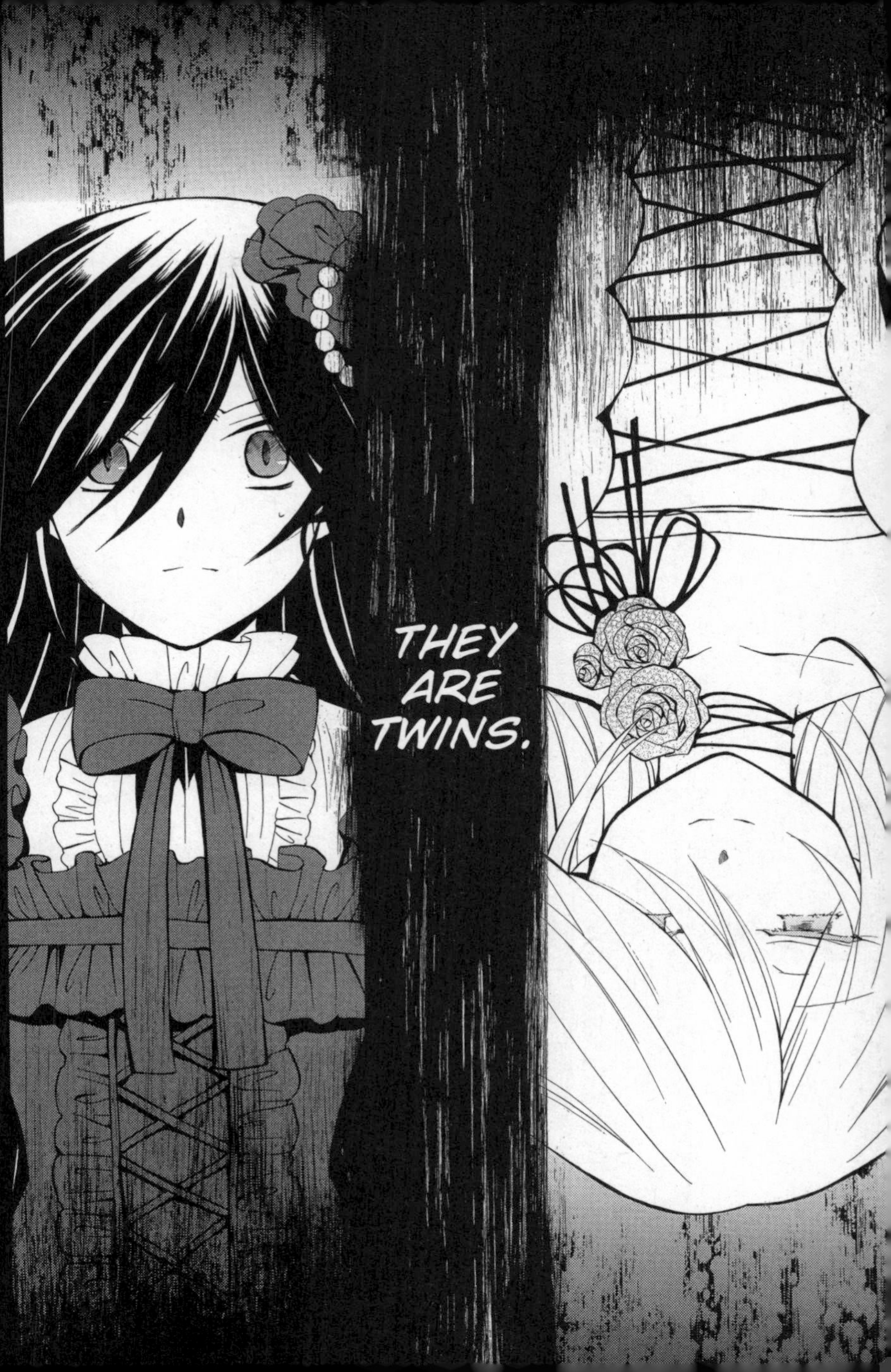
THEY ARE TWINS.

Retrace:XXXII Snow dome

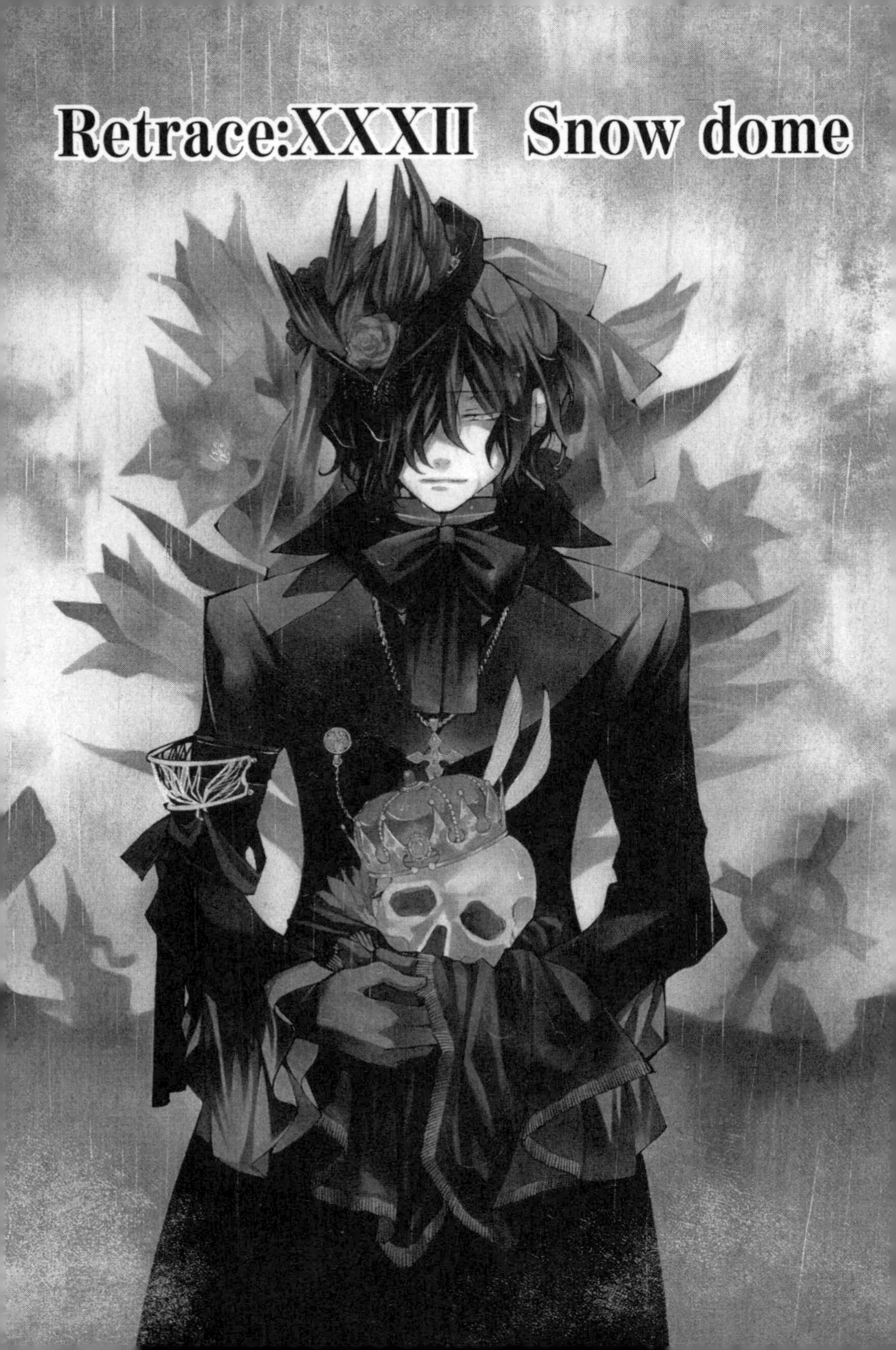

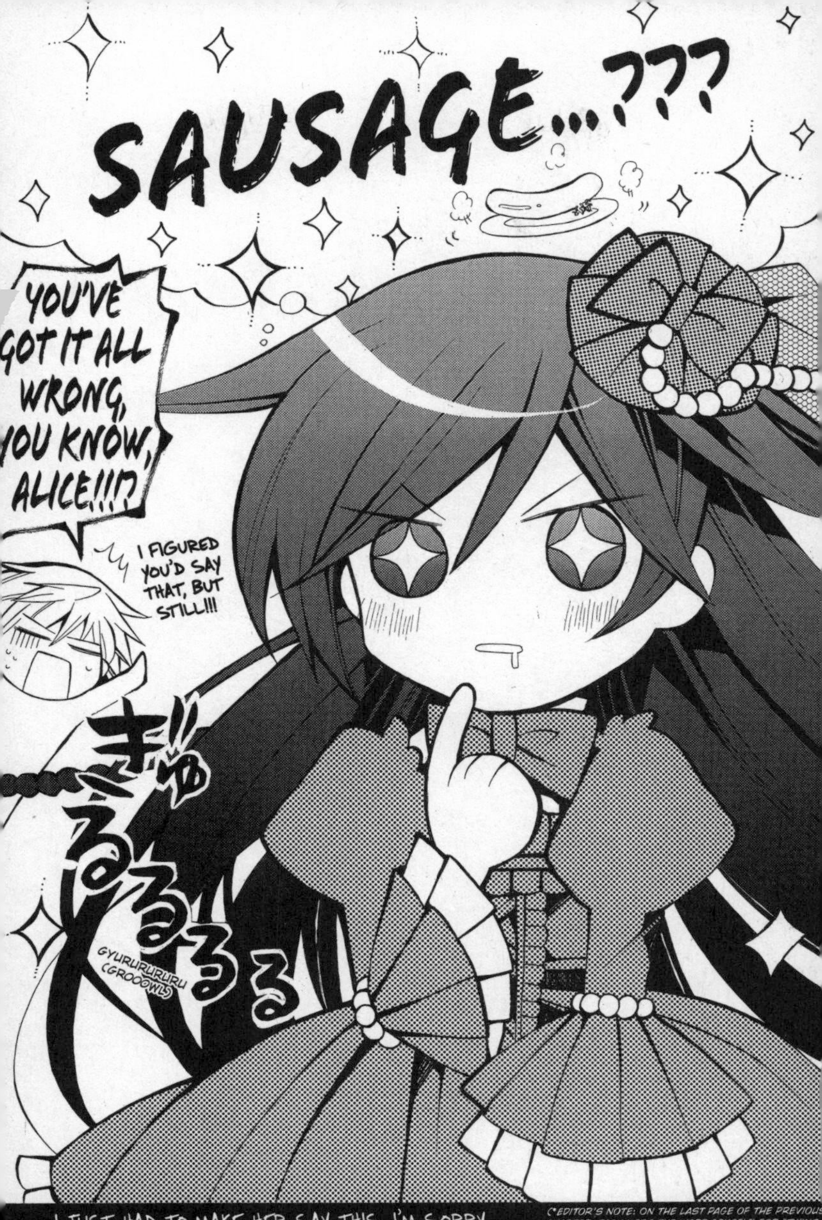
SAUSAGE...???
YOU'VE GOT IT ALL WRONG, YOU KNOW, ALICE!!!?
I FIGURED YOU'D SAY THAT, BUT STILL!!!
ぎゅるるるるる
GYURURURURU (GROOOWL)
I JUST HAD TO MAKE HER SAY THIS...I'M SORRY...
(*EDITOR'S NOTE: ON THE LAST PAGE OF THE PREVIOUS
CHAPTER, JACK USES THE WORD SOUSEIJI FOR "TWINS

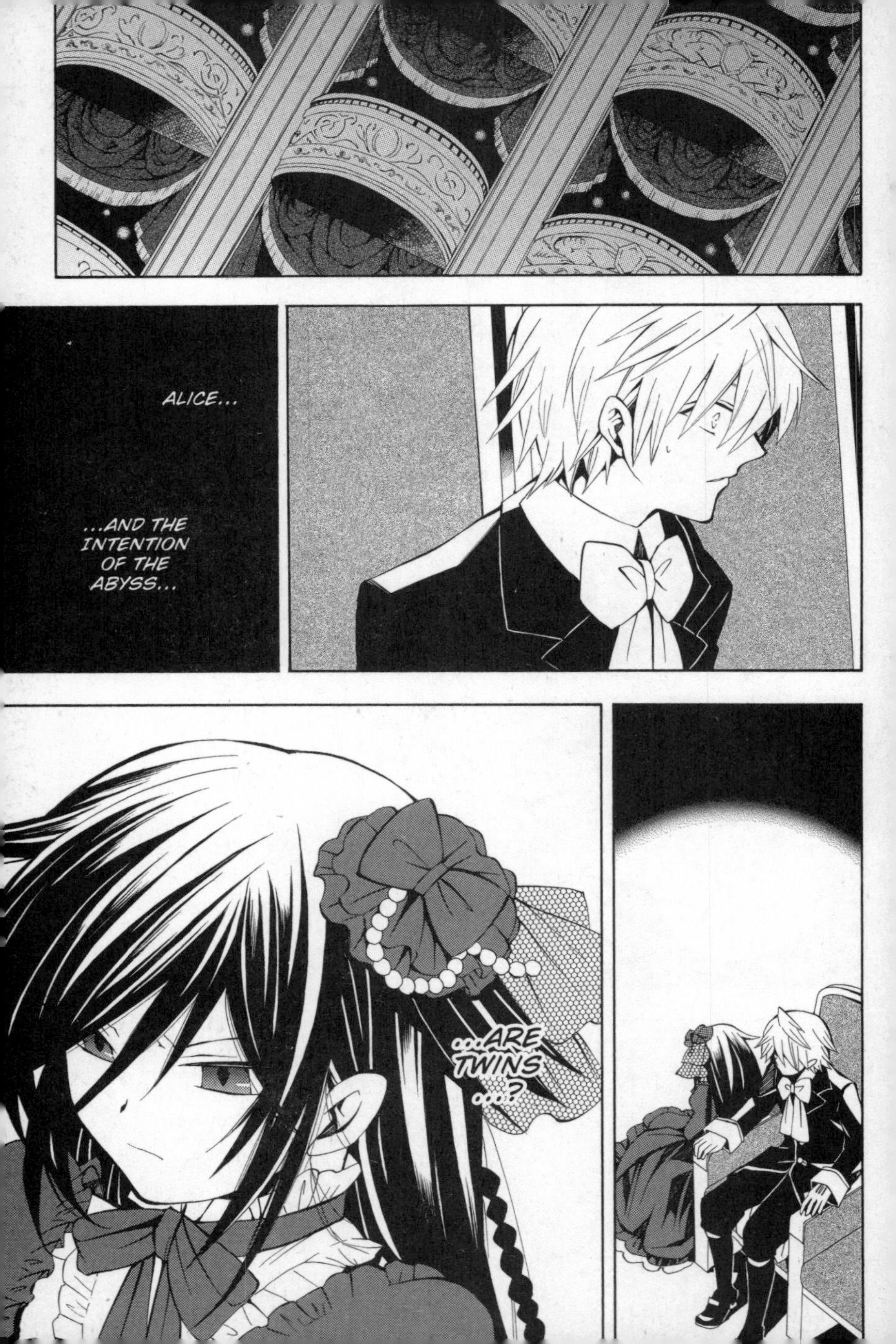
ALICE...
...AND THE INTENTION OF THE ABYSS...
...ARE TWINS...?

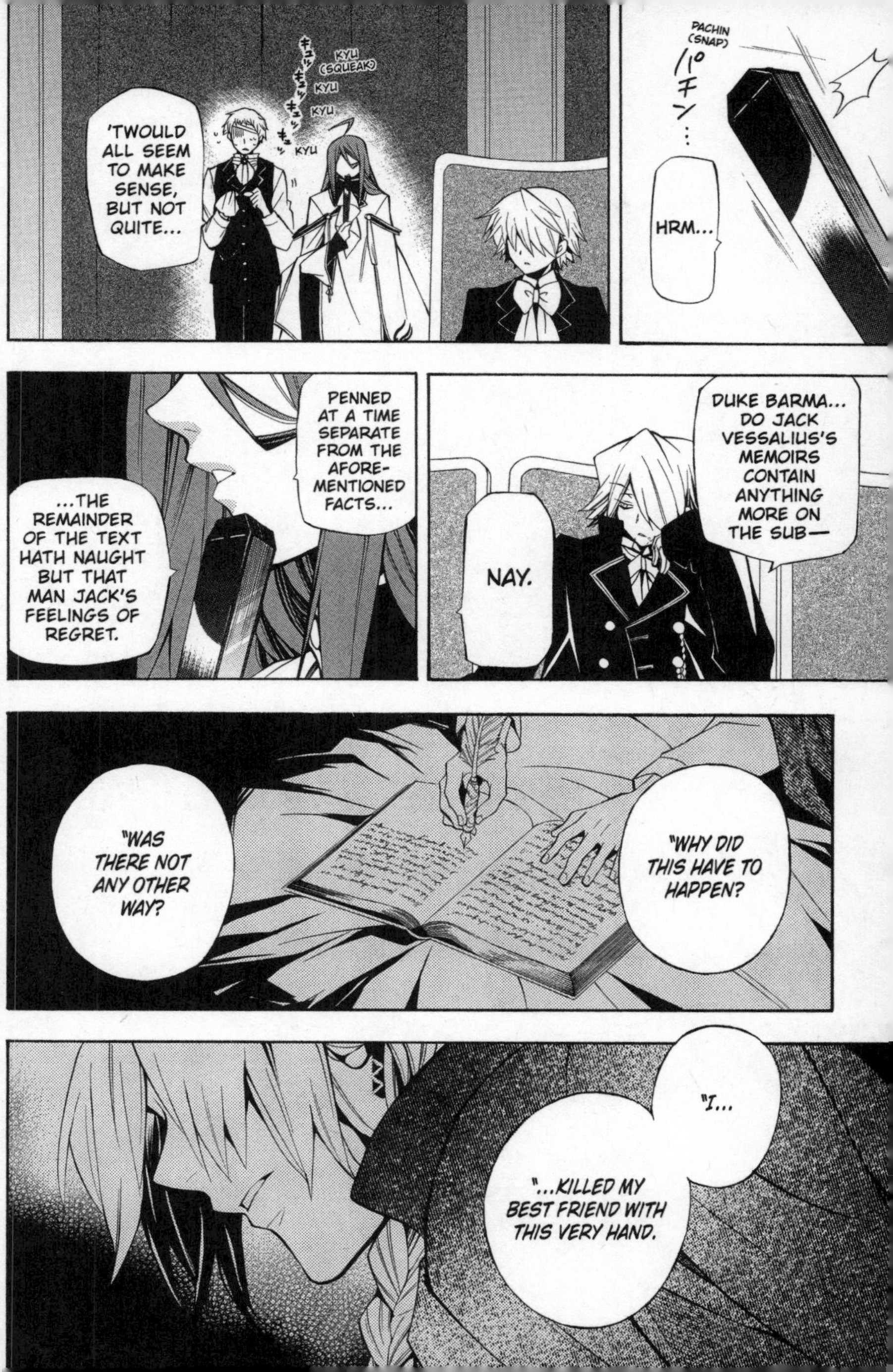

PACHIN (SNAP)
パチン…
HRM…
KYU (SQUEAK)
KYU
KYU
KYU
'TWOULD ALL SEEM TO MAKE SENSE, BUT NOT QUITE…
DUKE BARMA… DO JACK VESSALIUS'S MEMOIRS CONTAIN ANYTHING MORE ON THE SUB—
NAY.
PENNED AT A TIME SEPARATE FROM THE AFORE-MENTIONED FACTS…
…THE REMAINDER OF THE TEXT HATH NAUGHT BUT THAT MAN JACK'S FEELINGS OF REGRET.
"WHY DID THIS HAVE TO HAPPEN?
"WAS THERE NOT ANY OTHER WAY?
"I…
"…KILLED MY BEST FRIEND WITH THIS VERY HAND.

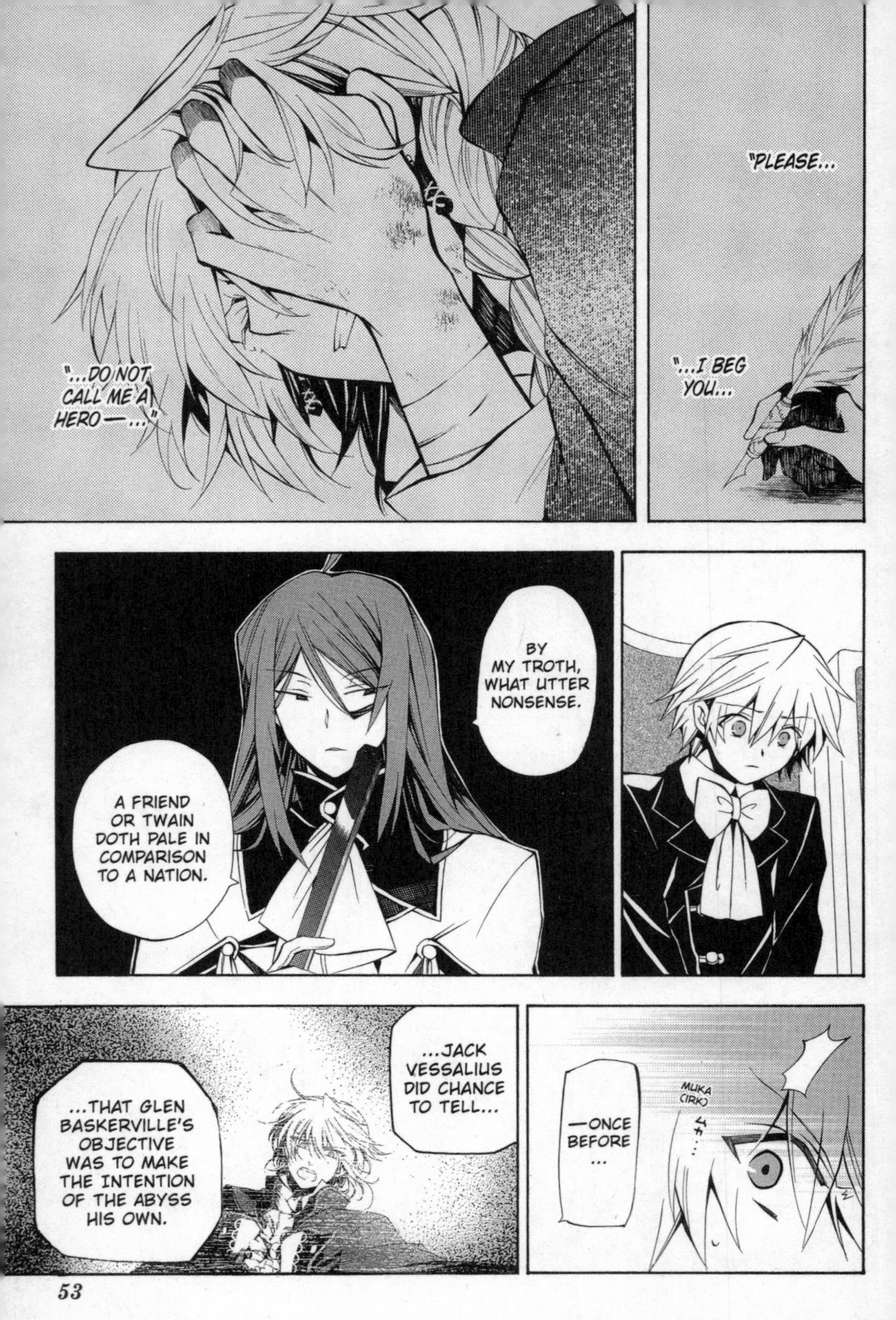
"PLEASE...
"...I BEG YOU...
"...DO NOT CALL ME A HERO—..."
BY MY TROTH, WHAT UTTER NONSENSE.
A FRIEND OR TWAIN DOTH PALE IN COMPARISON TO A NATION.
MUKA (IRK)
—ONCE BEFORE ...
...JACK VESSALIUS DID CHANCE TO TELL...
...THAT GLEN BASKERVILLE'S OBJECTIVE WAS TO MAKE THE INTENTION OF THE ABYSS HIS OWN.

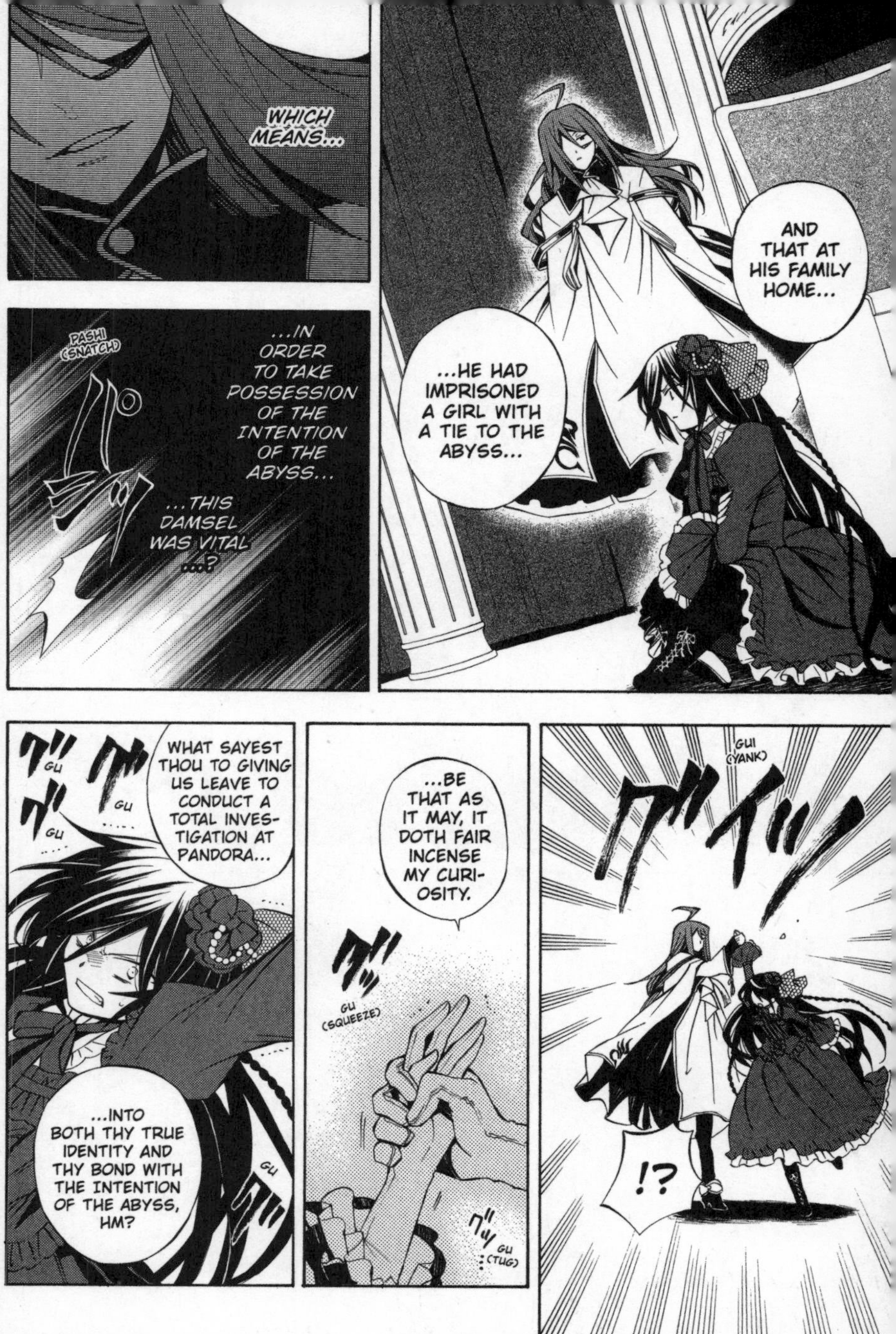
AND THAT AT HIS FAMILY HOME...
...HE HAD IMPRISONED A GIRL WITH A TIE TO THE ABYSS...
WHICH MEANS...
PASHI (SNATCH)
...IN ORDER TO TAKE POSSESSION OF THE INTENTION OF THE ABYSS...
...THIS DAMSEL WAS VITAL ...?
GUI (YANK)
!?
...BE THAT AS IT MAY, IT DOTH FAIR INCENSE MY CURI-OSITY.
GU (SQUEEZE)
GU (TUG)
GU
GU
GU
WHAT SAYEST THOU TO GIVING US LEAVE TO CONDUCT A TOTAL INVES-TIGATION AT PANDORA...
...INTO BOTH THY TRUE IDENTITY AND THY BOND WITH THE INTENTION OF THE ABYSS, HM?
GU

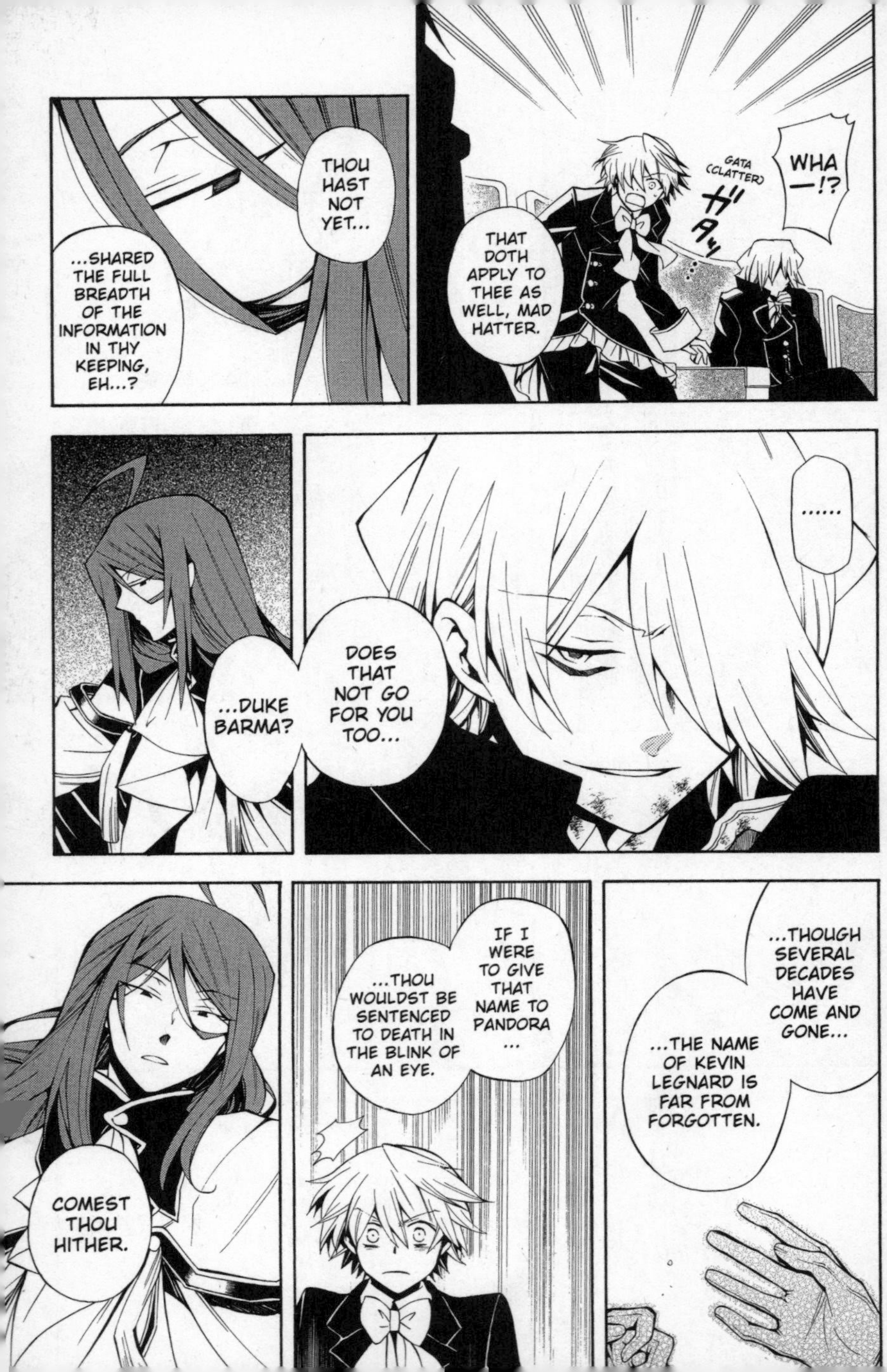
WHA—!?
GATA (CLATTER)
ガタッ
THAT DOTH APPLY TO THEE AS WELL, MAD HATTER.
THOU HAST NOT YET...
...SHARED THE FULL BREADTH OF THE INFORMATION IN THY KEEPING, EH...?
......
DOES THAT NOT GO FOR YOU TOO...
...DUKE BARMA?
...THOUGH SEVERAL DECADES HAVE COME AND GONE...
...THE NAME OF KEVIN LEGNARD IS FAR FROM FORGOTTEN.
IF I WERE TO GIVE THAT NAME TO PANDORA ...
...THOU WOULDST BE SENTENCED TO DEATH IN THE BLINK OF AN EYE.
COMEST THOU HITHER.

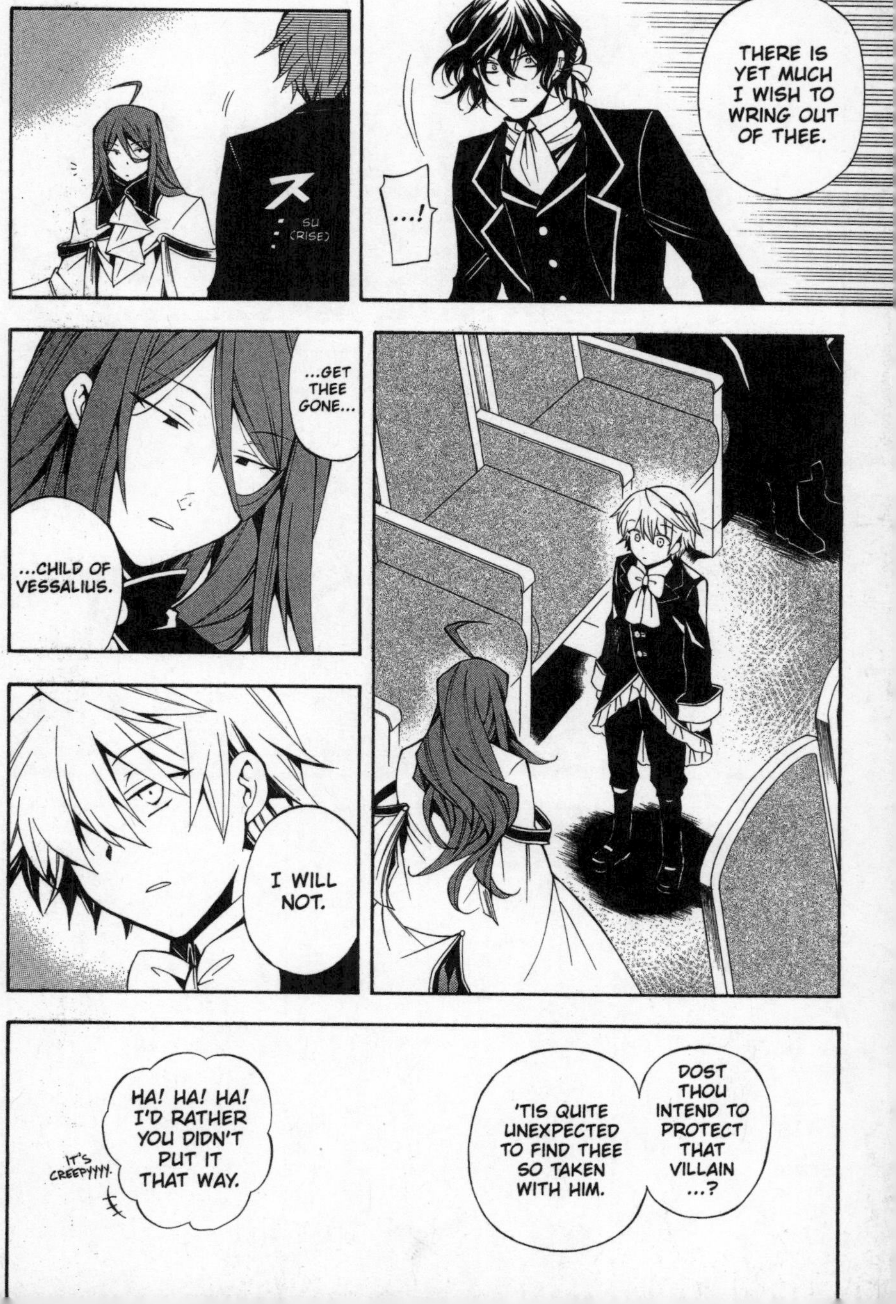
THERE IS YET MUCH I WISH TO WRING OUT OF THEE.
...!
ス
SU (RISE)
...GET THEE GONE...
...CHILD OF VESSALIUS.
I WILL NOT.
DOST THOU INTEND TO PROTECT THAT VILLAIN ...?
'TIS QUITE UNEXPECTED TO FIND THEE SO TAKEN WITH HIM.
HA! HA! HA! I'D RATHER YOU DIDN'T PUT IT THAT WAY.
IT'S CREEPYYYY.

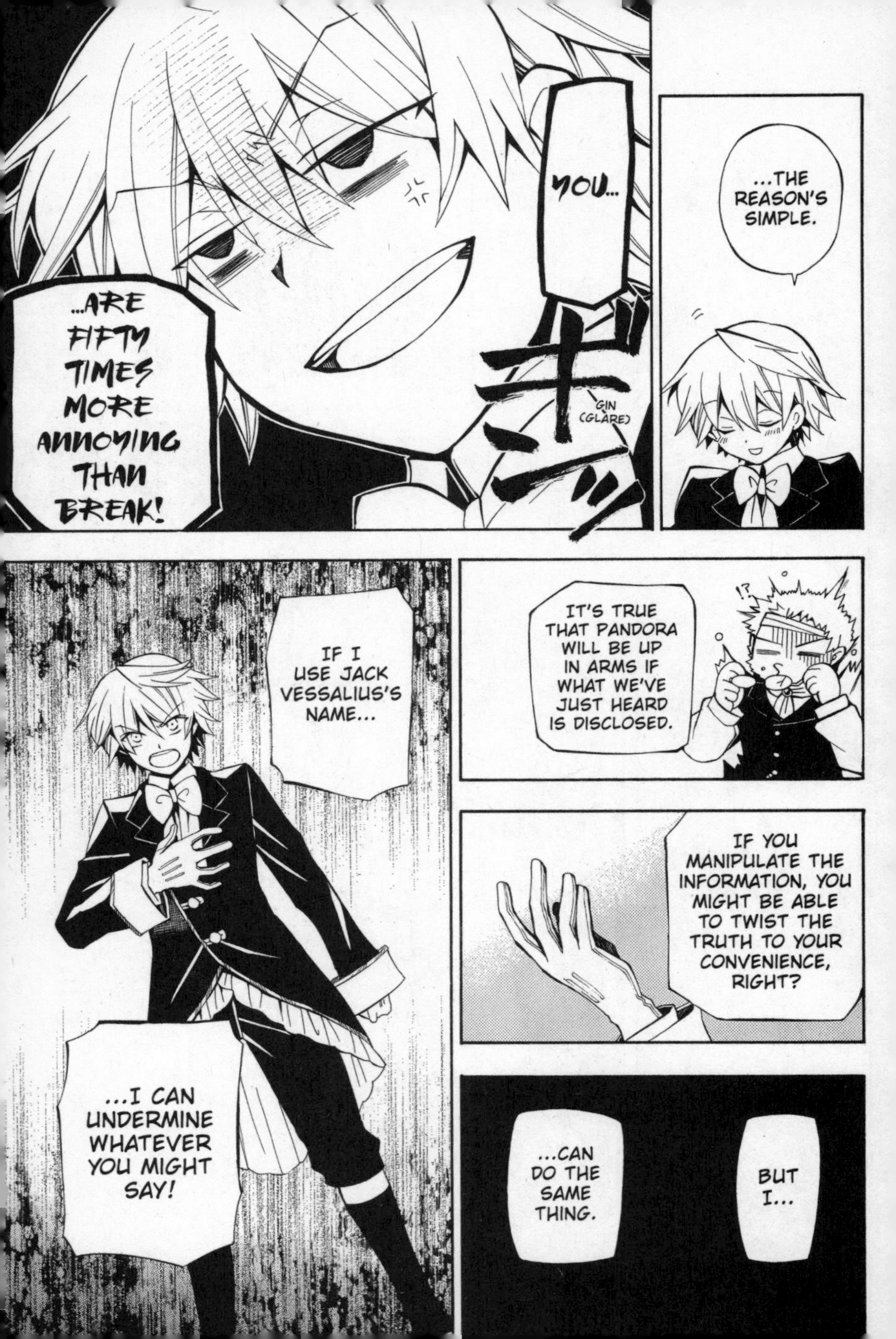
...THE REASON'S SIMPLE.
YOU...
GIN (GLARE)
...ARE FIFTY TIMES MORE ANNOYING THAN BREAK!
!?
IT'S TRUE THAT PANDORA WILL BE UP IN ARMS IF WHAT WE'VE JUST HEARD IS DISCLOSED.
IF YOU MANIPULATE THE INFORMATION, YOU MIGHT BE ABLE TO TWIST THE TRUTH TO YOUR CONVENIENCE, RIGHT?
BUT I...
...CAN DO THE SAME THING.
IF I USE JACK VESSALIUS'S NAME...
...I CAN UNDERMINE WHATEVER YOU MIGHT SAY!

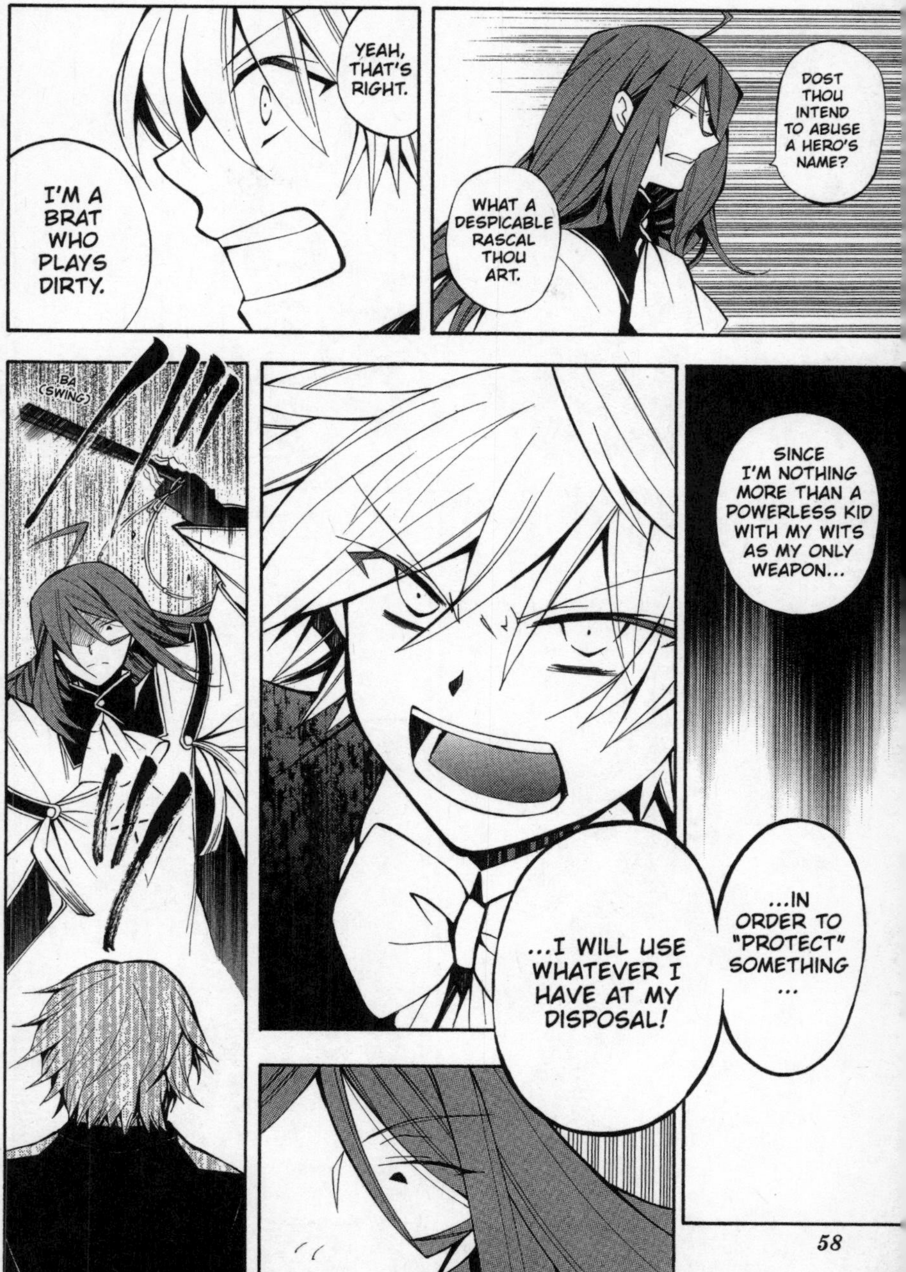
DOST THOU INTEND TO ABUSE A HERO'S NAME?
WHAT A DESPICABLE RASCAL THOU ART.
YEAH, THAT'S RIGHT.
I'M A BRAT WHO PLAYS DIRTY.
SINCE I'M NOTHING MORE THAN A POWERLESS KID WITH MY WITS AS MY ONLY WEAPON...
...IN ORDER TO "PROTECT" SOMETHING...
...I WILL USE WHATEVER I HAVE AT MY DISPOSAL!
BA (SWING)

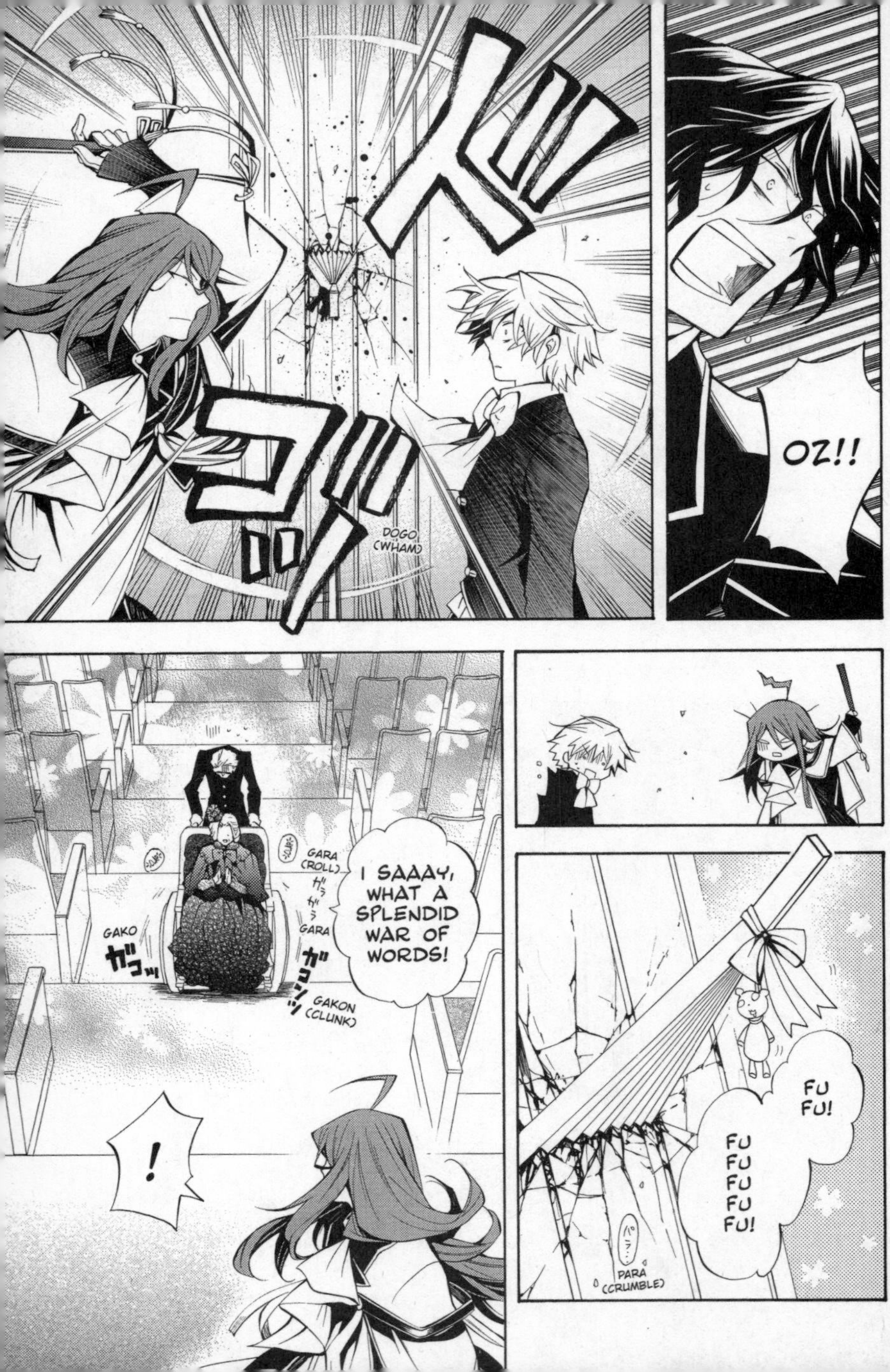
OZ!!
DOGO (WHAM)
FU FU!
FU FU FU FU FU!
PARA (CRUMBLE)
GARA (ROLL)
GARA
I SAAAY, WHAT A SPLENDID WAR OF WORDS!
GAKO
GAKON (CLUNK)
!

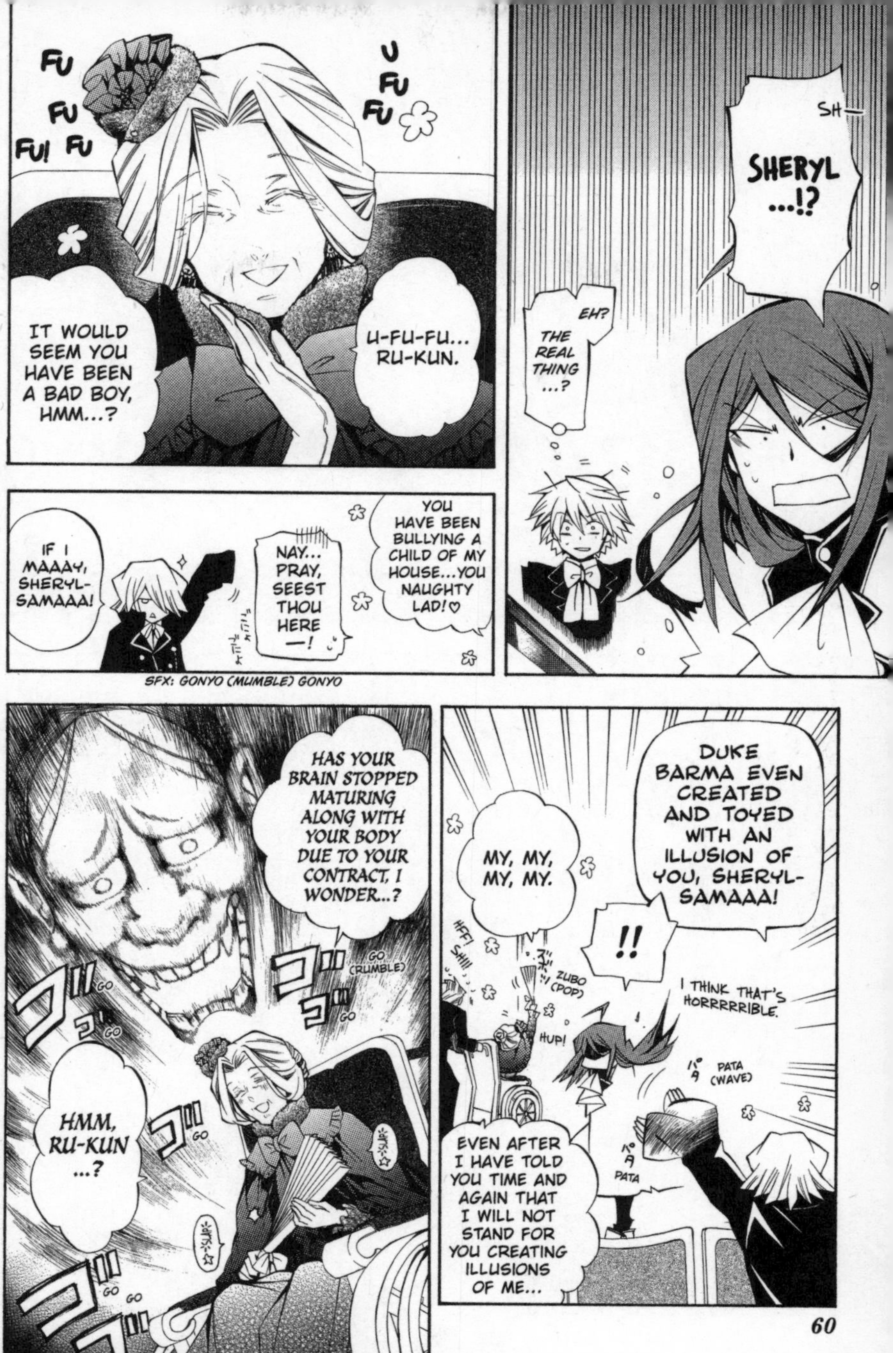
SH—
SHERYL ...!?
EH? THE REAL THING ...?
FU FU FU! FU
U FU FU
U-FU-FU... RU-KUN.
IT WOULD SEEM YOU HAVE BEEN A BAD BOY, HMM...?
YOU HAVE BEEN BULLYING A CHILD OF MY HOUSE...YOU NAUGHTY LAD!♡
NAY... PRAY, SEEST THOU HERE—!
IF I MAAAY, SHERYL-SAMAAA!
SFX: GONYO (MUMBLE) GONYO
DUKE BARMA EVEN CREATED AND TOYED WITH AN ILLUSION OF YOU, SHERYL-SAMAAA!
MY, MY, MY, MY.
!!
HFF! SH!!
ZUBO (POP)
HUP!
I THINK THAT'S HORRRRRIBLE.
PATA (WAVE)
PATA
EVEN AFTER I HAVE TOLD YOU TIME AND AGAIN THAT I WILL NOT STAND FOR YOU CREATING ILLUSIONS OF ME...
HAS YOUR BRAIN STOPPED MATURING ALONG WITH YOUR BODY DUE TO YOUR CONTRACT, I WONDER...?
GO (RUMBLE)
GO
HMM, RU-KUN ...?
GO GO

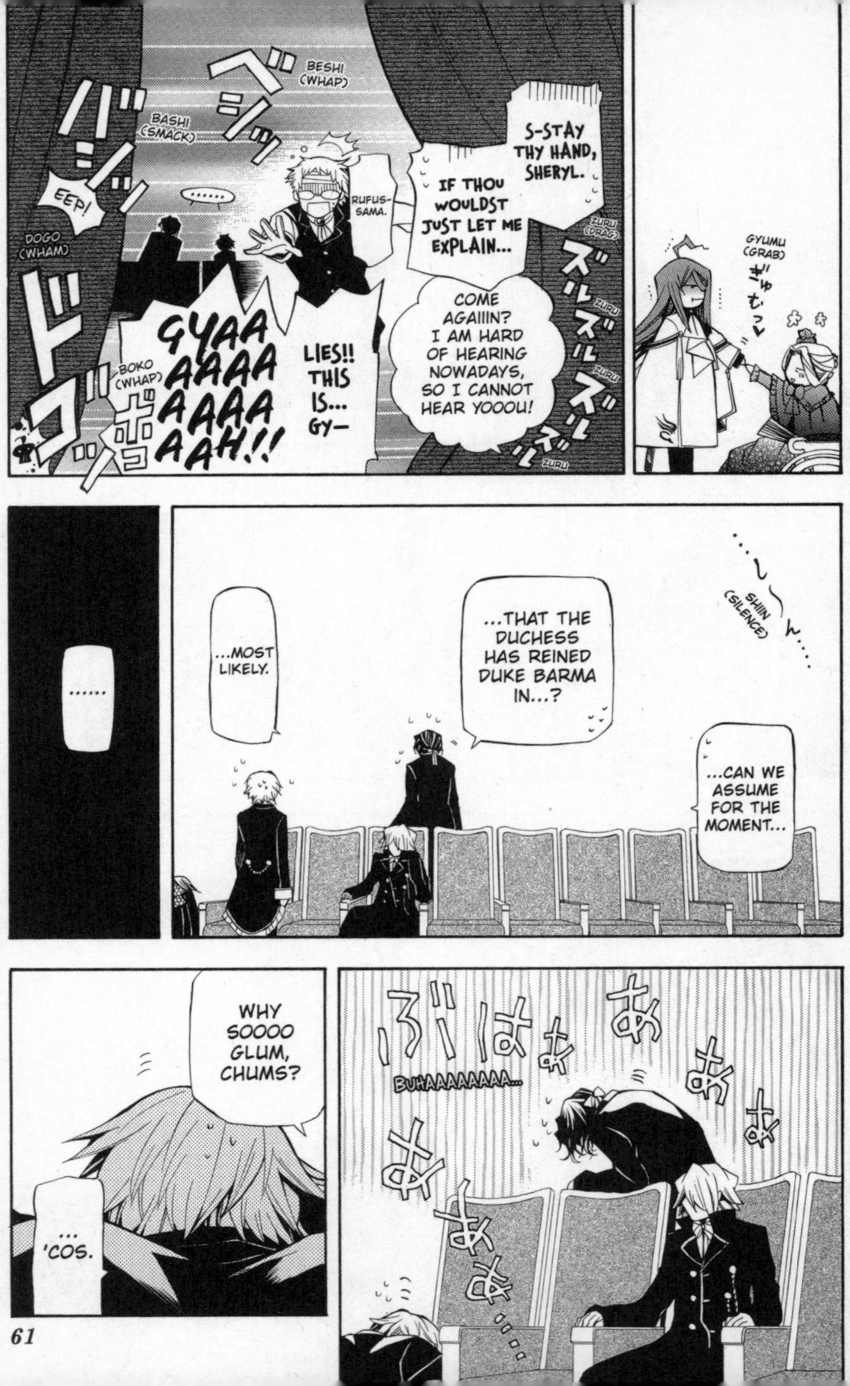
GYUMU (GRAB)
ぎゅむっ
S-STAY THY HAND, SHERYL.
IF THOU WOULDST JUST LET ME EXPLAIN...
ZURU (DRAG)
ZURU
ZURU
ZURU
COME AGAIIIN? I AM HARD OF HEARING NOWADAYS, SO I CANNOT HEAR YOOOU!
RUFUS-SAMA.
BESHI (WHAP)
BASHI (SMACK)
......
EEP!
LIES!! THIS IS... GY—
GYAAAAAAAAAAAAH!!!
DOGO (WHAM)
BOKO (WHAP)
SHIN (SILENCE)
...CAN WE ASSUME FOR THE MOMENT...
...THAT THE DUCHESS HAS REINED DUKE BARMA IN...?
...MOST LIKELY.
......
BUHAAAAAAAA...
WHY SOOOO GLUM, CHUMS?
...'COS.

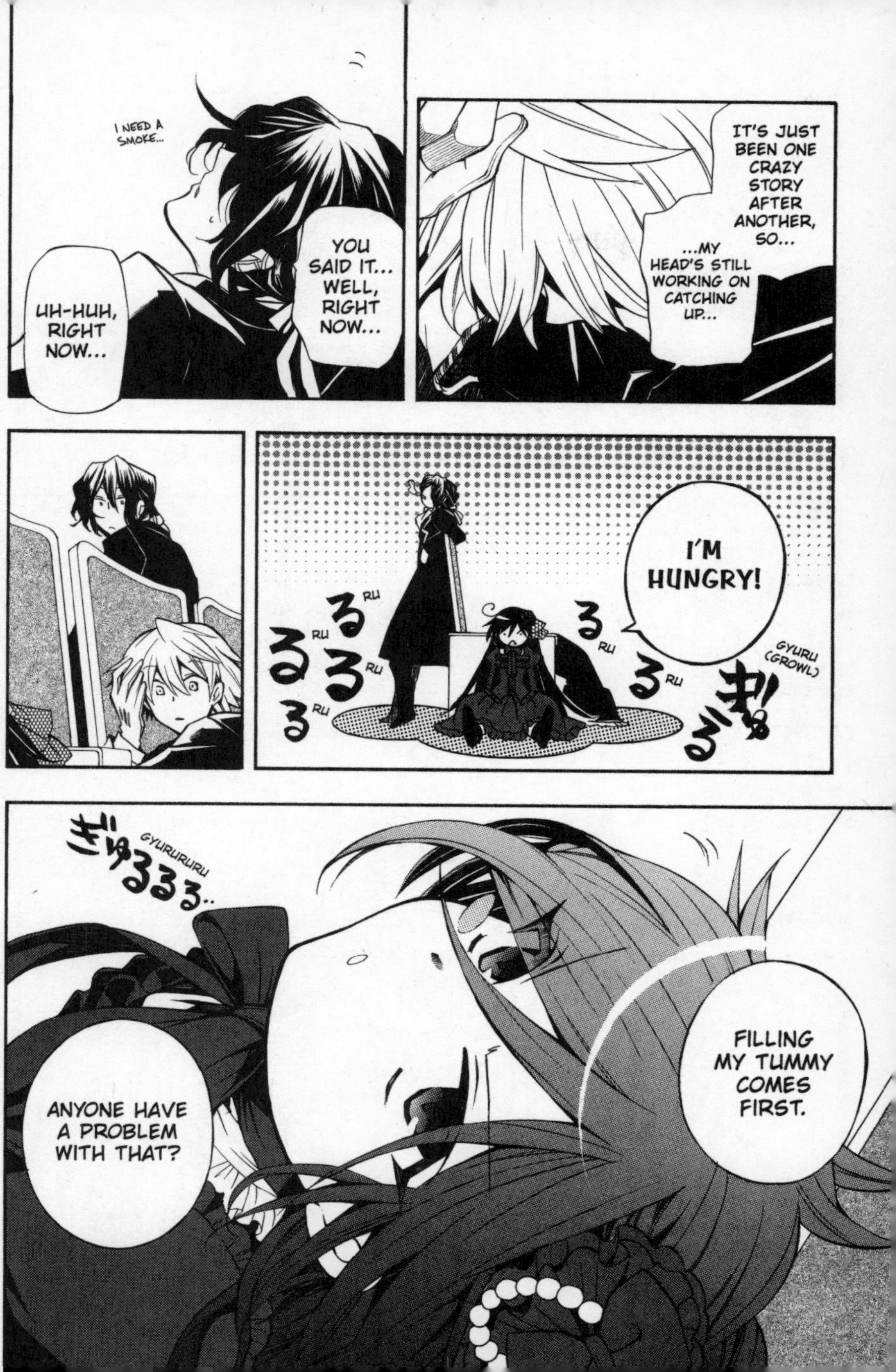
IT'S JUST BEEN ONE CRAZY STORY AFTER ANOTHER, SO...
...MY HEAD'S STILL WORKING ON CATCHING UP...
YOU SAID IT... WELL, RIGHT NOW...
UH-HUH, RIGHT NOW...
I NEED A SMOKE...
I'M HUNGRY!
GYURU (GROWL)
RU
RU
RU
RU
RU
RU
RU
GYURURURU
FILLING MY TUMMY COMES FIRST.
ANYONE HAVE A PROBLEM WITH THAT?

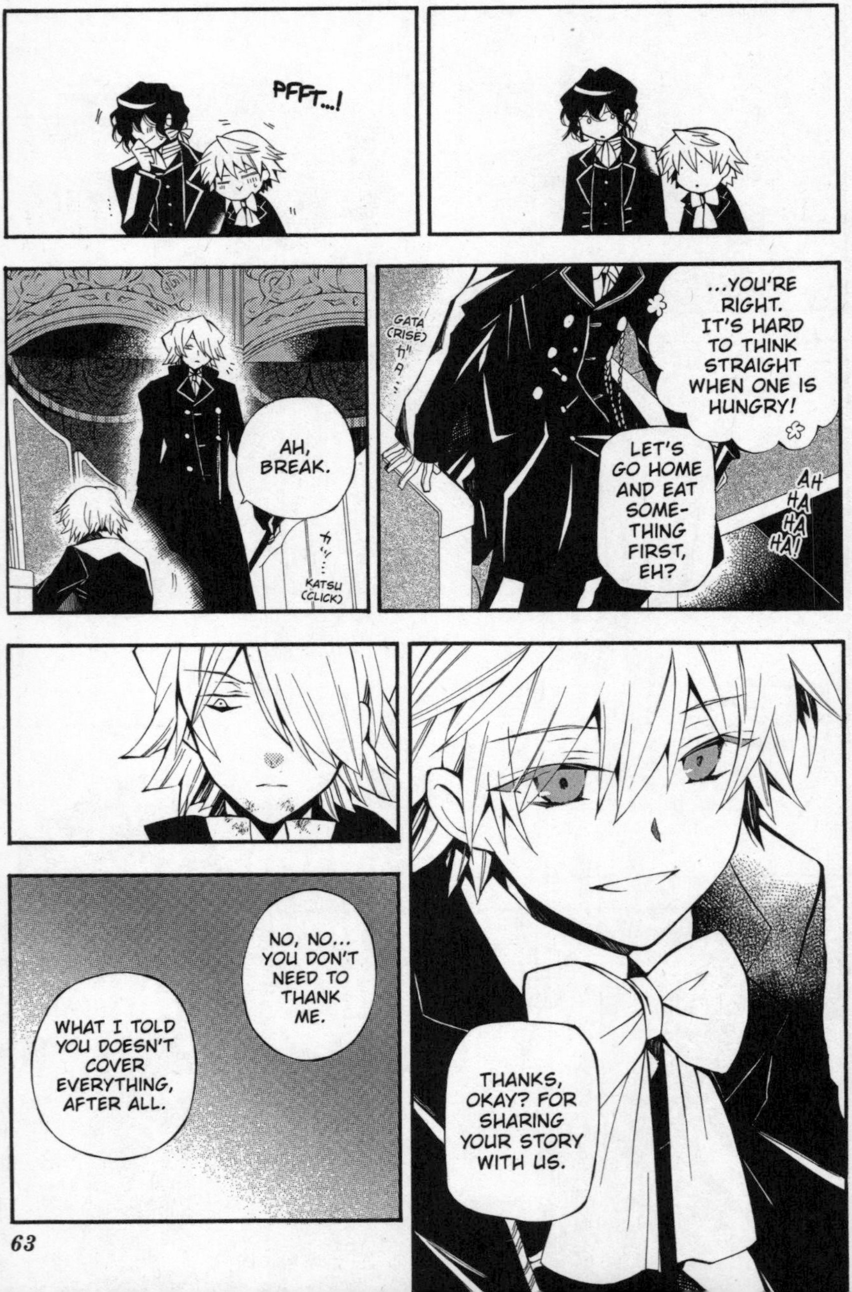
PFFT...!
GATA (RISE)
...YOU'RE RIGHT. IT'S HARD TO THINK STRAIGHT WHEN ONE IS HUNGRY!
LET'S GO HOME AND EAT SOME-THING FIRST, EH?
AH HA HA HA!
AH, BREAK.
KATSU (CLICK)
THANKS, OKAY? FOR SHARING YOUR STORY WITH US.
NO, NO... YOU DON'T NEED TO THANK ME.
WHAT I TOLD YOU DOESN'T COVER EVERYTHING, AFTER ALL.

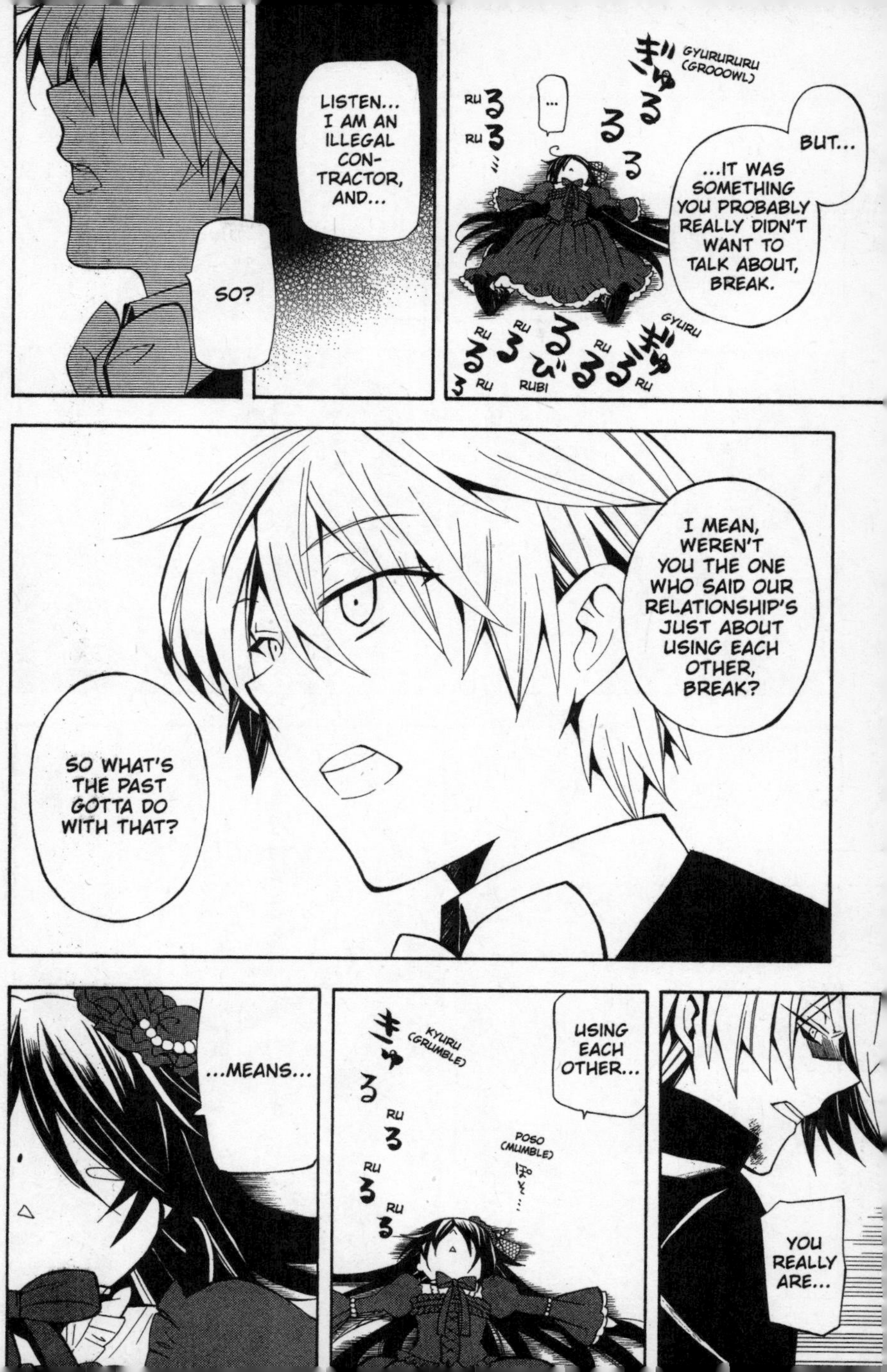
GYURURURU (GROOOWL)
BUT...
...IT WAS SOMETHING YOU PROBABLY REALLY DIDN'T WANT TO TALK ABOUT, BREAK.
...
RU RU
GYURU RU RU RUBI RU RU RU
LISTEN... I AM AN ILLEGAL CON-TRACTOR, AND...
SO?
I MEAN, WEREN'T YOU THE ONE WHO SAID OUR RELATIONSHIP'S JUST ABOUT USING EACH OTHER, BREAK?
SO WHAT'S THE PAST GOTTA DO WITH THAT?
YOU REALLY ARE...
USING EACH OTHER...
KYURU (GRUMBLE)
RU RU RU
POSO (MUMBLE)
...MEANS...

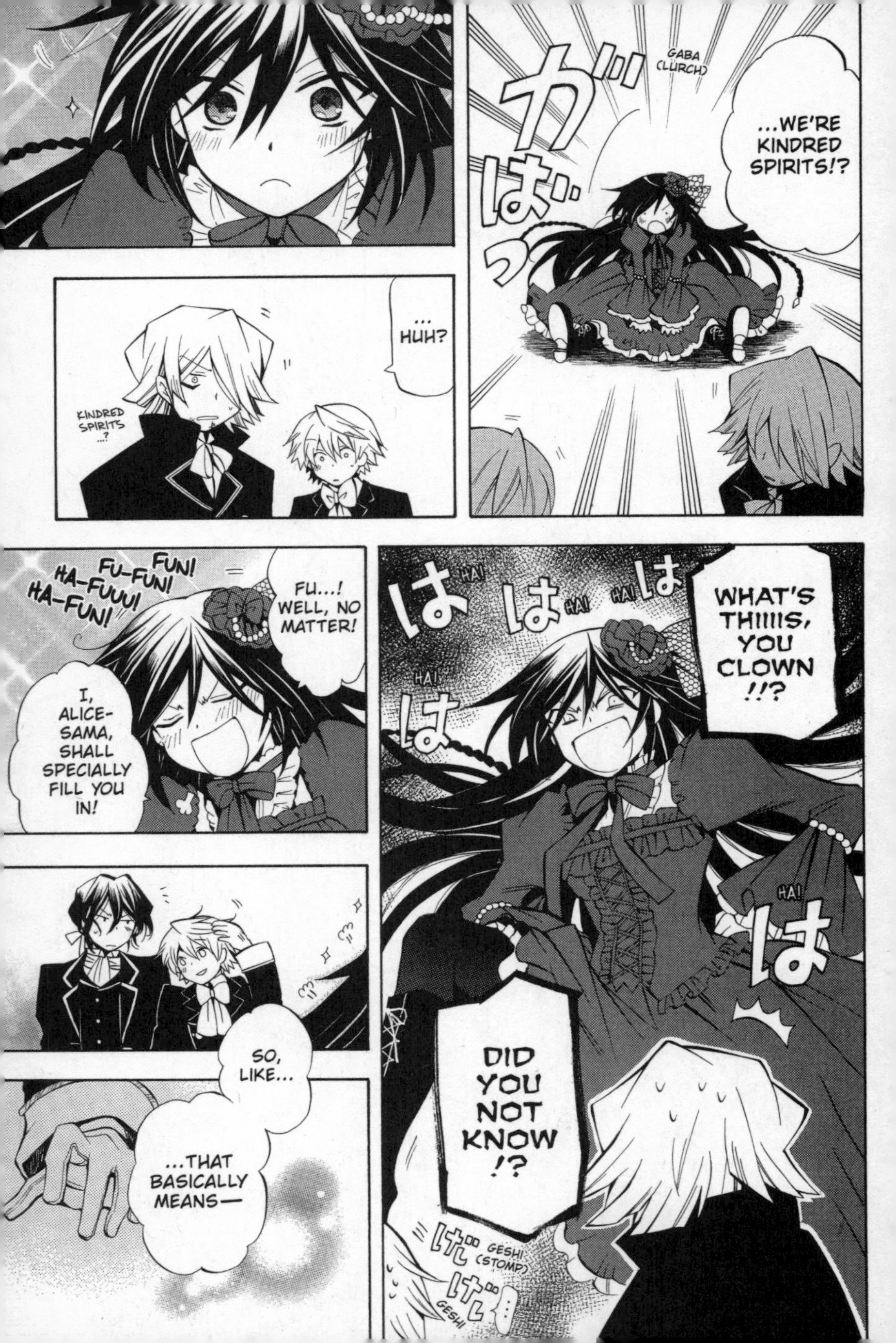
GABA (LURCH)
...WE'RE KINDRED SPIRITS!?
...HUH?
KINDRED SPIRITS ...?
HA! HA! HA!
WHAT'S THIIIIS, YOU CLOWN!!?
HA!
HA!
DID YOU NOT KNOW!?
GESHI (STOMP)
GESHI
FU...! WELL, NO MATTER!
FU-FUN! HA-FUUUN! HA-FUN!
I, ALICE-SAMA, SHALL SPECIALLY FILL YOU IN!
SO, LIKE...
...THAT BASICALLY MEANS—

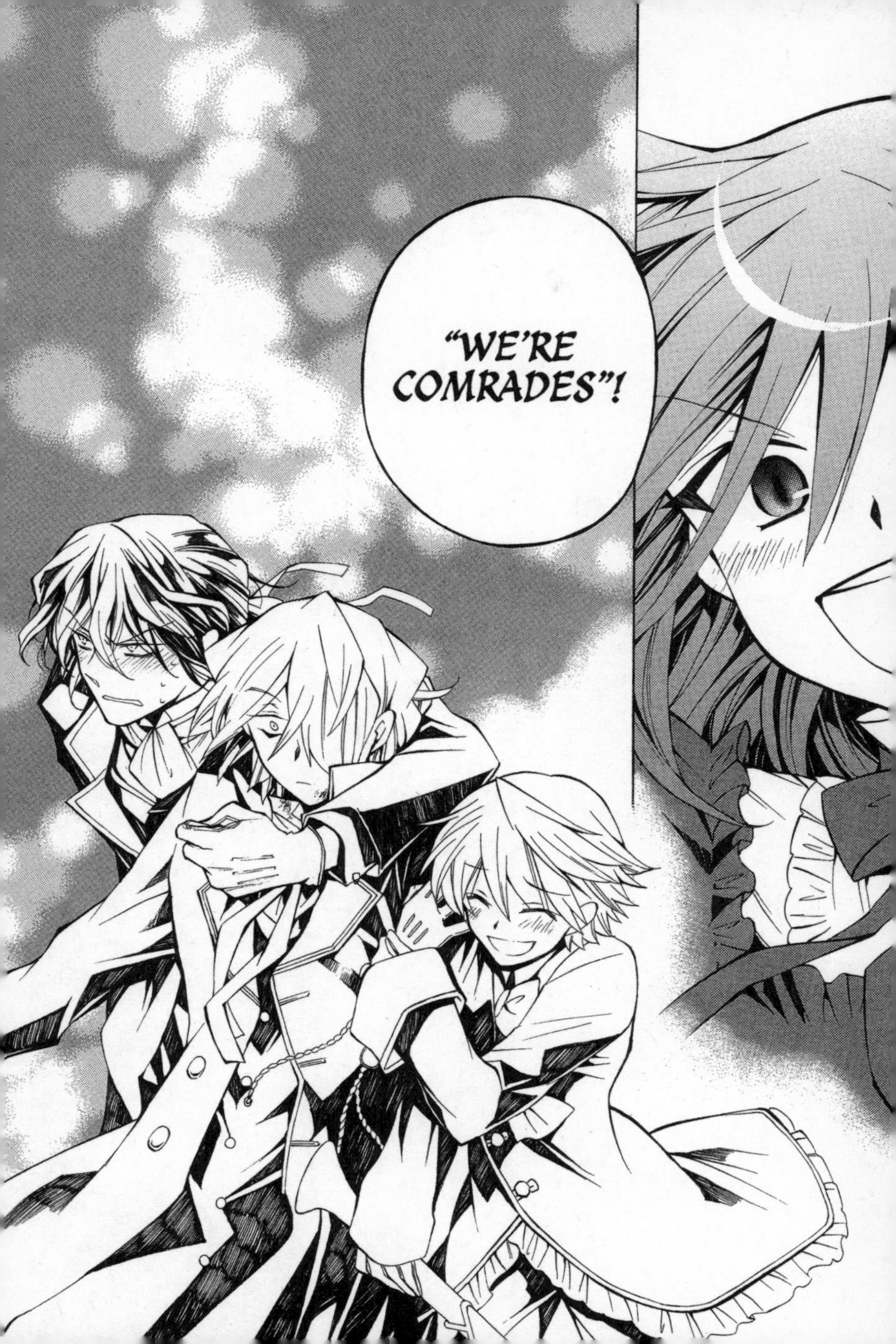
"WE'RE COMRADES"!

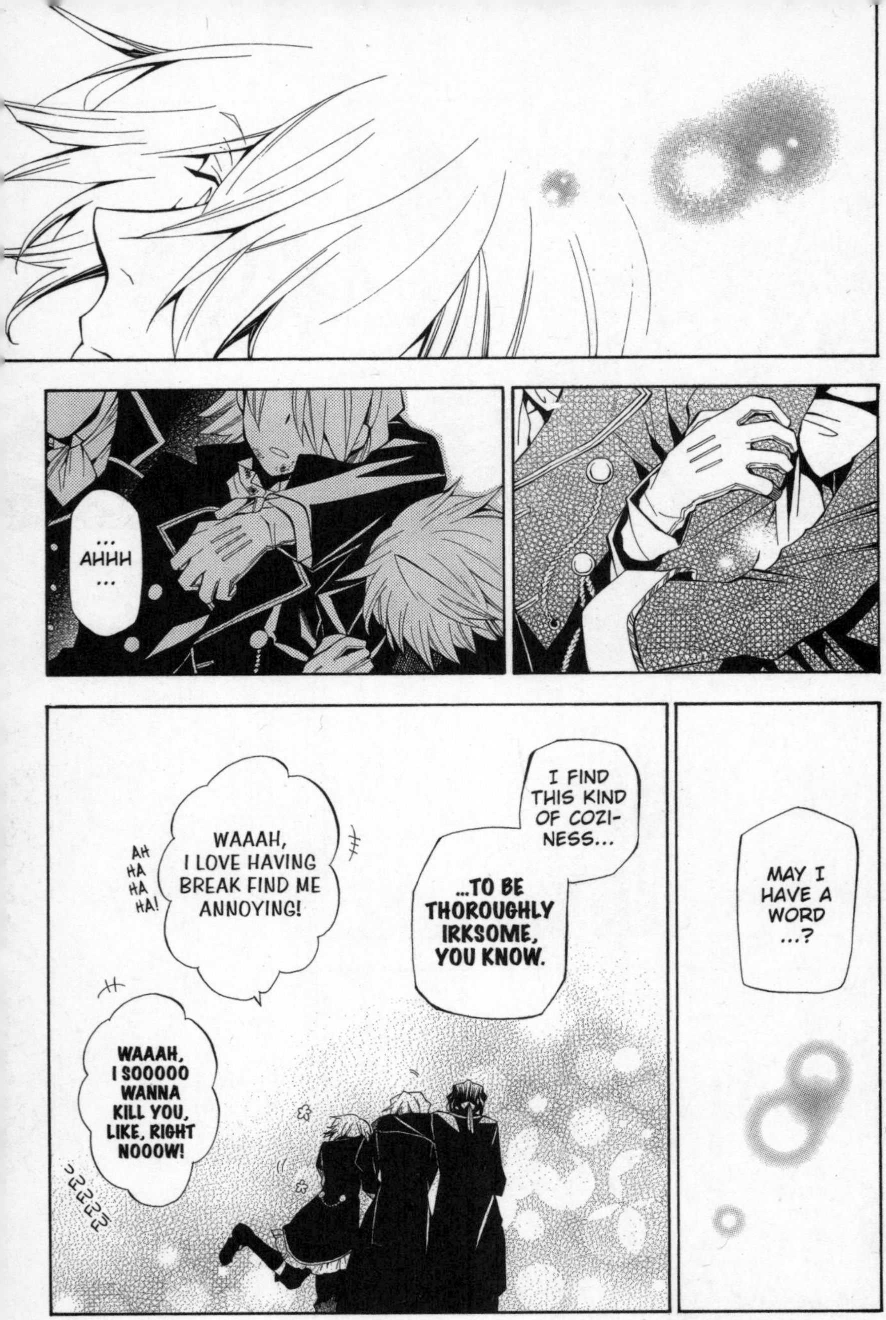
...AHHH...
MAY I HAVE A WORD ...?
I FIND THIS KIND OF COZI-NESS...
...TO BE THOROUGHLY IRKSOME, YOU KNOW.
WAAAH, I LOVE HAVING BREAK FIND ME ANNOYING!
AH HA HA HA!
WAAAH, I SOOOOO WANNA KILL YOU, LIKE, RIGHT NOOOW!

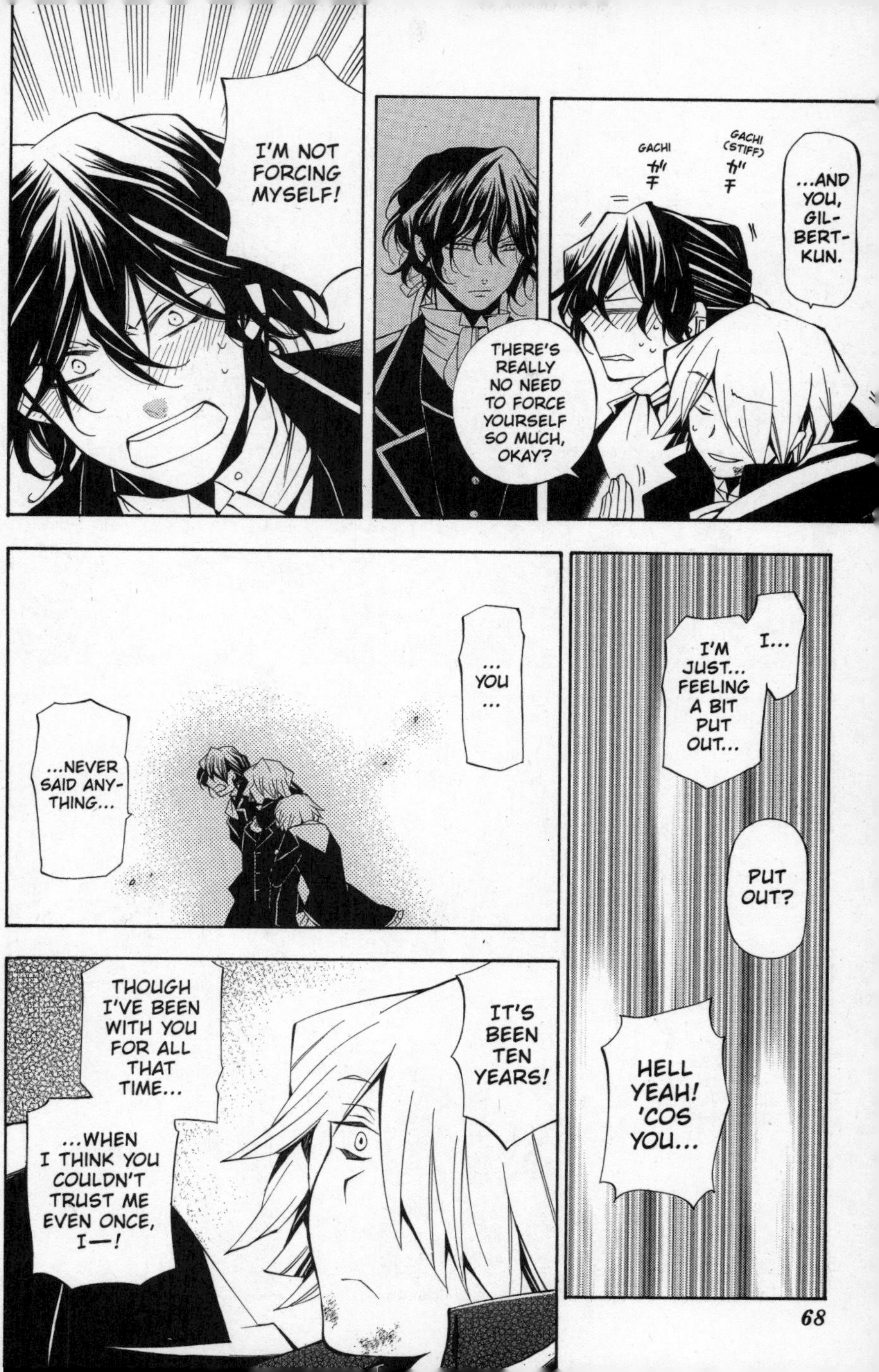
...AND YOU, GILBERT-KUN.
GACHI (STIFF)
ガチ
GACHI
ガチ
THERE'S REALLY NO NEED TO FORCE YOURSELF SO MUCH, OKAY?
I'M NOT FORCING MYSELF!
I...
I'M JUST... FEELING A BIT PUT OUT...
PUT OUT?
HELL YEAH! 'COS YOU...
...YOU...
...NEVER SAID ANYTHING...
IT'S BEEN TEN YEARS!
THOUGH I'VE BEEN WITH YOU FOR ALL THAT TIME...
...WHEN I THINK YOU COULDN'T TRUST ME EVEN ONCE, I—!

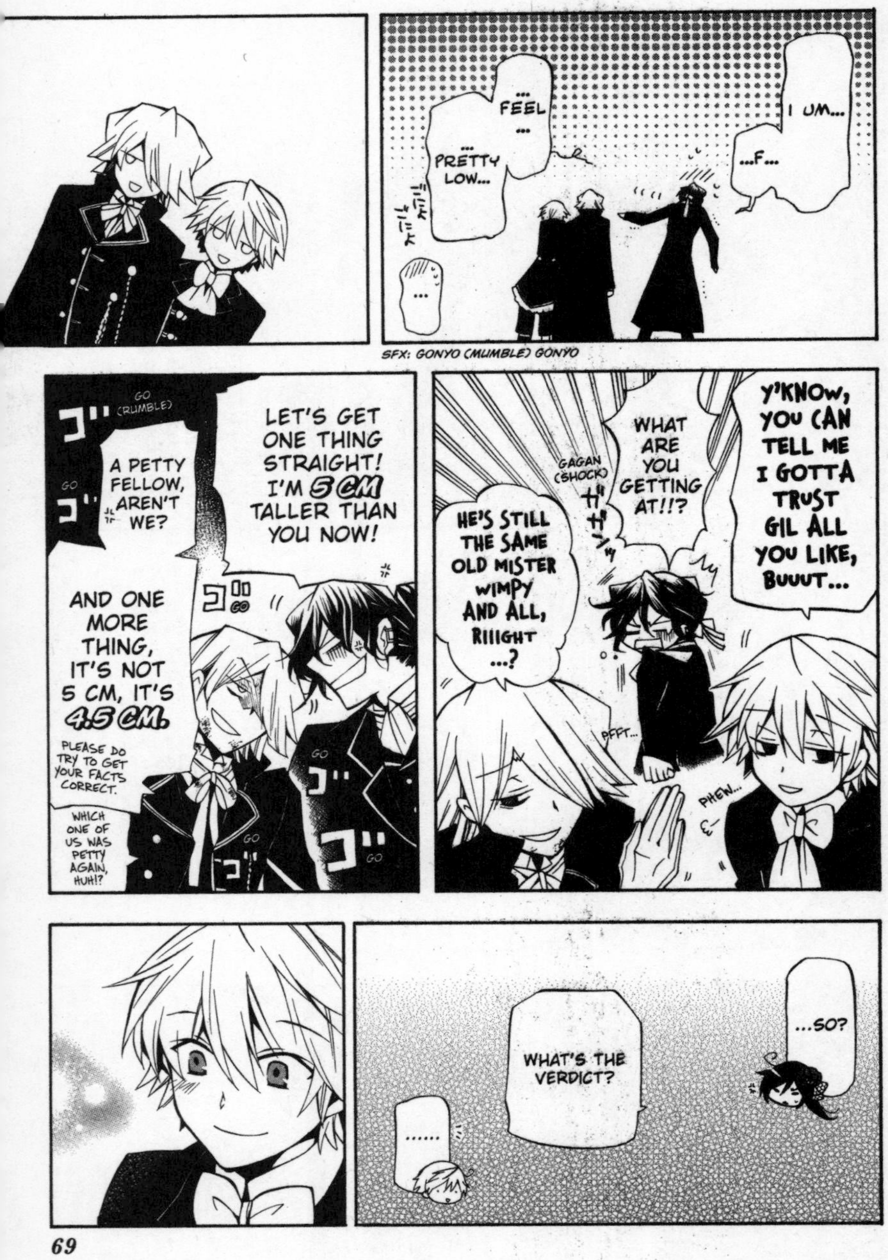
I UM...
...F...
...FEEL...
...PRETTY LOW...
...
SFX: GONYO (MUMBLE) GONYO
Y'KNOW, YOU CAN TELL ME I GOTTA TRUST GIL ALL YOU LIKE, BUUUT...
WHAT ARE YOU GETTING AT!!?
GAGAN (SHOCK)
HE'S STILL THE SAME OLD MISTER WIMPY AND ALL, RIIIGHT...?
PFFT...
PHEW...
LET'S GET ONE THING STRAIGHT! I'M 5 CM TALLER THAN YOU NOW!
GO (RUMBLE)
A PETTY FELLOW, AREN'T WE?
GO
AND ONE MORE THING, IT'S NOT 5 CM, IT'S 4.5 CM.
PLEASE DO TRY TO GET YOUR FACTS CORRECT.
WHICH ONE OF US WAS PETTY AGAIN, HUH!?
...SO?
WHAT'S THE VERDICT?
....

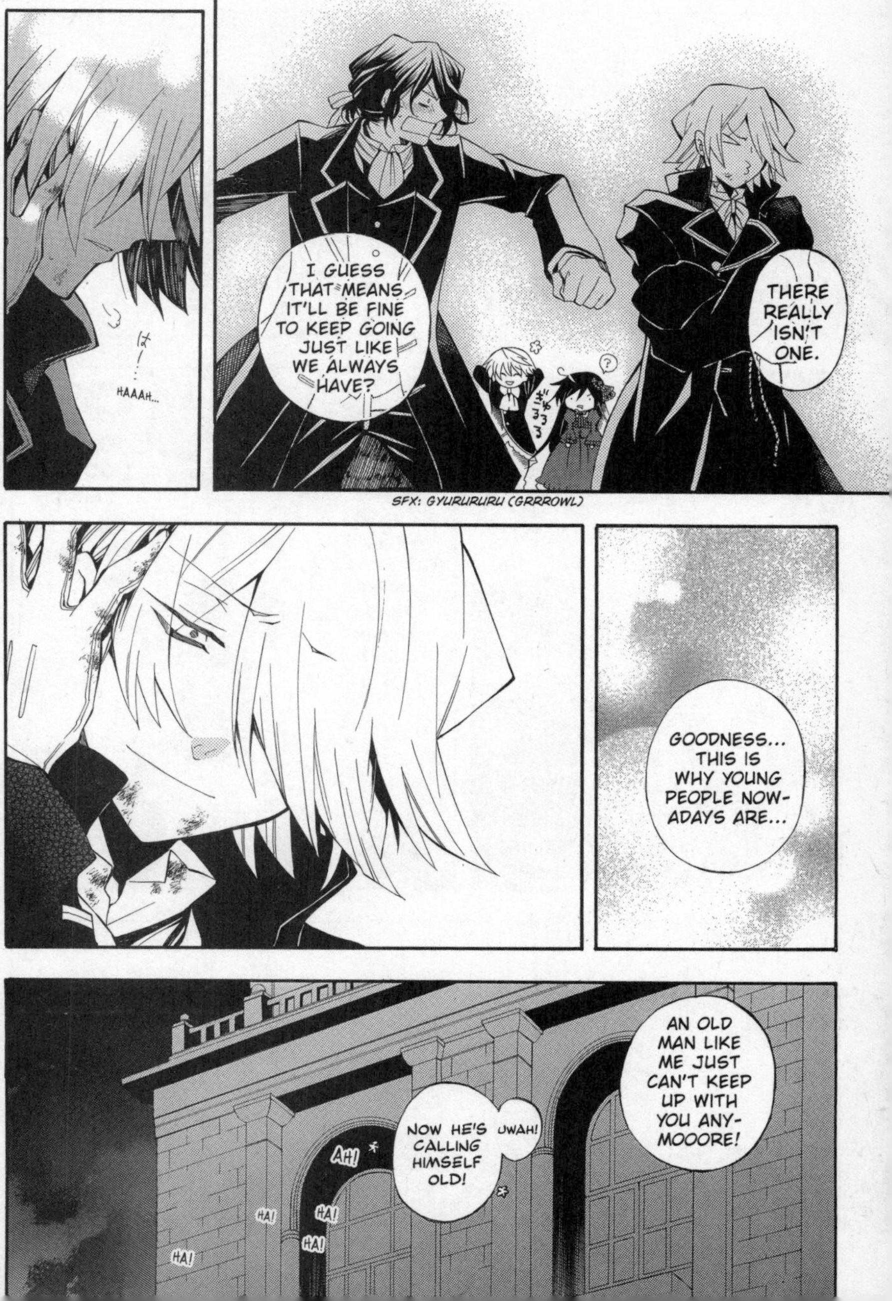
THERE REALLY ISN'T ONE.
I GUESS THAT MEANS IT'LL BE FINE TO KEEP GOING JUST LIKE WE ALWAYS HAVE?
ぎゅるるる
SFX: GYURURURU (GRRROWL)
は―…
HAAAH...
GOODNESS... THIS IS WHY YOUNG PEOPLE NOWADAYS ARE...
AN OLD MAN LIKE ME JUST CAN'T KEEP UP WITH YOU ANYMOOORE!
UWAH!
NOW HE'S CALLING HIMSELF OLD!
AH!
HA!
HA!
HA!
HA!

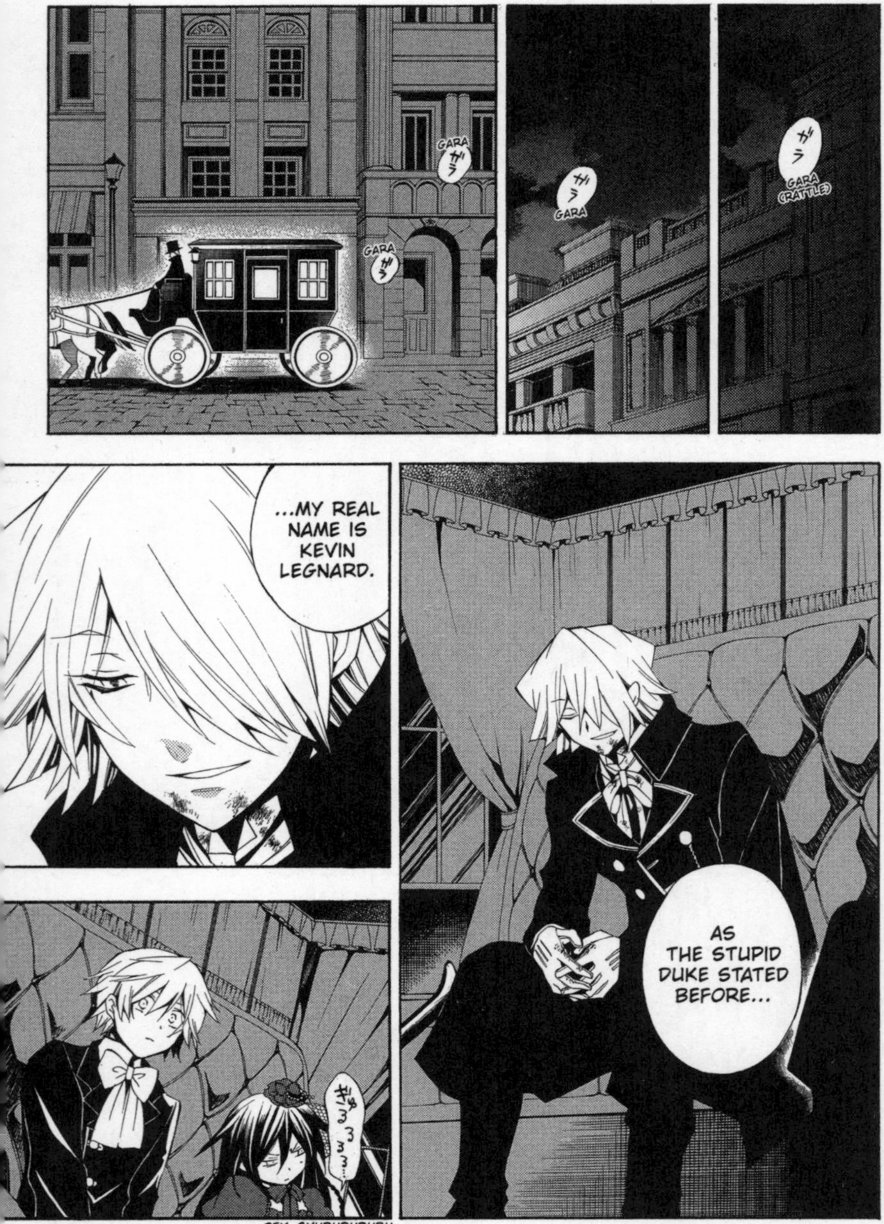
ガラ
GARA (RATTLE)
ガラ
GARA
GARA
ガラ
GARA
ガラ
AS THE STUPID DUKE STATED BEFORE...
...MY REAL NAME IS KEVIN LEGNARD.

SFX: GYURURURURU

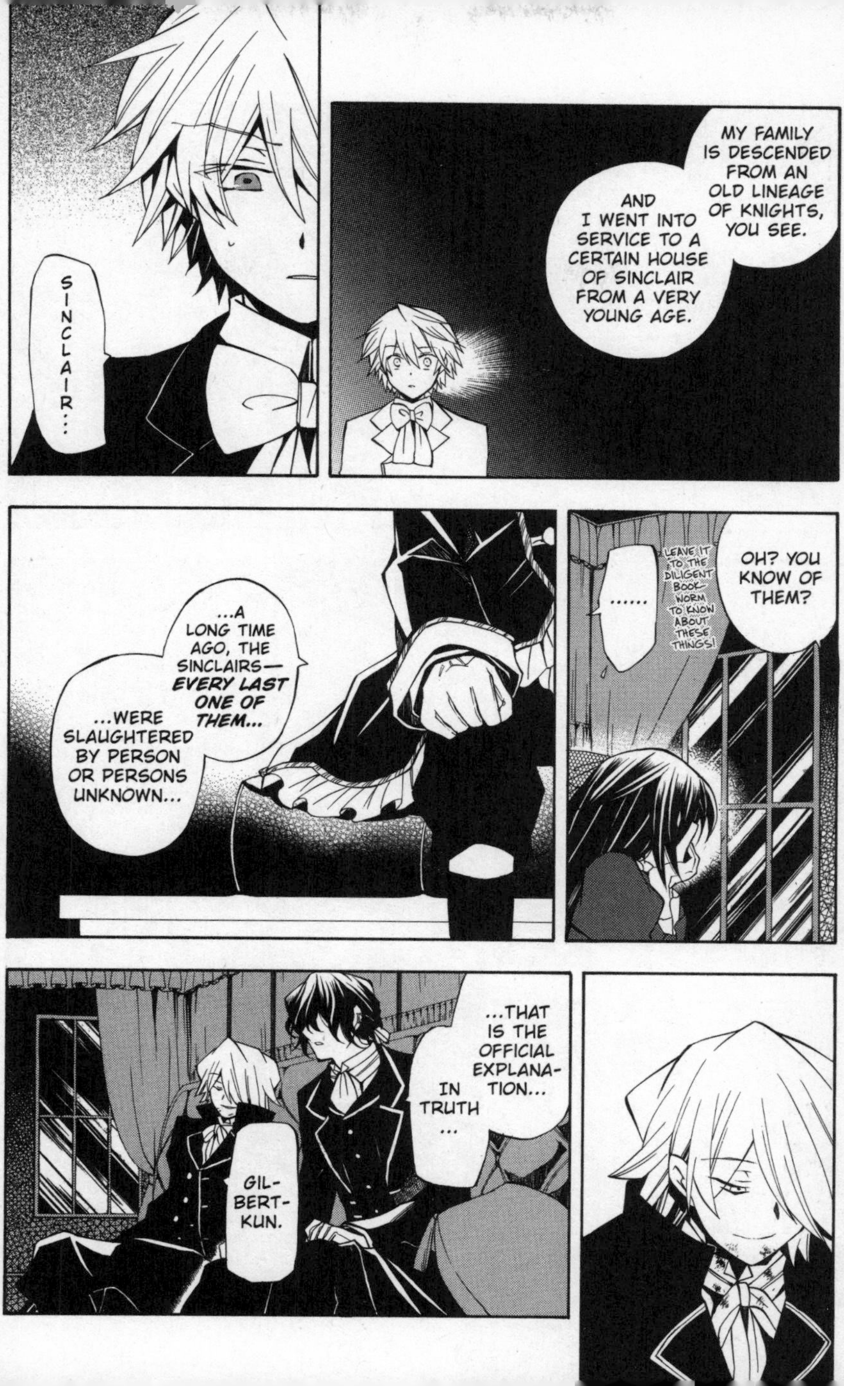
MY FAMILY IS DESCENDED FROM AN OLD LINEAGE OF KNIGHTS, YOU SEE.
AND I WENT INTO SERVICE TO A CERTAIN HOUSE OF SINCLAIR FROM A VERY YOUNG AGE.
SINCLAIR...
OH? YOU KNOW OF THEM?
LEAVE IT TO THE DILIGENT BOOK-WORM TO KNOW ABOUT THESE THINGS!
......
...A LONG TIME AGO, THE SINCLAIRS—*EVERY LAST ONE OF THEM...*
...WERE SLAUGHTERED BY PERSON OR PERSONS UNKNOWN...
...THAT IS THE OFFICIAL EXPLANATION...
IN TRUTH ...
GILBERT-KUN.

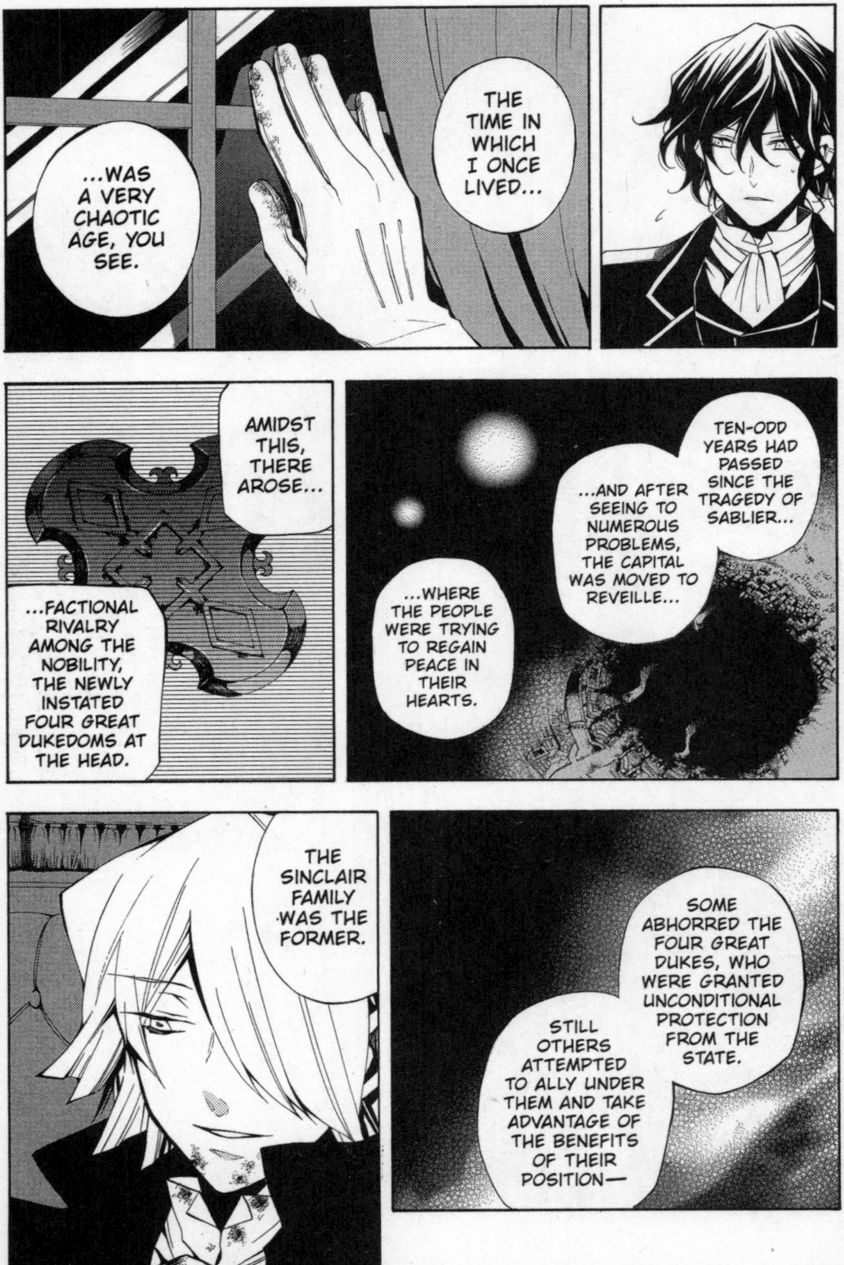
THE TIME IN WHICH I ONCE LIVED...
...WAS A VERY CHAOTIC AGE, YOU SEE.
TEN-ODD YEARS HAD PASSED SINCE THE TRAGEDY OF SABLIER...
...AND AFTER SEEING TO NUMEROUS PROBLEMS, THE CAPITAL WAS MOVED TO REVEILLE...
...WHERE THE PEOPLE WERE TRYING TO REGAIN PEACE IN THEIR HEARTS.
AMIDST THIS, THERE AROSE...
...FACTIONAL RIVALRY AMONG THE NOBILITY, THE NEWLY INSTATED FOUR GREAT DUKEDOMS AT THE HEAD.
SOME ABHORRED THE FOUR GREAT DUKES, WHO WERE GRANTED UNCONDITIONAL PROTECTION FROM THE STATE.
STILL OTHERS ATTEMPTED TO ALLY UNDER THEM AND TAKE ADVANTAGE OF THE BENEFITS OF THEIR POSITION—
THE SINCLAIR FAMILY WAS THE FORMER.

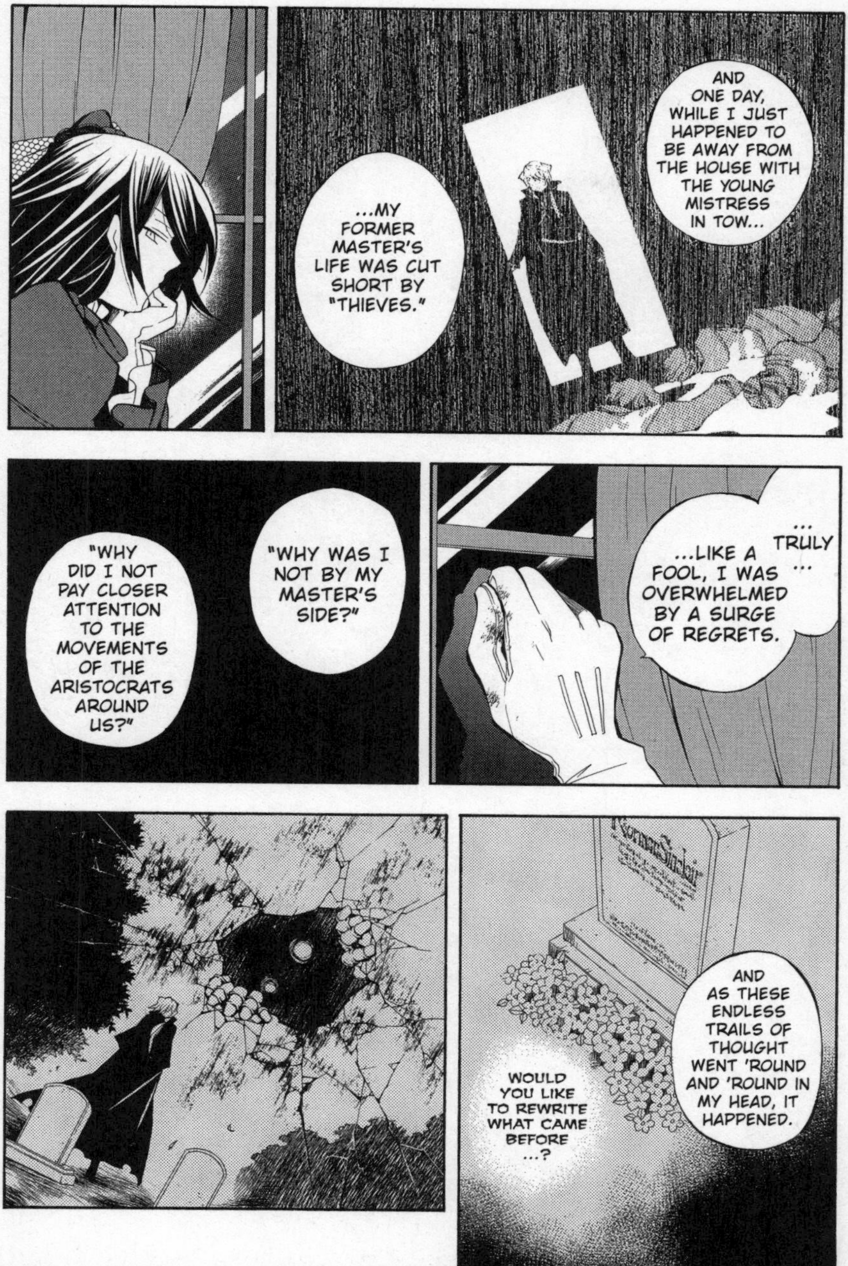
AND ONE DAY, WHILE I JUST HAPPENED TO BE AWAY FROM THE HOUSE WITH THE YOUNG MISTRESS IN TOW...
...MY FORMER MASTER'S LIFE WAS CUT SHORT BY "THIEVES."
... TRULY ...
...LIKE A FOOL, I WAS OVERWHELMED BY A SURGE OF REGRETS.
"WHY WAS I NOT BY MY MASTER'S SIDE?"
"WHY DID I NOT PAY CLOSER ATTENTION TO THE MOVEMENTS OF THE ARISTOCRATS AROUND US?"
AND AS THESE ENDLESS TRAILS OF THOUGHT WENT 'ROUND AND 'ROUND IN MY HEAD, IT HAPPENED.
WOULD YOU LIKE TO REWRITE WHAT CAME BEFORE ...?

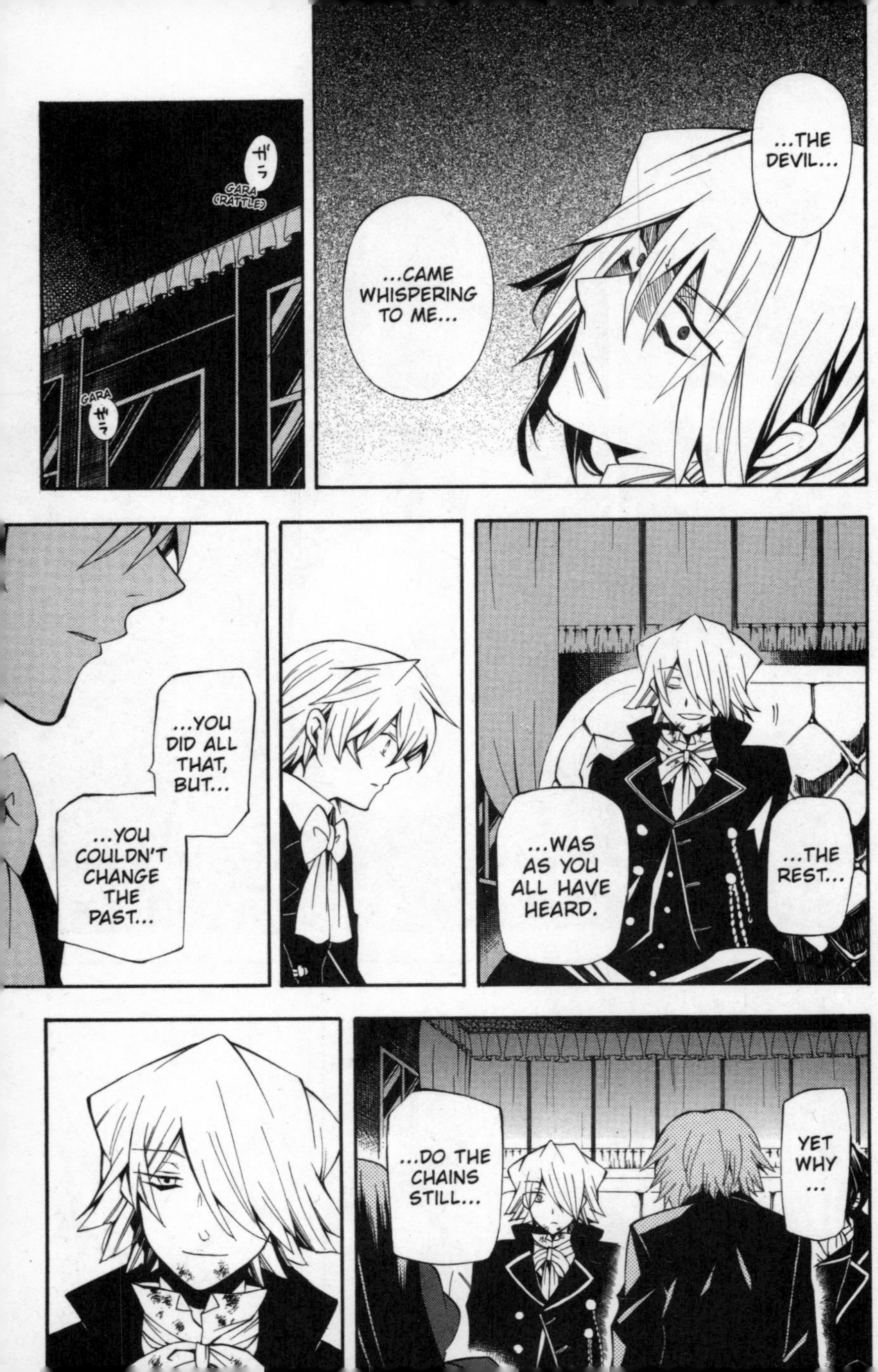
...THE DEVIL...
...CAME WHISPERING TO ME...
ガラ
GARA (RATTLE)
GARA
ガラ
...THE REST...
...WAS AS YOU ALL HAVE HEARD.
...YOU DID ALL THAT, BUT...
...YOU COULDN'T CHANGE THE PAST...
YET WHY...
...DO THE CHAINS STILL...

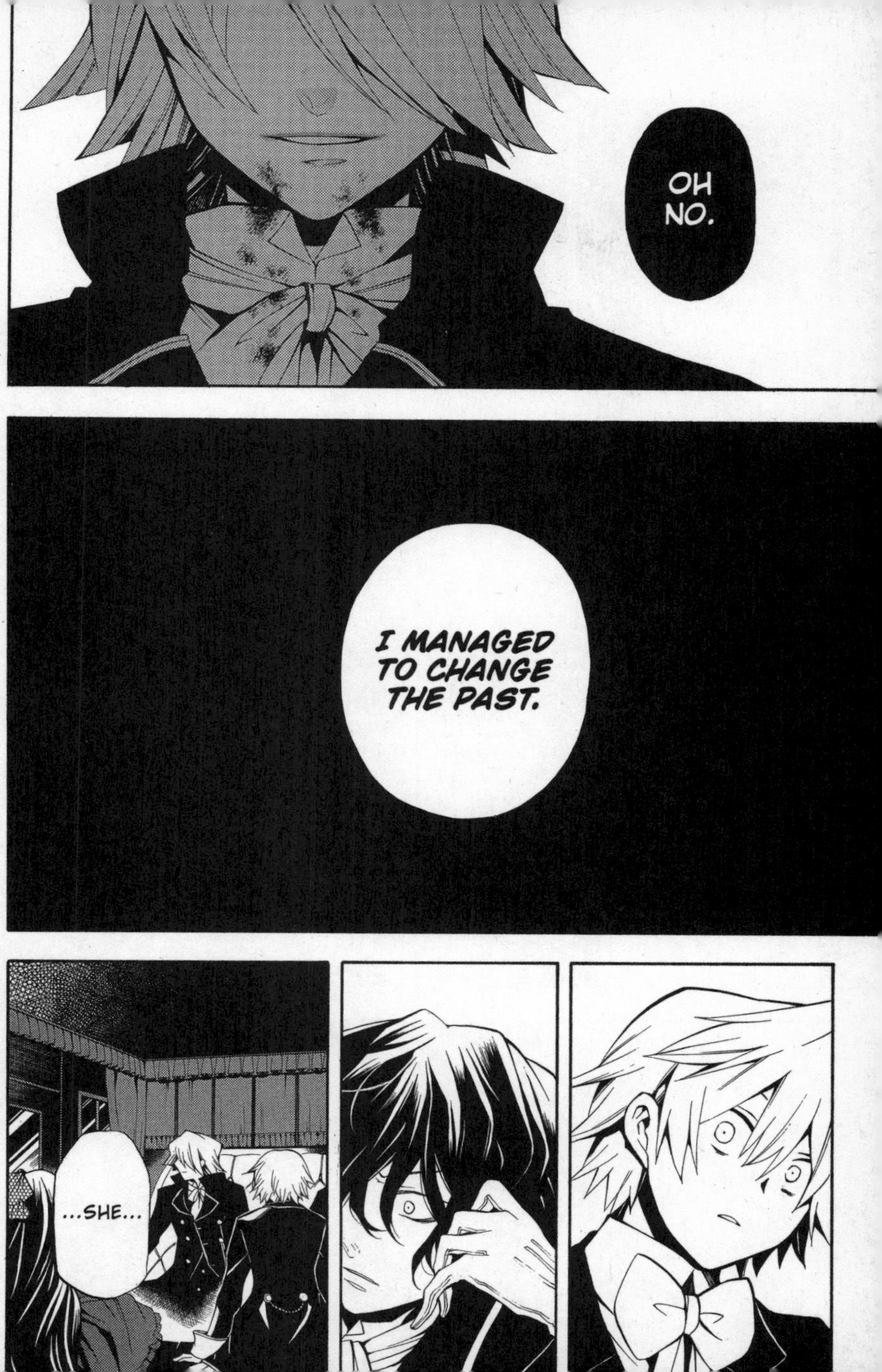
OH NO.
I MANAGED TO CHANGE THE PAST.
...SHE...

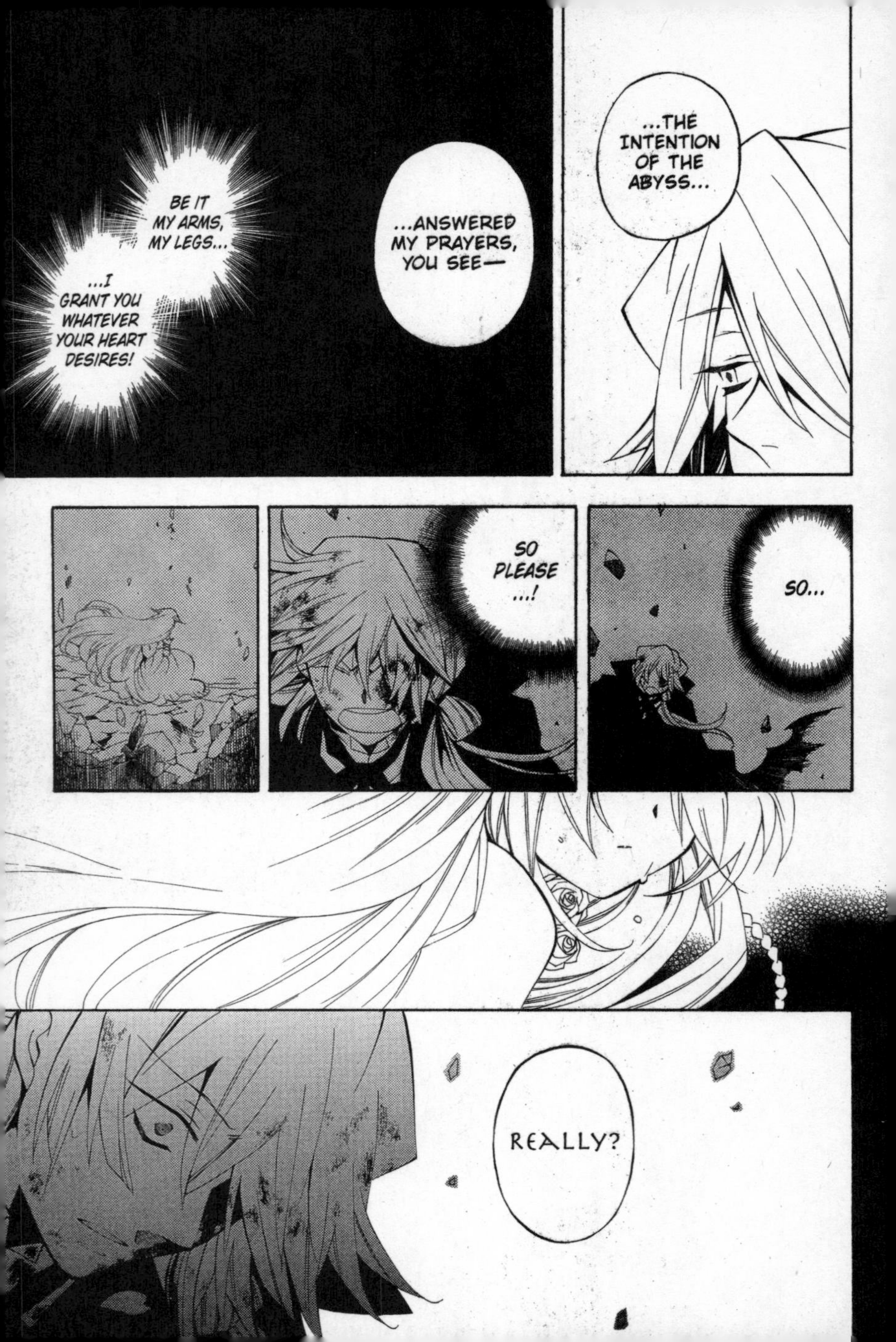
...THE INTENTION OF THE ABYSS...
...ANSWERED MY PRAYERS, YOU SEE—
BE IT MY ARMS, MY LEGS...
...I GRANT YOU WHATEVER YOUR HEART DESIRES!
SO...
SO PLEASE ...!
REALLY?

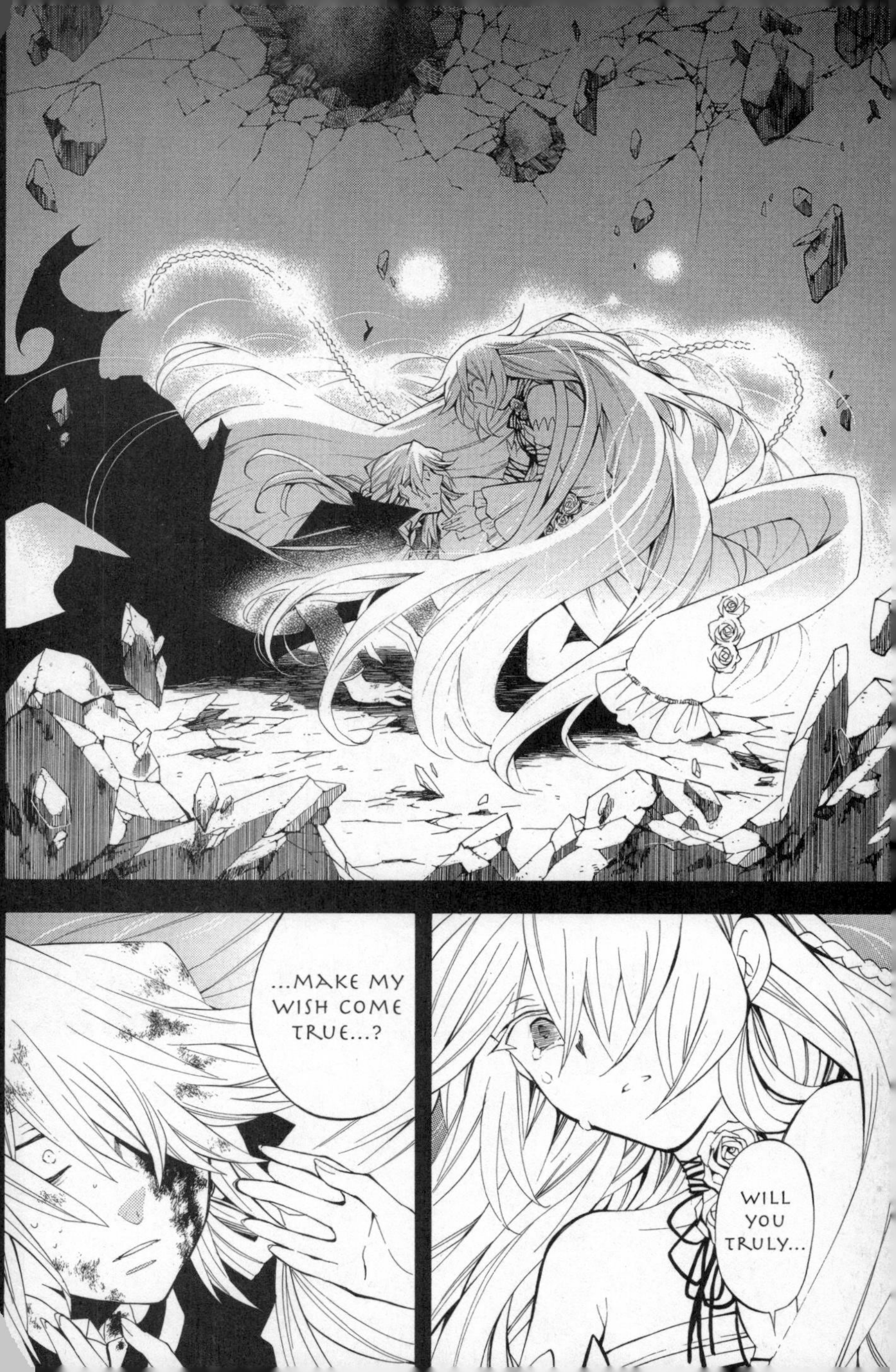
WILL YOU TRULY...
...MAKE MY WISH COME TRUE...?

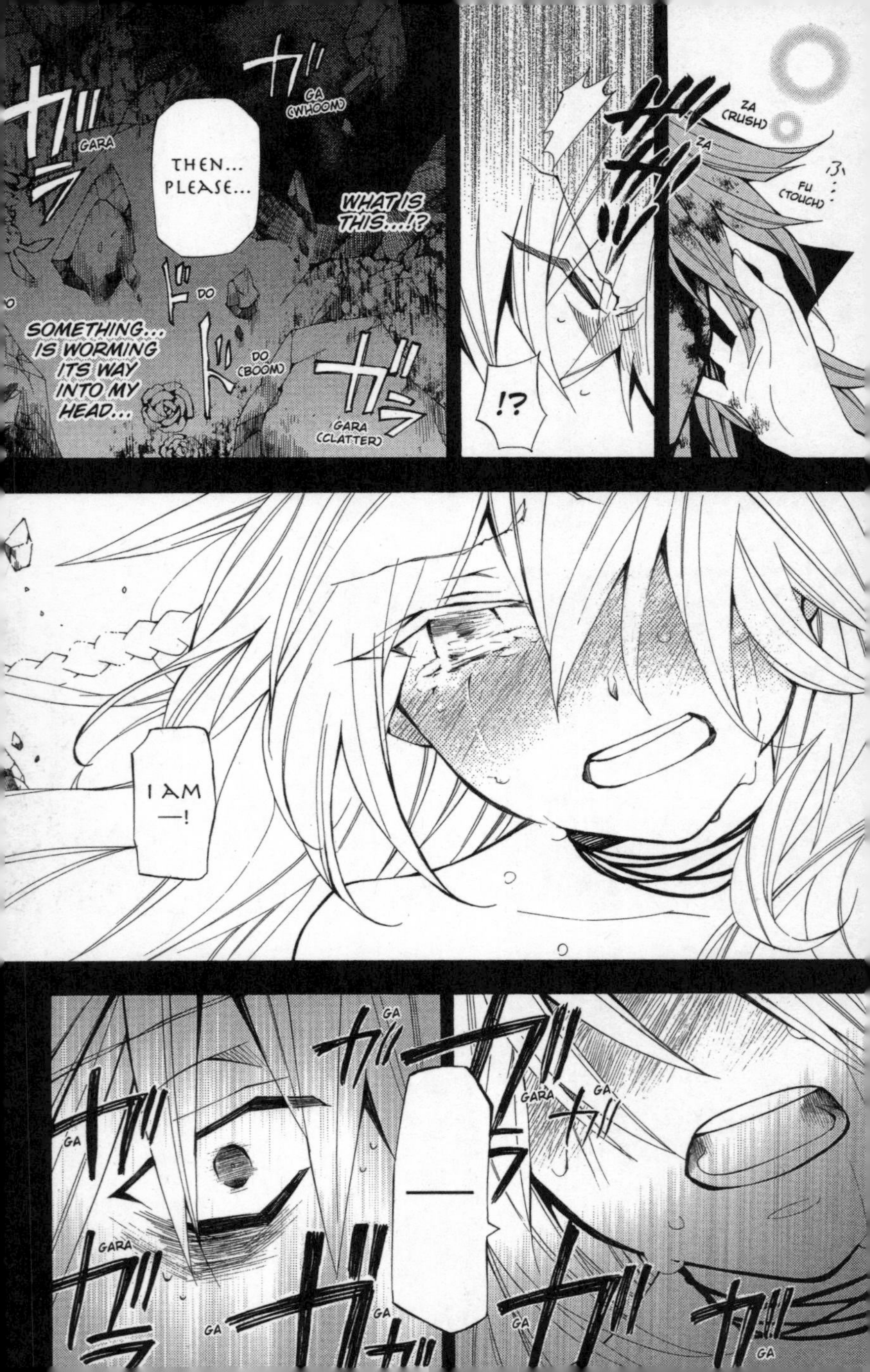

ふ…
FU (TOUCH)
ZA (RUSH)
ZA
!?
GA (WHOOM)
THEN... PLEASE...
WHAT IS THIS...!?
GARA
DO
DO (BOOM)
SOMETHING... IS WORMING ITS WAY INTO MY HEAD...
GARA (CLATTER)
I AM —!
GA
GARA
GA
GA
—
GA
GA
GARA
GA
GA

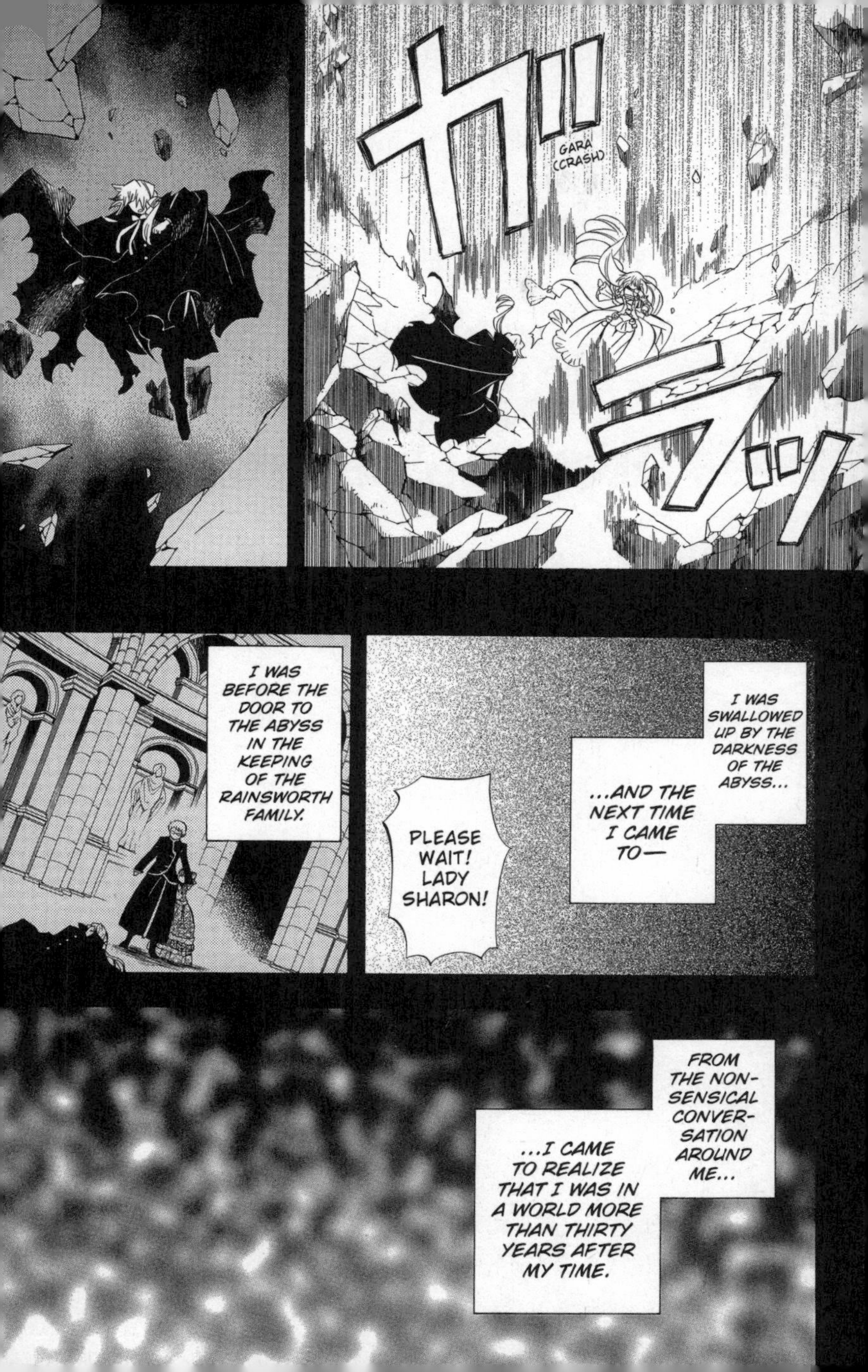

ガラッ
GARA (CRASH)
I WAS SWALLOWED UP BY THE DARKNESS OF THE ABYSS...
...AND THE NEXT TIME I CAME TO—
PLEASE WAIT! LADY SHARON!
I WAS BEFORE THE DOOR TO THE ABYSS IN THE KEEPING OF THE RAINSWORTH FAMILY.
FROM THE NON-SENSICAL CONVER-SATION AROUND ME...
...I CAME TO REALIZE THAT I WAS IN A WORLD MORE THAN THIRTY YEARS AFTER MY TIME.

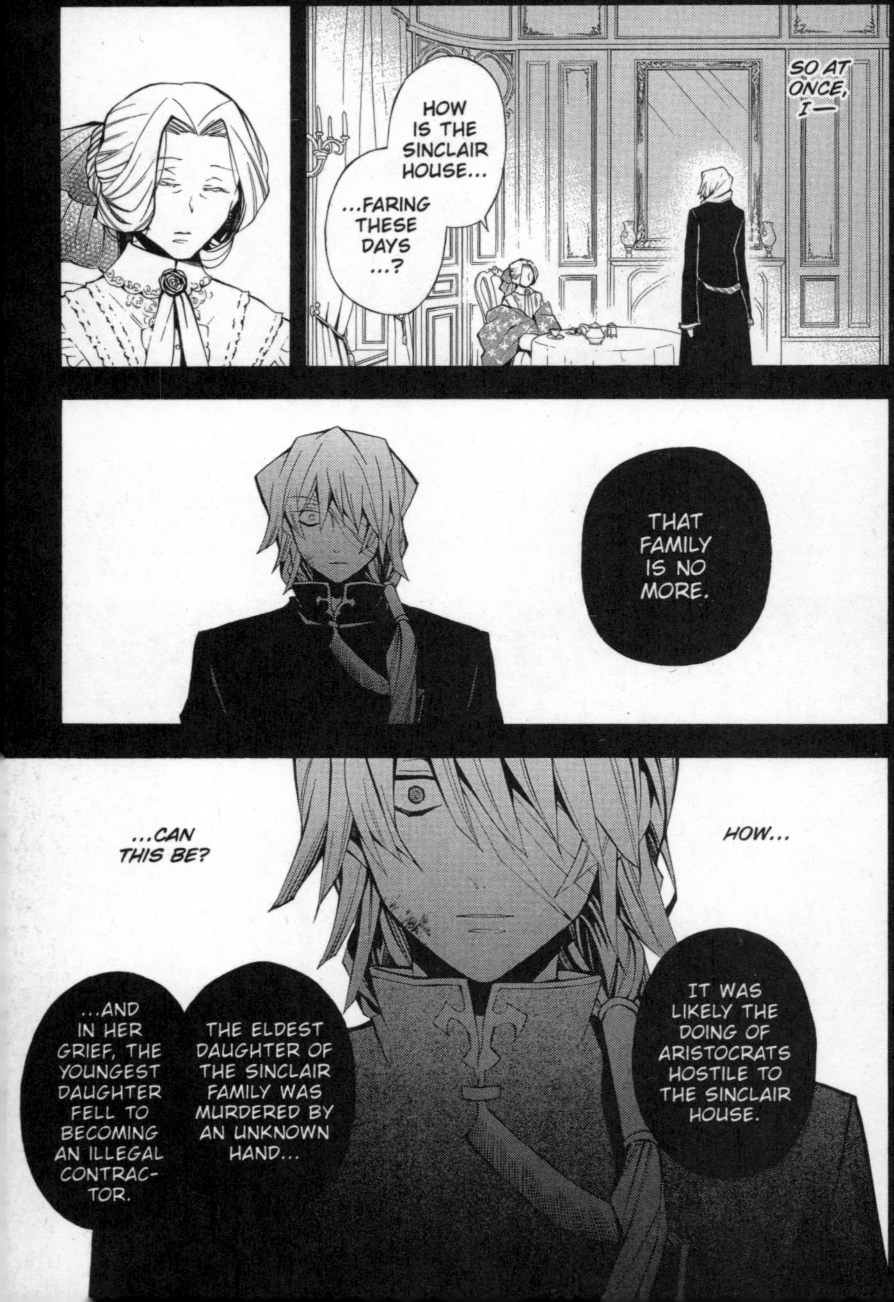
SO AT ONCE, I—
HOW IS THE SINCLAIR HOUSE...
...FARING THESE DAYS...?
THAT FAMILY IS NO MORE.
HOW...
...CAN THIS BE?
IT WAS LIKELY THE DOING OF ARISTOCRATS HOSTILE TO THE SINCLAIR HOUSE.
THE ELDEST DAUGHTER OF THE SINCLAIR FAMILY WAS MURDERED BY AN UNKNOWN HAND...
...AND IN HER GRIEF, THE YOUNGEST DAUGHTER FELL TO BECOMING AN ILLEGAL CONTRAC-TOR.

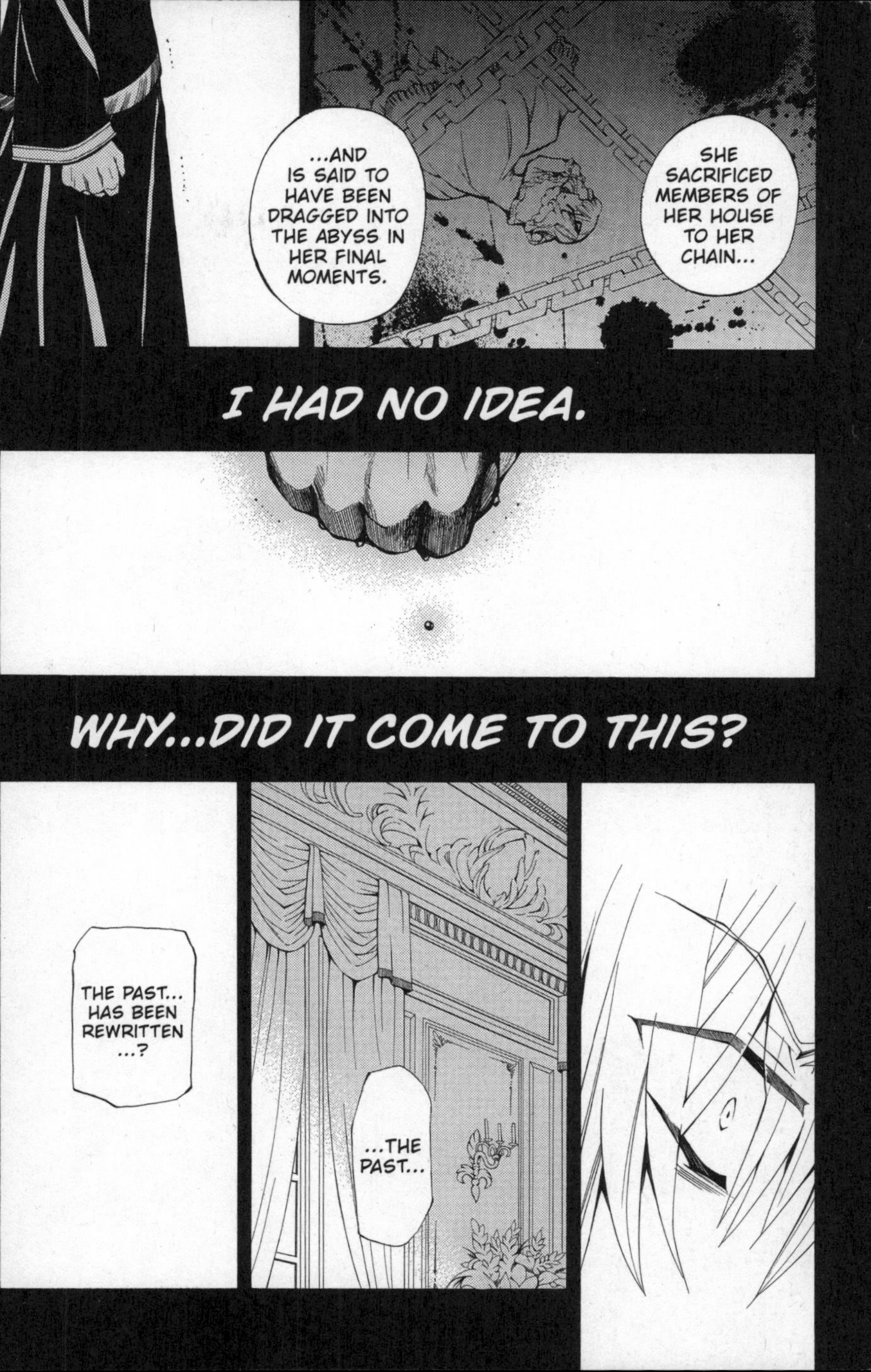
SHE SACRIFICED MEMBERS OF HER HOUSE TO HER CHAIN...
...AND IS SAID TO HAVE BEEN DRAGGED INTO THE ABYSS IN HER FINAL MOMENTS.
I HAD NO IDEA.
WHY...DID IT COME TO THIS?
...THE PAST...
THE PAST... HAS BEEN REWRITTEN ...?

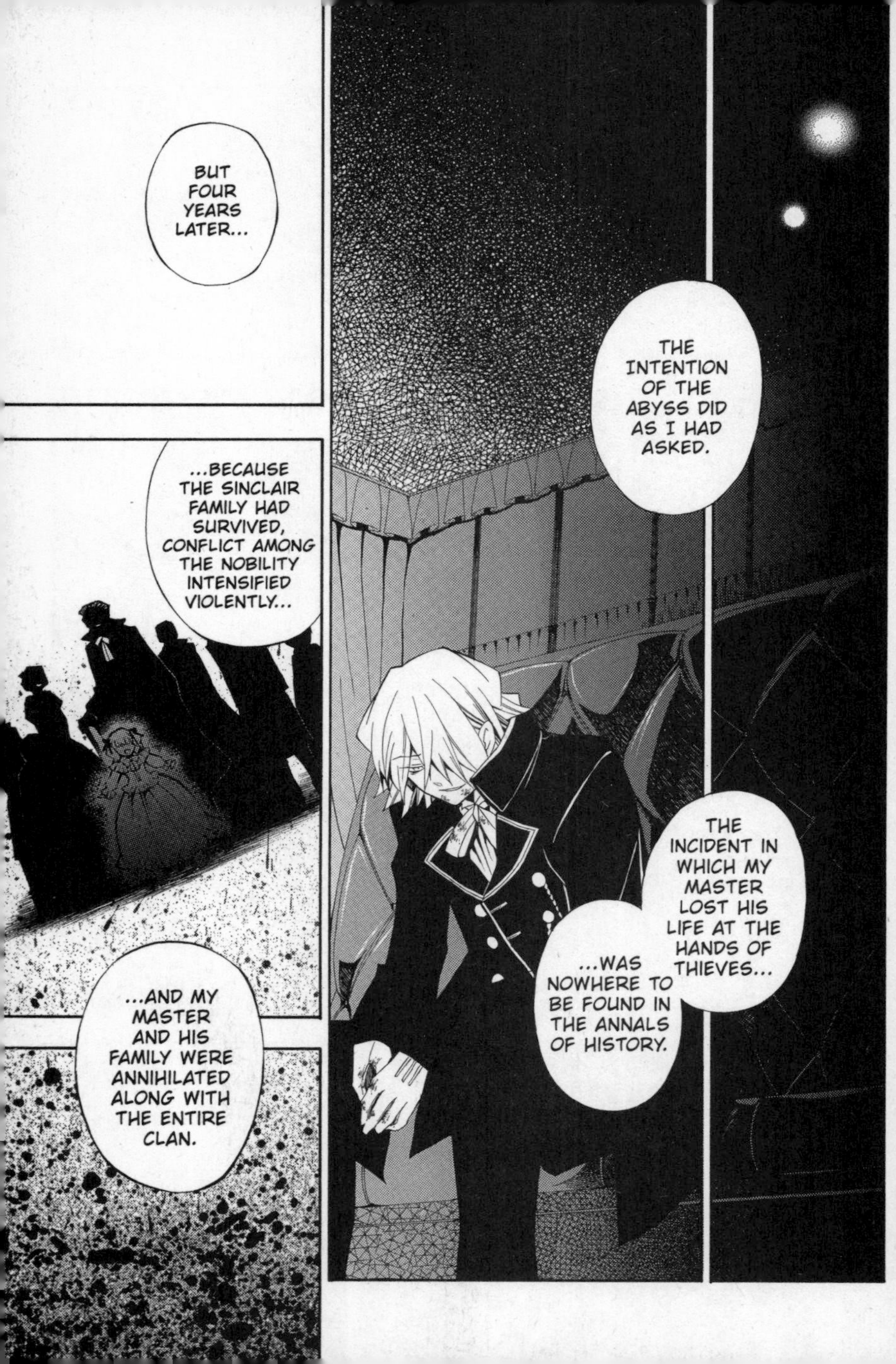
THE INTENTION OF THE ABYSS DID AS I HAD ASKED.
THE INCIDENT IN WHICH MY MASTER LOST HIS LIFE AT THE HANDS OF THIEVES...
...WAS NOWHERE TO BE FOUND IN THE ANNALS OF HISTORY.
BUT FOUR YEARS LATER...
...BECAUSE THE SINCLAIR FAMILY HAD SURVIVED, CONFLICT AMONG THE NOBILITY INTENSIFIED VIOLENTLY...
...AND MY MASTER AND HIS FAMILY WERE ANNIHILATED ALONG WITH THE ENTIRE CLAN.

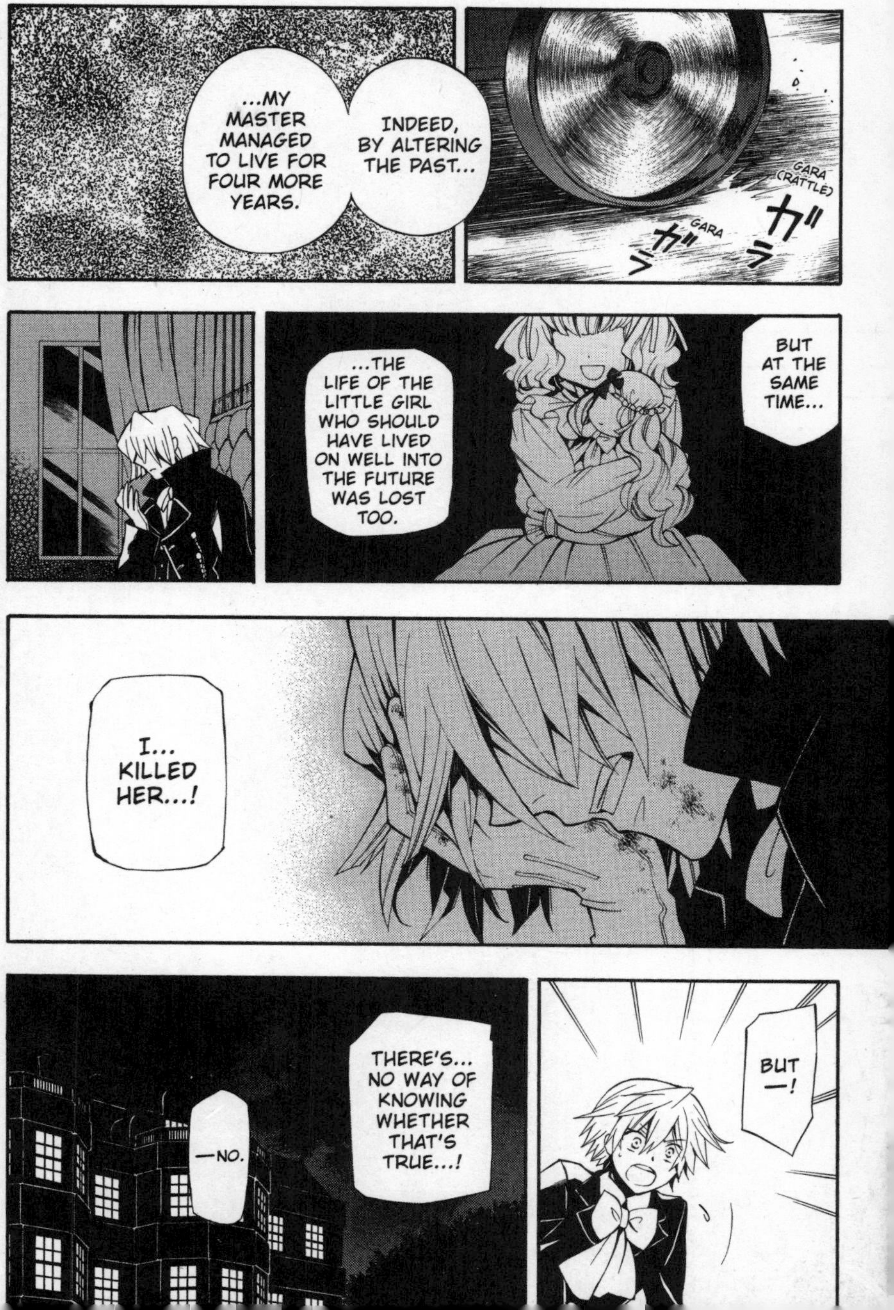
GARA (RATTLE)
ガラ
GARA
ガラ
INDEED, BY ALTERING THE PAST...
...MY MASTER MANAGED TO LIVE FOR FOUR MORE YEARS.
BUT AT THE SAME TIME...
...THE LIFE OF THE LITTLE GIRL WHO SHOULD HAVE LIVED ON WELL INTO THE FUTURE WAS LOST TOO.
I... KILLED HER...!
BUT—!
THERE'S... NO WAY OF KNOWING WHETHER THAT'S TRUE...!
—NO.

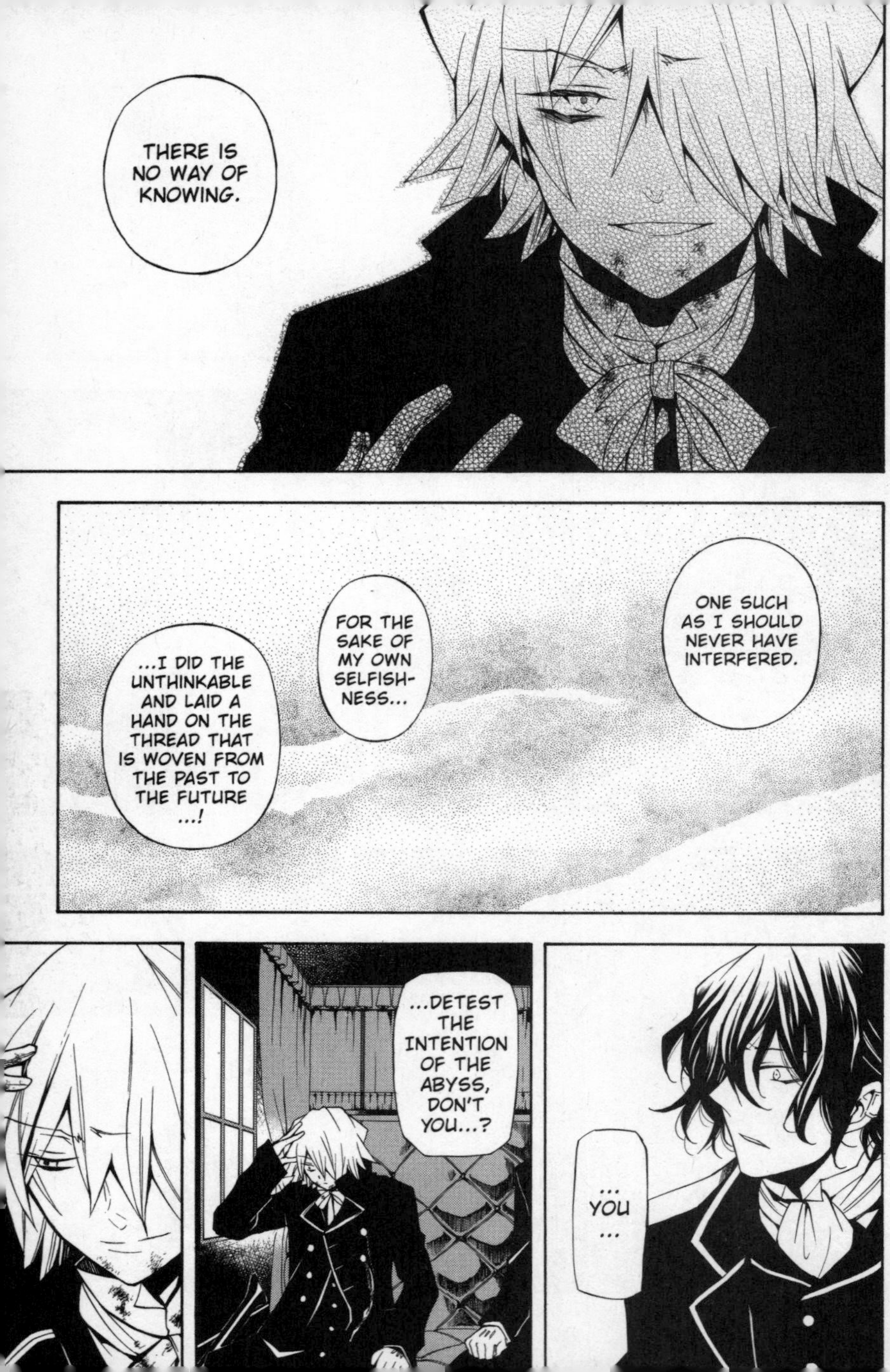
THERE IS NO WAY OF KNOWING.
ONE SUCH AS I SHOULD NEVER HAVE INTERFERED.
FOR THE SAKE OF MY OWN SELFISH-NESS...
...I DID THE UNTHINKABLE AND LAID A HAND ON THE THREAD THAT IS WOVEN FROM THE PAST TO THE FUTURE ...!
... YOU ...
...DETEST THE INTENTION OF THE ABYSS, DON'T YOU...?

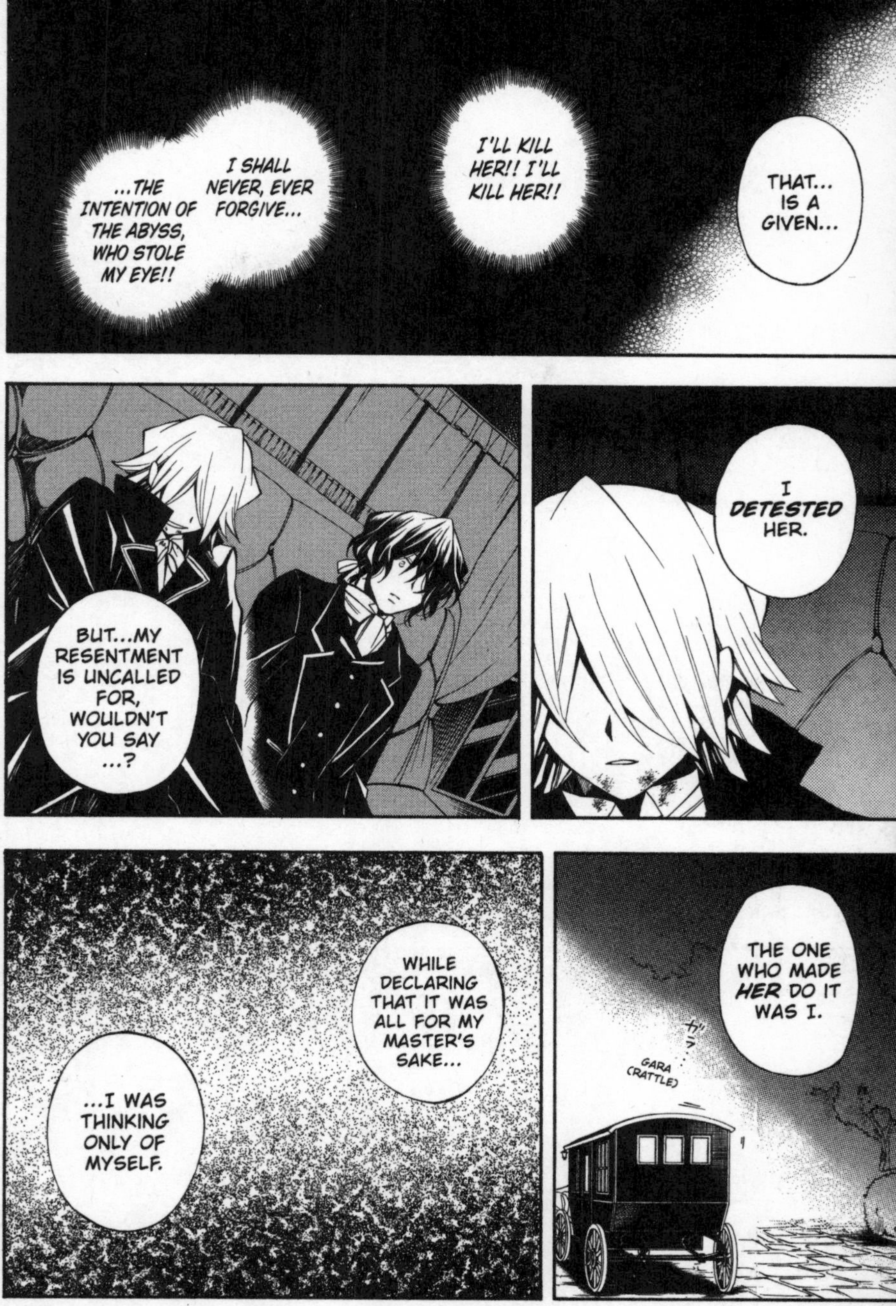

THAT... IS A GIVEN...
I'LL KILL HER!! I'LL KILL HER!!
I SHALL NEVER, EVER FORGIVE...
...THE INTENTION OF THE ABYSS, WHO STOLE MY EYE!!
I DETESTED HER.
BUT...MY RESENTMENT IS UNCALLED FOR, WOULDN'T YOU SAY ...?
THE ONE WHO MADE HER DO IT WAS I.
GARA (RATTLE)
WHILE DECLARING THAT IT WAS ALL FOR MY MASTER'S SAKE...
...I WAS THINKING ONLY OF MYSELF.

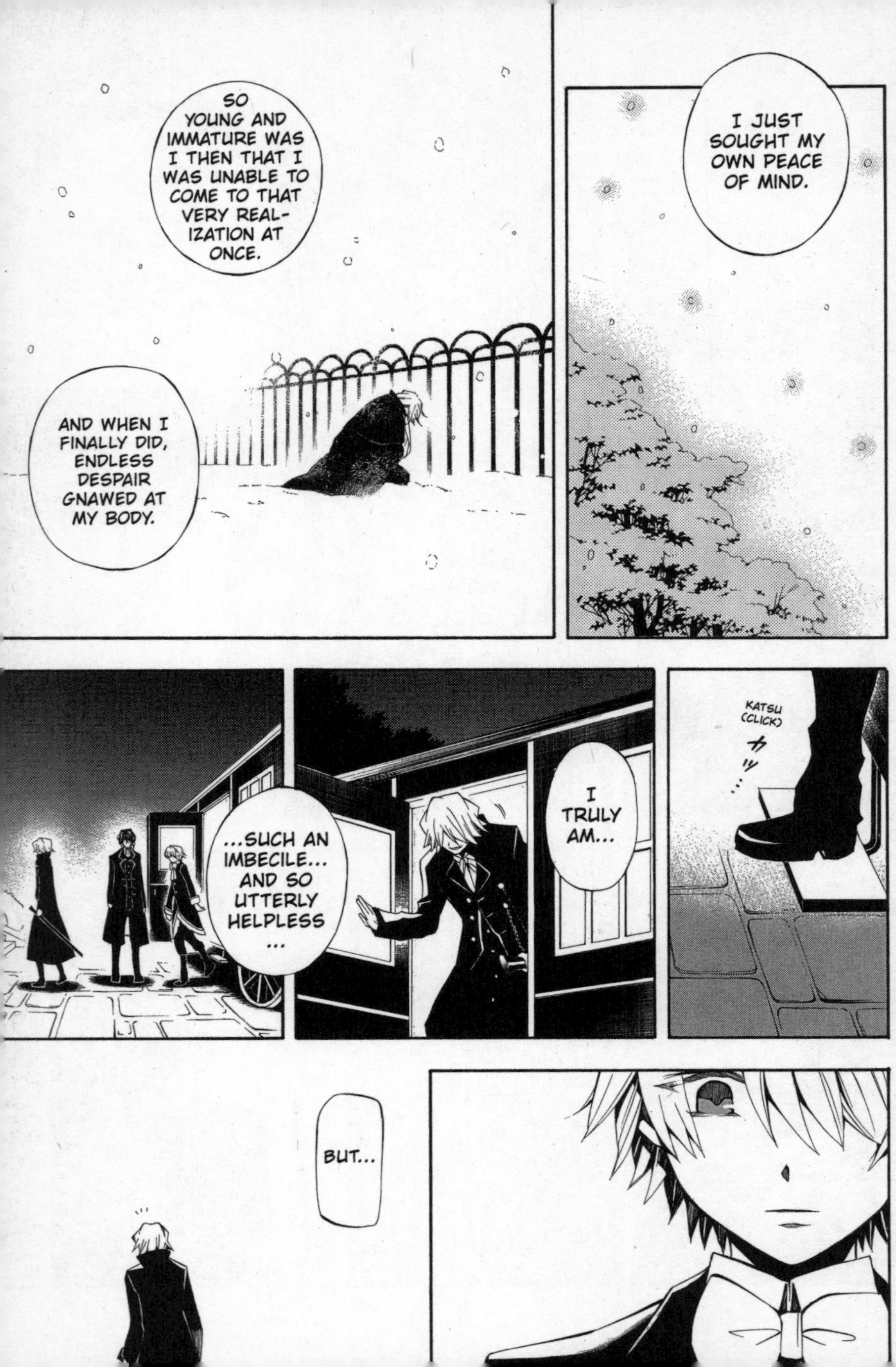
I JUST SOUGHT MY OWN PEACE OF MIND.
SO YOUNG AND IMMATURE WAS I THEN THAT I WAS UNABLE TO COME TO THAT VERY REAL-IZATION AT ONCE.
AND WHEN I FINALLY DID, ENDLESS DESPAIR GNAWED AT MY BODY.
KATSU (CLICK)
I TRULY AM...
...SUCH AN IMBECILE... AND SO UTTERLY HELPLESS ...
BUT...

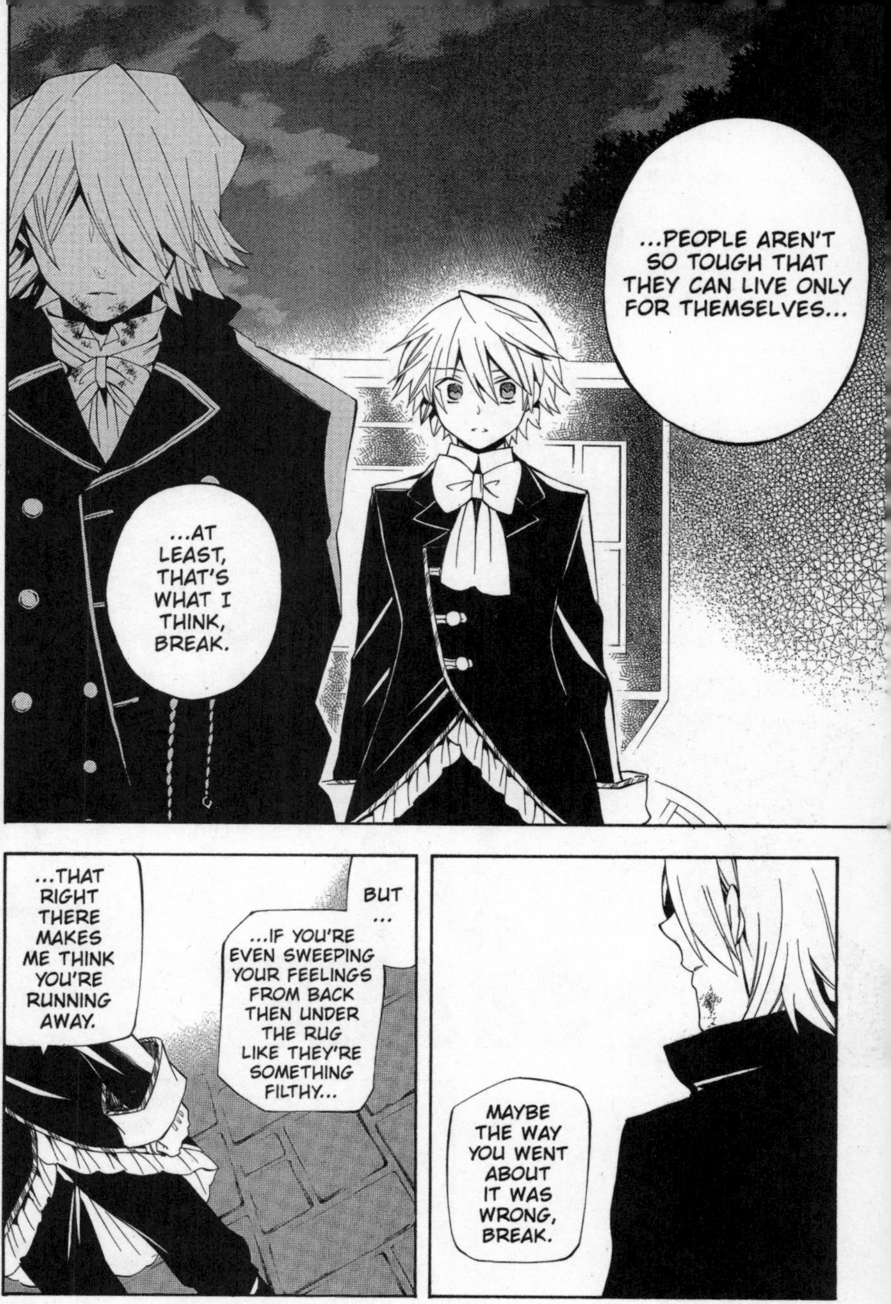
...PEOPLE AREN'T SO TOUGH THAT THEY CAN LIVE ONLY FOR THEMSELVES...
...AT LEAST, THAT'S WHAT I THINK, BREAK.
MAYBE THE WAY YOU WENT ABOUT IT WAS WRONG, BREAK.
BUT ...
...IF YOU'RE EVEN SWEEPING YOUR FEELINGS FROM BACK THEN UNDER THE RUG LIKE THEY'RE SOMETHING FILTHY...
...THAT RIGHT THERE MAKES ME THINK YOU'RE RUNNING AWAY.

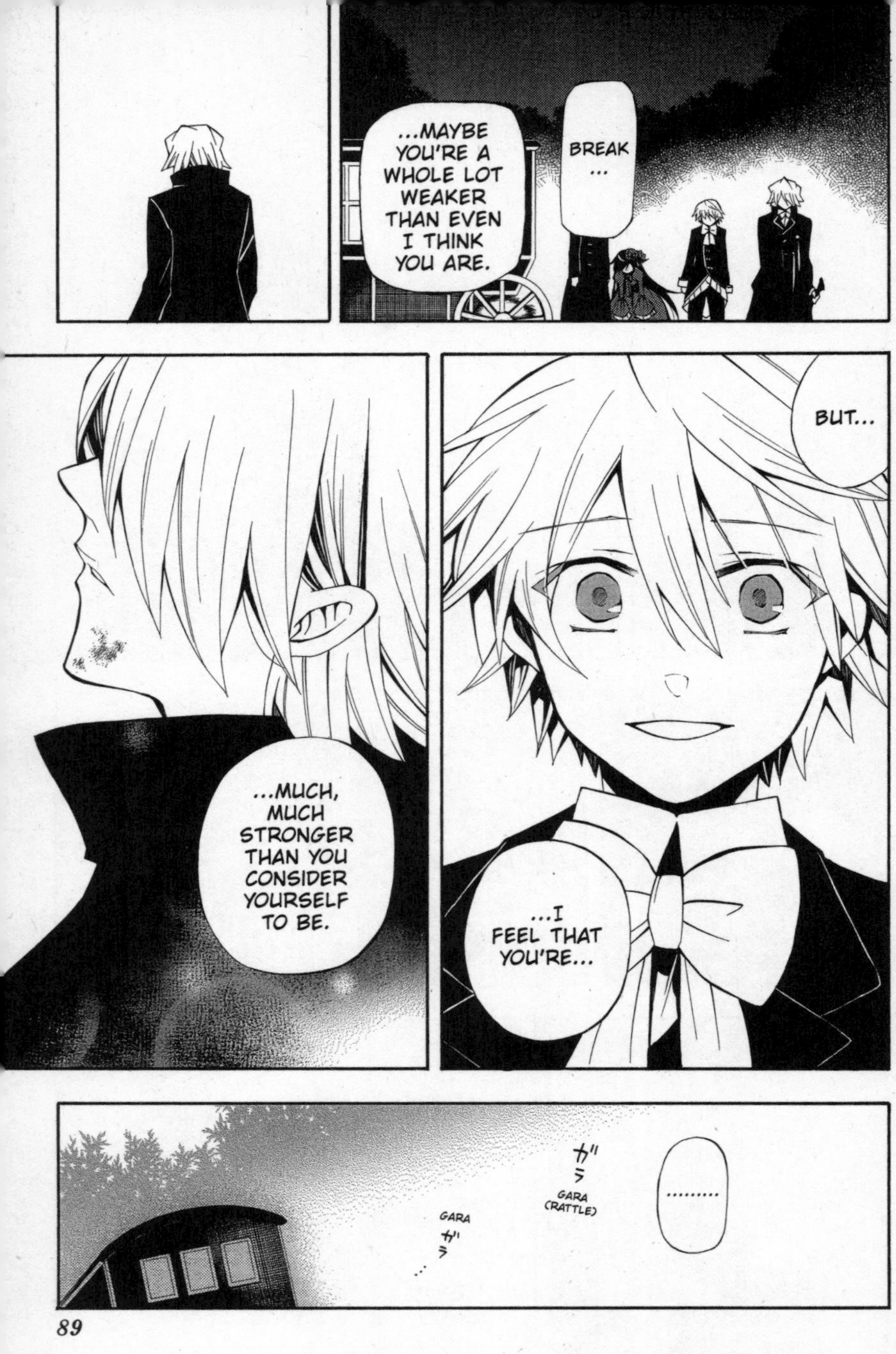
BREAK ...
...MAYBE YOU'RE A WHOLE LOT WEAKER THAN EVEN I THINK YOU ARE.
BUT...
...I FEEL THAT YOU'RE...
...MUCH, MUCH STRONGER THAN YOU CONSIDER YOURSELF TO BE.
....
ガラ
GARA (RATTLE)
GARA
ガラ

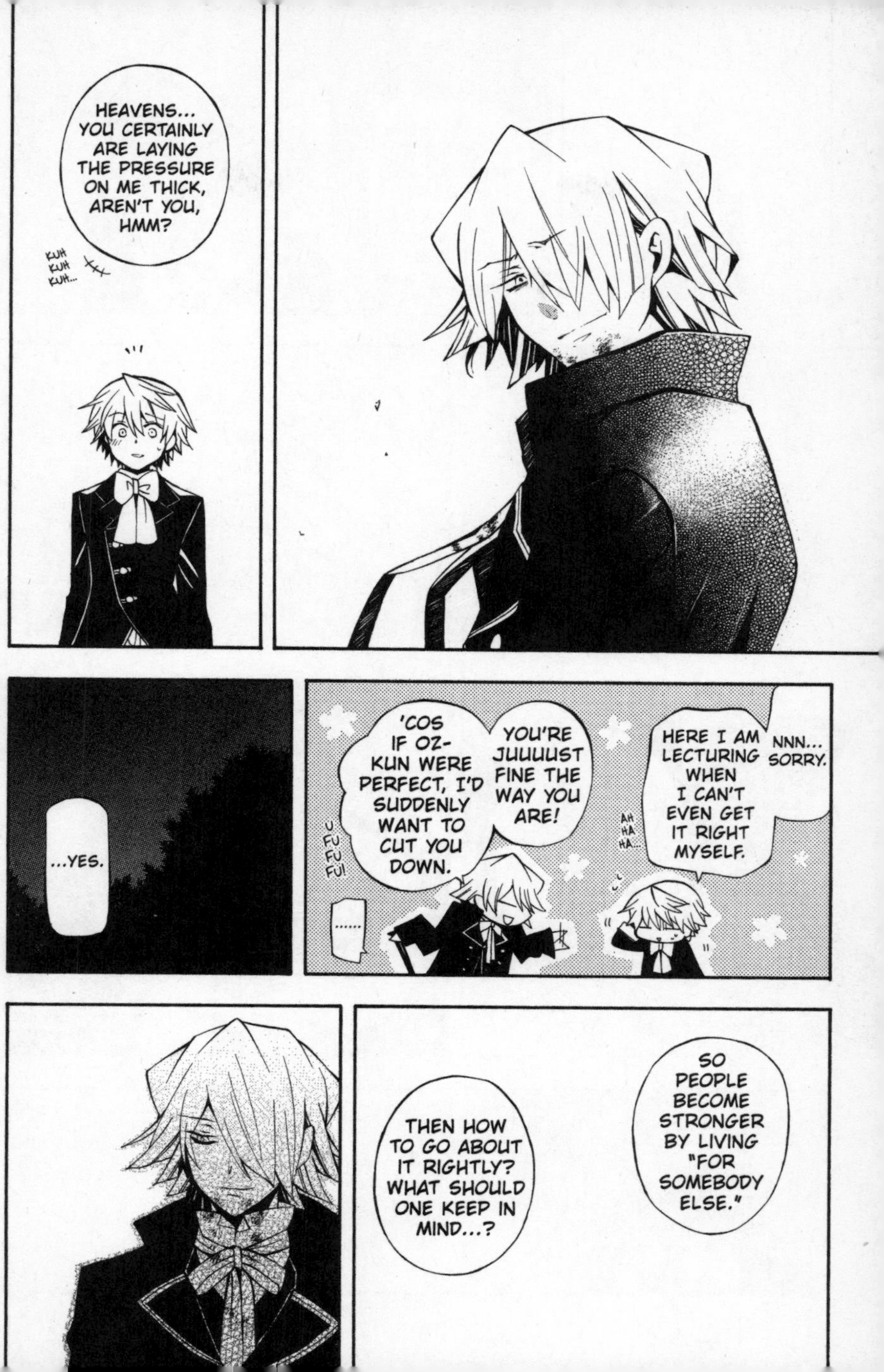
HEAVENS... YOU CERTAINLY ARE LAYING THE PRESSURE ON ME THICK, AREN'T YOU, HMM?
KUH KUH KUH...
NNN... SORRY.
HERE I AM LECTURING WHEN I CAN'T EVEN GET IT RIGHT MYSELF.
AH HA HA...
YOU'RE JUUUUST FINE THE WAY YOU ARE!
'COS IF OZ-KUN WERE PERFECT, I'D SUDDENLY WANT TO CUT YOU DOWN.
U FU FU FU!
......
...YES.
SO PEOPLE BECOME STRONGER BY LIVING "FOR SOMEBODY ELSE."
THEN HOW TO GO ABOUT IT RIGHTLY? WHAT SHOULD ONE KEEP IN MIND...?

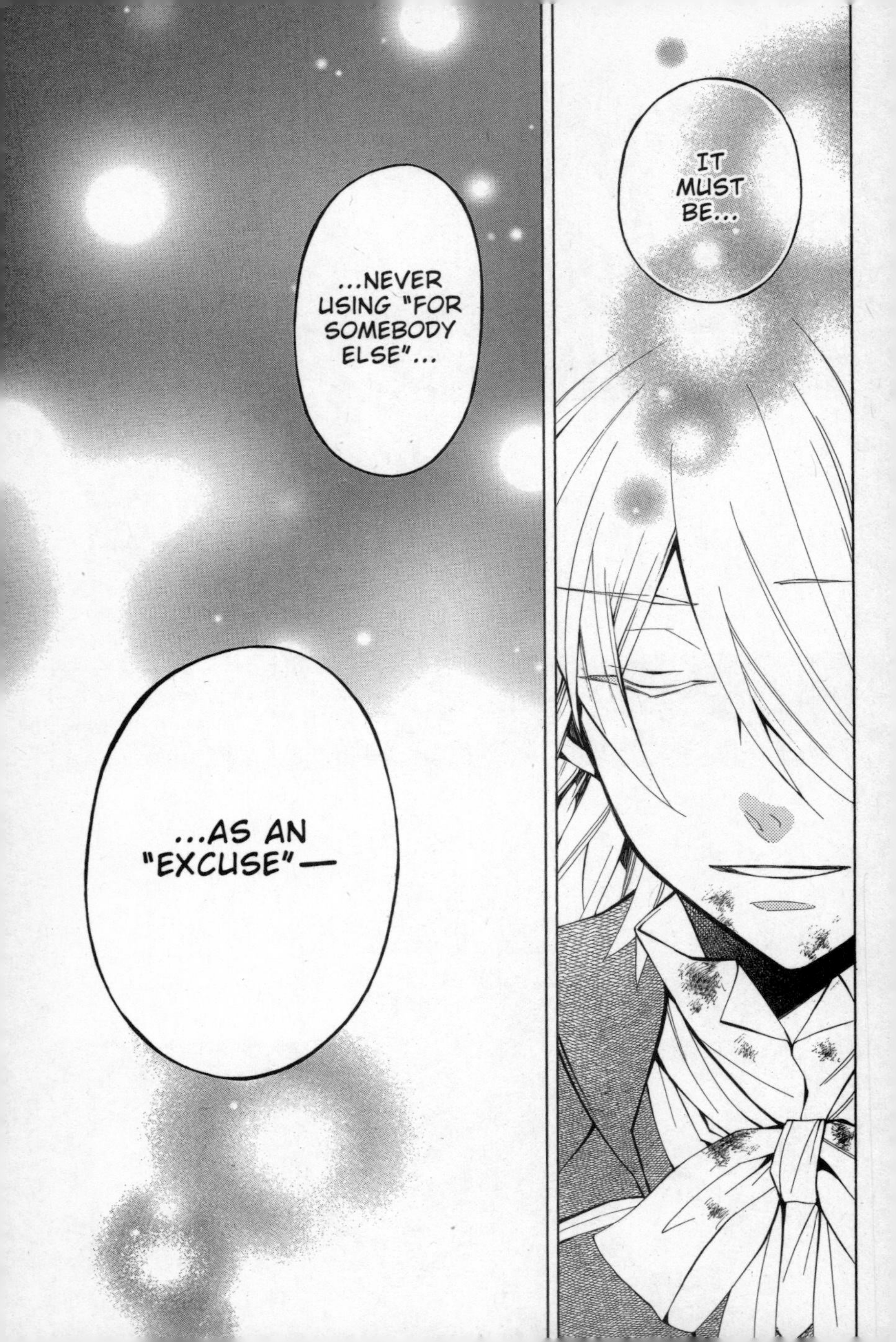
IT MUST BE...
...NEVER USING "FOR SOMEBODY ELSE"...
...AS AN "EXCUSE"—

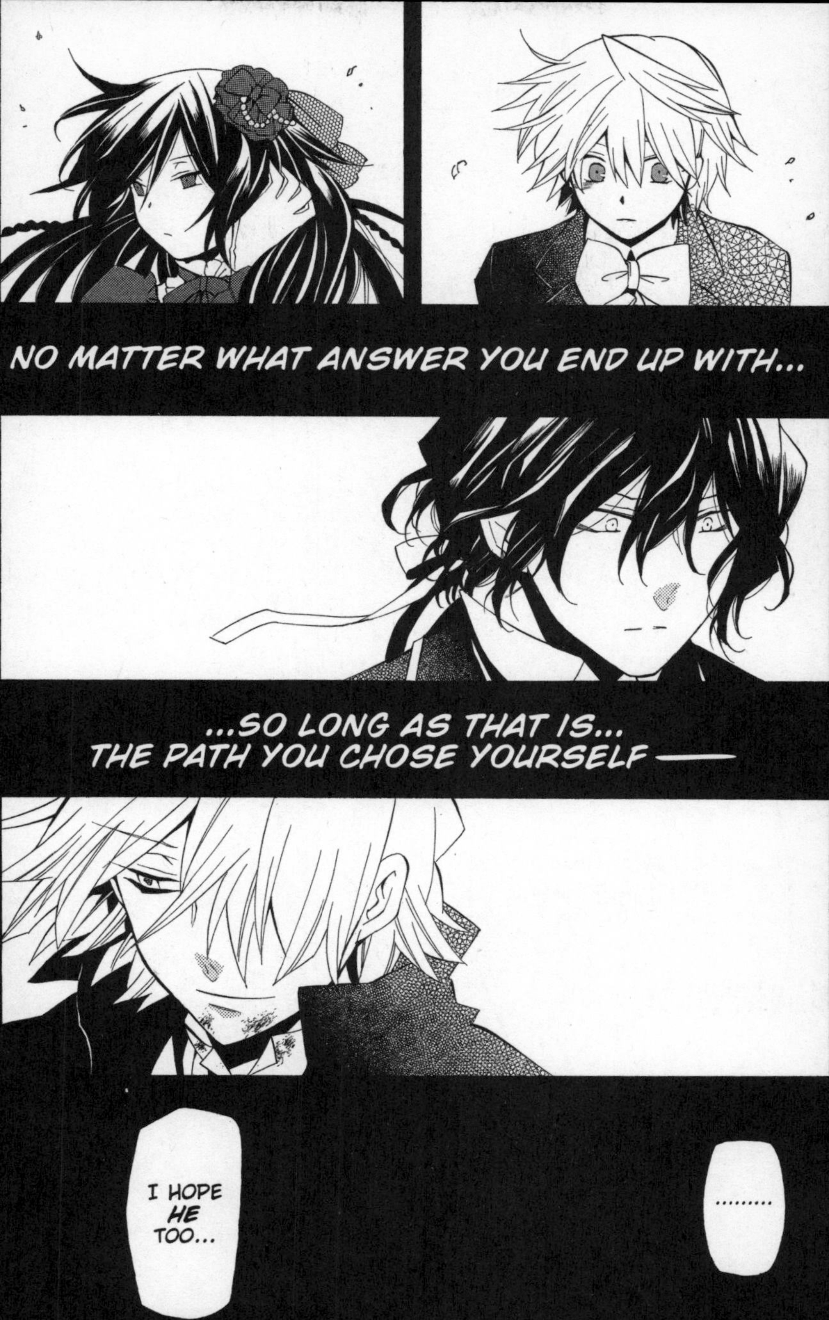
NO MATTER WHAT ANSWER YOU END UP WITH...
...SO LONG AS THAT IS... THE PATH YOU CHOSE YOURSELF —
....
I HOPE HE TOO...

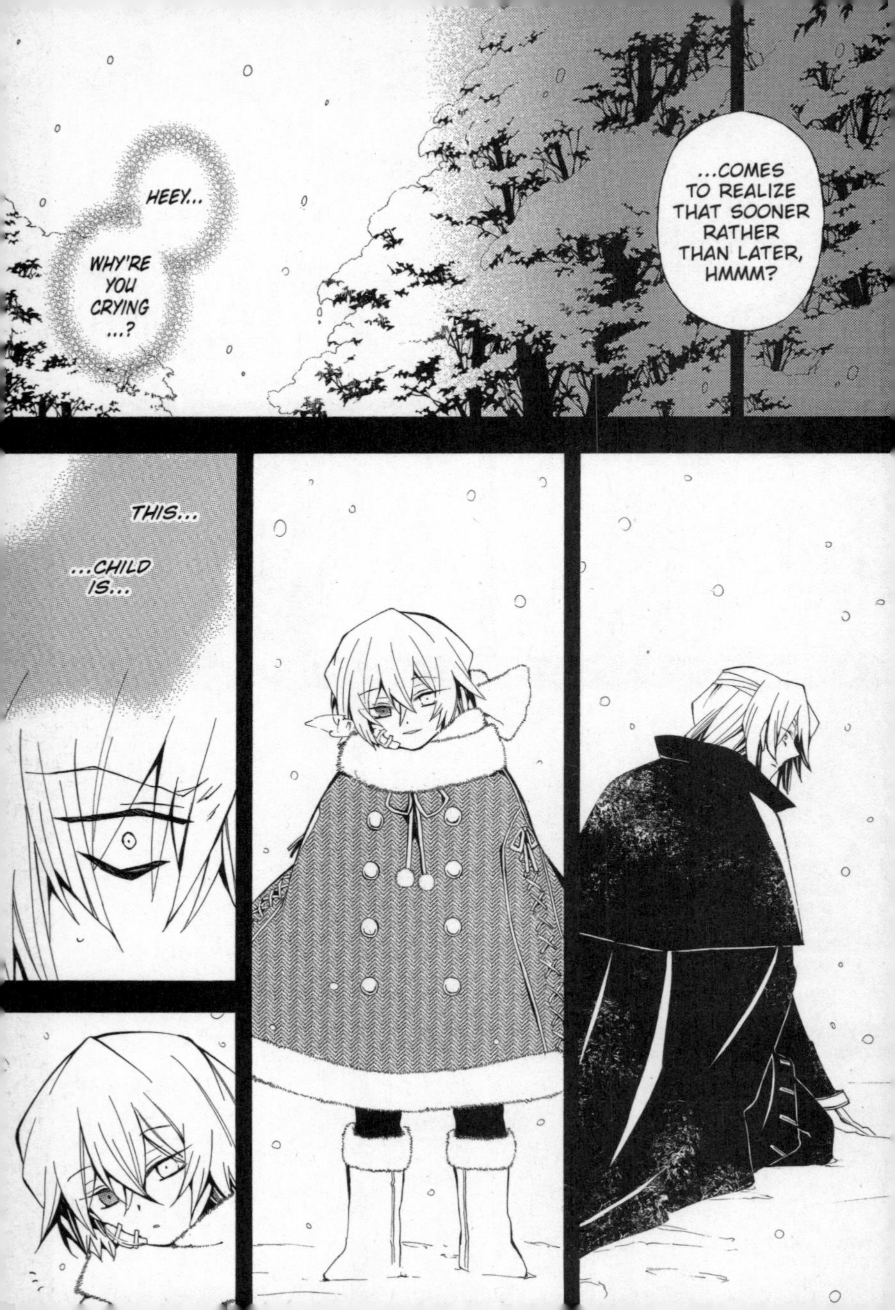
...COMES TO REALIZE THAT SOONER RATHER THAN LATER, HMMM?
HEEY...
WHY'RE YOU CRYING ...?
THIS...
...CHILD IS...

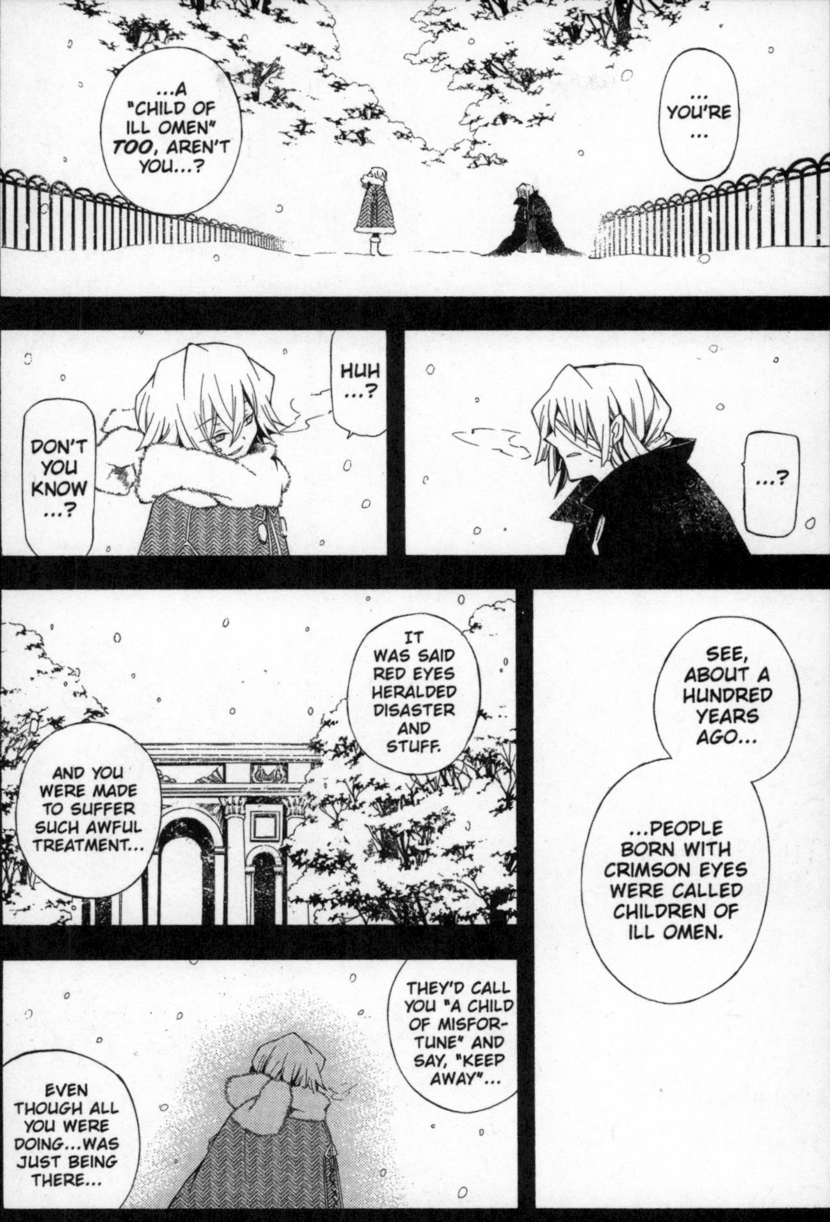
... YOU'RE ...
...A "CHILD OF ILL OMEN" TOO, AREN'T YOU...?
...?
HUH ...?
DON'T YOU KNOW ...?
SEE, ABOUT A HUNDRED YEARS AGO...
...PEOPLE BORN WITH CRIMSON EYES WERE CALLED CHILDREN OF ILL OMEN.
IT WAS SAID RED EYES HERALDED DISASTER AND STUFF.
AND YOU WERE MADE TO SUFFER SUCH AWFUL TREATMENT...
THEY'D CALL YOU "A CHILD OF MISFOR-TUNE" AND SAY, "KEEP AWAY"...
EVEN THOUGH ALL YOU WERE DOING...WAS JUST BEING THERE...

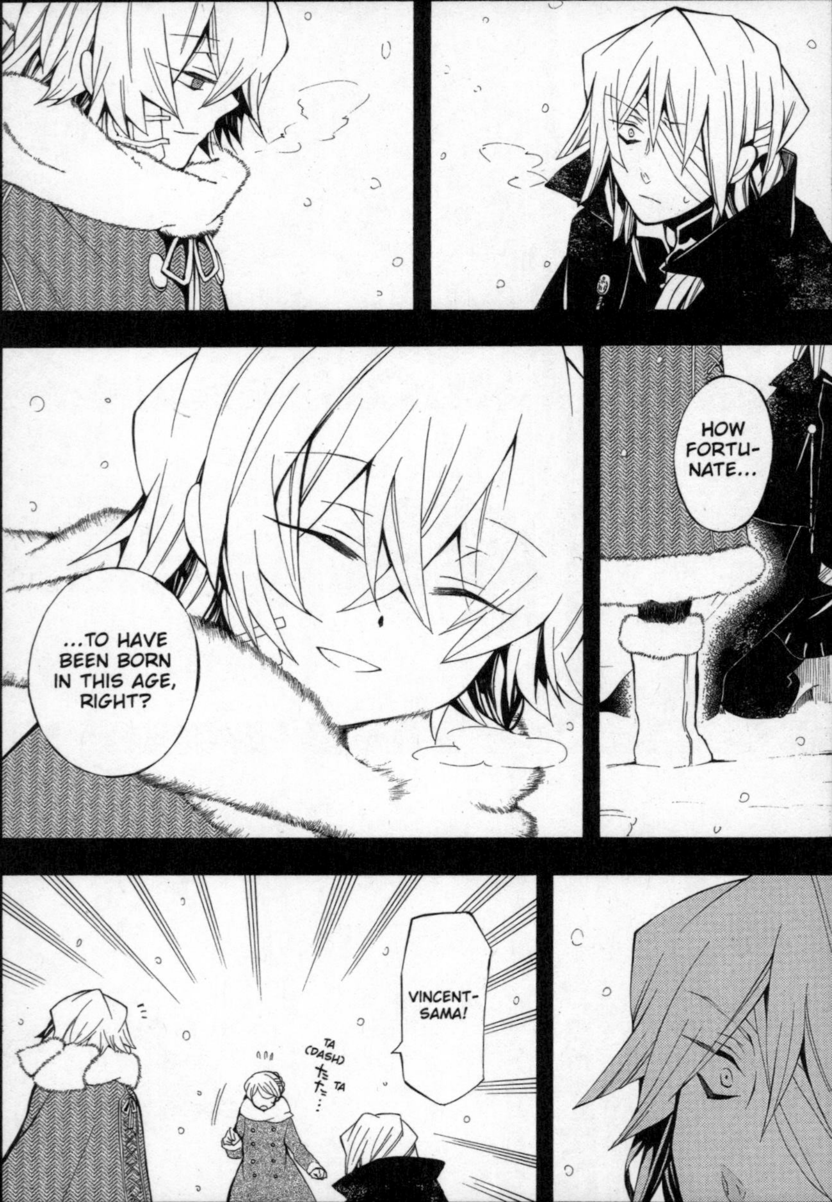
HOW FORTUNATE...
...TO HAVE BEEN BORN IN THIS AGE, RIGHT?
VINCENT-SAMA!
TA (DASH) TA

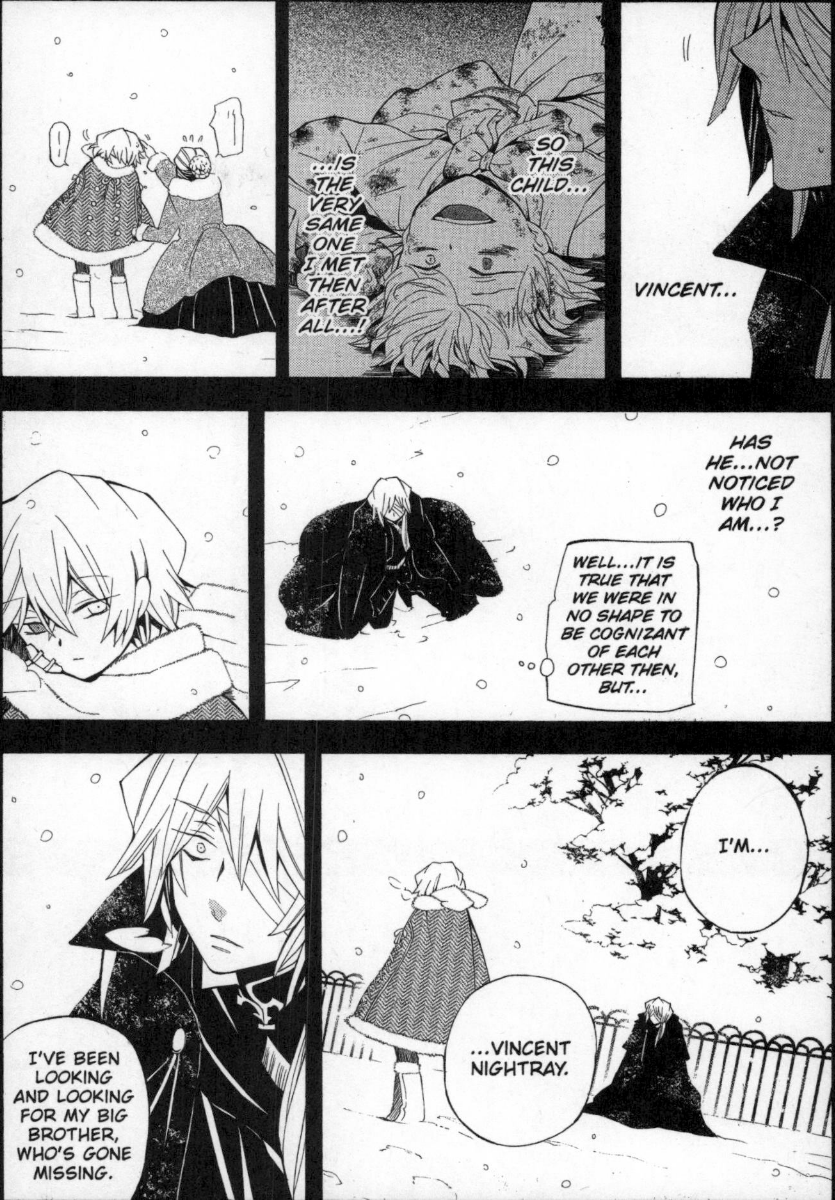
VINCENT...
SO THIS CHILD...
...IS THE VERY SAME ONE I MET THEN AFTER ALL...!
HAS HE...NOT NOTICED WHO I AM...?
WELL...IT IS TRUE THAT WE WERE IN NO SHAPE TO BE COGNIZANT OF EACH OTHER THEN, BUT...
I'M...
...VINCENT NIGHTRAY.
I'VE BEEN LOOKING AND LOOKING FOR MY BIG BROTHER, WHO'S GONE MISSING.

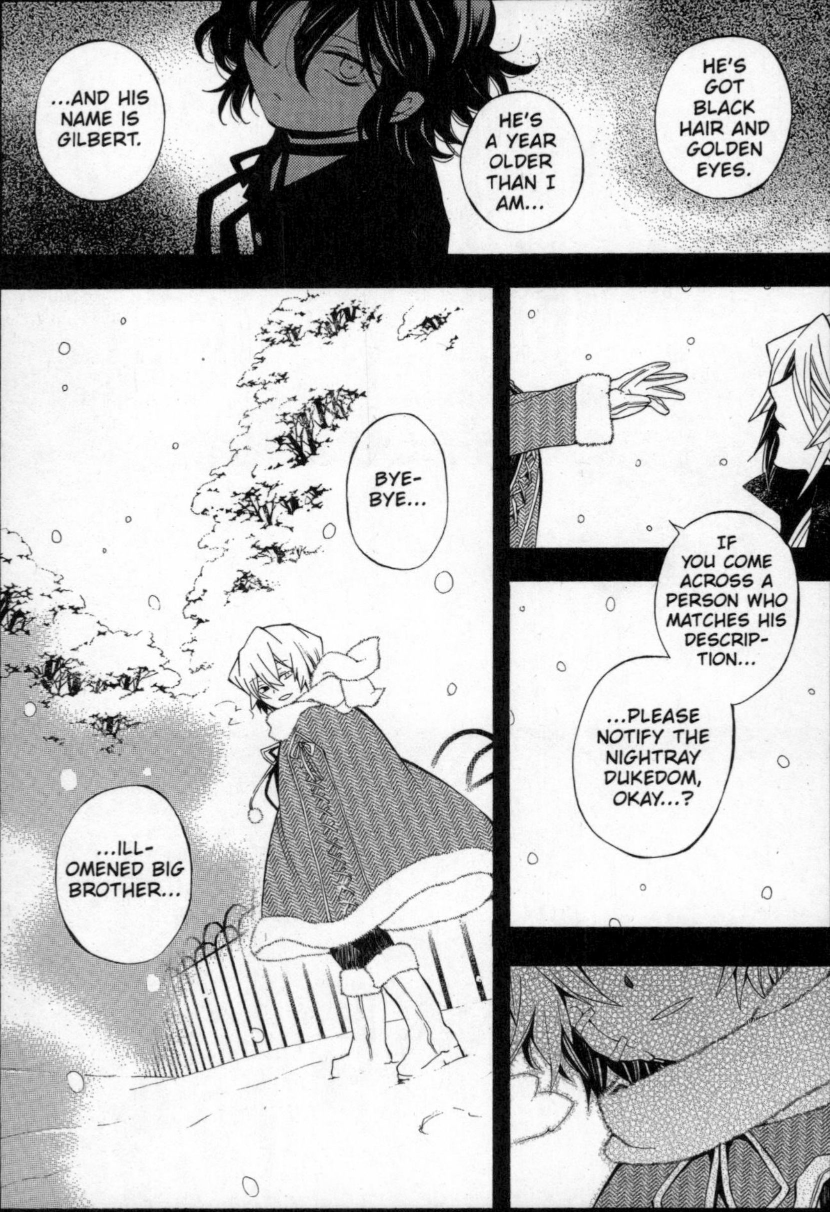
HE'S GOT BLACK HAIR AND GOLDEN EYES.
HE'S A YEAR OLDER THAN I AM...
...AND HIS NAME IS GILBERT.
IF YOU COME ACROSS A PERSON WHO MATCHES HIS DESCRIPTION...
...PLEASE NOTIFY THE NIGHTRAY DUKEDOM, OKAY...?
BYE-BYE...
...ILL-OMENED BIG BROTHER...

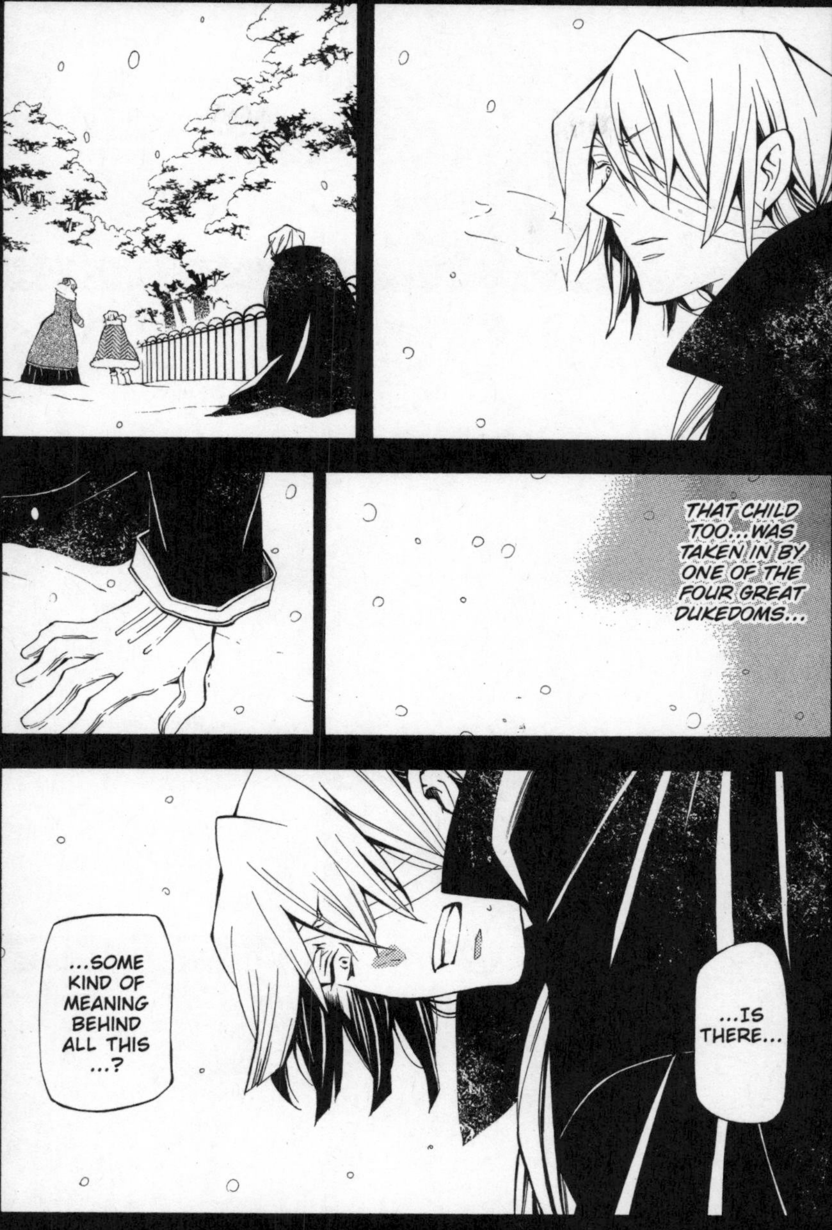
THAT CHILD TOO…WAS TAKEN IN BY ONE OF THE FOUR GREAT DUKEDOMS…
…IS THERE…
…SOME KIND OF MEANING BEHIND ALL THIS …?

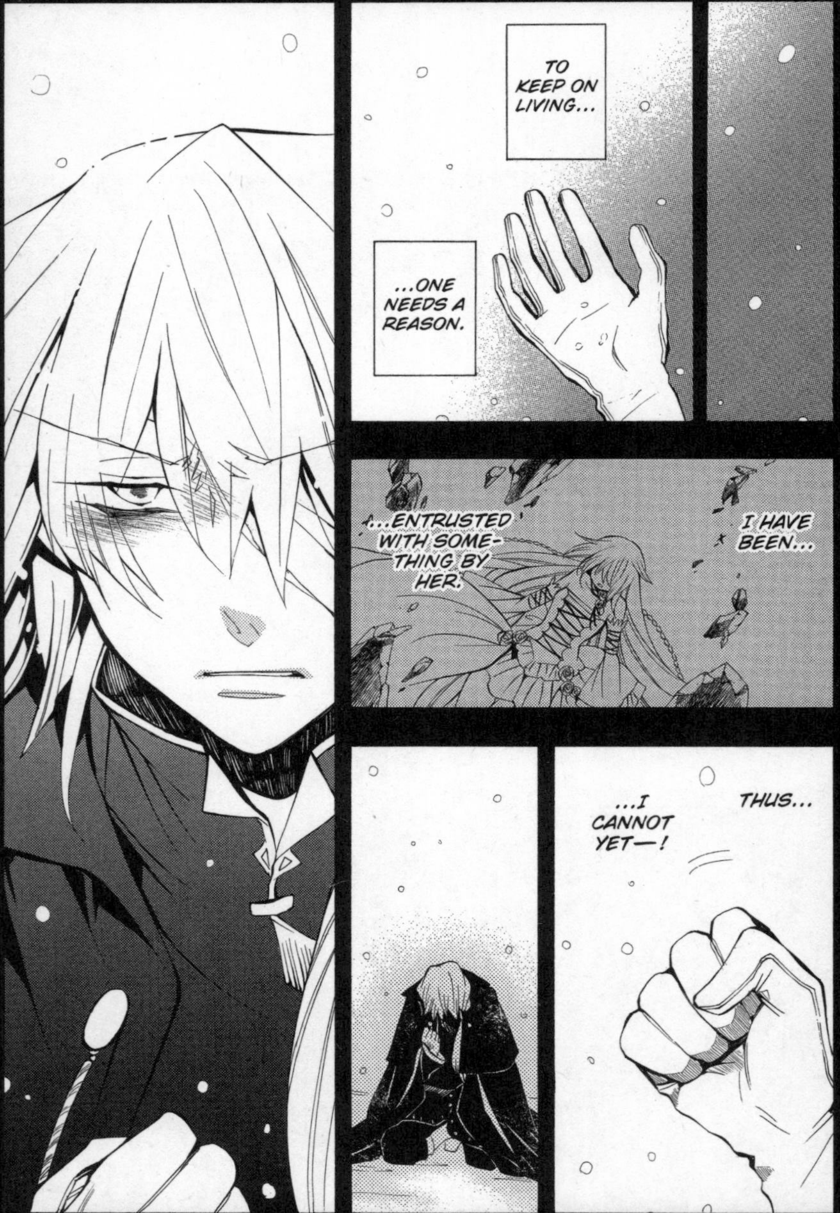
TO KEEP ON LIVING...
...ONE NEEDS A REASON.
I HAVE BEEN...
...ENTRUSTED WITH SOME-THING BY HER.
THUS...
...I CANNOT YET—!

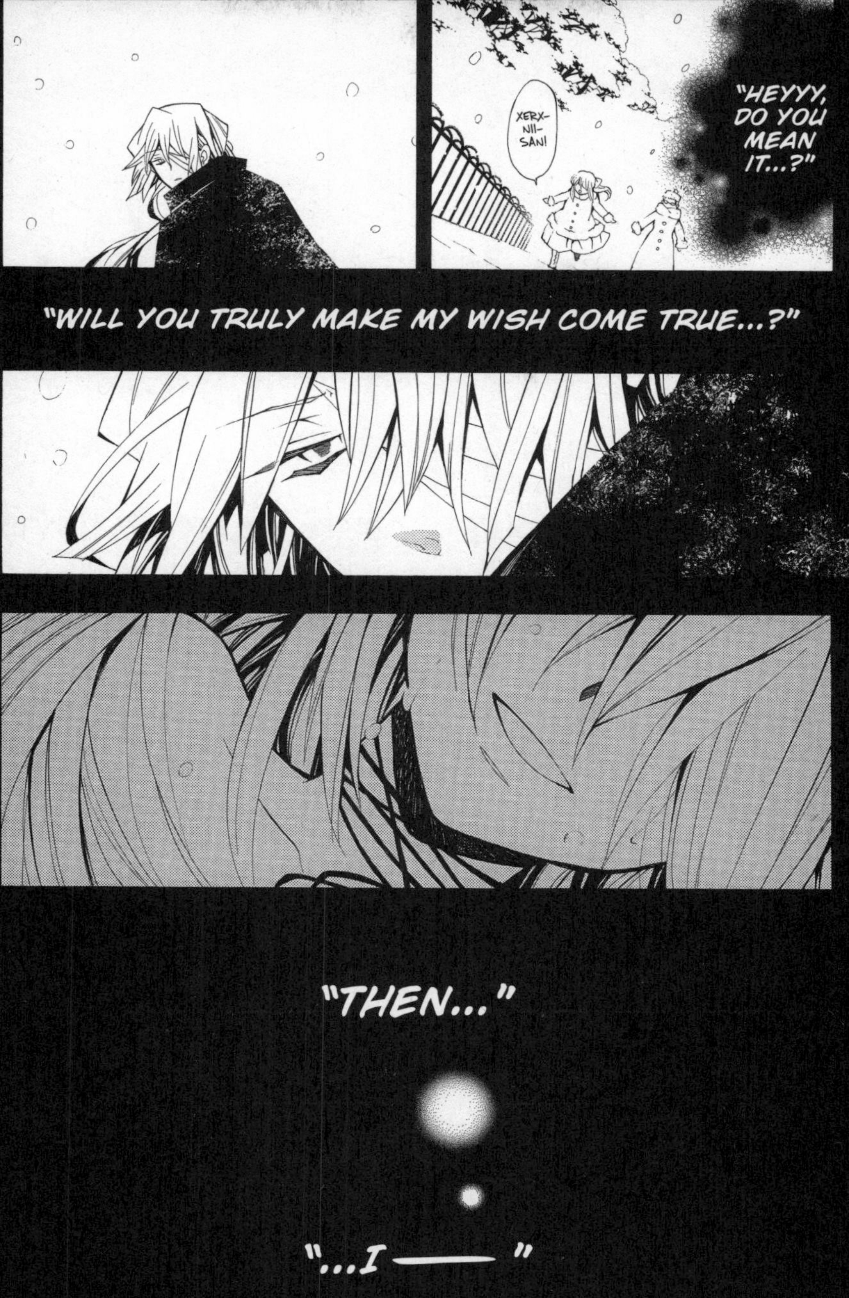
"HEYYY, DO YOU MEAN IT...?"
XERX-NII-SAN!
"WILL YOU TRULY MAKE MY WISH COME TRUE...?"
"THEN..."
"...I——"

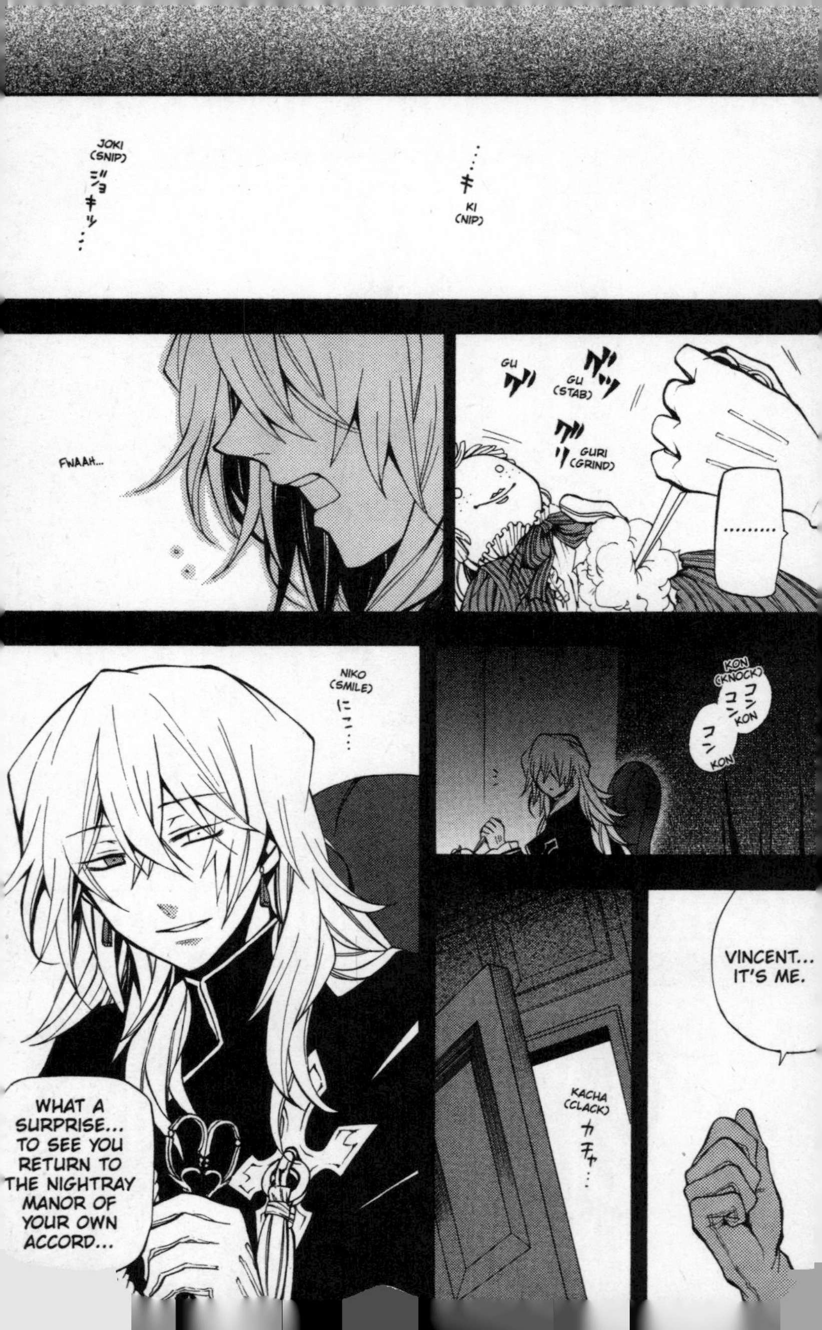
...キ
KI (NIP)
JOKI (SNIP)
ジョキッ...
GU (STAB)
グッ
GU
グ
GURI (GRIND)
グリ
....
FWAAH...
KON (KNOCK)
コン
KON
コン
KON
コン
VINCENT... IT'S ME.
KACHA (CLACK)
カチャ...
NIKO (SMILE)
にこ...
WHAT A SURPRISE... TO SEE YOU RETURN TO THE NIGHTRAY MANOR OF YOUR OWN ACCORD...

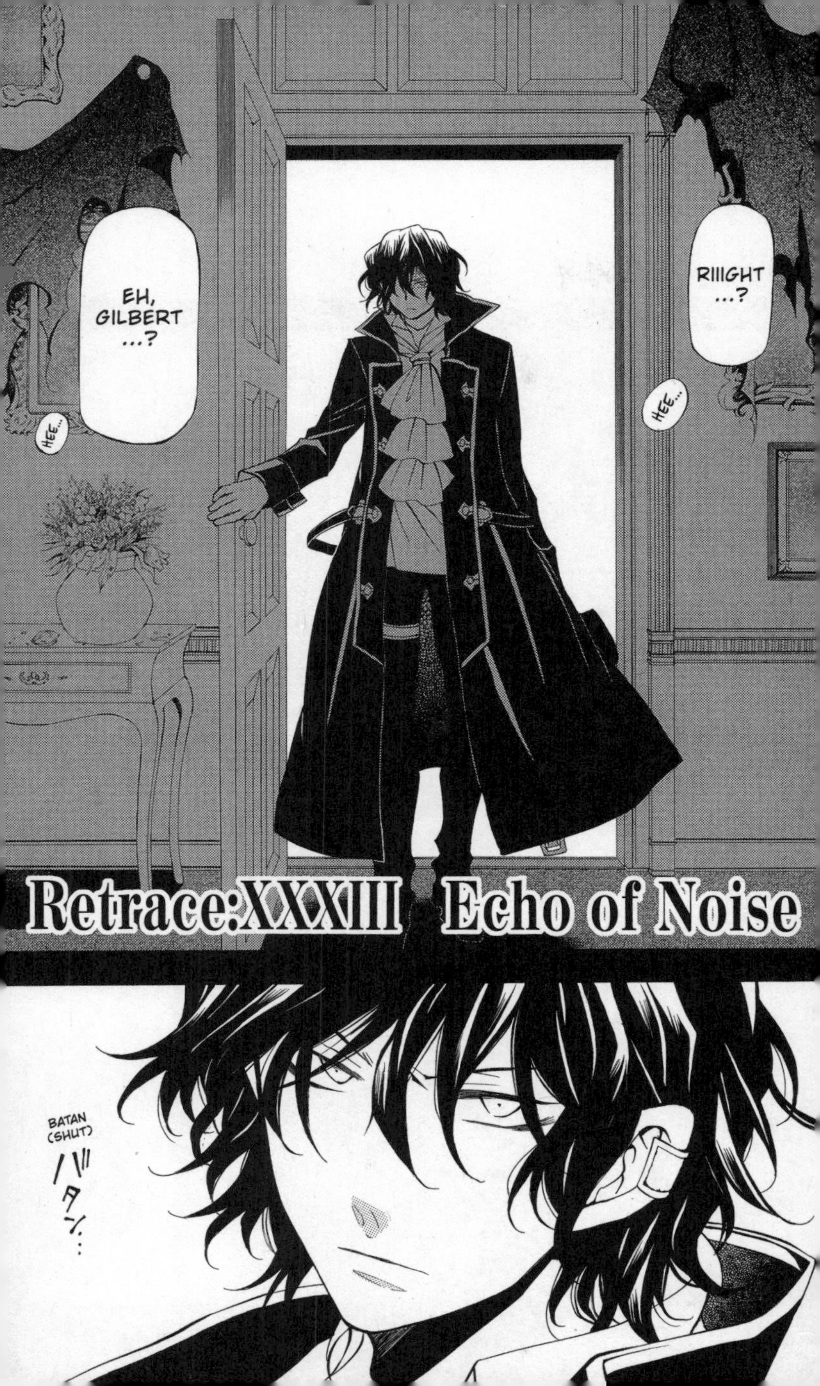
RIIIGHT ...?
HEE...
EH, GILBERT ...?
HEE...
Retrace:XXXIII Echo of Noise
BATAN (SHUT)
バタン…

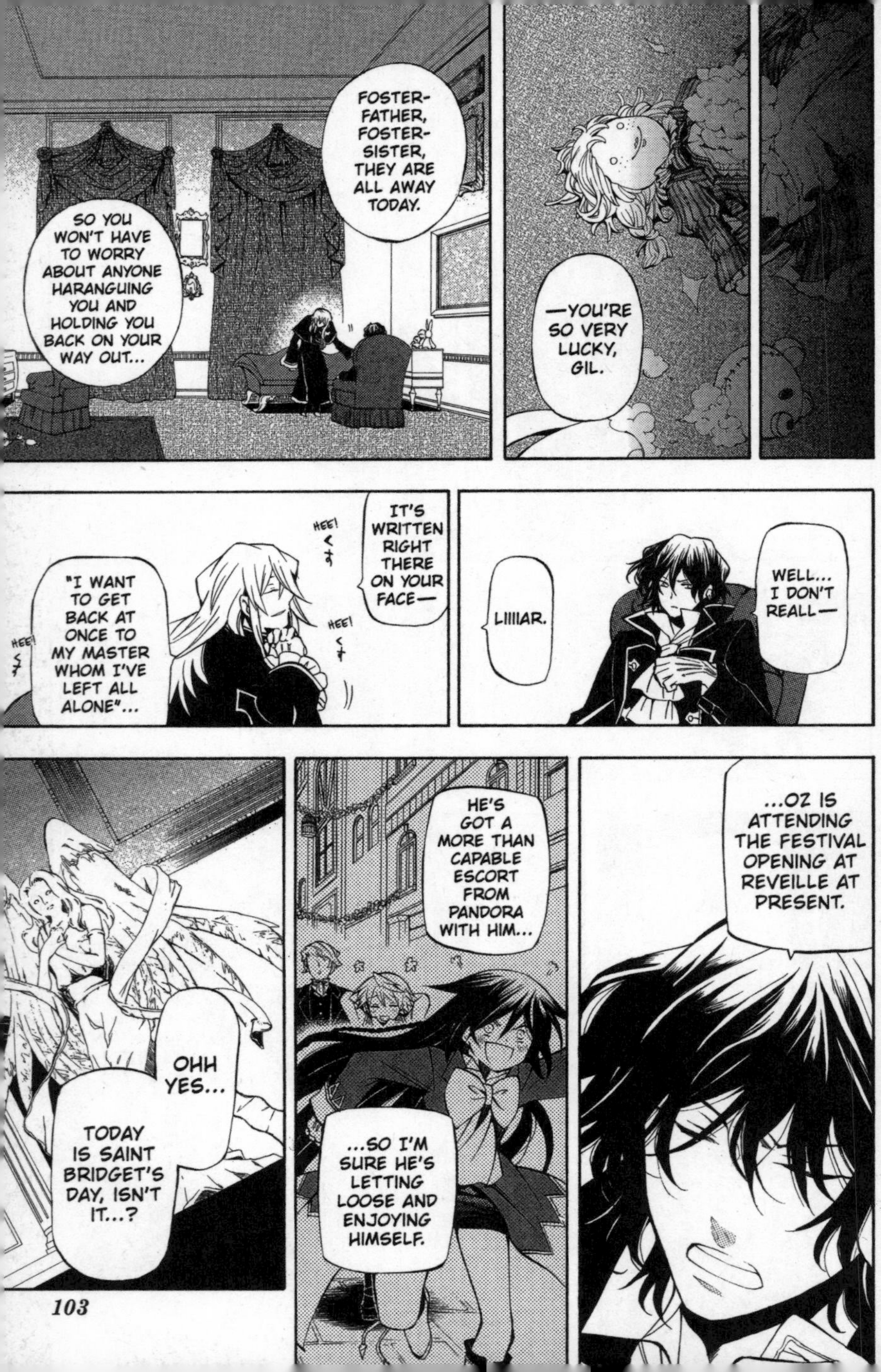
—YOU'RE SO VERY LUCKY, GIL.
FOSTER-FATHER, FOSTER-SISTER, THEY ARE ALL AWAY TODAY.
SO YOU WON'T HAVE TO WORRY ABOUT ANYONE HARANGUING YOU AND HOLDING YOU BACK ON YOUR WAY OUT...
WELL... I DON'T REALL—
LIIIIAR.
IT'S WRITTEN RIGHT THERE ON YOUR FACE—
HEE!
HEE!
"I WANT TO GET BACK AT ONCE TO MY MASTER WHOM I'VE LEFT ALL ALONE"...
HEE!
...OZ IS ATTENDING THE FESTIVAL OPENING AT REVEILLE AT PRESENT.
HE'S GOT A MORE THAN CAPABLE ESCORT FROM PANDORA WITH HIM...
...SO I'M SURE HE'S LETTING LOOSE AND ENJOYING HIMSELF.
OHH YES...
TODAY IS SAINT BRIDGET'S DAY, ISN'T IT...?

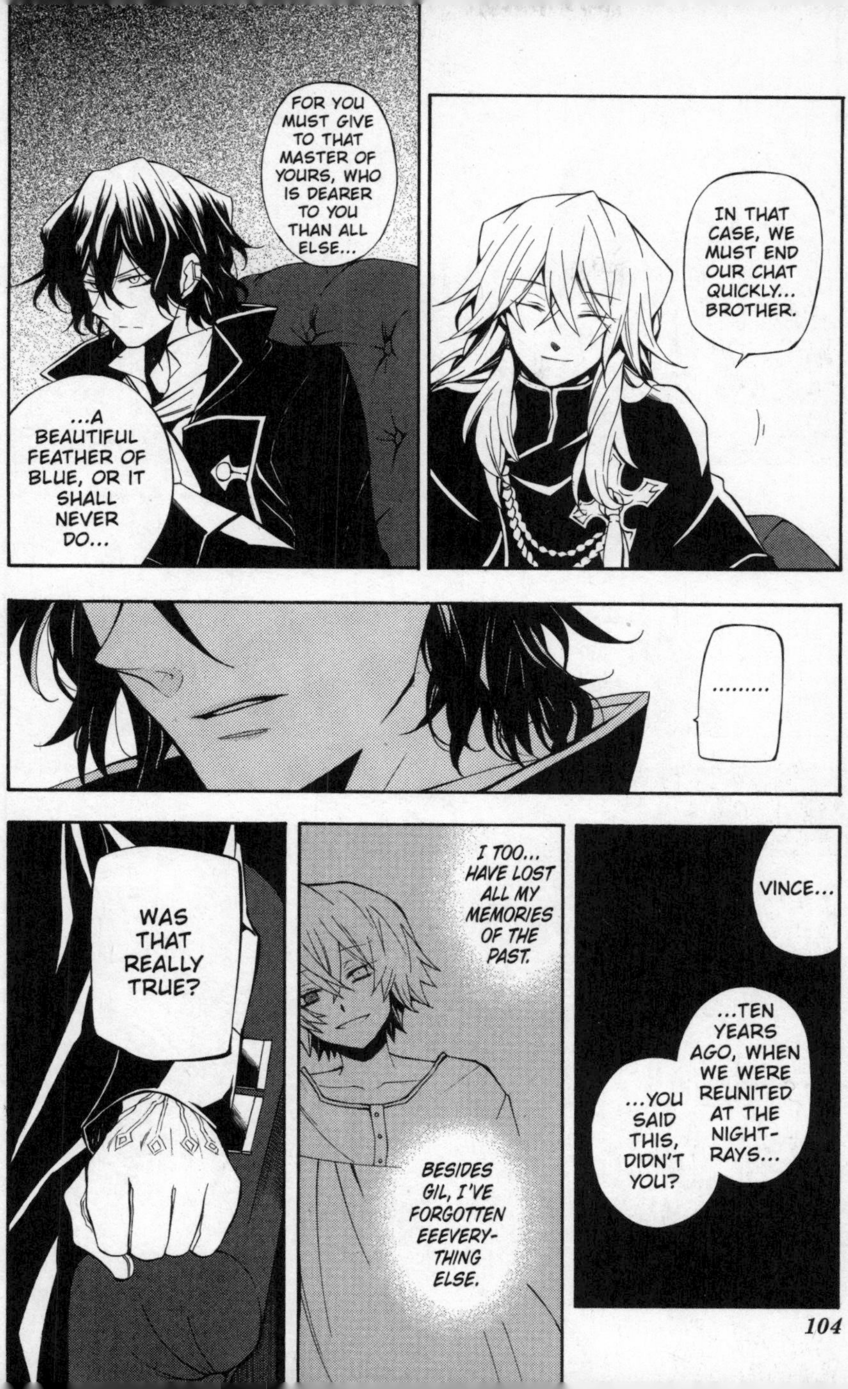
IN THAT CASE, WE MUST END OUR CHAT QUICKLY... BROTHER.
FOR YOU MUST GIVE TO THAT MASTER OF YOURS, WHO IS DEARER TO YOU THAN ALL ELSE...
...A BEAUTIFUL FEATHER OF BLUE, OR IT SHALL NEVER DO...
....
VINCE...
...TEN YEARS AGO, WHEN WE WERE REUNITED AT THE NIGHT-RAYS...
...YOU SAID THIS, DIDN'T YOU?
I TOO... HAVE LOST ALL MY MEMORIES OF THE PAST.
BESIDES GIL, I'VE FORGOTTEN EEEVERY-THING ELSE.
WAS THAT REALLY TRUE?

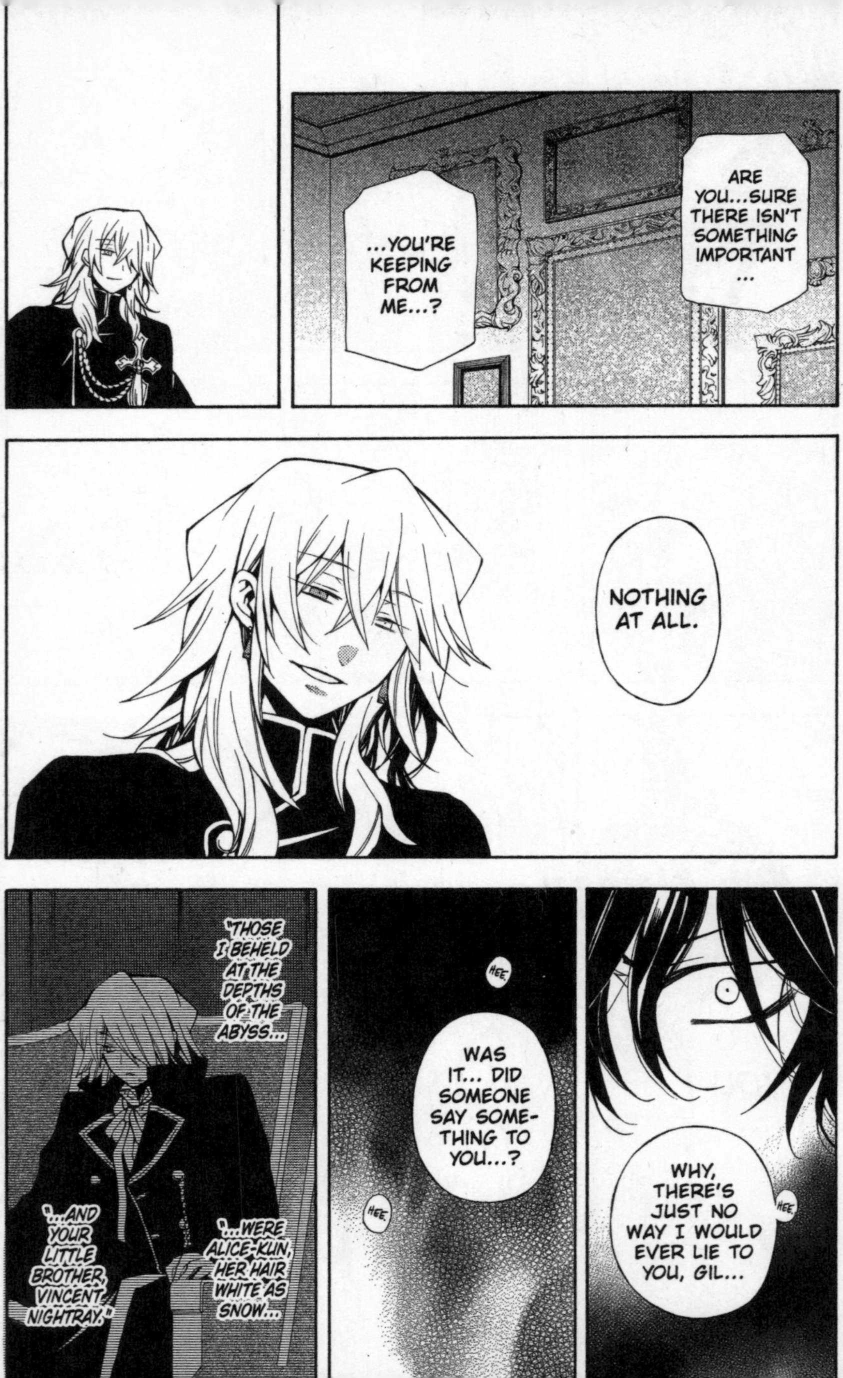
ARE YOU...SURE THERE ISN'T SOMETHING IMPORTANT ...
...YOU'RE KEEPING FROM ME...?
NOTHING AT ALL.
WHY, THERE'S JUST NO WAY I WOULD EVER LIE TO YOU, GIL...
HEE.
HEE.
WAS IT... DID SOMEONE SAY SOME-THING TO YOU...?
HEE.
"THOSE I BEHELD AT THE DEPTHS OF THE ABYSS...
"...WERE ALICE-KUN, HER HAIR WHITE AS SNOW...
"...AND YOUR LITTLE BROTHER, VINCENT NIGHTRAY."

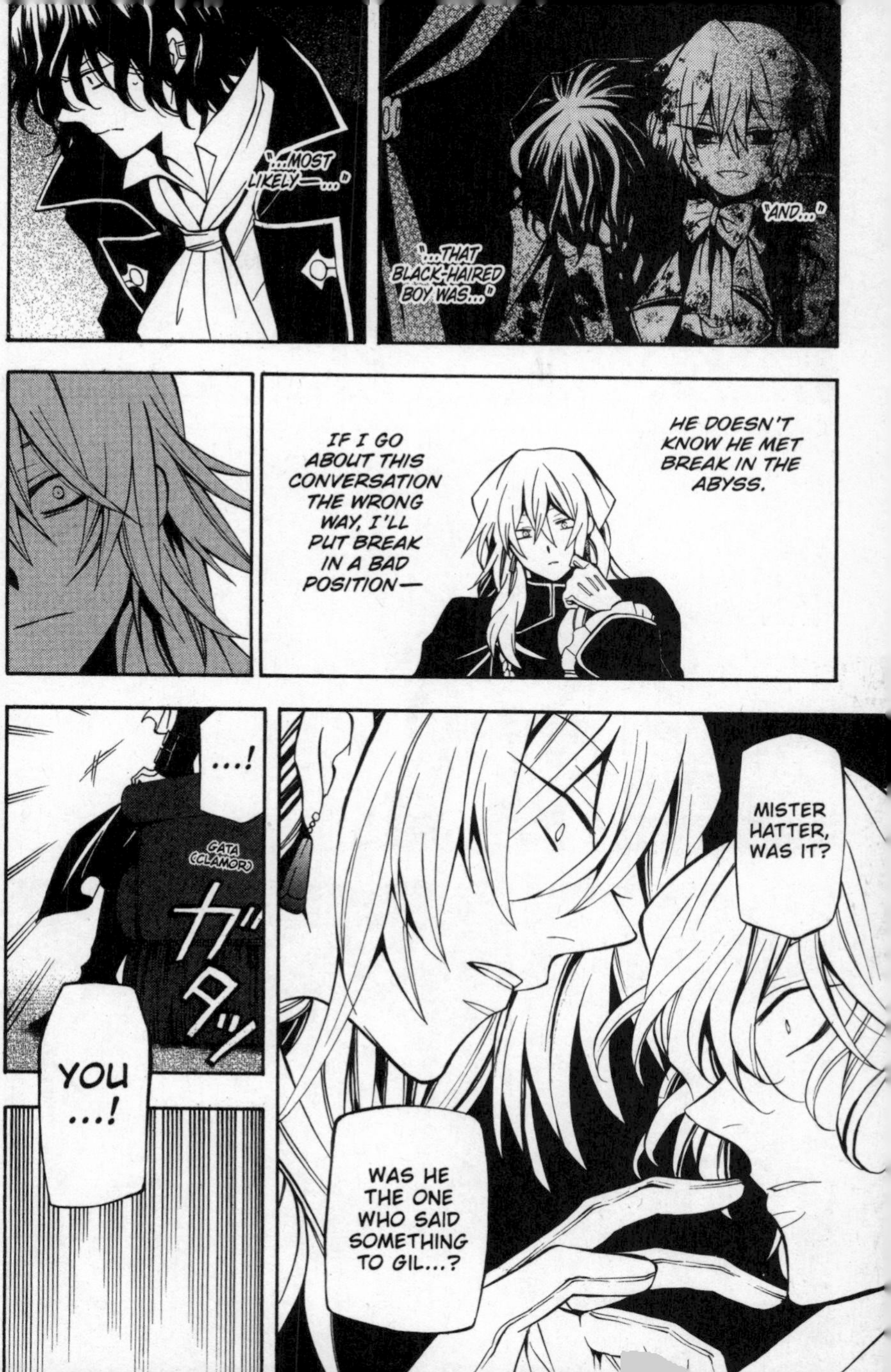

"AND..."
"...THAT BLACK-HAIRED BOY WAS..."
"...MOST LIKELY—..."
HE DOESN'T KNOW HE MET BREAK IN THE ABYSS.
IF I GO ABOUT THIS CONVERSATION THE WRONG WAY, I'LL PUT BREAK IN A BAD POSITION—
MISTER HATTER, WAS IT?
WAS HE THE ONE WHO SAID SOMETHING TO GIL...?
...!
GATA (CLAMOR)
ガタッ
YOU ...!

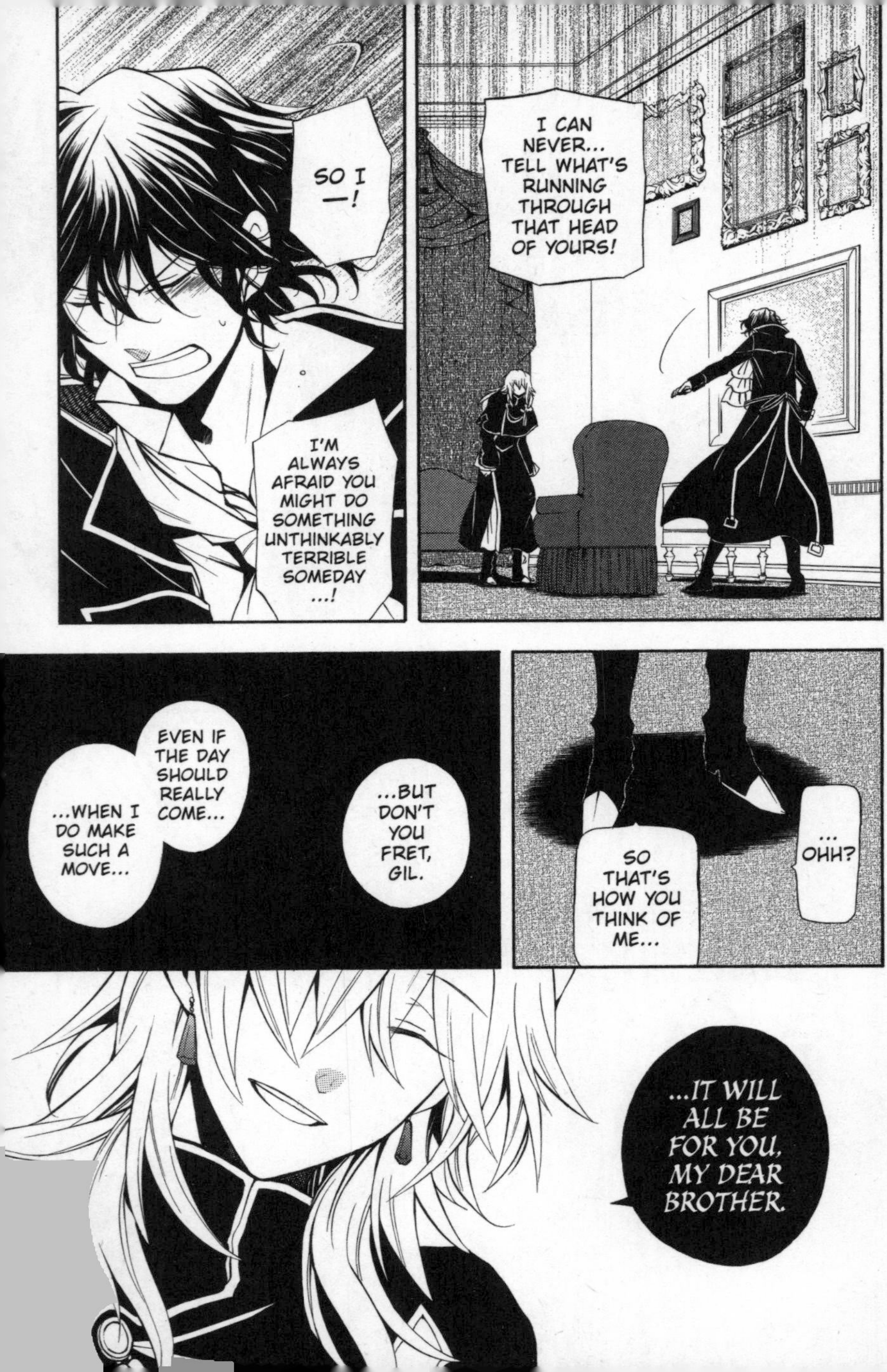
I CAN NEVER... TELL WHAT'S RUNNING THROUGH THAT HEAD OF YOURS!
SO I —!
I'M ALWAYS AFRAID YOU MIGHT DO SOMETHING UNTHINKABLY TERRIBLE SOMEDAY ...!
...OHH?
SO THAT'S HOW YOU THINK OF ME...
...BUT DON'T YOU FRET, GIL.
EVEN IF THE DAY SHOULD REALLY COME...
...WHEN I DO MAKE SUCH A MOVE...
...IT WILL ALL BE FOR YOU, MY DEAR BROTHER.

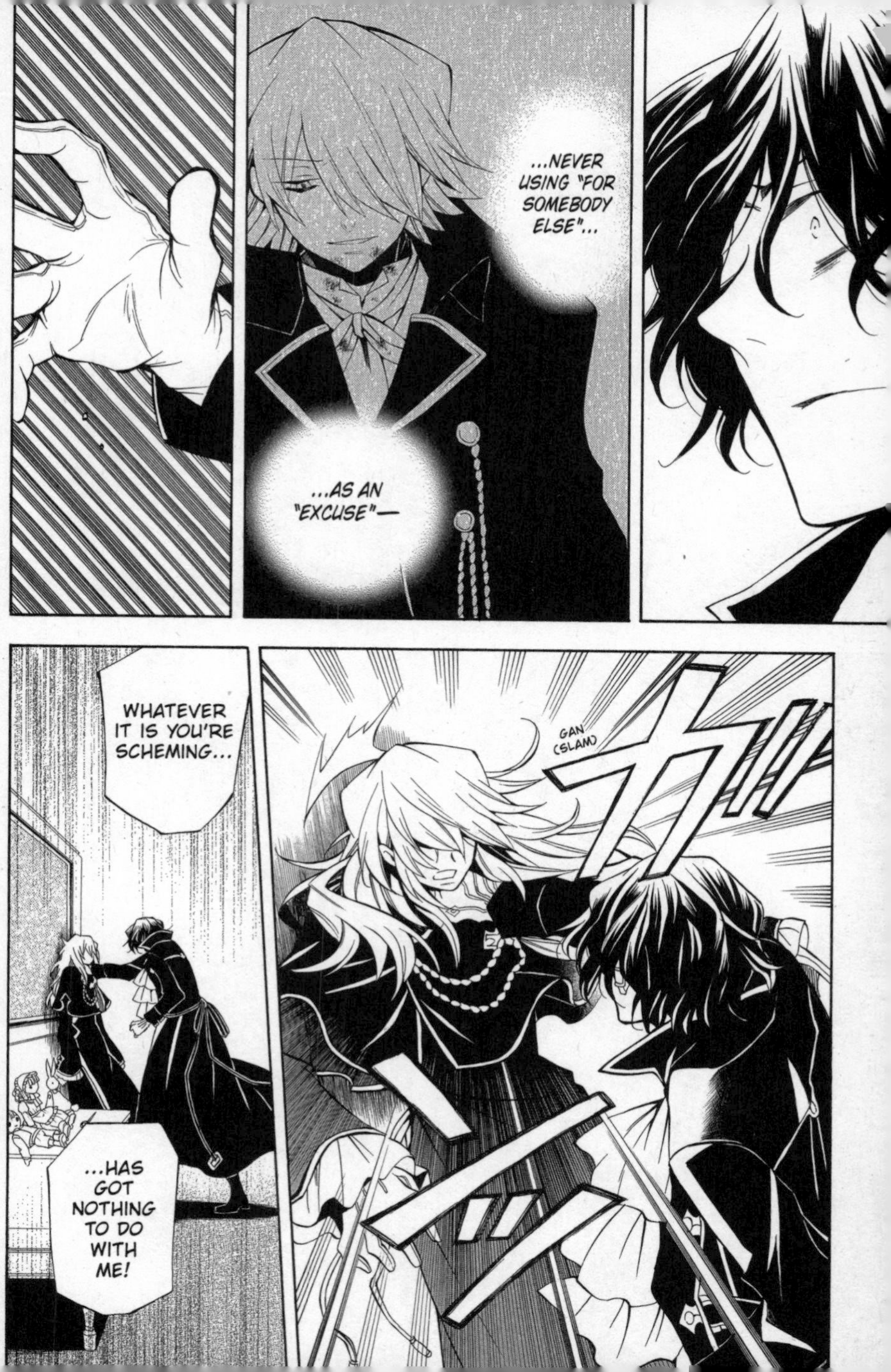
...NEVER USING "FOR SOMEBODY ELSE"...
...AS AN "EXCUSE"—
GAN (SLAM)
WHATEVER IT IS YOU'RE SCHEMING...
...HAS GOT NOTHING TO DO WITH ME!

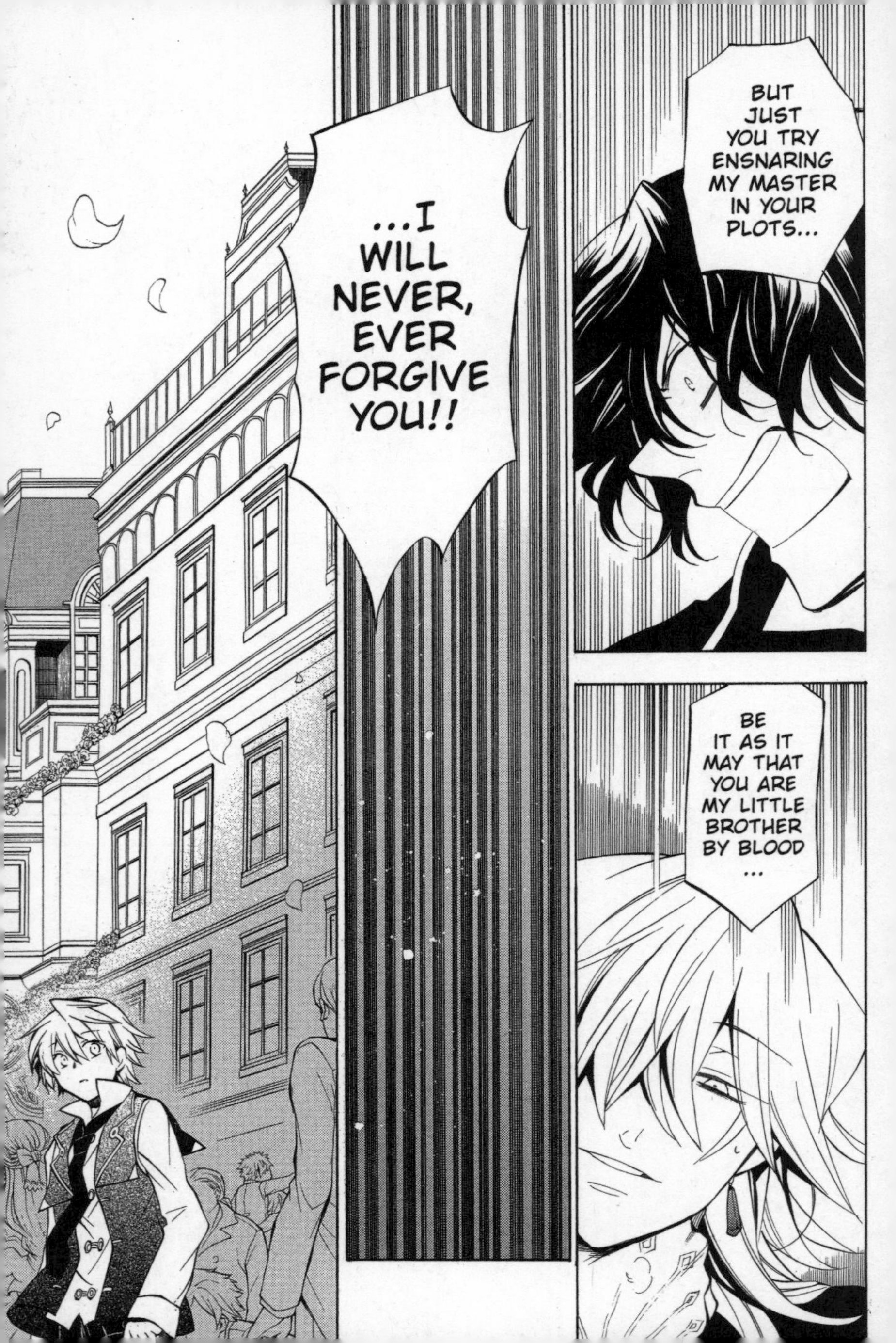
BUT JUST YOU TRY ENSNARING MY MASTER IN YOUR PLOTS...
BE IT AS IT MAY THAT YOU ARE MY LITTLE BROTHER BY BLOOD...
...I WILL NEVER, EVER FORGIVE YOU!!

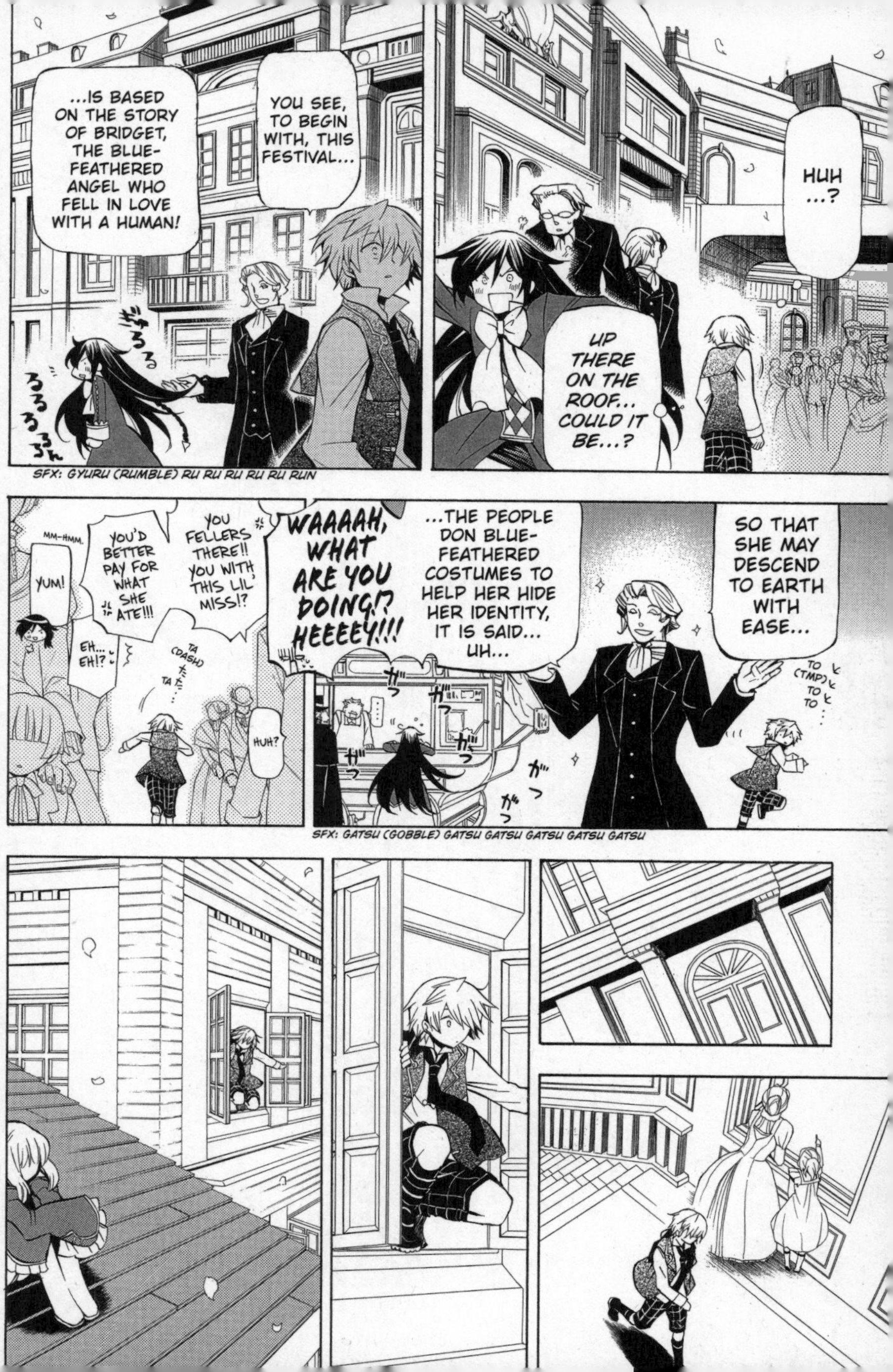
HUH ...?
UP THERE ON THE ROOF... COULD IT BE...?
YOU SEE, TO BEGIN WITH, THIS FESTIVAL...
...IS BASED ON THE STORY OF BRIDGET, THE BLUE-FEATHERED ANGEL WHO FELL IN LOVE WITH A HUMAN!
SFX: GYURU (RUMBLE) RU RU RU RU RU RUN
SO THAT SHE MAY DESCEND TO EARTH WITH EASE...
TO (TMP) TO TO
...THE PEOPLE DON BLUE-FEATHERED COSTUMES TO HELP HER HIDE HER IDENTITY, IT IS SAID... UH...
WAAAAH, WHAT ARE YOU DOING!? HEEEEY!!!
YOU FELLERS THERE!! YOU WITH THIS LIL' MISS!?
YOU'D BETTER PAY FOR WHAT SHE ATE!!!
MM-HMM.
YUM!
EH... EH!?
TA (DASH) TA
HUH?
SFX: GATSU (GOBBLE) GATSU GATSU GATSU GATSU GATSU

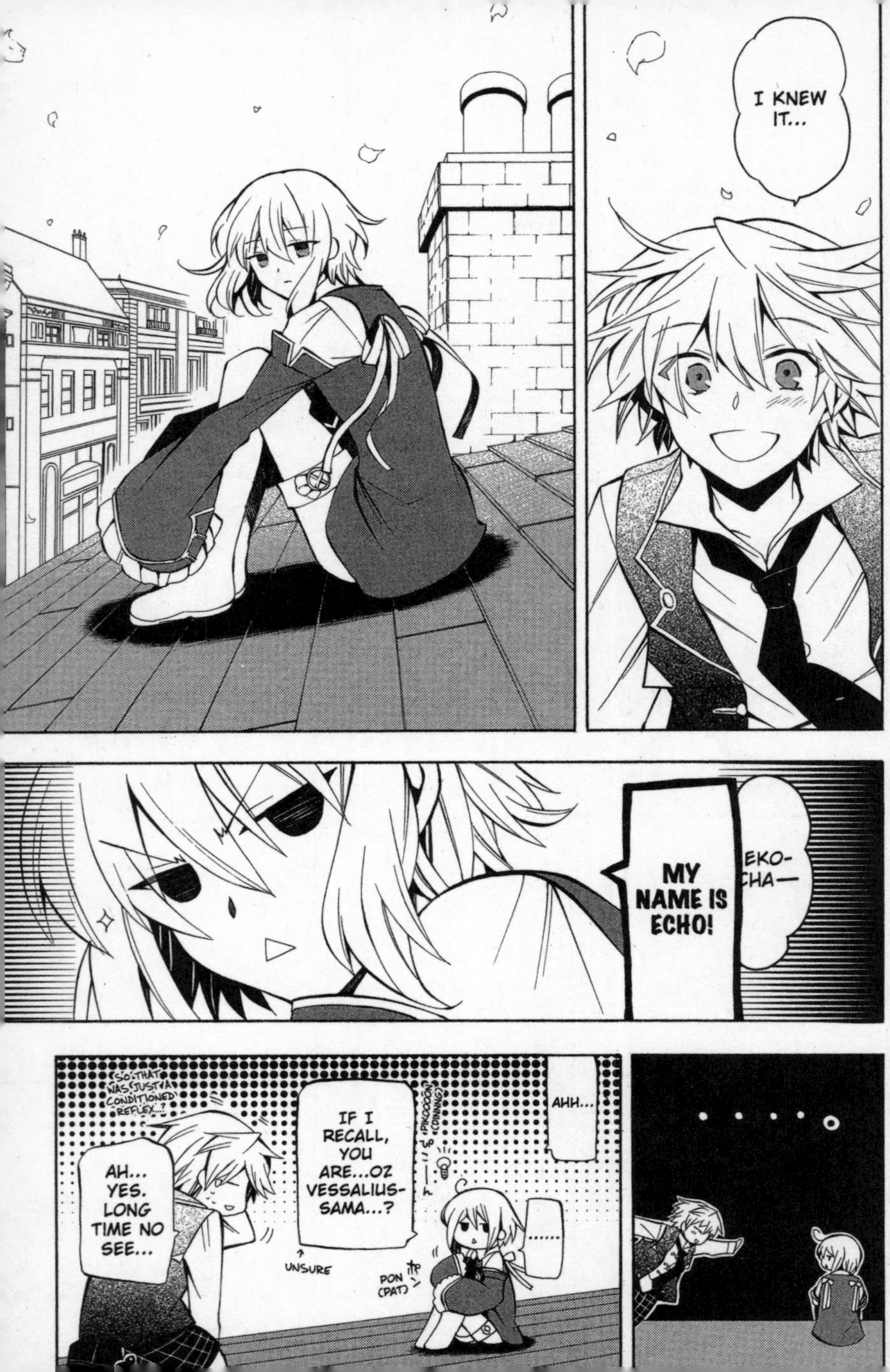
I KNEW IT...
EKO-CHA—
MY NAME IS ECHO!
. . . . o
AHH...
PIKOOOON (DINNNG)
IF I RECALL, YOU ARE...OZ VESSALIUS-SAMA...?
UNSURE
......
PON (PAT)
SO THAT WAS JUST A CONDITIONED REFLEX...?
AH... YES. LONG TIME NO SEE...

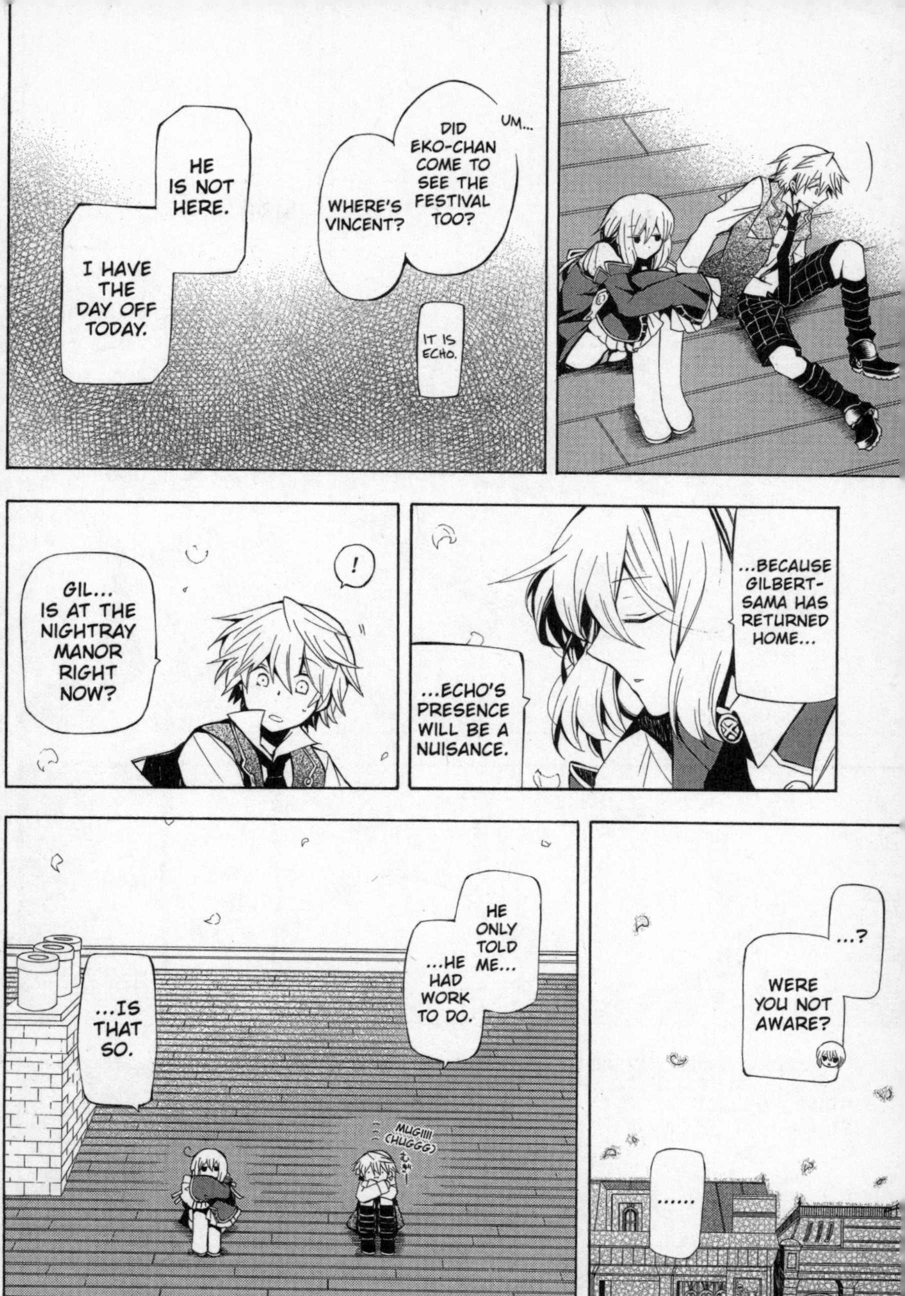
UM...
DID EKO-CHAN COME TO SEE THE FESTIVAL TOO?
IT IS ECHO.
WHERE'S VINCENT?
HE IS NOT HERE.
I HAVE THE DAY OFF TODAY.
...BECAUSE GILBERT-SAMA HAS RETURNED HOME...
...ECHO'S PRESENCE WILL BE A NUISANCE.
!
GIL... IS AT THE NIGHTRAY MANOR RIGHT NOW?
...?
WERE YOU NOT AWARE?
......
HE ONLY TOLD ME...
...HE HAD WORK TO DO.
...IS THAT SO.
MUGIIII (HUGGG)

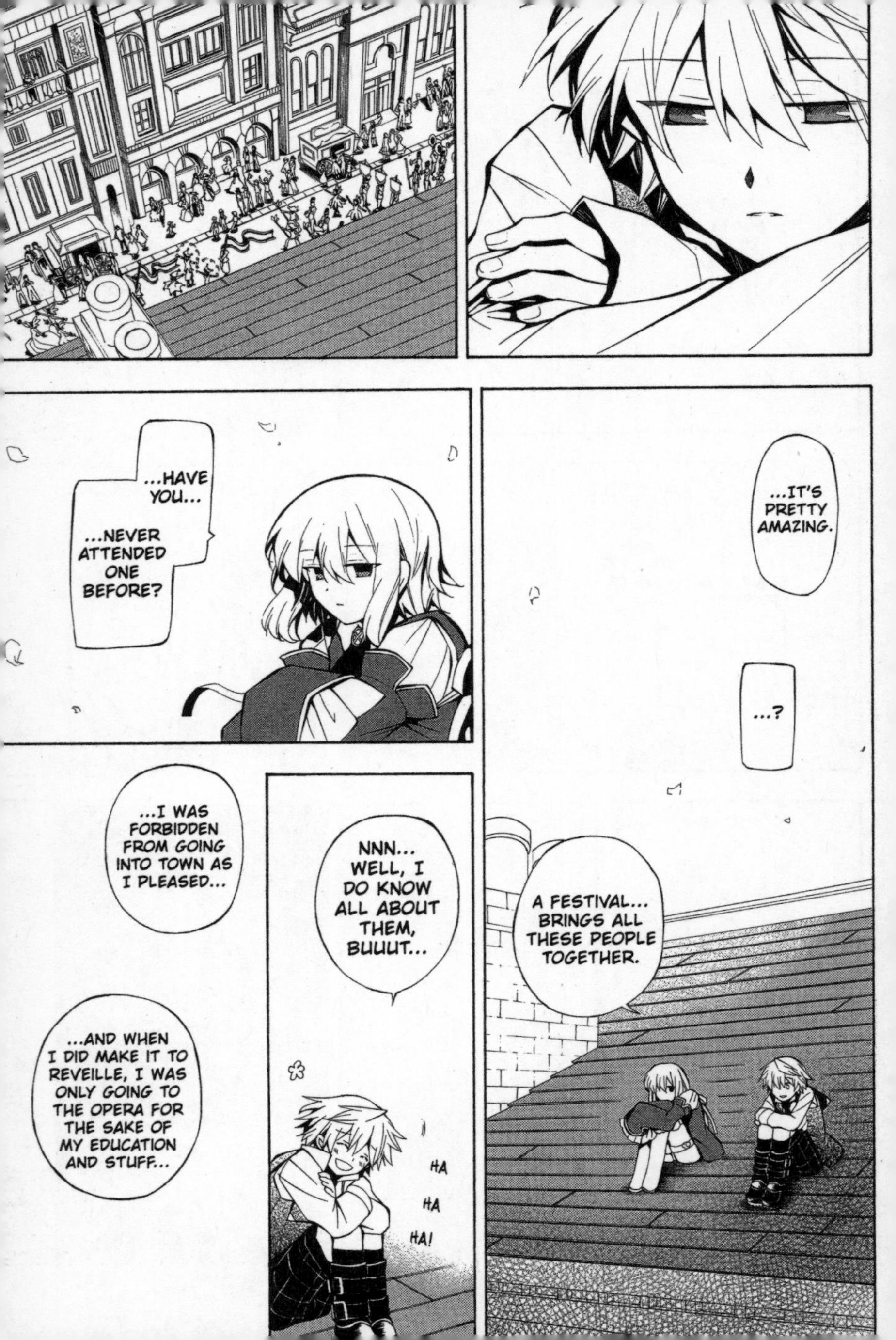
...IT'S PRETTY AMAZING.
...?
A FESTIVAL... BRINGS ALL THESE PEOPLE TOGETHER.
...HAVE YOU...
...NEVER ATTENDED ONE BEFORE?
NNN... WELL, I DO KNOW ALL ABOUT THEM, BUUUT...
...I WAS FORBIDDEN FROM GOING INTO TOWN AS I PLEASED...
...AND WHEN I DID MAKE IT TO REVEILLE, I WAS ONLY GOING TO THE OPERA FOR THE SAKE OF MY EDUCATION AND STUFF...
HA HA HA!

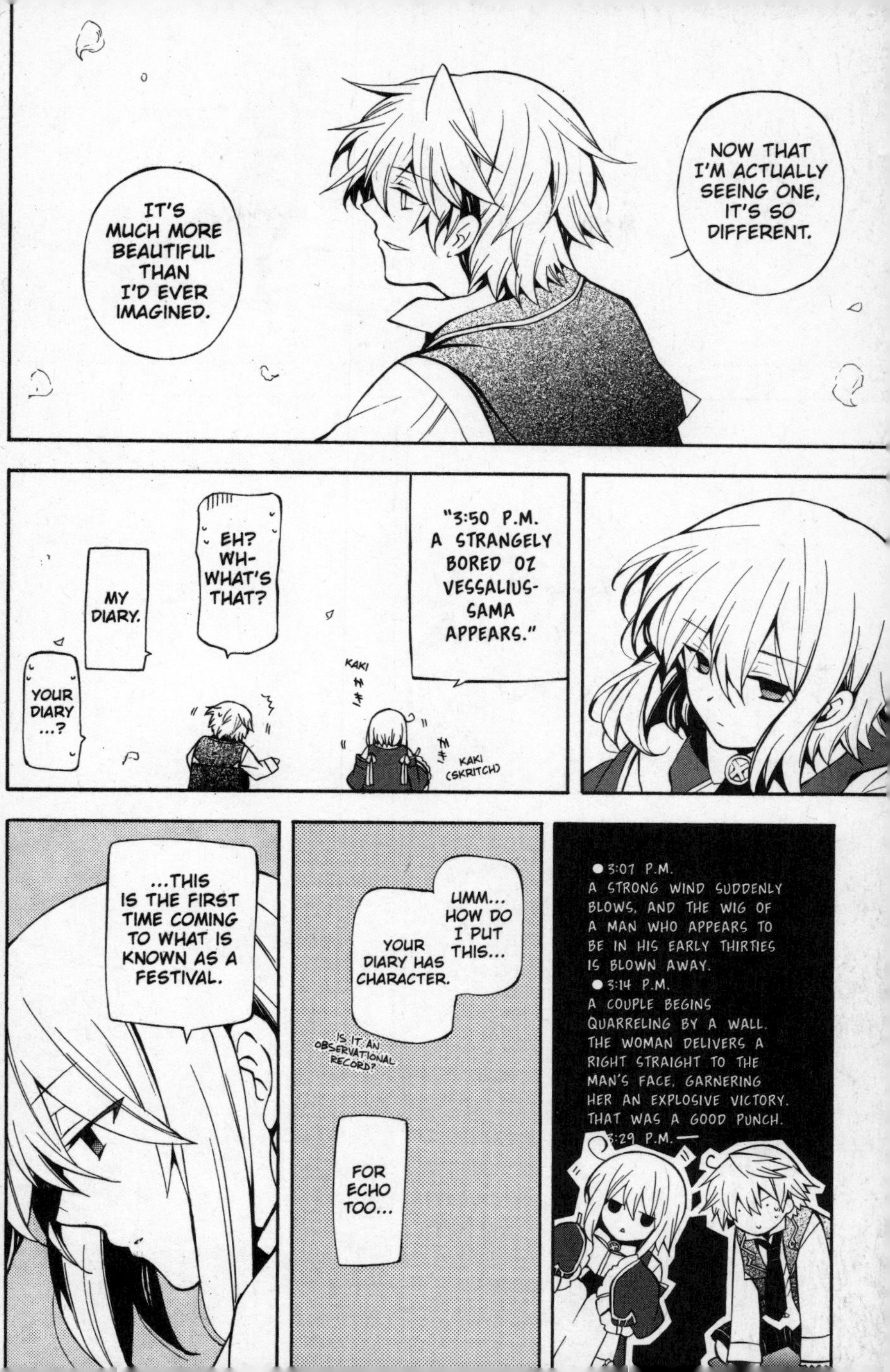
NOW THAT I'M ACTUALLY SEEING ONE, IT'S SO DIFFERENT.
IT'S MUCH MORE BEAUTIFUL THAN I'D EVER IMAGINED.
"3:50 P.M. A STRANGELY BORED OZ VESSALIUS-SAMA APPEARS."
EH? WH-WHAT'S THAT?
MY DIARY.
KAKI
YOUR DIARY ...?
KAKI (SKRITCH)
●3:07 P.M.
A STRONG WIND SUDDENLY BLOWS, AND THE WIG OF A MAN WHO APPEARS TO BE IN HIS EARLY THIRTIES IS BLOWN AWAY.
●3:14 P.M.
A COUPLE BEGINS QUARRELING BY A WALL. THE WOMAN DELIVERS A RIGHT STRAIGHT TO THE MAN'S FACE, GARNERING HER AN EXPLOSIVE VICTORY. THAT WAS A GOOD PUNCH.
3:29 P.M.—
UMM... HOW DO I PUT THIS...
YOUR DIARY HAS CHARACTER.
IS IT AN OBSERVATIONAL RECORD?
FOR ECHO TOO...
...THIS IS THE FIRST TIME COMING TO WHAT IS KNOWN AS A FESTIVAL.

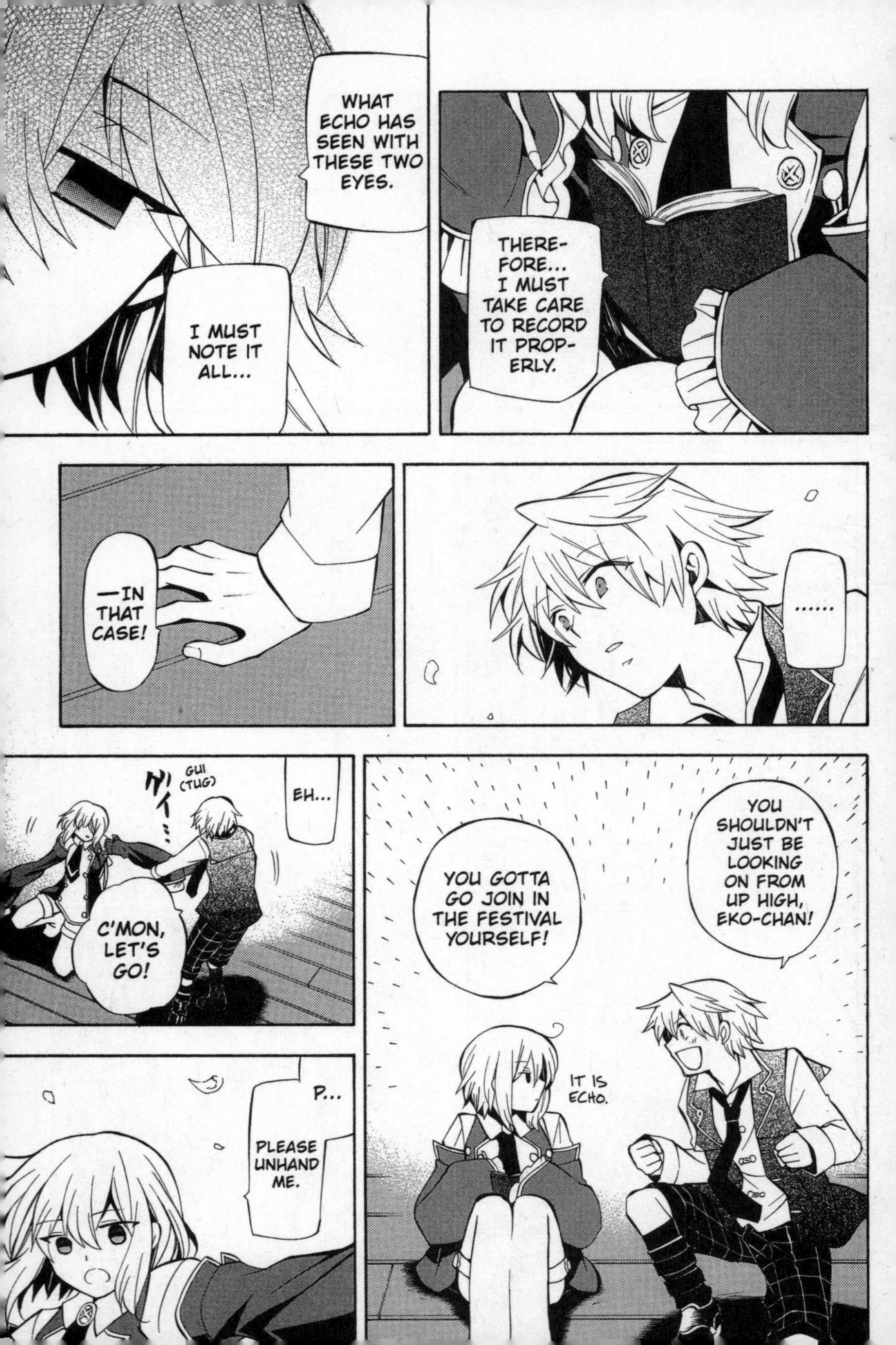
THERE-FORE... I MUST TAKE CARE TO RECORD IT PROP-ERLY.
WHAT ECHO HAS SEEN WITH THESE TWO EYES.
I MUST NOTE IT ALL...
......
—IN THAT CASE!
YOU SHOULDN'T JUST BE LOOKING ON FROM UP HIGH, EKO-CHAN!
YOU GOTTA GO JOIN IN THE FESTIVAL YOURSELF!
IT IS ECHO.
EH...
GUI (TUG)
C'MON, LET'S GO!
P...
PLEASE UNHAND ME.

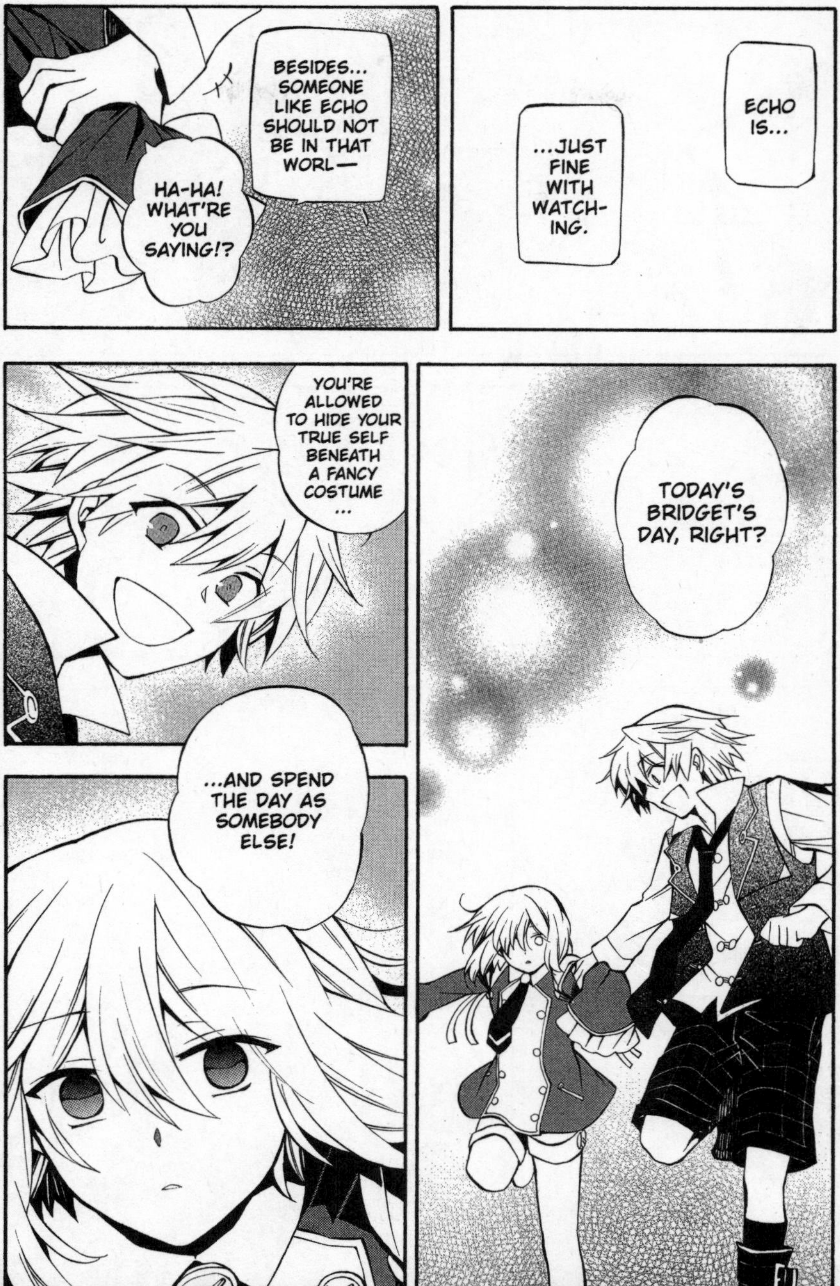
ECHO IS...
...JUST FINE WITH WATCHING.
BESIDES... SOMEONE LIKE ECHO SHOULD NOT BE IN THAT WORL—
HA-HA! WHAT'RE YOU SAYING!?
TODAY'S BRIDGET'S DAY, RIGHT?
YOU'RE ALLOWED TO HIDE YOUR TRUE SELF BENEATH A FANCY COSTUME ...
...AND SPEND THE DAY AS SOMEBODY ELSE!

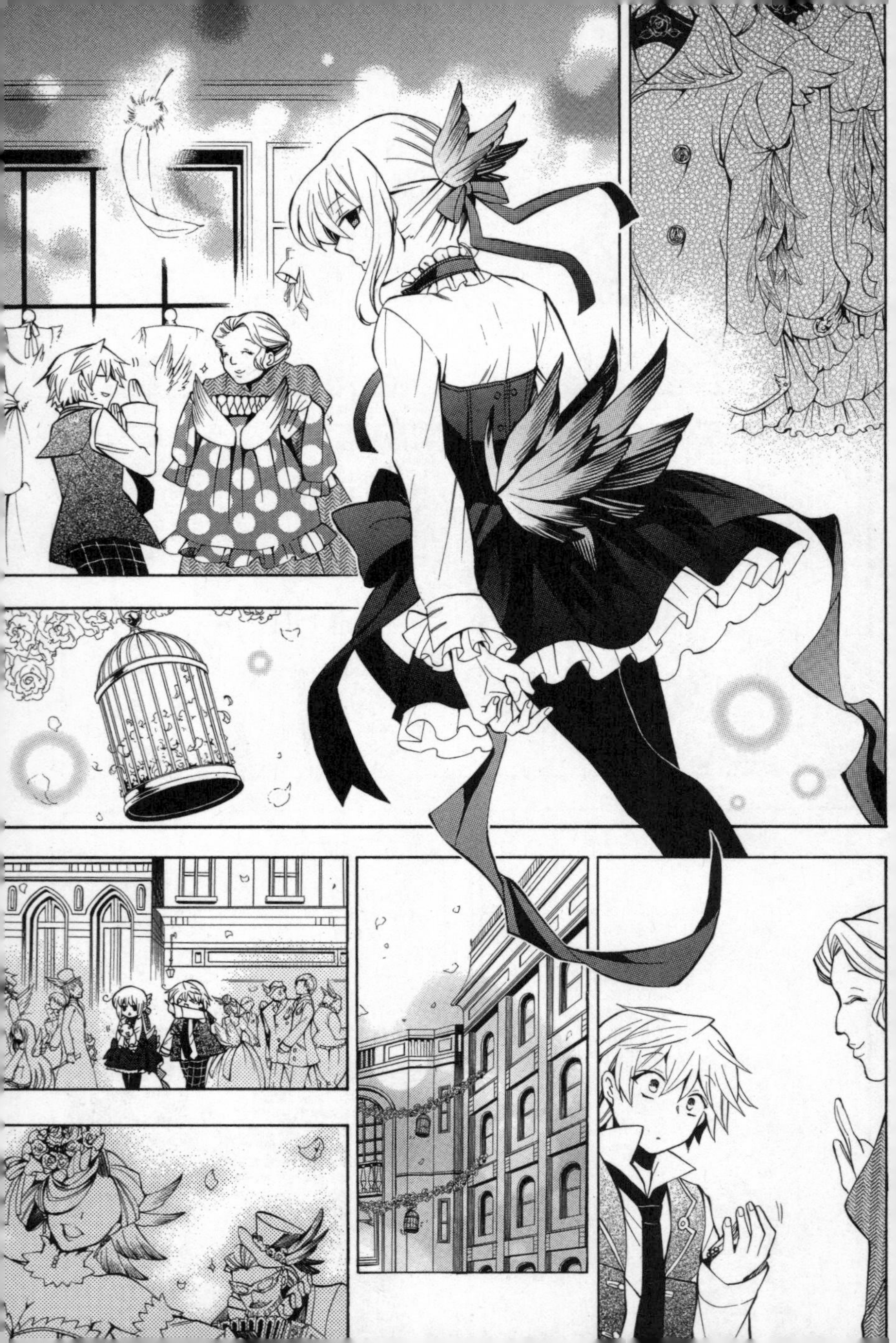

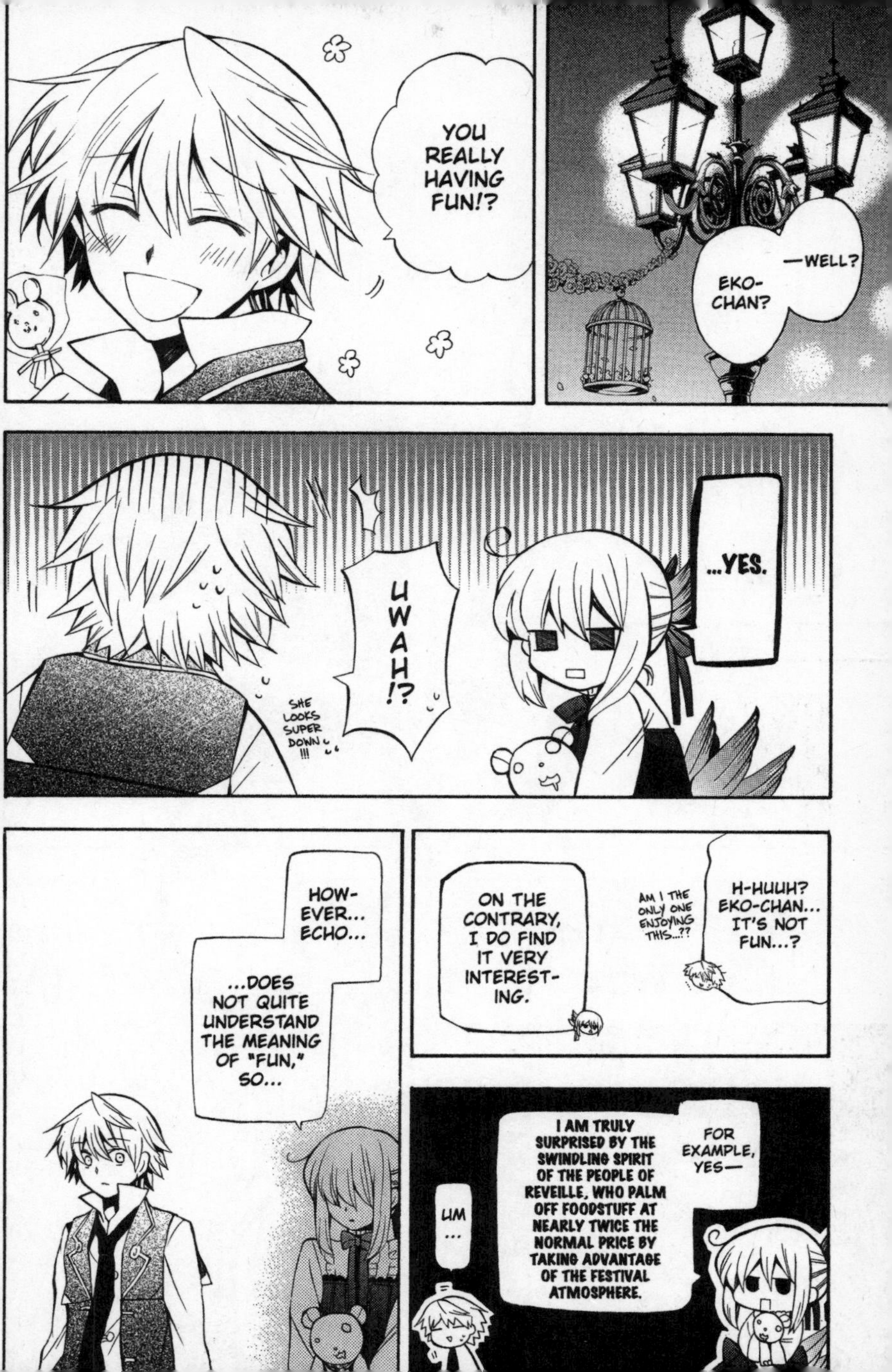
—WELL?
EKO-CHAN?
YOU REALLY HAVING FUN!?
...YES.
UWAH!?
SHE LOOKS SUPER DOWN!!!
H-HUUH? EKO-CHAN... IT'S NOT FUN...?
AM I THE ONLY ONE ENJOYING THIS...??
ON THE CONTRARY, I DO FIND IT VERY INTEREST-ING.
FOR EXAMPLE, YES—
I AM TRULY SURPRISED BY THE SWINDLING SPIRIT OF THE PEOPLE OF REVEILLE, WHO PALM OFF FOODSTUFF AT NEARLY TWICE THE NORMAL PRICE BY TAKING ADVANTAGE OF THE FESTIVAL ATMOSPHERE.
UM ...
HOW-EVER... ECHO...
...DOES NOT QUITE UNDERSTAND THE MEANING OF "FUN," SO...

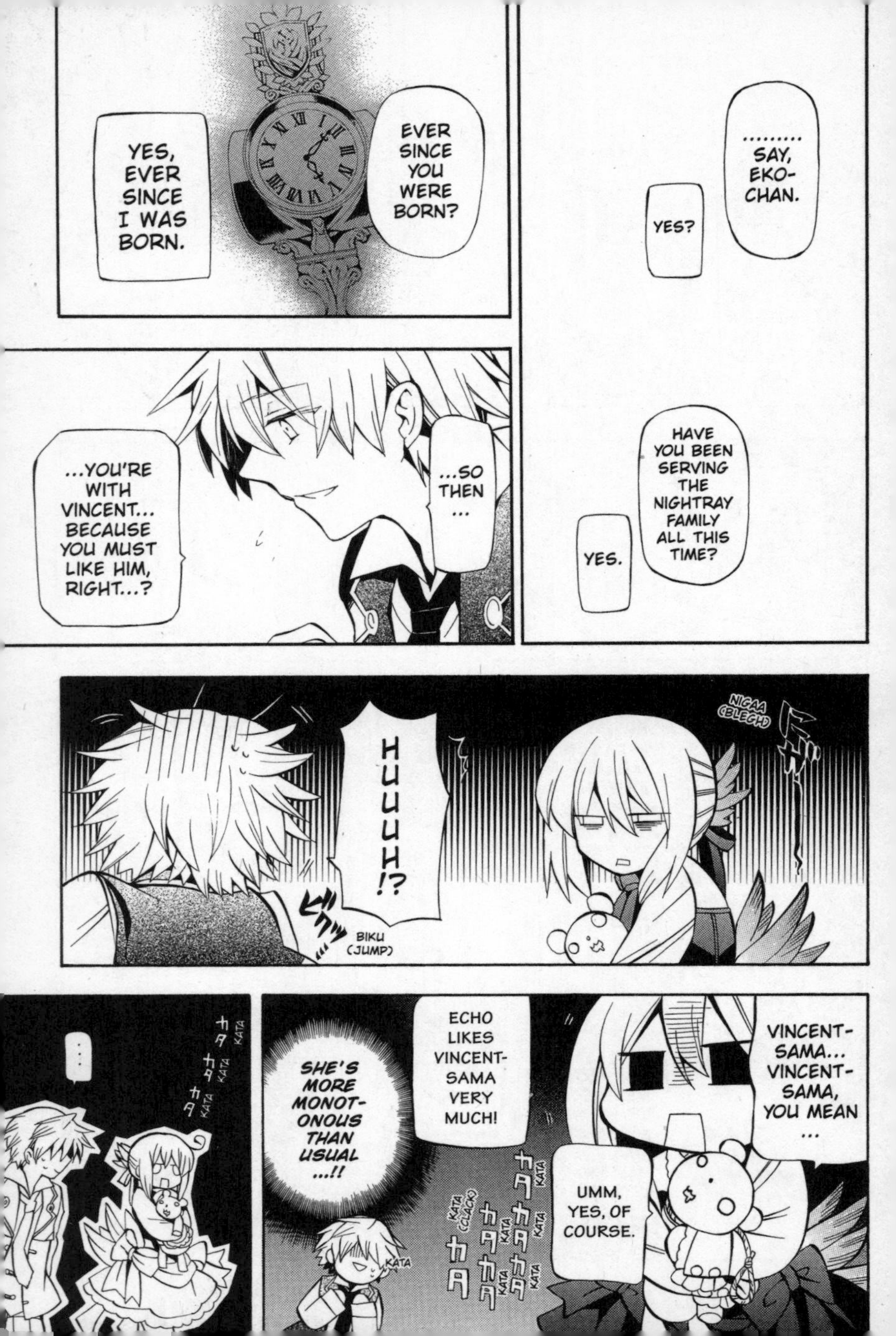
....
SAY, EKO-CHAN.
YES?
HAVE YOU BEEN SERVING THE NIGHTRAY FAMILY ALL THIS TIME?
YES.
EVER SINCE YOU WERE BORN?
YES, EVER SINCE I WAS BORN.
...SO THEN...
...YOU'RE WITH VINCENT... BECAUSE YOU MUST LIKE HIM, RIGHT...?
NIGAA (BLEGH)
HUUUUH!?
BIKU (JUMP)
VINCENT-SAMA... VINCENT-SAMA, YOU MEAN...
ECHO LIKES VINCENT-SAMA VERY MUCH!
UMM, YES, OF COURSE.
SHE'S MORE MONOTONOUS THAN USUAL...!!
KATA KATA KATA KATA KATA (CLACK) KATA KATA KATA
KATA
KATA KATA KATA
...

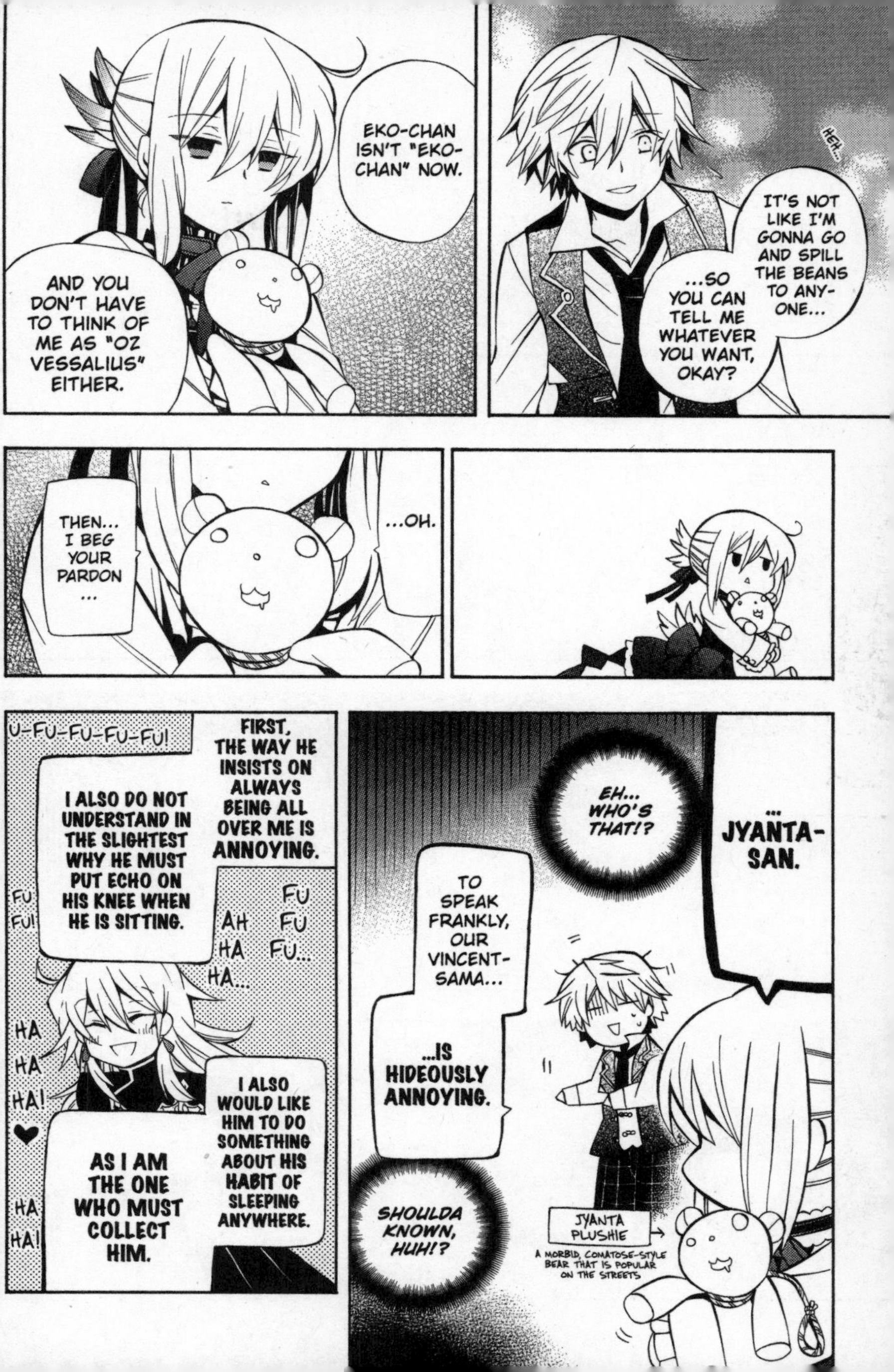
HEH...
IT'S NOT LIKE I'M GONNA GO AND SPILL THE BEANS TO ANYONE...
...SO YOU CAN TELL ME WHATEVER YOU WANT, OKAY?
EKO-CHAN ISN'T "EKO-CHAN" NOW.
AND YOU DON'T HAVE TO THINK OF ME AS "OZ VESSALIUS" EITHER.
...OH.
THEN... I BEG YOUR PARDON...
...JYANTA-SAN.
EH... WHO'S THAT!?
TO SPEAK FRANKLY, OUR VINCENT-SAMA...
...IS HIDEOUSLY ANNOYING.
SHOULDA KNOWN, HUH!?
JYANTA PLUSHIE
A MORBID, COMATOSE-STYLE BEAR THAT IS POPULAR ON THE STREETS
U-FU-FU-FU-FU!
FIRST, THE WAY HE INSISTS ON ALWAYS BEING ALL OVER ME IS ANNOYING.
I ALSO DO NOT UNDERSTAND IN THE SLIGHTEST WHY HE MUST PUT ECHO ON HIS KNEE WHEN HE IS SITTING.
FU FU FU...
FU FU!
AH HA HA...
HA HA HA! ❤
I ALSO WOULD LIKE HIM TO DO SOMETHING ABOUT HIS HABIT OF SLEEPING ANYWHERE.
AS I AM THE ONE WHO MUST COLLECT HIM.
HA HA!

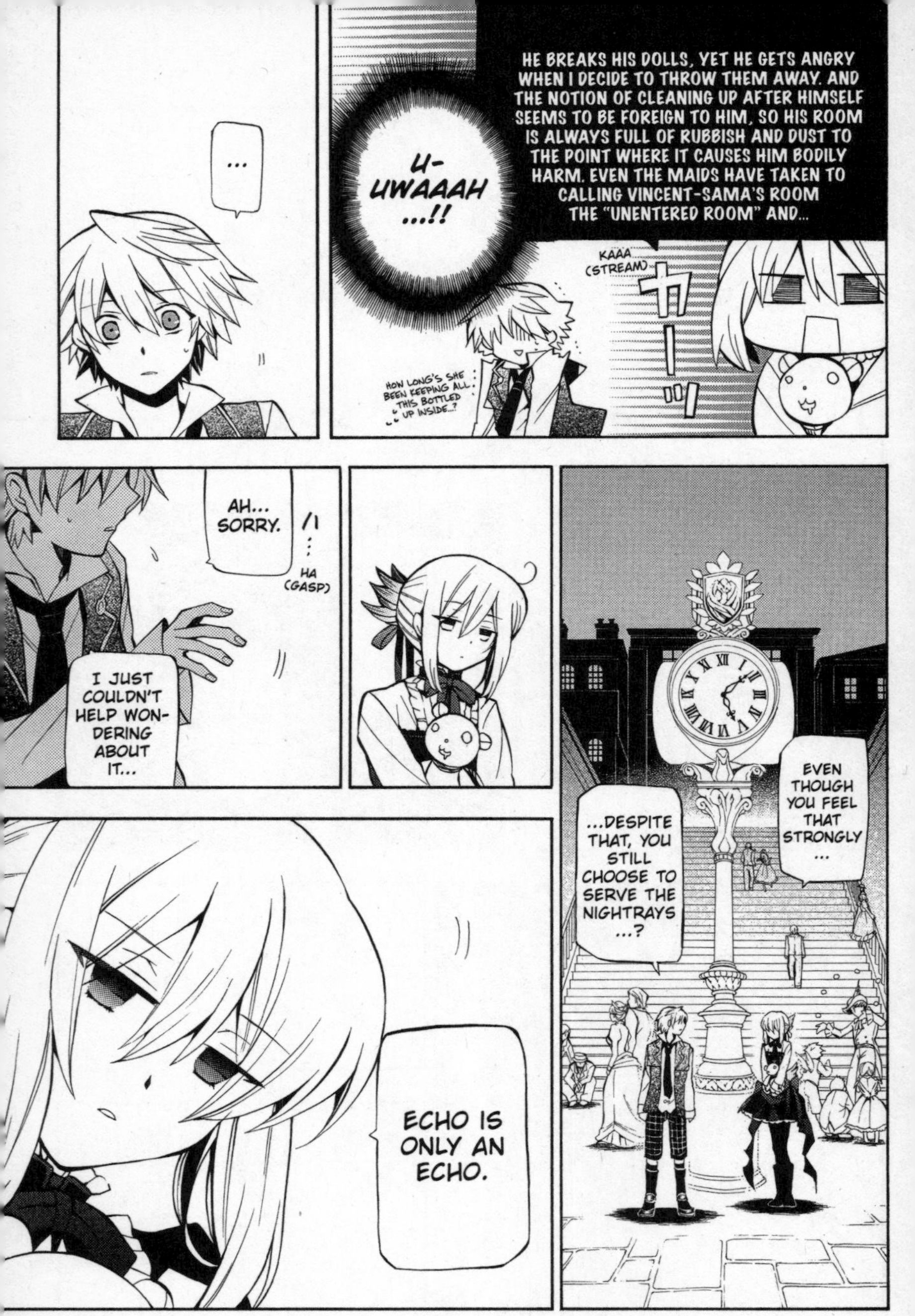
HE BREAKS HIS DOLLS, YET HE GETS ANGRY WHEN I DECIDE TO THROW THEM AWAY. AND THE NOTION OF CLEANING UP AFTER HIMSELF SEEMS TO BE FOREIGN TO HIM, SO HIS ROOM IS ALWAYS FULL OF RUBBISH AND DUST TO THE POINT WHERE IT CAUSES HIM BODILY HARM. EVEN THE MAIDS HAVE TAKEN TO CALLING VINCENT-SAMA'S ROOM THE "UNENTERED ROOM" AND...
KAAA (STREAM)
U-UWAAAH ...!!
HOW LONG'S SHE BEEN KEEPING ALL THIS BOTTLED UP INSIDE...?
...
EVEN THOUGH YOU FEEL THAT STRONGLY ...
...DESPITE THAT, YOU STILL CHOOSE TO SERVE THE NIGHTRAYS ...?
AH... SORRY.
HA (GASP)
I JUST COULDN'T HELP WONDERING ABOUT IT...
ECHO IS ONLY AN ECHO.

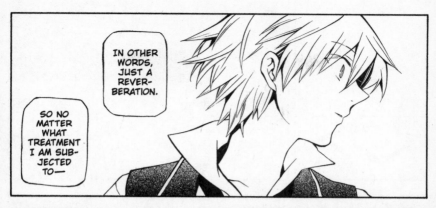

IN OTHER WORDS, JUST A REVERBERATION.

SO NO MATTER WHAT TREATMENT I AM SUBJECTED TO—

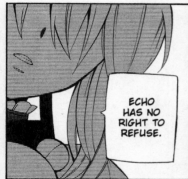

ECHO HAS NO RIGHT TO REFUSE.

...HUMILIATION—

...ABUSE...

...TORTURE...

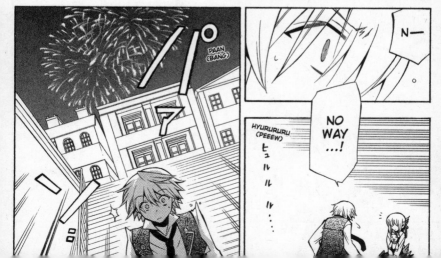

PAAN (BANG)

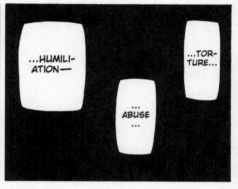

N—

HYURURURU (PEEEW)
ヒュルルル...

NO WAY...!

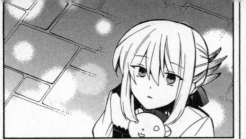

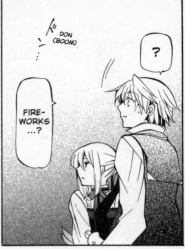

DON
(BOOM)

?

FIRE-
WORKS
...?

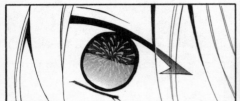

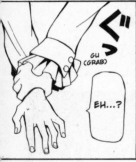

GU
(GRAB)

EH...?

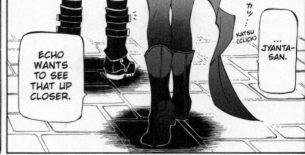

ECHO
WANTS
TO SEE
THAT UP
CLOSER.

KATSU
(CLICK)

...
JYANTA-
SAN.

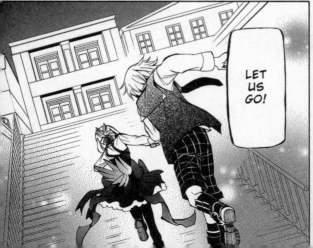

LET
US
GO!

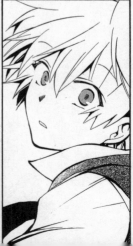

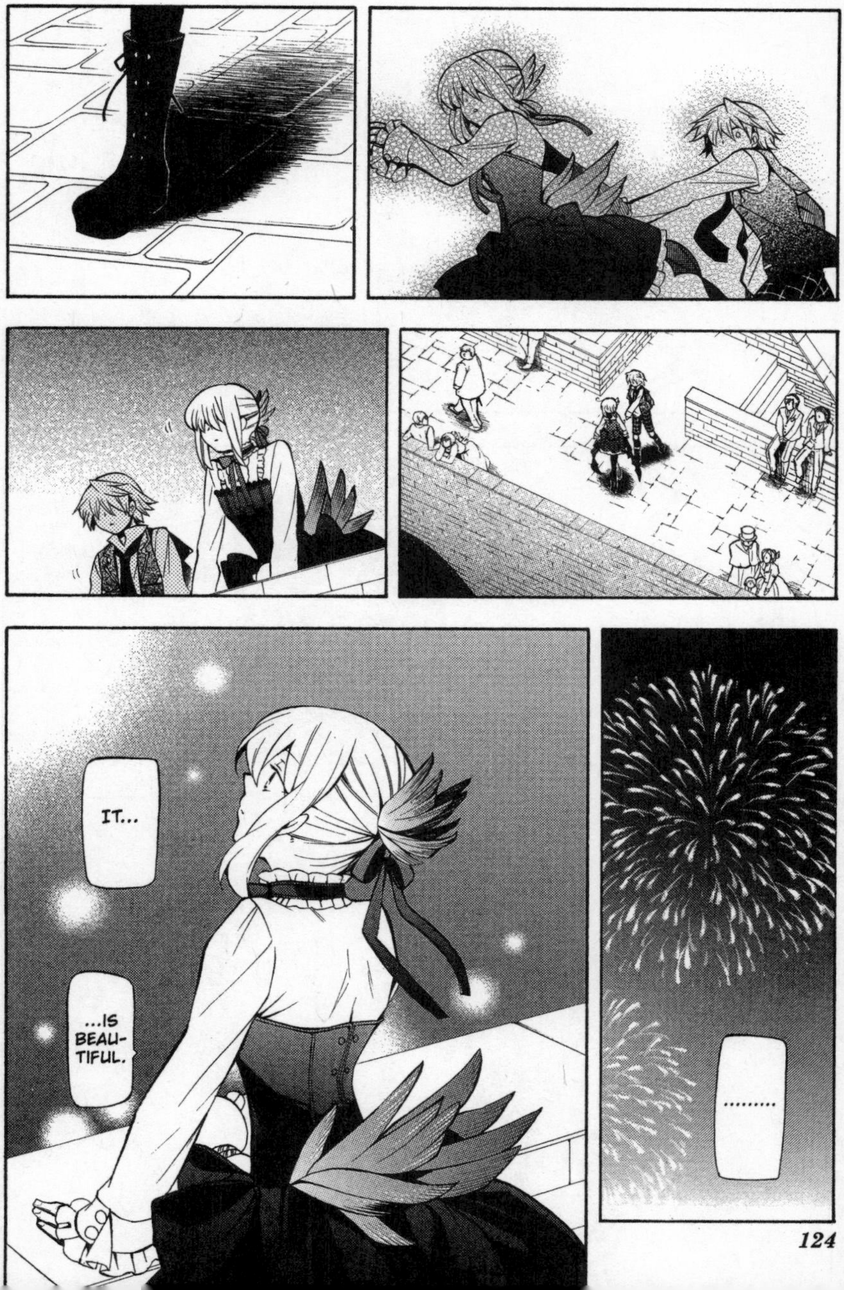
....
IT...
...IS BEAU-TIFUL.

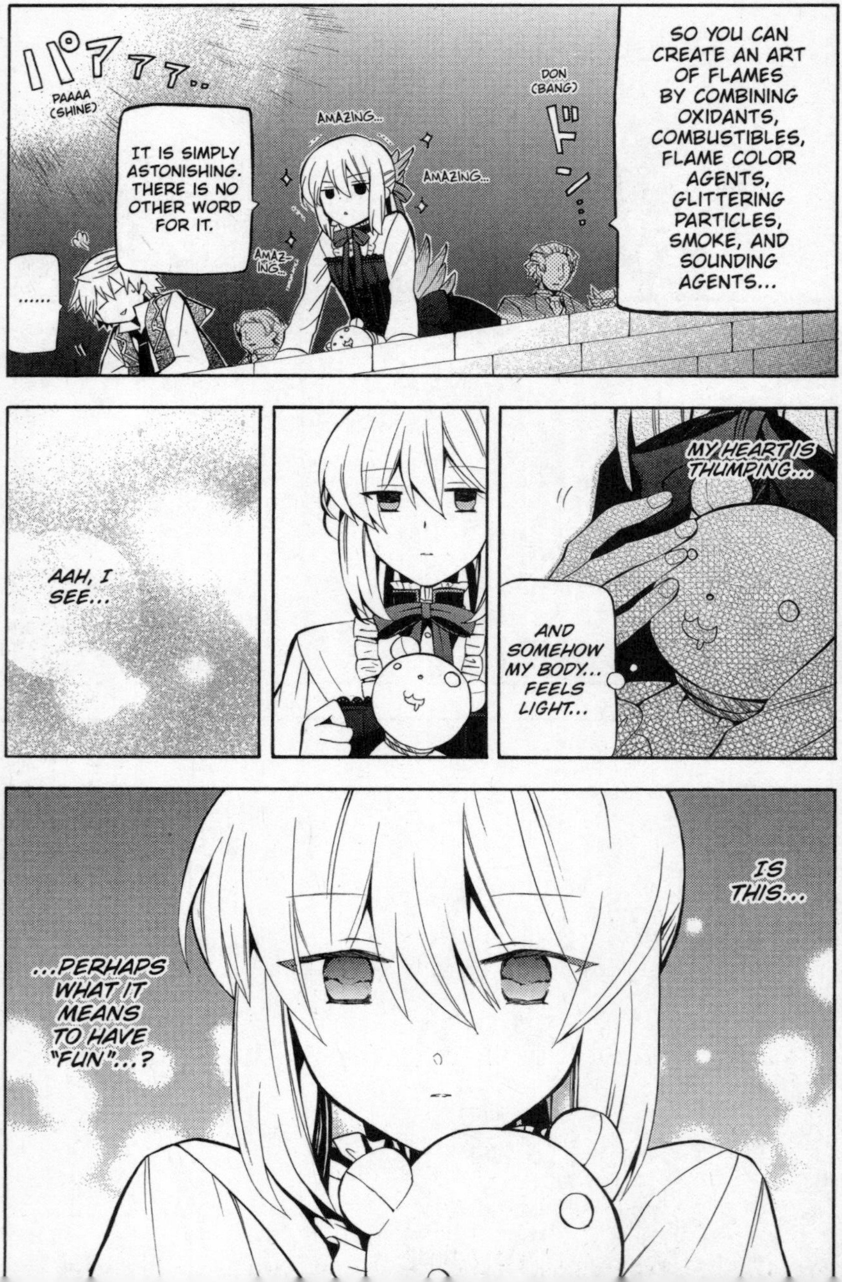
SO YOU CAN CREATE AN ART OF FLAMES BY COMBINING OXIDANTS, COMBUSTIBLES, FLAME COLOR AGENTS, GLITTERING PARTICLES, SMOKE, AND SOUNDING AGENTS...
DON (BANG)
AMAZING...
AMAZING...
AMAZ-ING...
IT IS SIMPLY ASTONISHING. THERE IS NO OTHER WORD FOR IT.
PAAAA (SHINE)
......
MY HEART IS THUMPING...
AND SOMEHOW MY BODY... FEELS LIGHT...
AAH, I SEE...
IS THIS...
...PERHAPS WHAT IT MEANS TO HAVE "FUN"...?

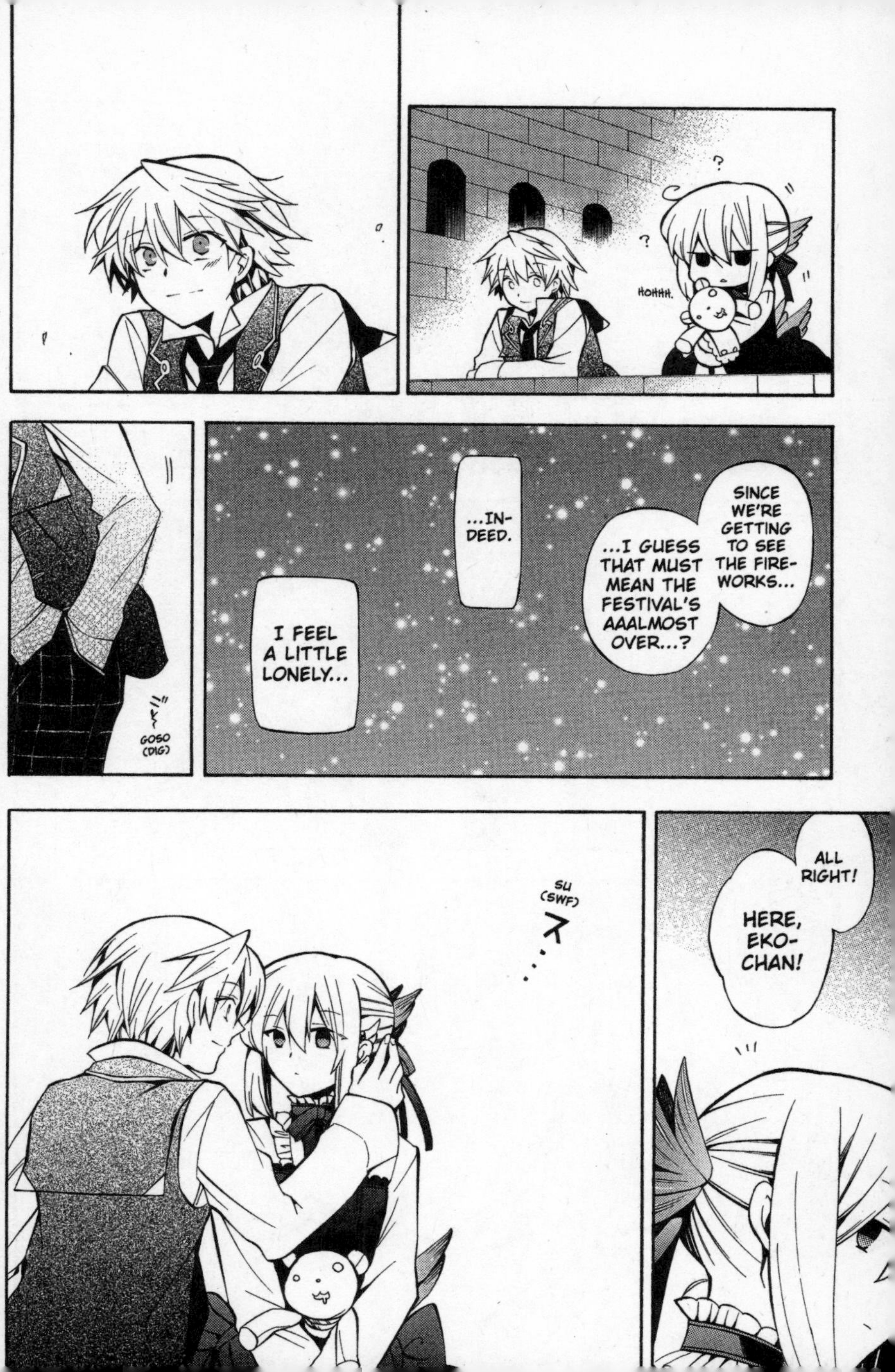
?
?
HOHHH.
SINCE WE'RE GETTING TO SEE THE FIRE-WORKS...
...I GUESS THAT MUST MEAN THE FESTIVAL'S AAALMOST OVER...?
...IN-DEED.
I FEEL A LITTLE LONELY...
GOSO (DIG)
ALL RIGHT!
HERE, EKO-CHAN!
SU (SWF)

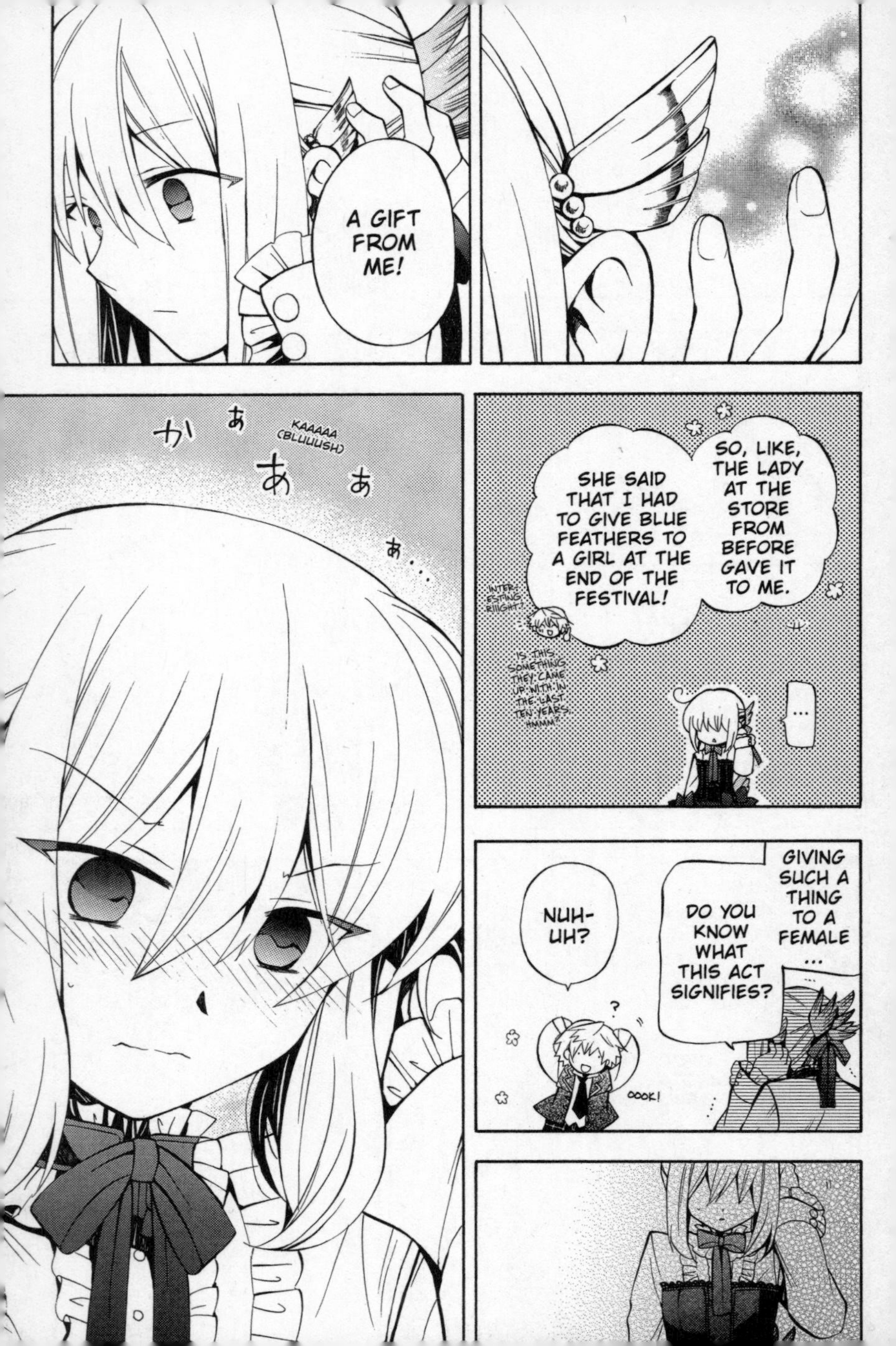
A GIFT FROM ME!
SO, LIKE, THE LADY AT THE STORE FROM BEFORE GAVE IT TO ME.
SHE SAID THAT I HAD TO GIVE BLUE FEATHERS TO A GIRL AT THE END OF THE FESTIVAL!
INTER-ESTING RIIIGHT?
IS THIS SOMETHING THEY CAME UP WITH IN THE LAST TEN YEARS, HMMM?
...
GIVING SUCH A THING TO A FEMALE ...
DO YOU KNOW WHAT THIS ACT SIGNIFIES?
NUH-UH?
?
OOOK!
かあああ
あ...
KAAAAA (BLUUUSH)

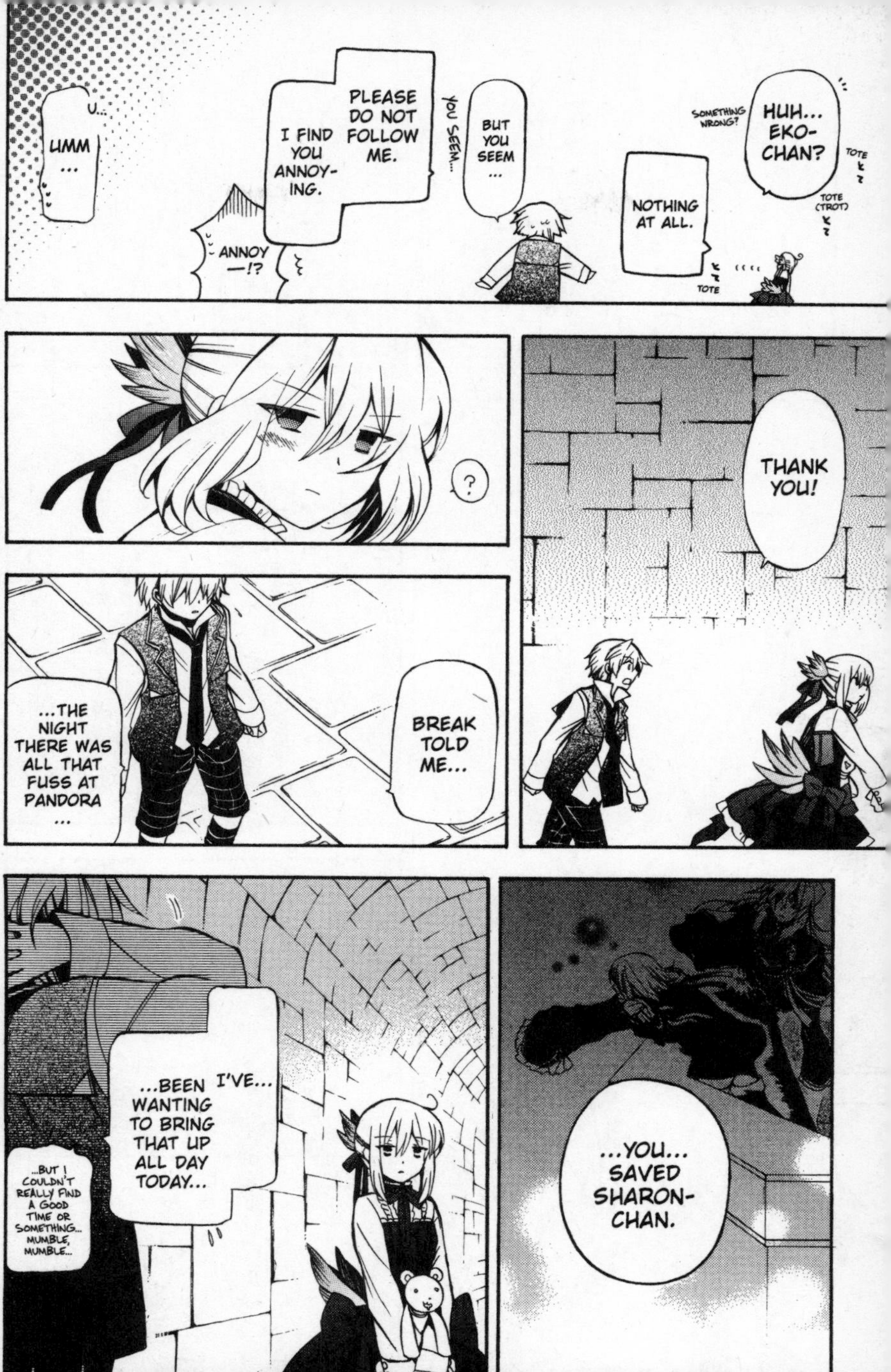
HUH... EKO-CHAN?
SOMETHING WRONG?
TOTE
TOTE (TROT)
NOTHING AT ALL.
TOTE
BUT YOU SEEM...
YOU SEEM...
PLEASE DO NOT FOLLOW ME.
I FIND YOU ANNOYING.
ANNOY—!?
U... UMM...
THANK YOU!
?
BREAK TOLD ME...
...THE NIGHT THERE WAS ALL THAT FUSS AT PANDORA...
...YOU... SAVED SHARON-CHAN.
I'VE... ...BEEN WANTING TO BRING THAT UP ALL DAY TODAY...
...BUT I COULDN'T REALLY FIND A GOOD TIME OR SOMETHING... MUMBLE, MUMBLE...

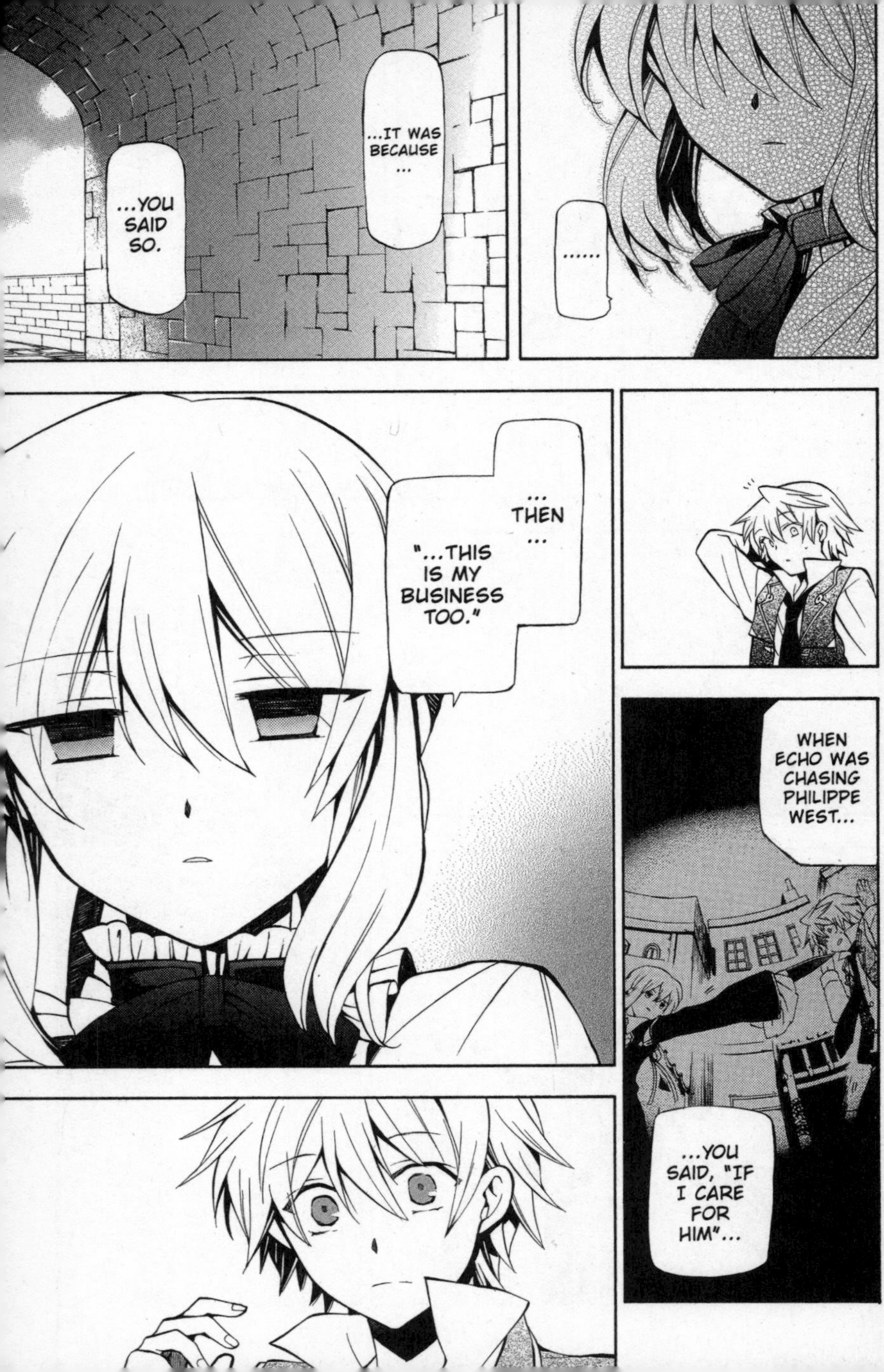
......
...IT WAS BECAUSE ...
...YOU SAID SO.
... THEN ...
"...THIS IS MY BUSINESS TOO."
WHEN ECHO WAS CHASING PHILIPPE WEST...
...YOU SAID, "IF I CARE FOR HIM"...

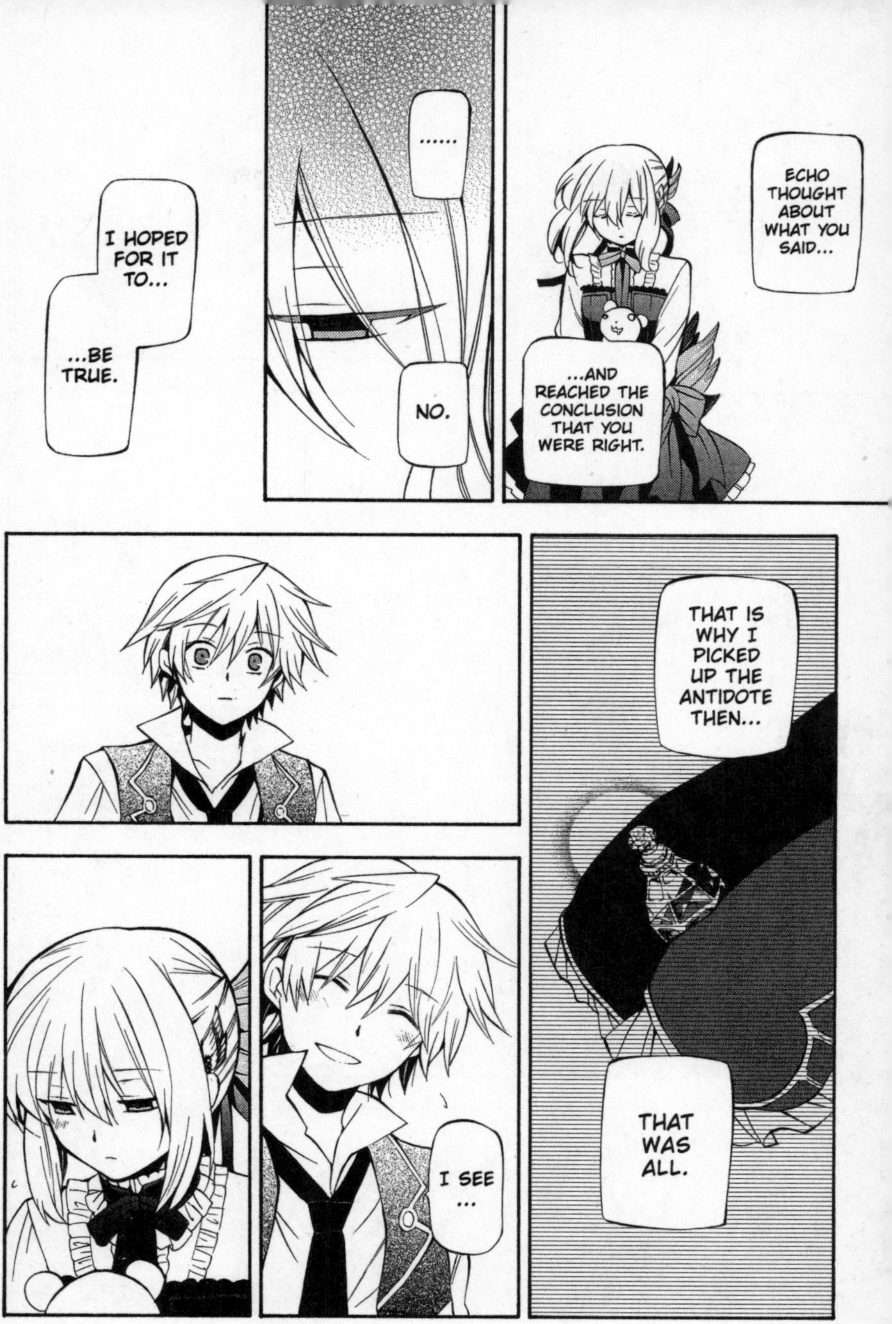
ECHO THOUGHT ABOUT WHAT YOU SAID...
...AND REACHED THE CONCLUSION THAT YOU WERE RIGHT.
......
NO.
I HOPED FOR IT TO...
...BE TRUE.
THAT IS WHY I PICKED UP THE ANTIDOTE THEN...
THAT WAS ALL.
I SEE ...

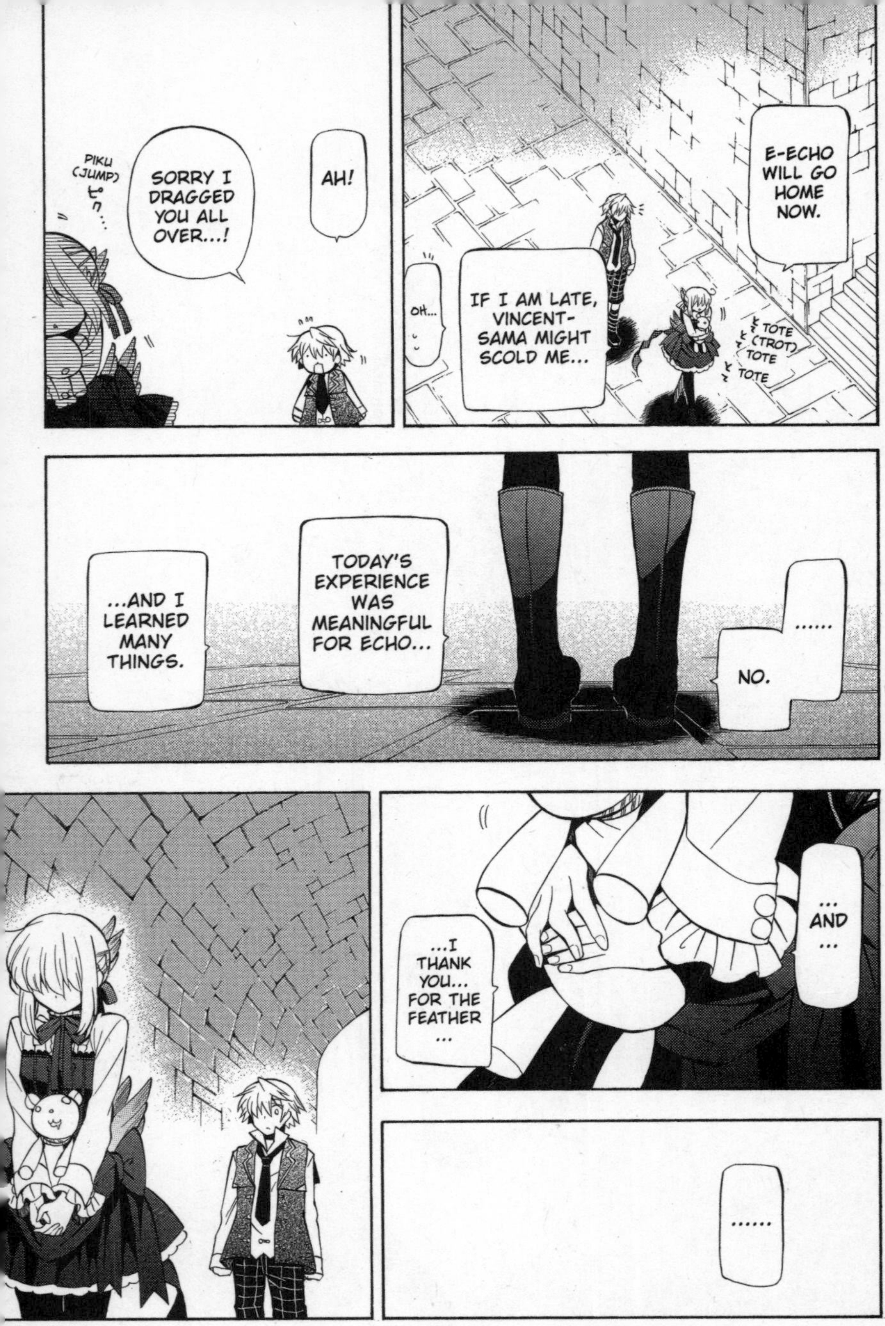
E-ECHO WILL GO HOME NOW.
IF I AM LATE, VINCENT-SAMA MIGHT SCOLD ME...
OH...
TOTE (TROT) TOTE TOTE
AH!
SORRY I DRAGGED YOU ALL OVER...!
PIKU (JUMP)
......
NO.
TODAY'S EXPERIENCE WAS MEANINGFUL FOR ECHO...
...AND I LEARNED MANY THINGS.
... AND ...
...I THANK YOU... FOR THE FEATHER ...
......

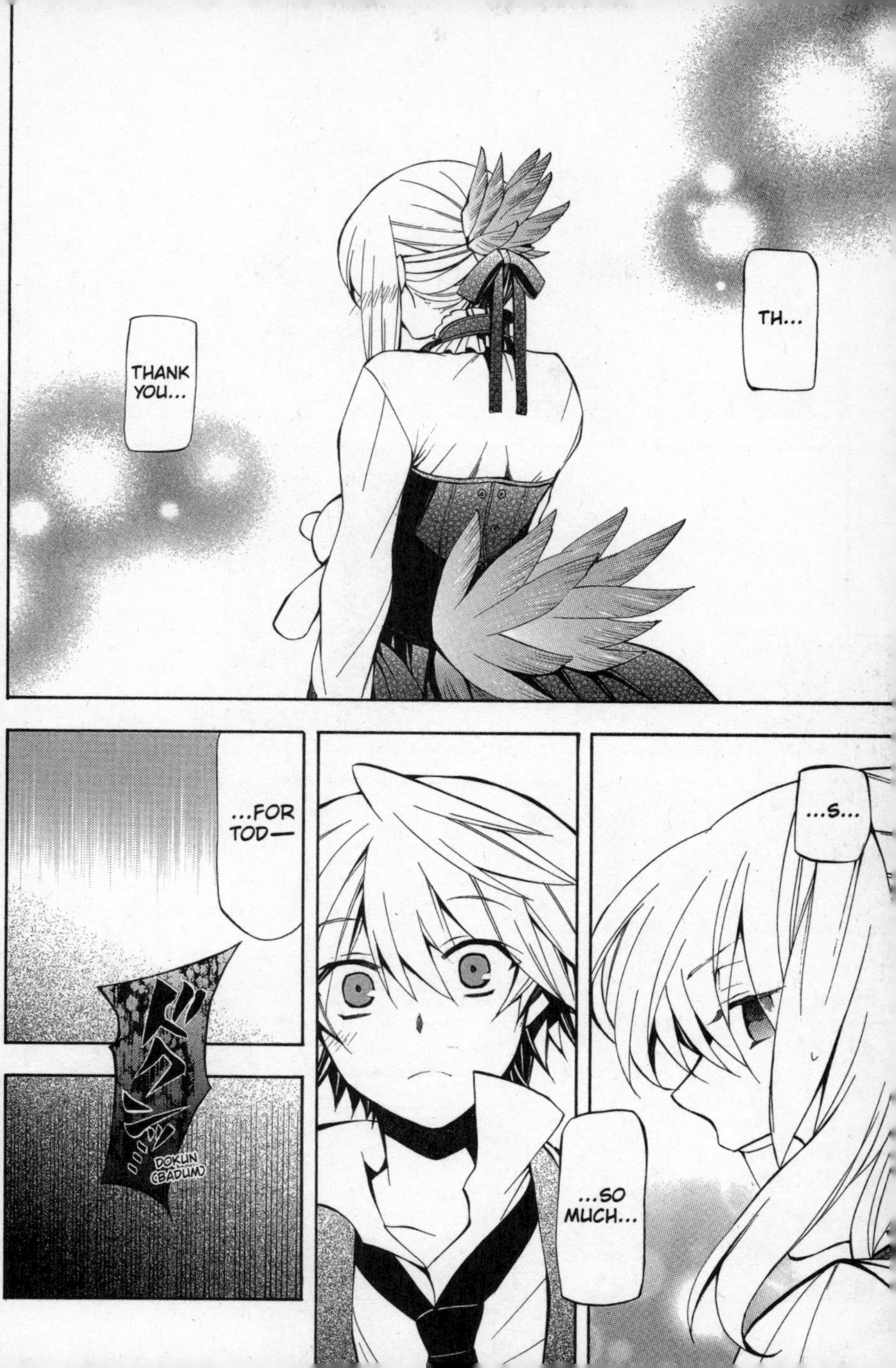
TH...
THANK YOU...
...S...
...SO MUCH...
...FOR TOD—
DOKUN (BADUM)

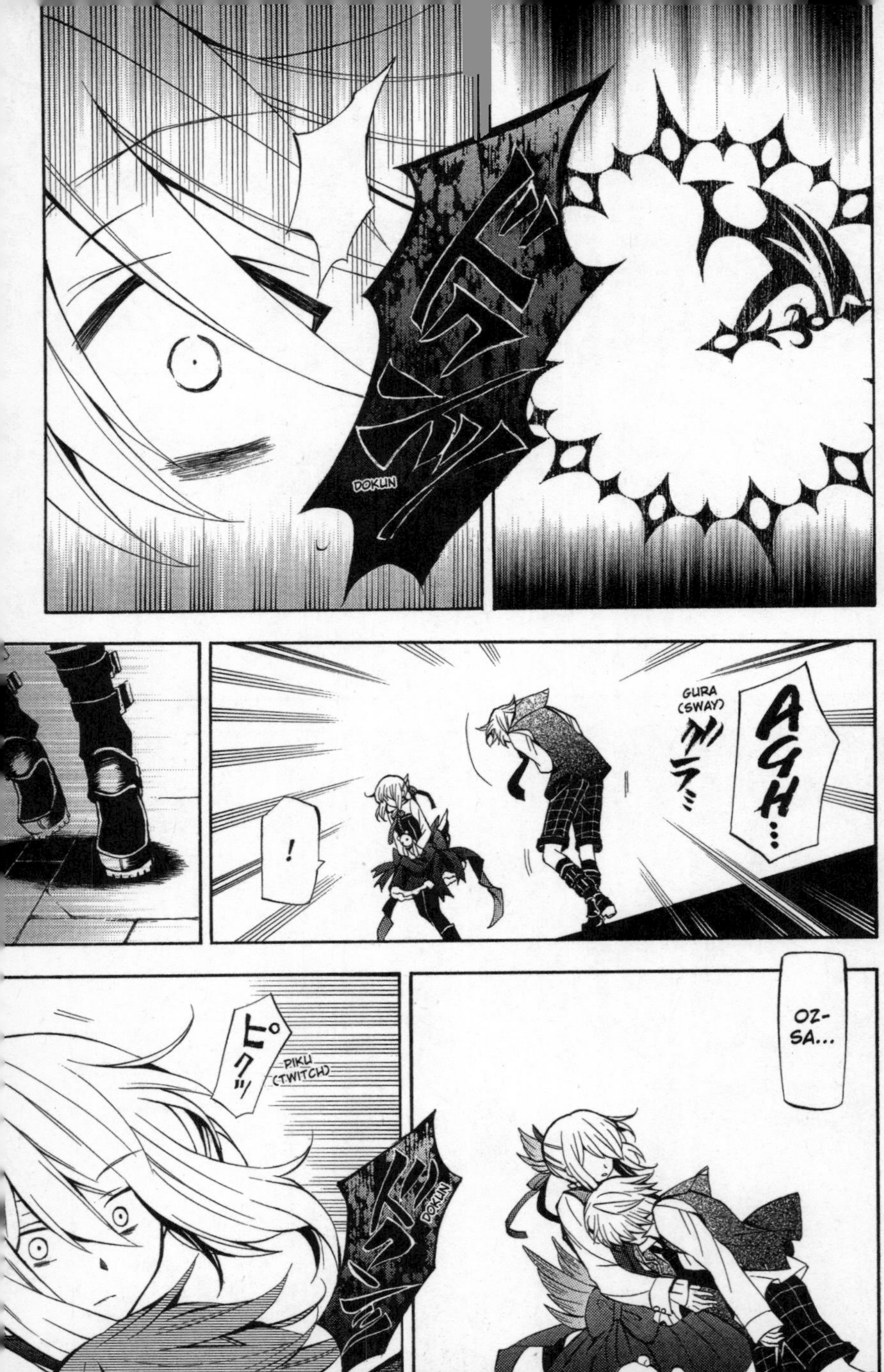

DOKUN
AGH...
GURA (SWAY)
!
OZ-SA...
PIKU (TWITCH)
DOKUN

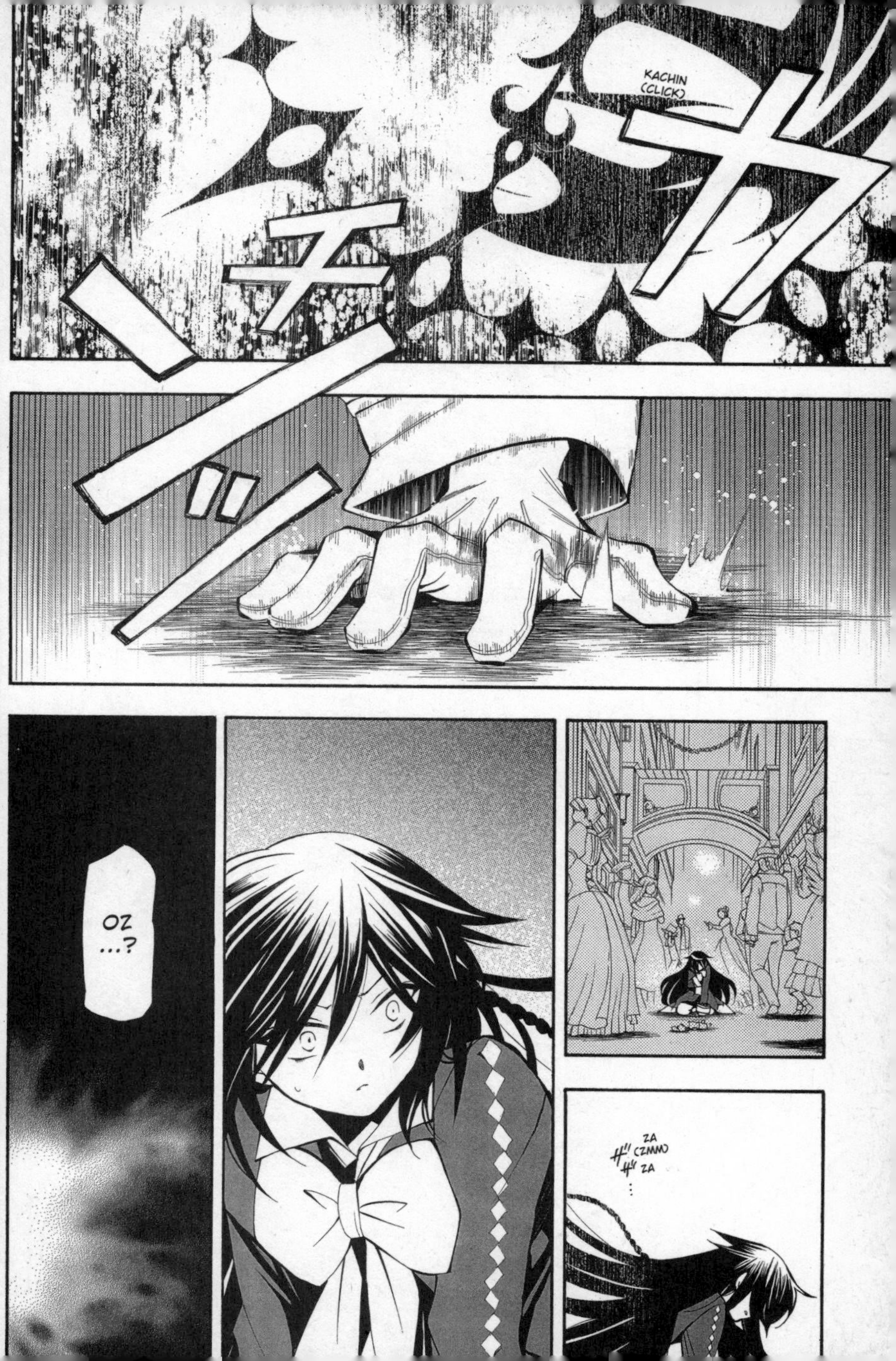
KACHIN (CLICK)
ZA (ZMM) ZA
...
OZ ...?

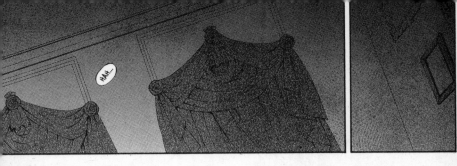

HAH...

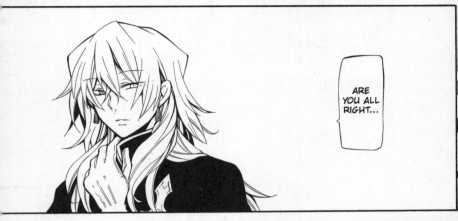

ARE YOU ALL RIGHT...

HAH...

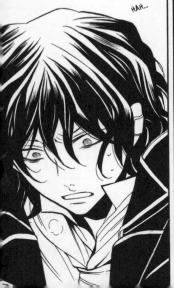

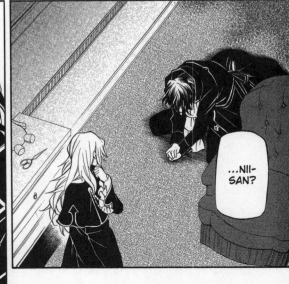

...NII-SAN?

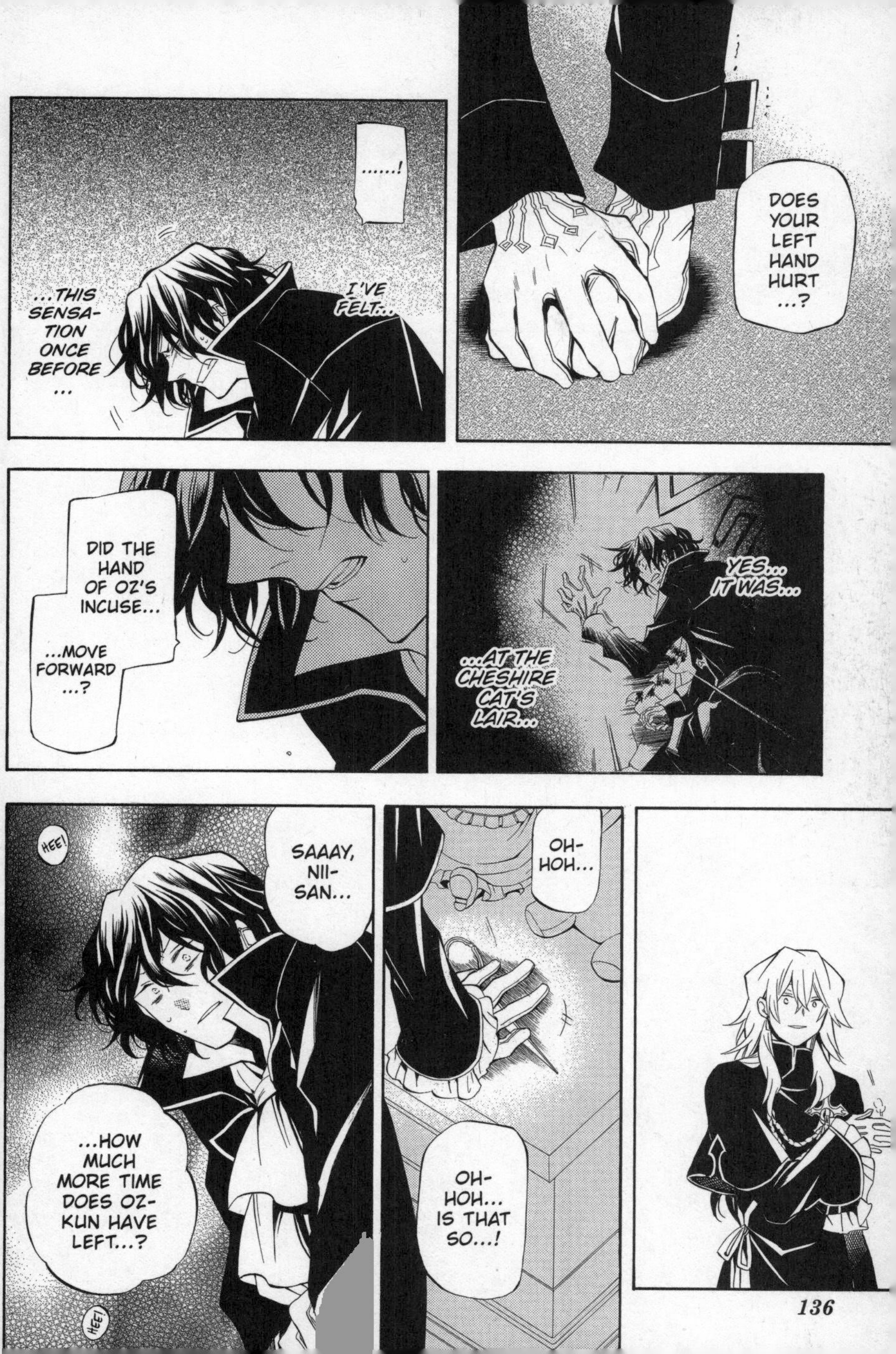
DOES YOUR LEFT HAND HURT...?
......!
I'VE FELT...
...THIS SENSATION ONCE BEFORE...
YES... IT WAS...
...AT THE CHESHIRE CAT'S LAIR...
DID THE HAND OF OZ'S INCUSE...
...MOVE FORWARD...?
OH-HOH...
OH-HOH... IS THAT SO...!
HEE!
SAAAY, NII-SAN...
...HOW MUCH MORE TIME DOES OZ-KUN HAVE LEFT...?
HEE!

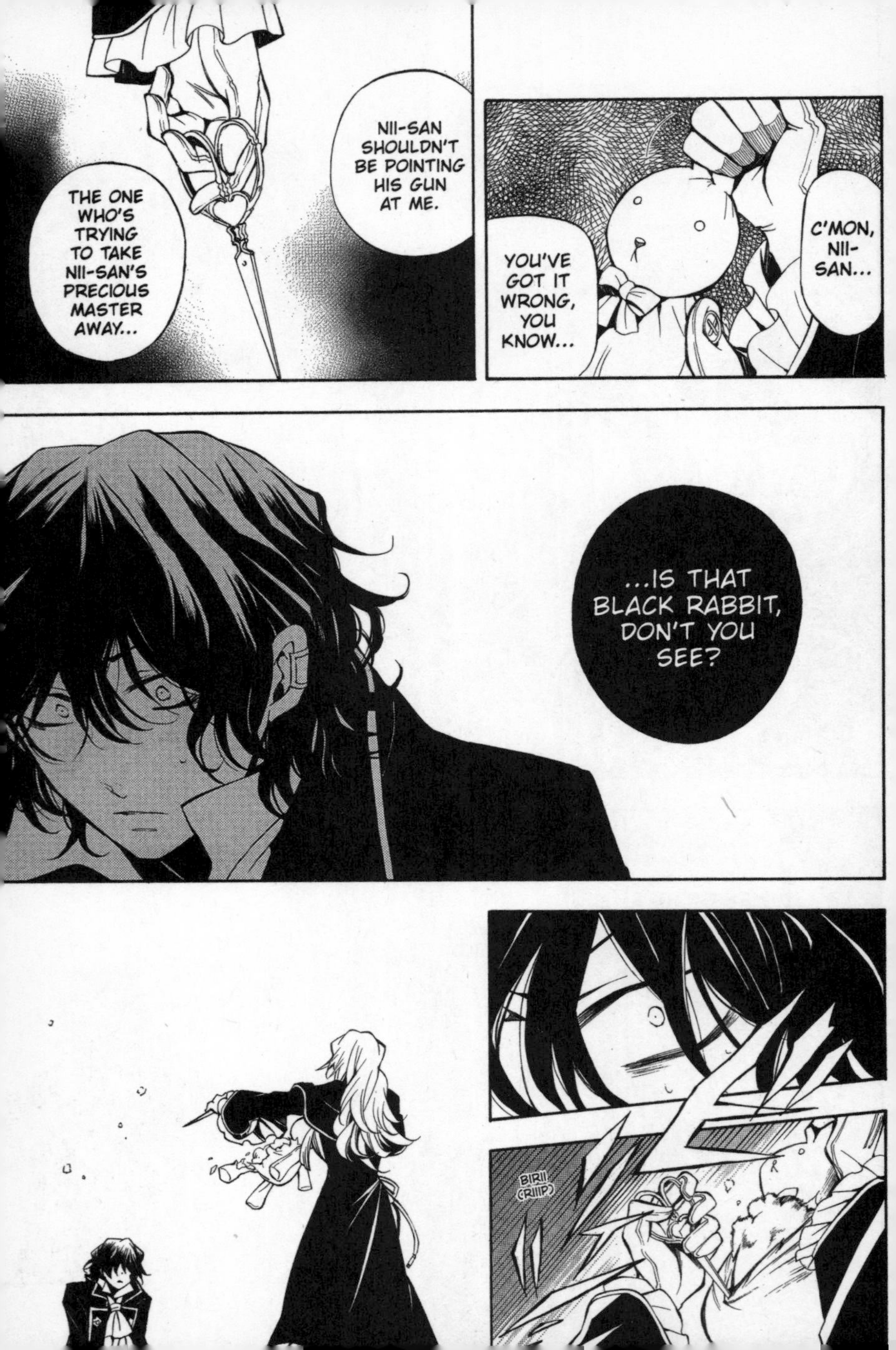
C'MON, NII-SAN...
YOU'VE GOT IT WRONG, YOU KNOW...
NII-SAN SHOULDN'T BE POINTING HIS GUN AT ME.
THE ONE WHO'S TRYING TO TAKE NII-SAN'S PRECIOUS MASTER AWAY...
...IS THAT BLACK RABBIT, DON'T YOU SEE?
BIRII (RIIIP)

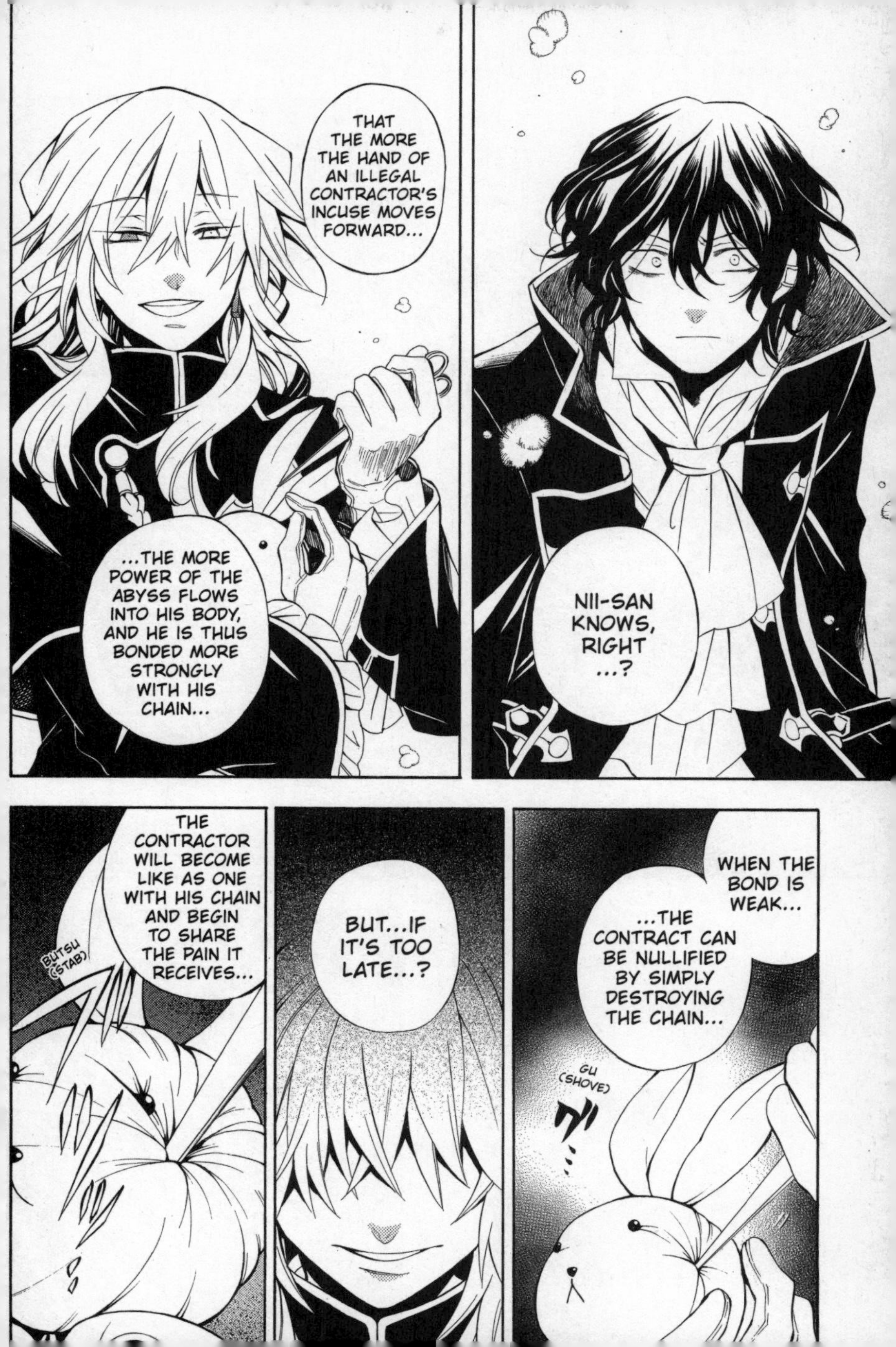
NII-SAN KNOWS, RIGHT ...?
THAT THE MORE THE HAND OF AN ILLEGAL CONTRACTOR'S INCUSE MOVES FORWARD...
...THE MORE POWER OF THE ABYSS FLOWS INTO HIS BODY, AND HE IS THUS BONDED MORE STRONGLY WITH HIS CHAIN...
WHEN THE BOND IS WEAK...
...THE CONTRACT CAN BE NULLIFIED BY SIMPLY DESTROYING THE CHAIN...
GU (SHOVE)
BUT...IF IT'S TOO LATE...?
THE CONTRACTOR WILL BECOME LIKE AS ONE WITH HIS CHAIN AND BEGIN TO SHARE THE PAIN IT RECEIVES...
BUTSU (STAB)

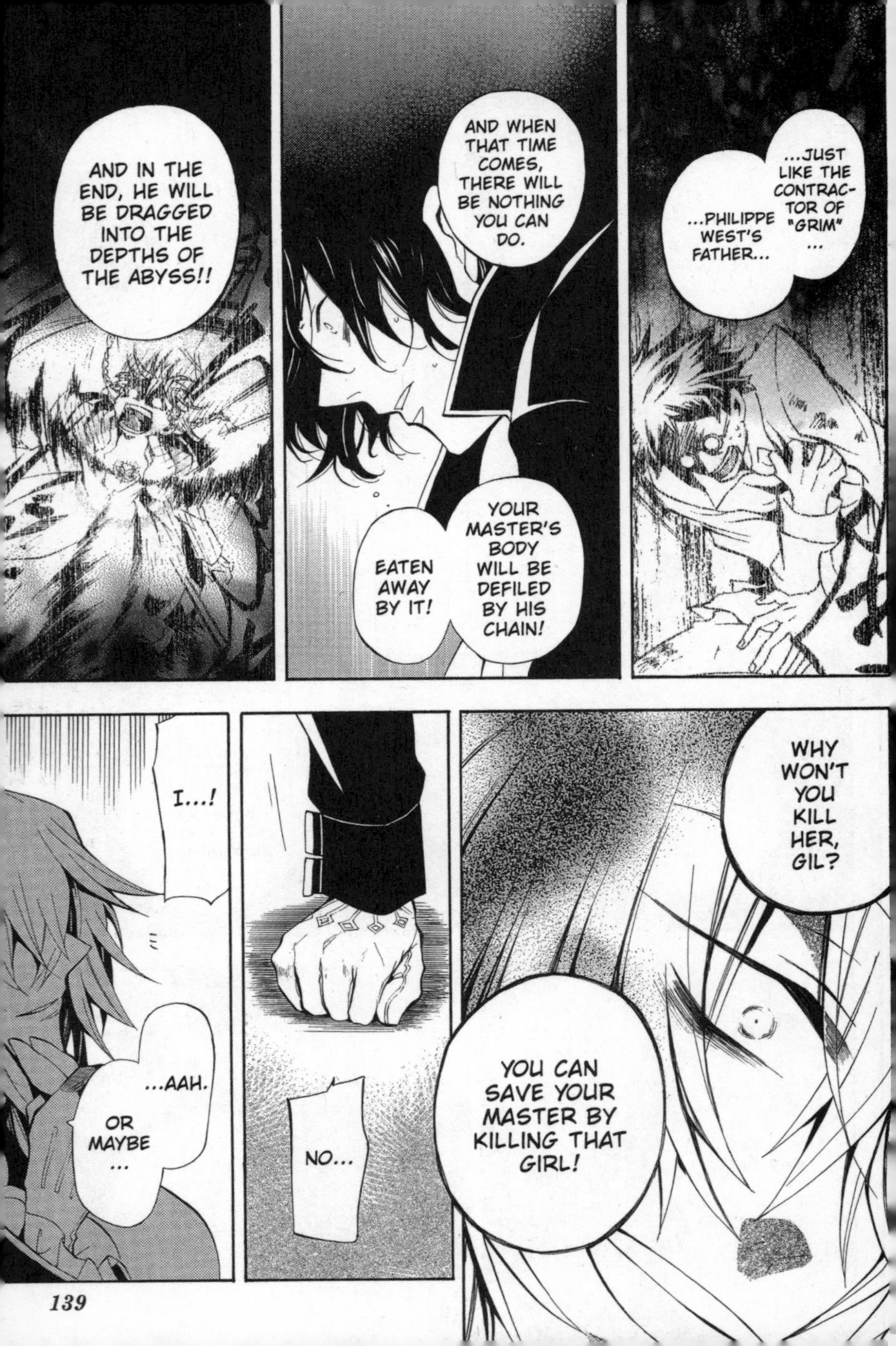
...JUST LIKE THE CONTRACTOR OF "GRIM"...
...PHILIPPE WEST'S FATHER...
AND WHEN THAT TIME COMES, THERE WILL BE NOTHING YOU CAN DO.
YOUR MASTER'S BODY WILL BE DEFILED BY HIS CHAIN!
EATEN AWAY BY IT!
AND IN THE END, HE WILL BE DRAGGED INTO THE DEPTHS OF THE ABYSS!!
WHY WON'T YOU KILL HER, GIL?
YOU CAN SAVE YOUR MASTER BY KILLING THAT GIRL!
NO...
I...!
...AAH.
OR MAYBE ...

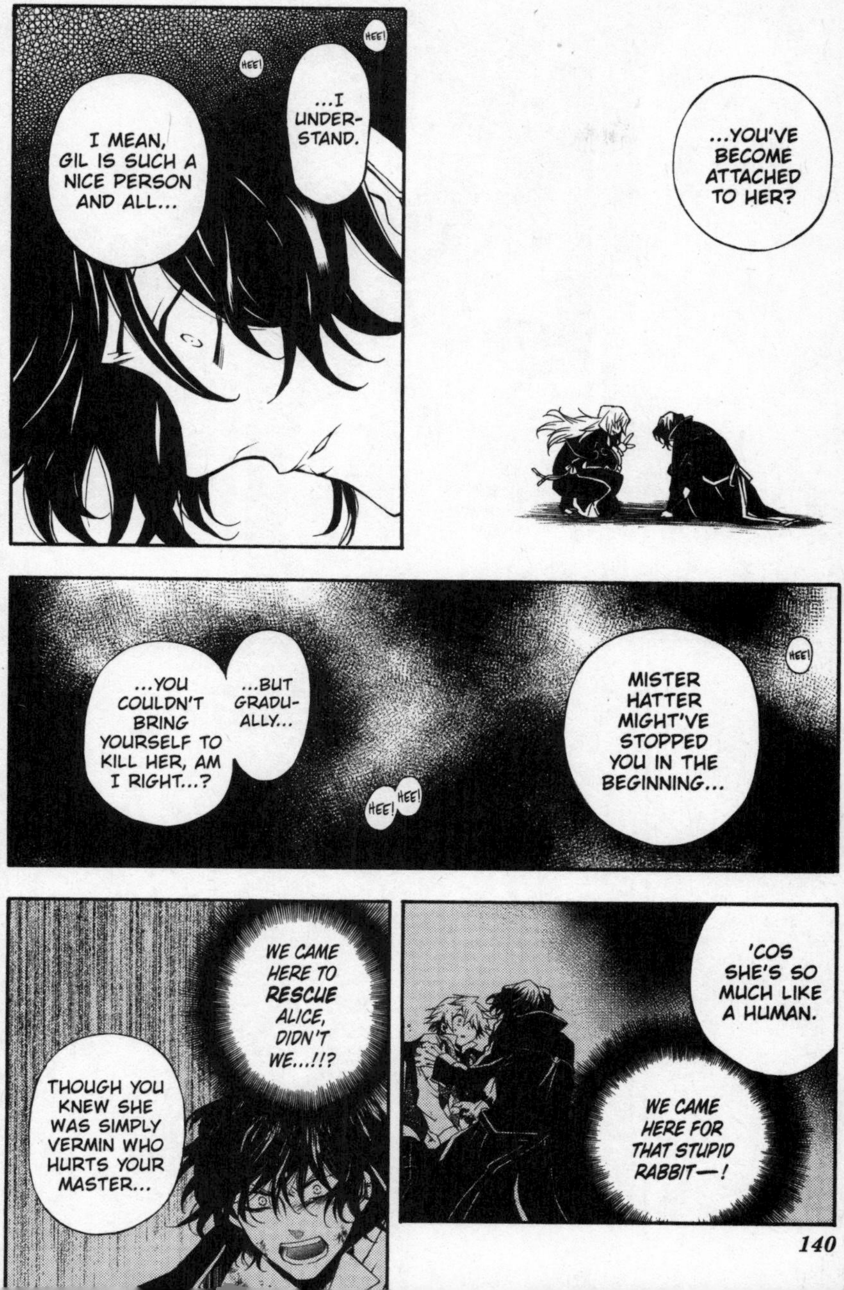
...YOU'VE BECOME ATTACHED TO HER?
HEE!
HEE!
...I UNDERSTAND.
I MEAN, GIL IS SUCH A NICE PERSON AND ALL...
HEE!
MISTER HATTER MIGHT'VE STOPPED YOU IN THE BEGINNING...
HEE! HEE!
...BUT GRADUALLY...
...YOU COULDN'T BRING YOURSELF TO KILL HER, AM I RIGHT...?
'COS SHE'S SO MUCH LIKE A HUMAN.
WE CAME HERE FOR THAT STUPID RABBIT—!
WE CAME HERE TO RESCUE ALICE, DIDN'T WE...!!?
THOUGH YOU KNEW SHE WAS SIMPLY VERMIN WHO HURTS YOUR MASTER...

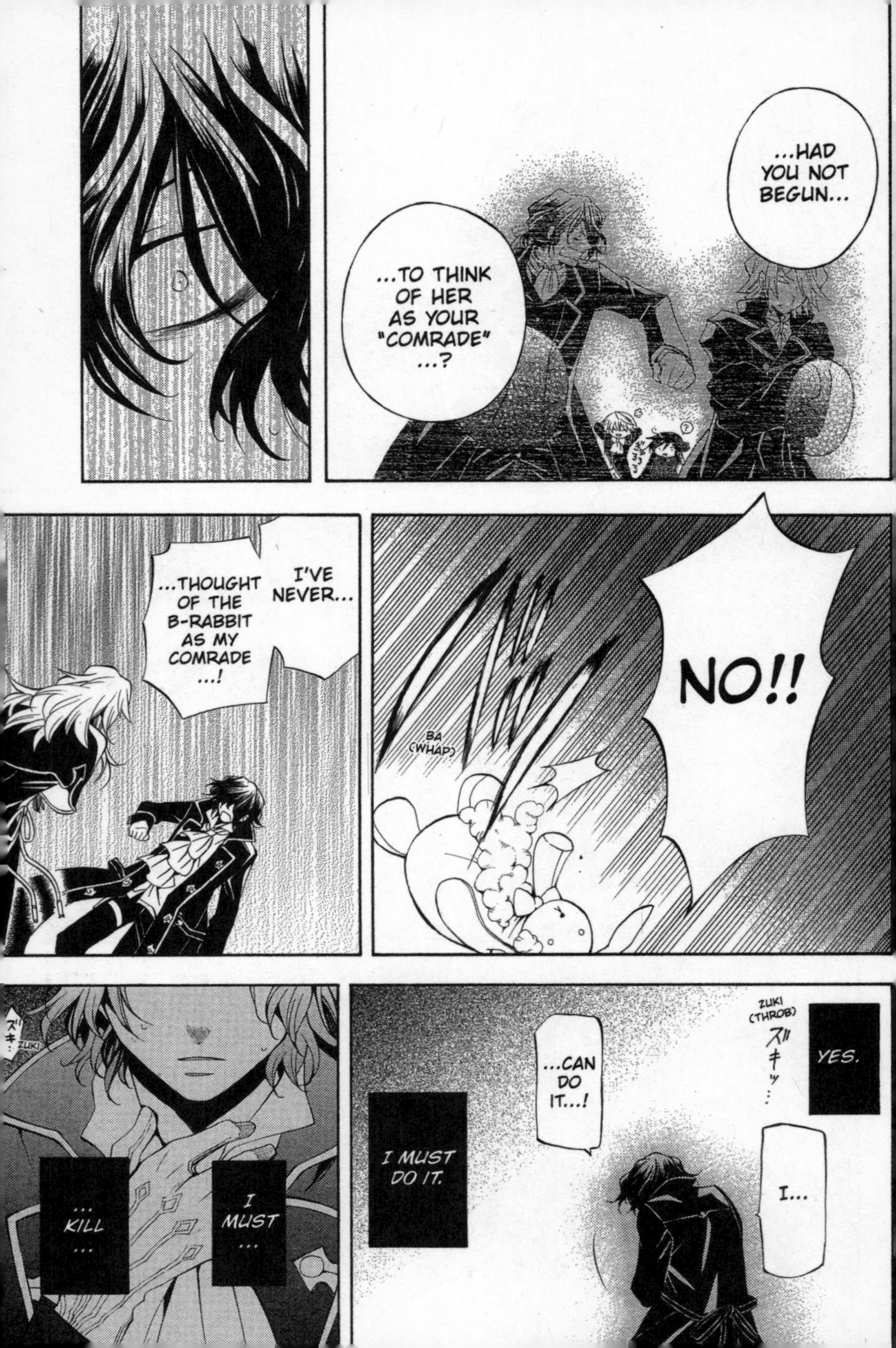
...HAD YOU NOT BEGUN...
...TO THINK OF HER AS YOUR "COMRADE" ...?
NO!!
BA (WHAP)
I'VE NEVER...
...THOUGHT OF THE B-RABBIT AS MY COMRADE ...!
YES.
ZUKI (THROB)
ズキッ…
I...
...CAN DO IT...!
I MUST DO IT.
ズキ…
ZUKI
I MUST ...
... KILL ...

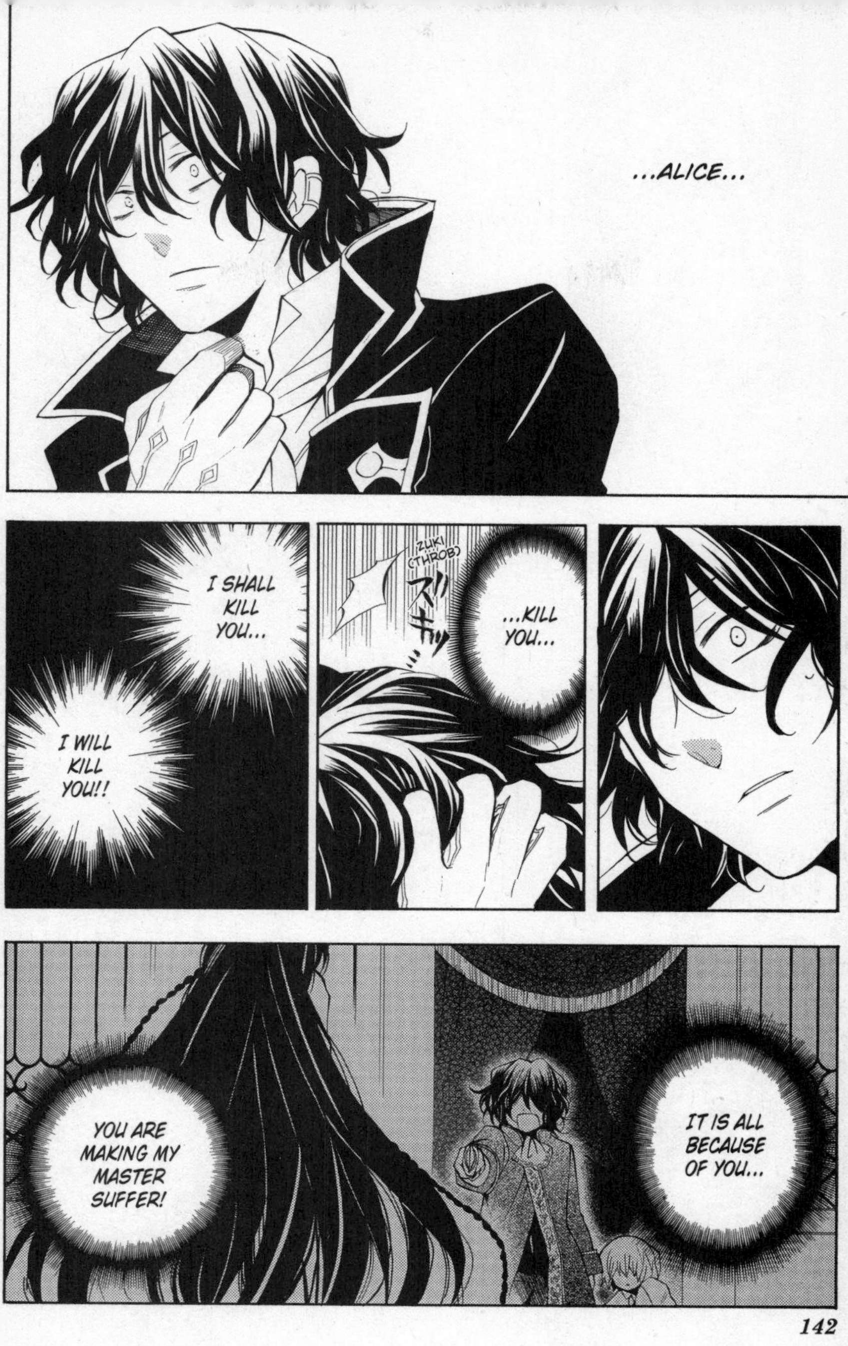
...ALICE...
ZUKI (THROB)
...KILL YOU...
I SHALL KILL YOU...
I WILL KILL YOU!!
IT IS ALL BECAUSE OF YOU...
YOU ARE MAKING MY MASTER SUFFER!

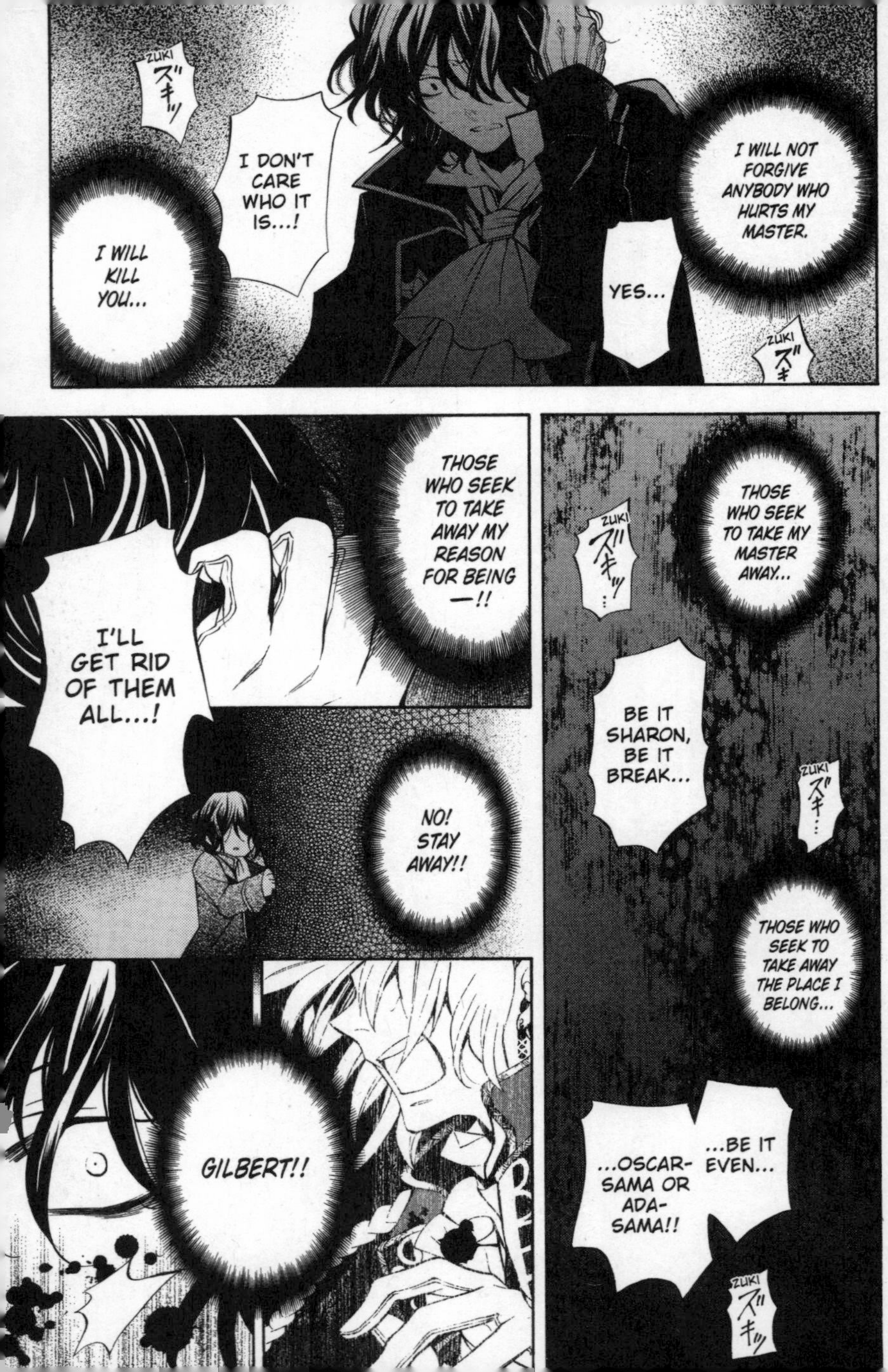
I WILL NOT FORGIVE ANYBODY WHO HURTS MY MASTER.
YES...
ZUKI
ズキ
I DON'T CARE WHO IT IS...!
ZUKI
ズキッ
I WILL KILL YOU...
THOSE WHO SEEK TO TAKE MY MASTER AWAY...
ZUKI
ズキッ...
BE IT SHARON, BE IT BREAK...
ZUKI
ズキ...
THOSE WHO SEEK TO TAKE AWAY THE PLACE I BELONG...
...BE IT EVEN...
...OSCAR-SAMA OR ADA-SAMA!!
ZUKI
ズキッ
THOSE WHO SEEK TO TAKE AWAY MY REASON FOR BEING—!!
I'LL GET RID OF THEM ALL...!
NO! STAY AWAY!!
GILBERT!!

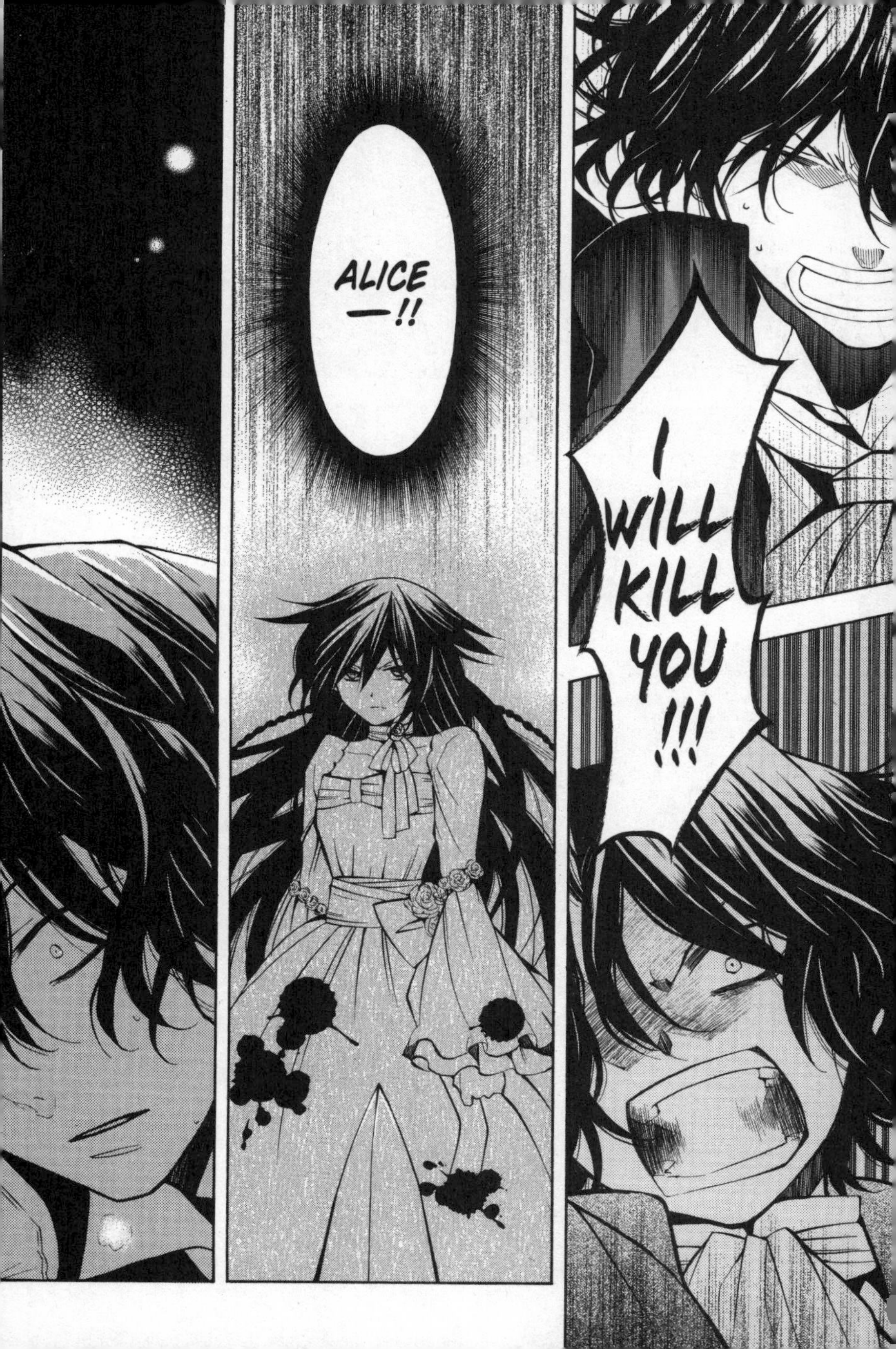
I WILL KILL YOU!!!
ALICE—!!

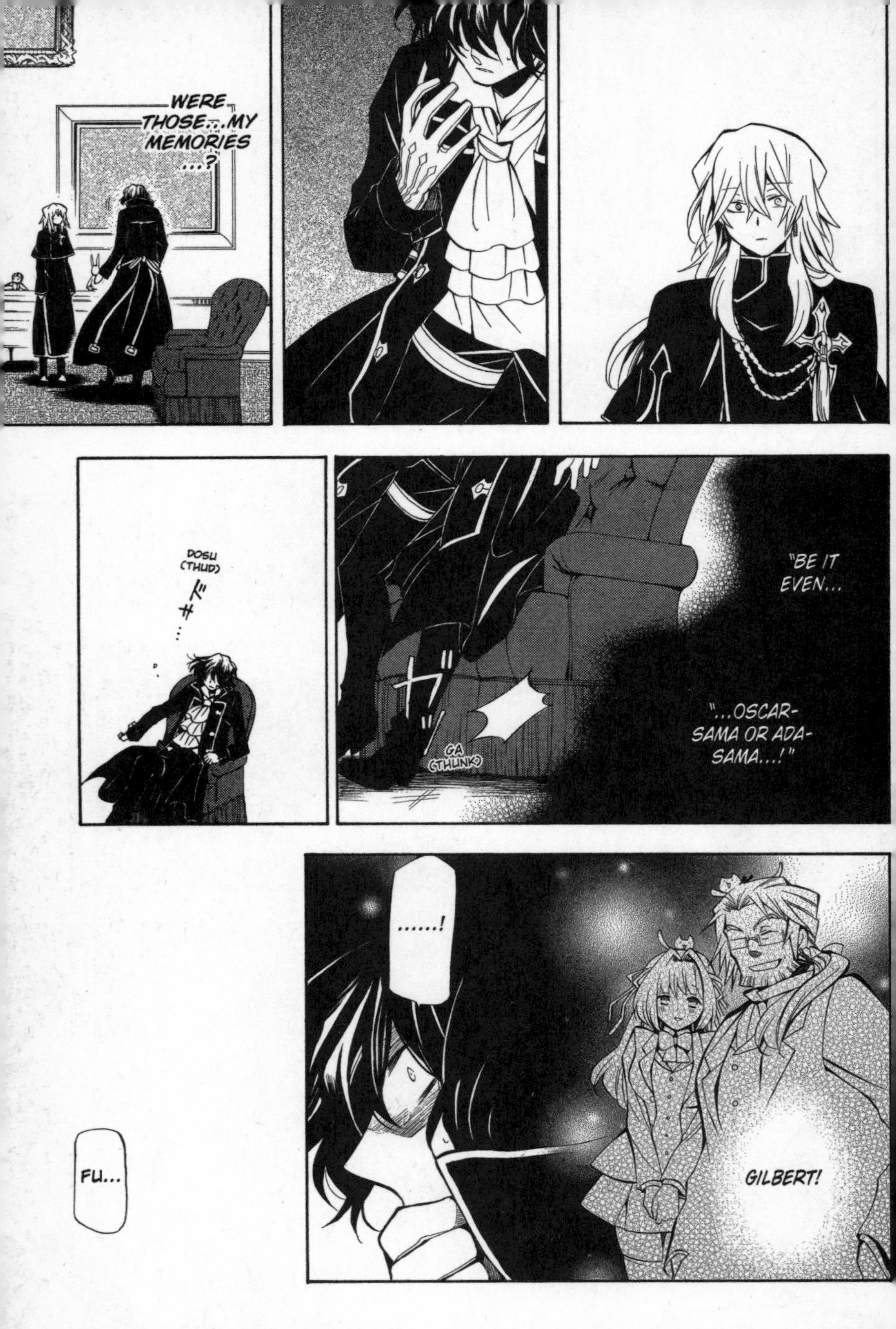
WERE THOSE...MY MEMORIES...?
"BE IT EVEN...
"...OSCAR-SAMA OR ADA-SAMA...!"
GA (THUNK)
DOSU (THUD)
ドサ...
......!
GILBERT!
FU...

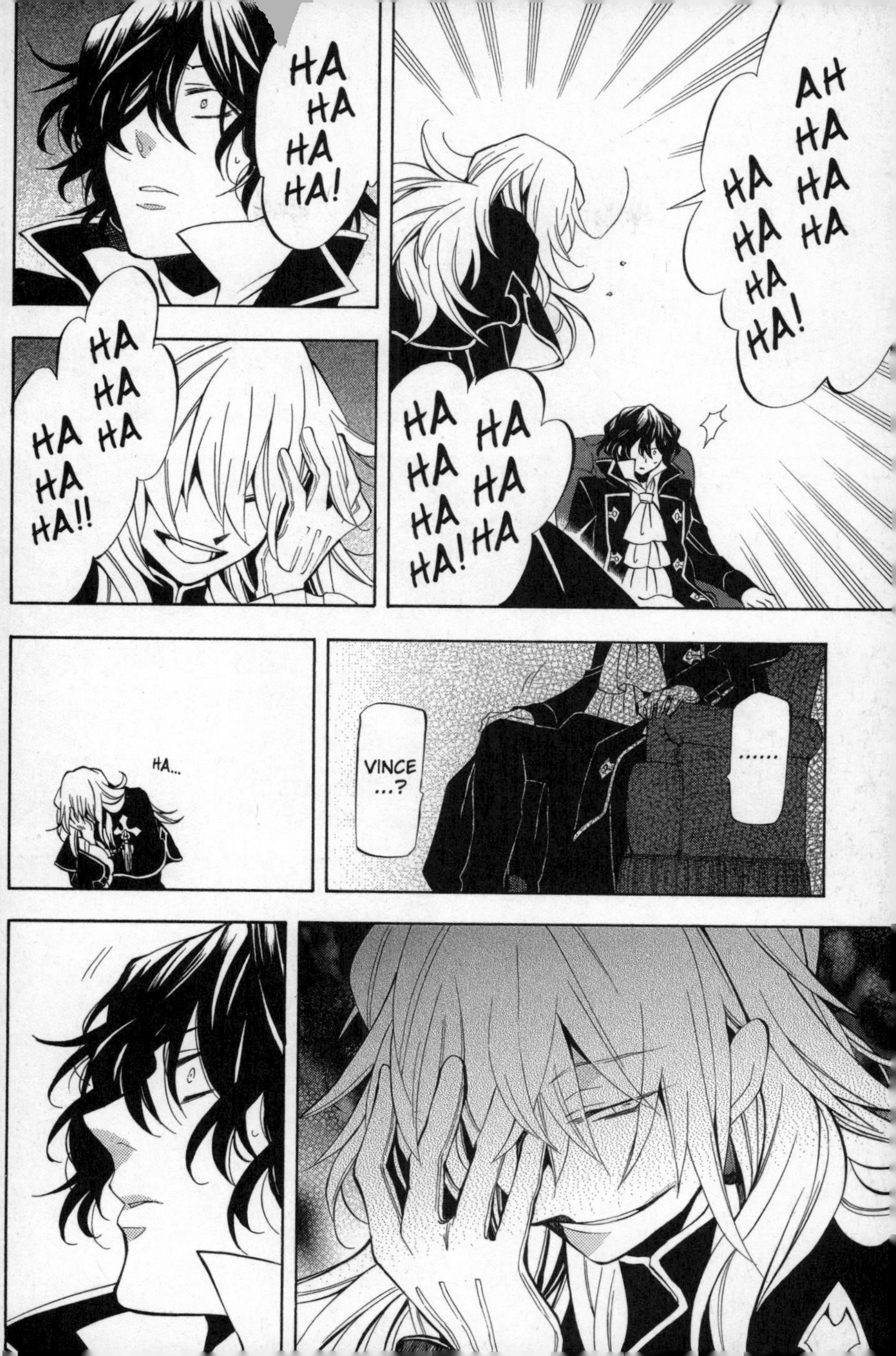
AH HA HA HA HA HA HA HA HA!
HA HA HA HA! HA HA HA HA
HA HA HA HA!
HA HA HA HA HA HA!!
VINCE ...?
......
HA...

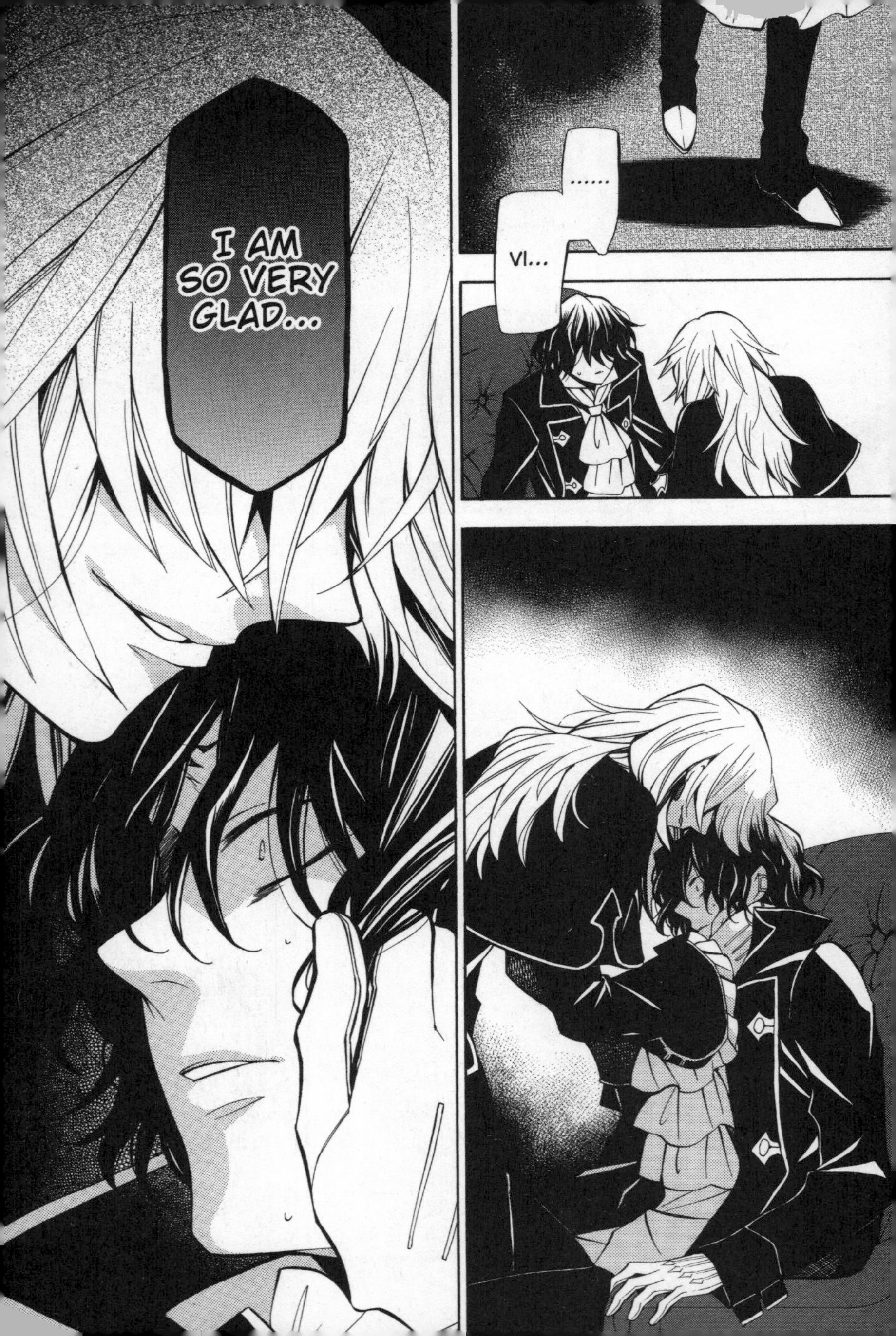
......
VI...
I AM SO VERY GLAD...

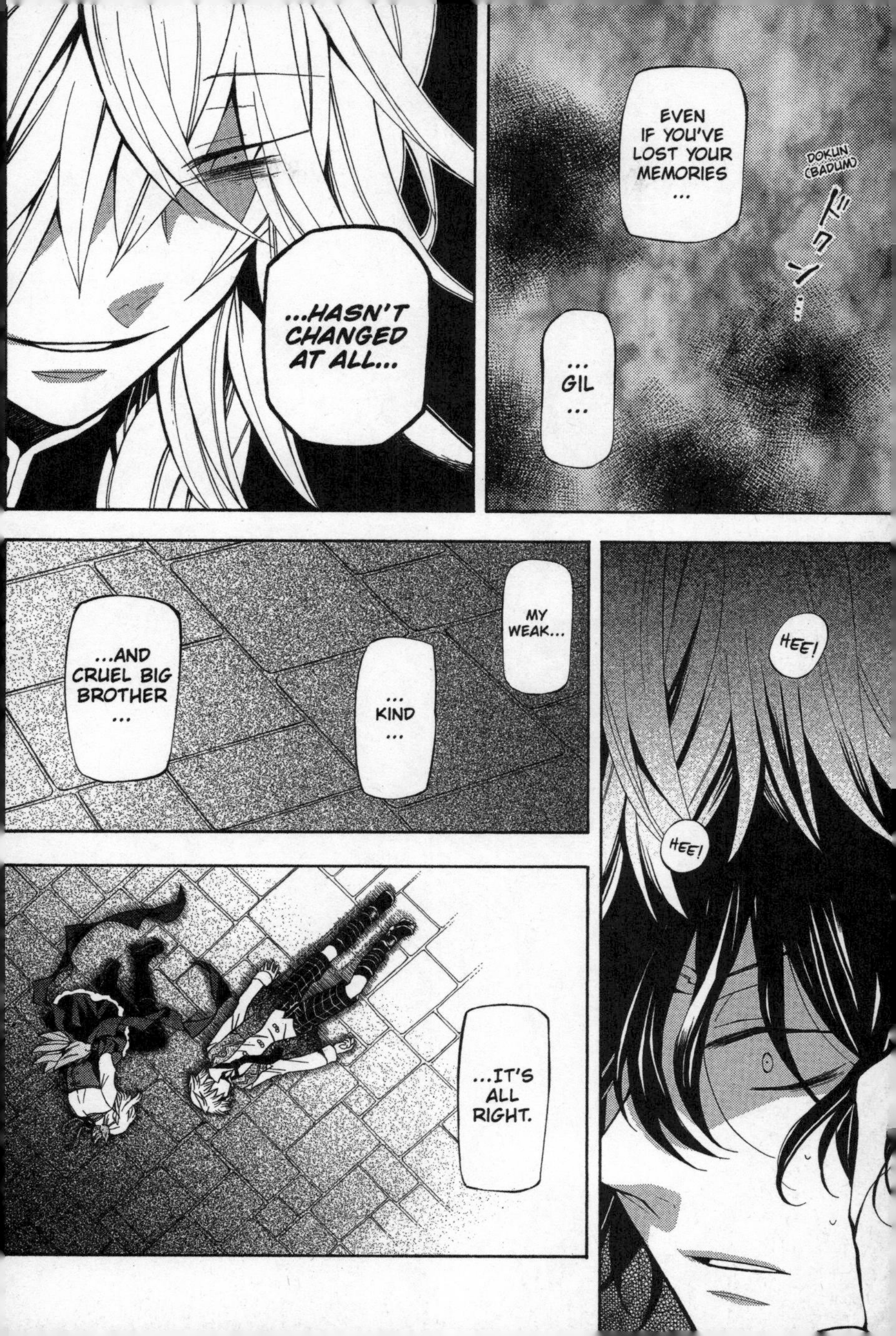
EVEN IF YOU'VE LOST YOUR MEMORIES ...
DOKUN (BADUMP)
ドクン…
... GIL ...
...HASN'T CHANGED AT ALL...
HEE!
HEE!
MY WEAK...
... KIND ...
...AND CRUEL BIG BROTHER ...
...IT'S ALL RIGHT.

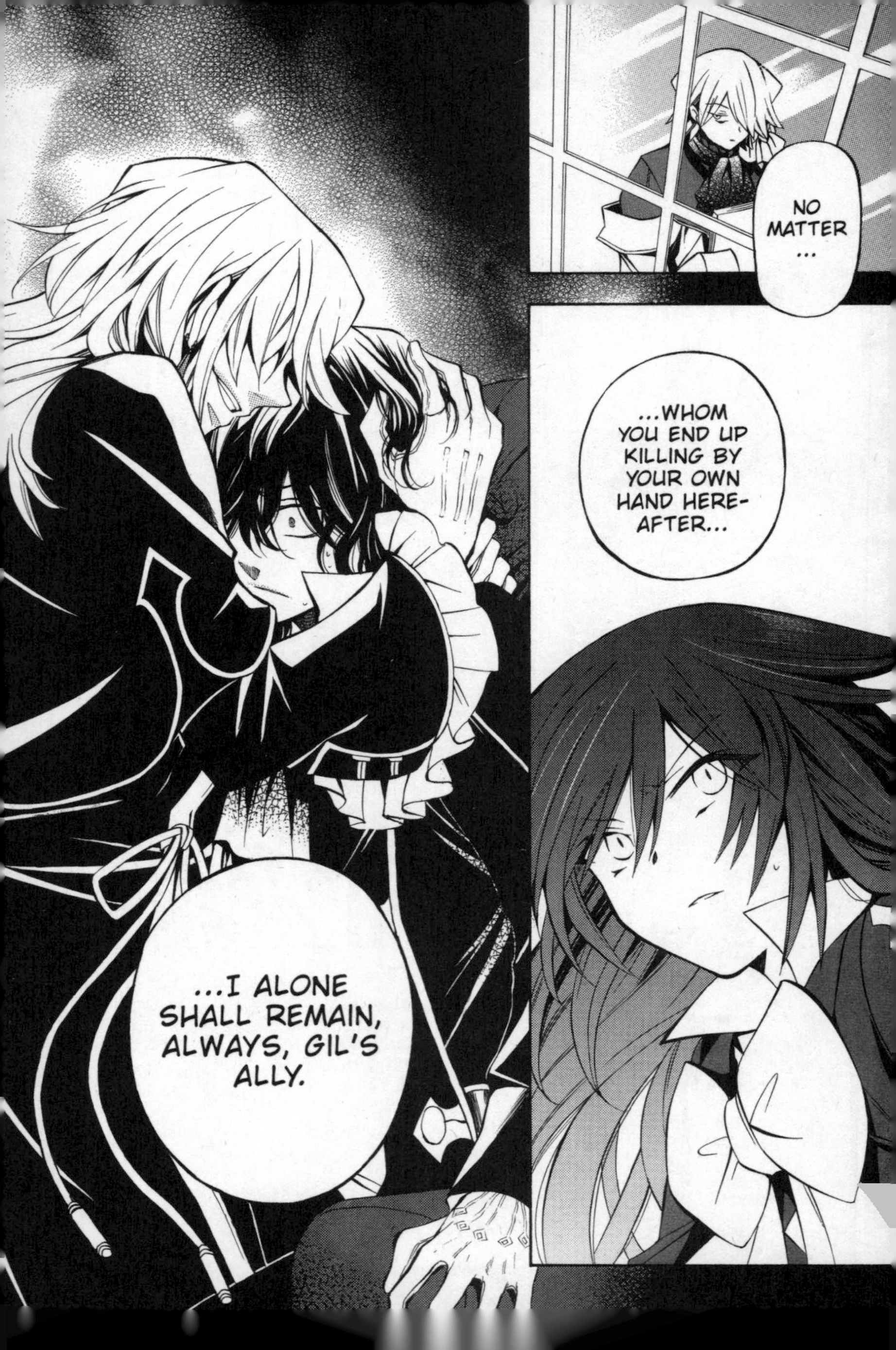
NO MATTER ...
...WHOM YOU END UP KILLING BY YOUR OWN HAND HERE-AFTER...
...I ALONE SHALL REMAIN, ALWAYS, GIL'S ALLY.

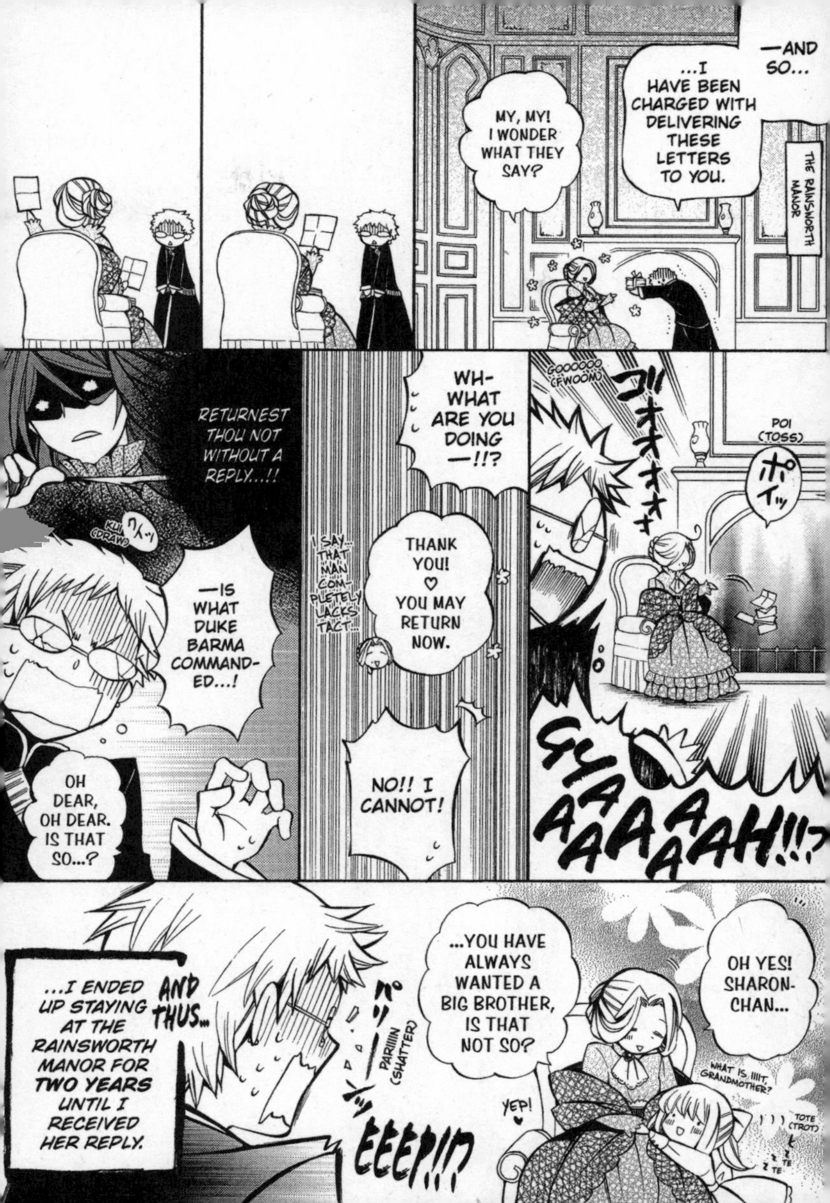
—AND SO...
...I HAVE BEEN CHARGED WITH DELIVERING THESE LETTERS TO YOU.
THE RAINSWORTH MANOR
MY, MY! I WONDER WHAT THEY SAY?
GOOOOOO (FWOOM)
POI (TOSS)
GYAAAAAAAH!!?
WH-WHAT ARE YOU DOING—!!?
THANK YOU! ♡ YOU MAY RETURN NOW.
I SAY... THAT MAN COMPLETELY LACKS TACT...
NO!! I CANNOT!
RETURNEST THOU NOT WITHOUT A REPLY...!!
KUI (DRAW)
—IS WHAT DUKE BARMA COMMANDED...!
OH DEAR, OH DEAR. IS THAT SO...?
OH YES! SHARON-CHAN...
...YOU HAVE ALWAYS WANTED A BIG BROTHER, IS THAT NOT SO?
WHAT IS IIIIT, GRANDMOTHER?
TOTE (TROT)
YEP! ♥
PARIIIIN (SHATTER)
EEEP!!?
AND THUS...
...I ENDED UP STAYING AT THE RAINSWORTH MANOR FOR TWO YEARS UNTIL I RECEIVED HER REPLY.

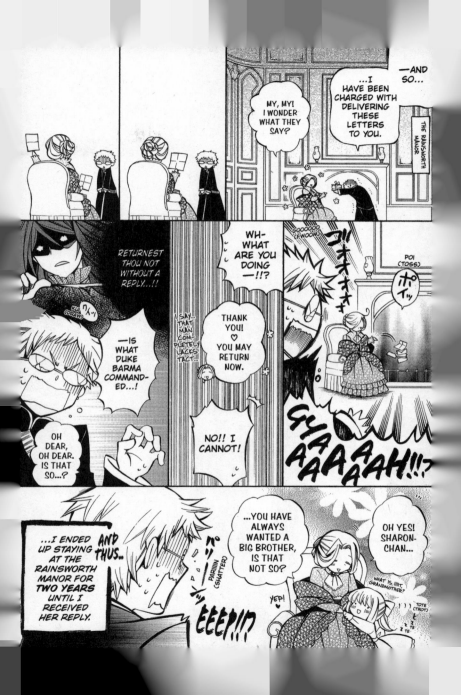

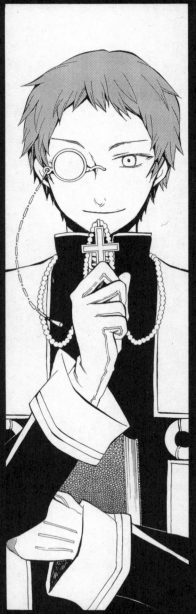

AFTERWORD...NO, MIDDLE-WORD.

"PANDORAHEARTS" ENDS HERE.

THANK YOU FOR READING!!!

....BECAUSE, YOU SEE...
IT BEGINS TWO PAGES LATER.
→SHAKE← →SHAKE← →SHAKE←

MY, JUN MOCHIZUKI'S, BITTER AND SALTY DEBUT WORK, THE ONE-SHOT VERSION OF......"PANDORAHEARTS"!!!
→SHAKE← →SHAKE← →SHAKE← →SHAKE←
→SHAKE← →SHAKE← →SHAKE← →SHAKE←

IT'S SO SALTY, ALL SORTS OF BODILY FLUIDS ARE ABOUT TO GUSH OUT FROM MY BODY.

THE TITLE HAS ONLY CHANGED FROM KATAKANA TO ENGLISH LETTERS, BUT I FEEL THE CONTENTS OF THIS ONE-SHOT ARE MORE LIKE A SHOUNEN MANGA.

THE GIRL ADA IS BASED ON IS CALLED "ALICE," AND THE MEANINGS OF "PANDORA" AND "THE ABYSS" ARE DIFFERENT, SO I'LL BE HAPPY IF YOU ENJOY THOSE DIFFERENCES.

PAINFUL

NOW, I LOOK BACK ON THE MEMORIES.

- o AMAZINGLY, 90% OF THIS ONE-SHOT WAS DRAWN WITH A MARU-PEN (AND TACHIKAWA—THEY'RE STIFF). OF COURSE I INJURED MY HAND AFTERWARD.

THE NIBS ARE SUITED FOR DRAWING THIN LINES. THE BACKGROUNDS WERE DRAWN WITH HI-TEC-C 0.3MM.

- o I TOOK HOME MY SCHOOL FRIENDS AS ASSISTANTS, TELLING THEM "IF YOU CAN COLOR AND CUT, YOU CAN DO IT!" LIKE A HUSTLER ON THE STREET, BUT BECAUSE I WAS LATE DOING MY WORK, THEY HAD NOTHING TO DO, AND EVERYONE WAS IN THE NEXT ROOM WATCHING TV, AND I WAS LONELY.

- o JUN MOCHIZUKI DRINKS ENERGY
  DRINKS FOR THE FIRST TIME!! (SAD)

- o I ONLY SLEPT FOR TEN HOURS IN FIVE DAYS.
  NOW I WANT THE PHYSICAL STRENGTH I HAD THEN....!!

- o NO MATTER WHAT PEOPLE SAY, THE HERO OF THE ONE-SHOT IS HARRIS-KUN!

(↑ THE PRIEST)

SPECIAL ONE-SHOT

PANDORAHEARTS

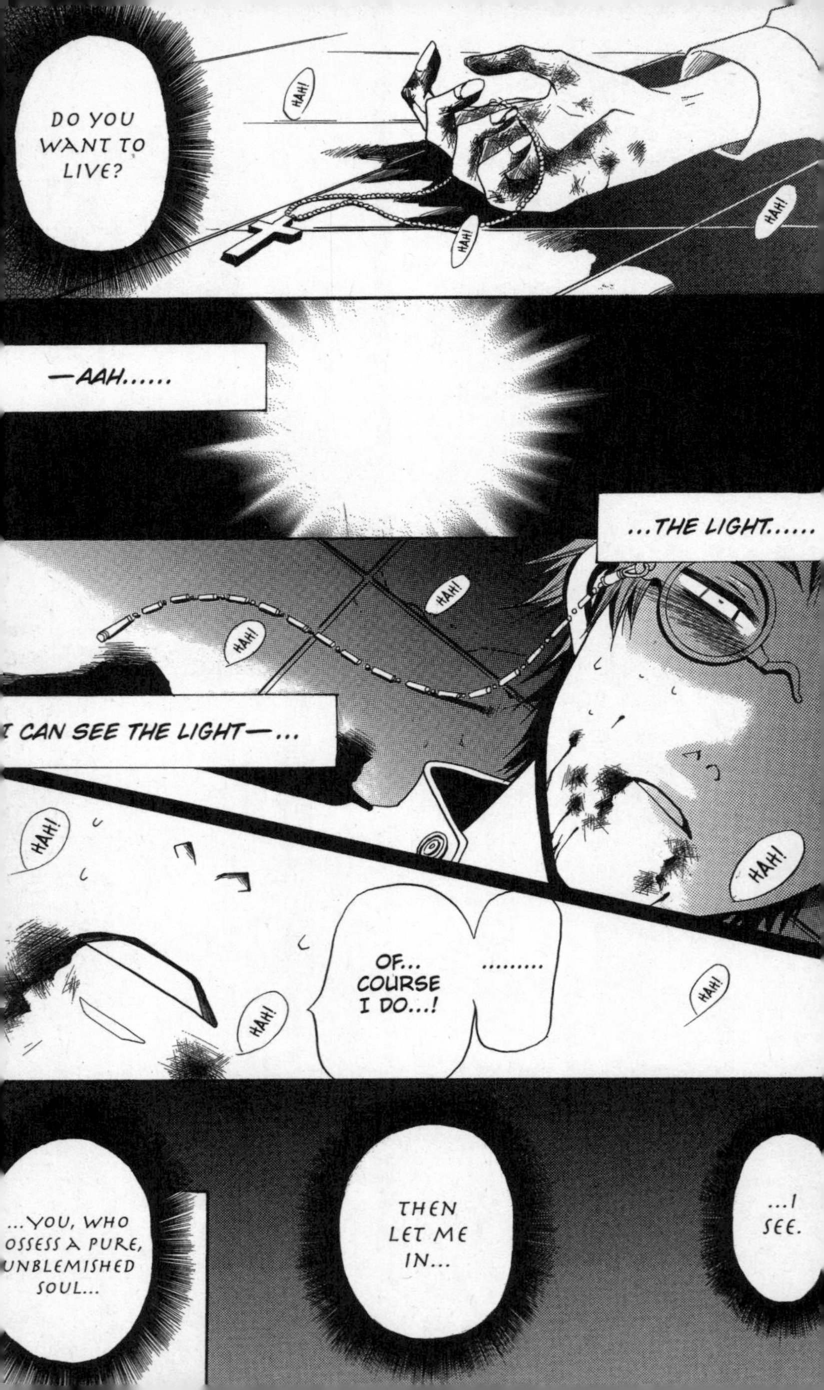
HAH!
HAH!
HAH!
DO YOU WANT TO LIVE?
—AAH......
...THE LIGHT......
HAH!
HAH!
CAN SEE THE LIGHT—...
HAH!
....
OF... COURSE I DO...!
HAH!
HAH!
HAH!
...I SEE.
THEN LET ME IN...
...YOU, WHO OSSESS A PURE, UNBLEMISHED SOUL...

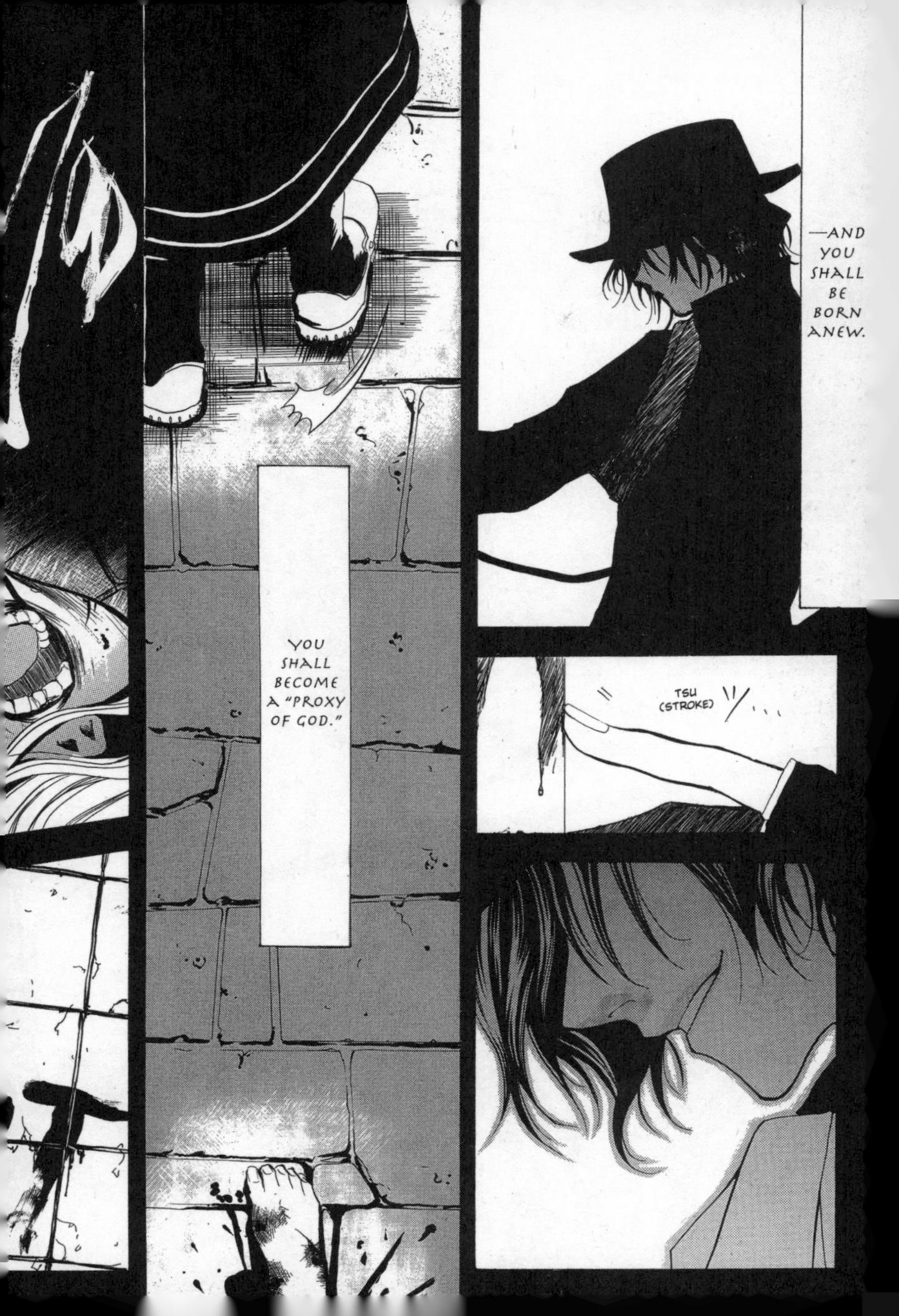
—AND YOU SHALL BE BORN ANEW.
TSU (STROKE)
YOU SHALL BECOME A "PROXY OF GOD."

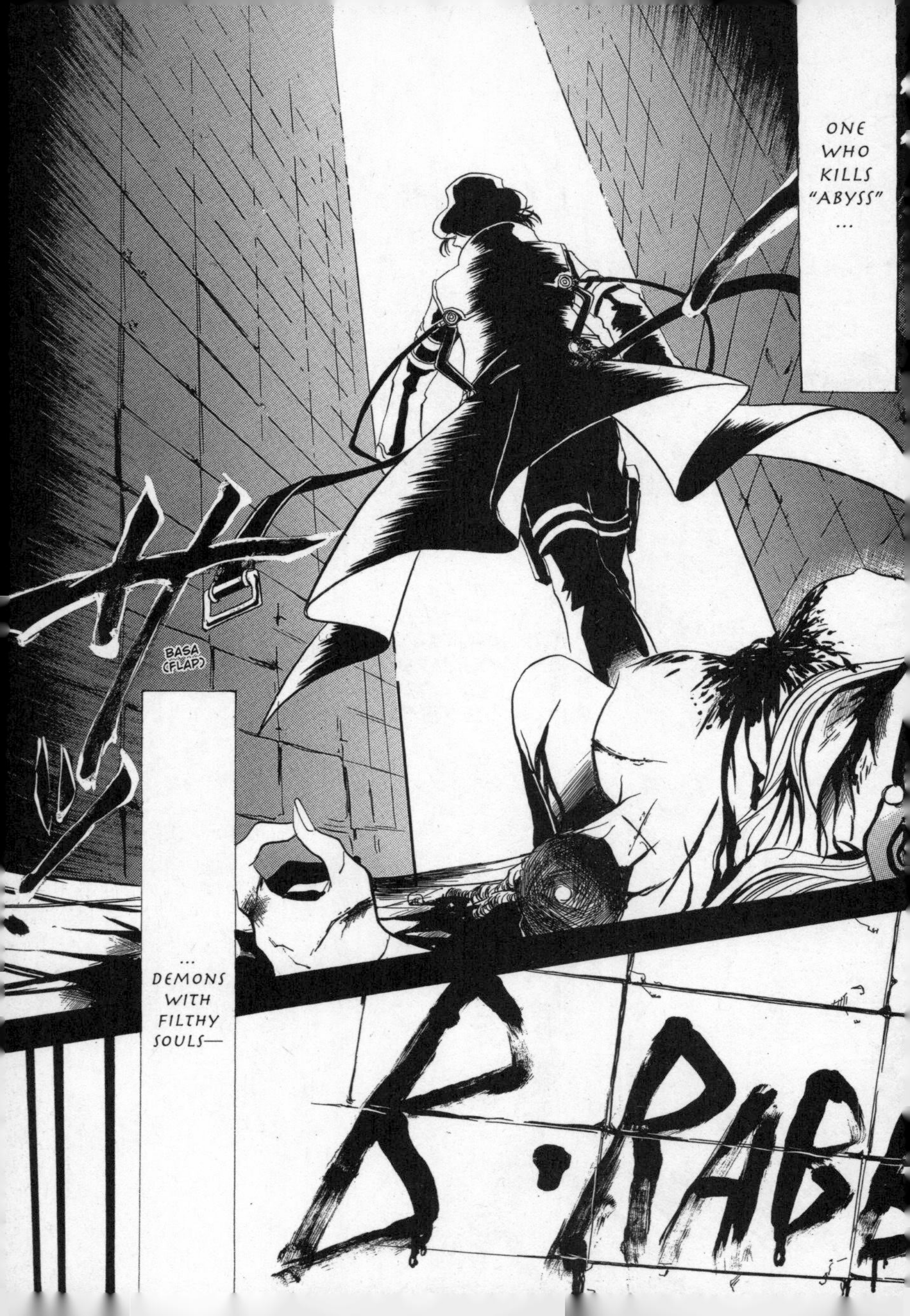
ONE WHO KILLS "ABYSS" ...
BASA (FLAP)
... DEMONS WITH FILTHY SOULS—

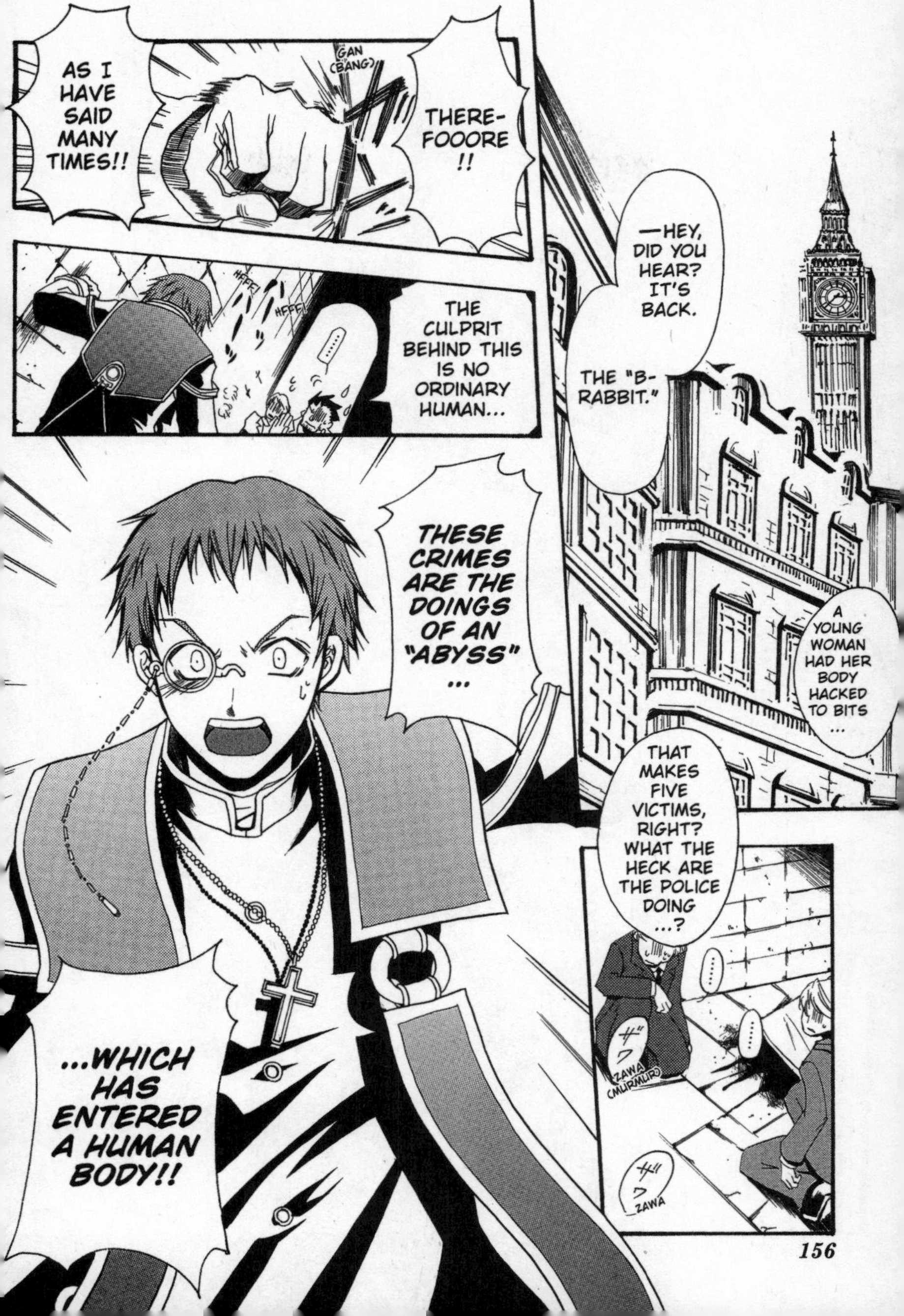
—HEY, DID YOU HEAR? IT'S BACK.
THE "B-RABBIT."
A YOUNG WOMAN HAD HER BODY HACKED TO BITS ...
THAT MAKES FIVE VICTIMS, RIGHT? WHAT THE HECK ARE THE POLICE DOING ...?
.....
.....
ZAWA (MURMUR)
ZAWA
AS I HAVE SAID MANY TIMES!!
GAN (BANG)
THERE-FOOORE !!
HFFF
HFFF
THE CULPRIT BEHIND THIS IS NO ORDINARY HUMAN...
.....
THESE CRIMES ARE THE DOINGS OF AN "ABYSS" ...
...WHICH HAS ENTERED A HUMAN BODY!!

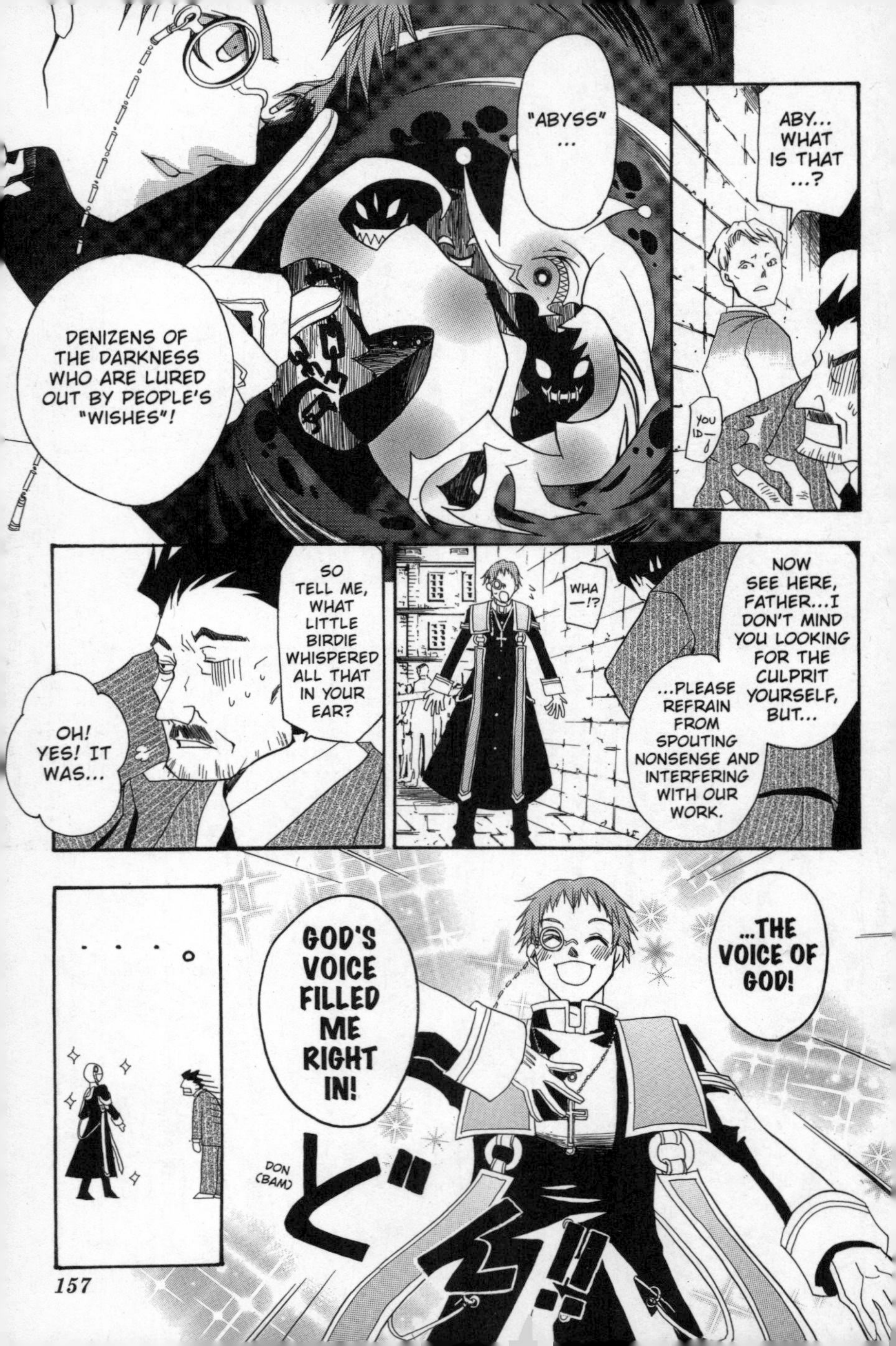
ABY... WHAT IS THAT ...?
YOU ID—
"ABYSS" ...
DENIZENS OF THE DARKNESS WHO ARE LURED OUT BY PEOPLE'S "WISHES"!
NOW SEE HERE, FATHER...I DON'T MIND YOU LOOKING FOR THE CULPRIT YOURSELF, BUT...
...PLEASE REFRAIN FROM SPOUTING NONSENSE AND INTERFERING WITH OUR WORK.
WHA—!?
SO TELL ME, WHAT LITTLE BIRDIE WHISPERED ALL THAT IN YOUR EAR?
OH! YES! IT WAS...
...THE VOICE OF GOD!
GOD'S VOICE FILLED ME RIGHT IN!
DON (BAM)
. . . .

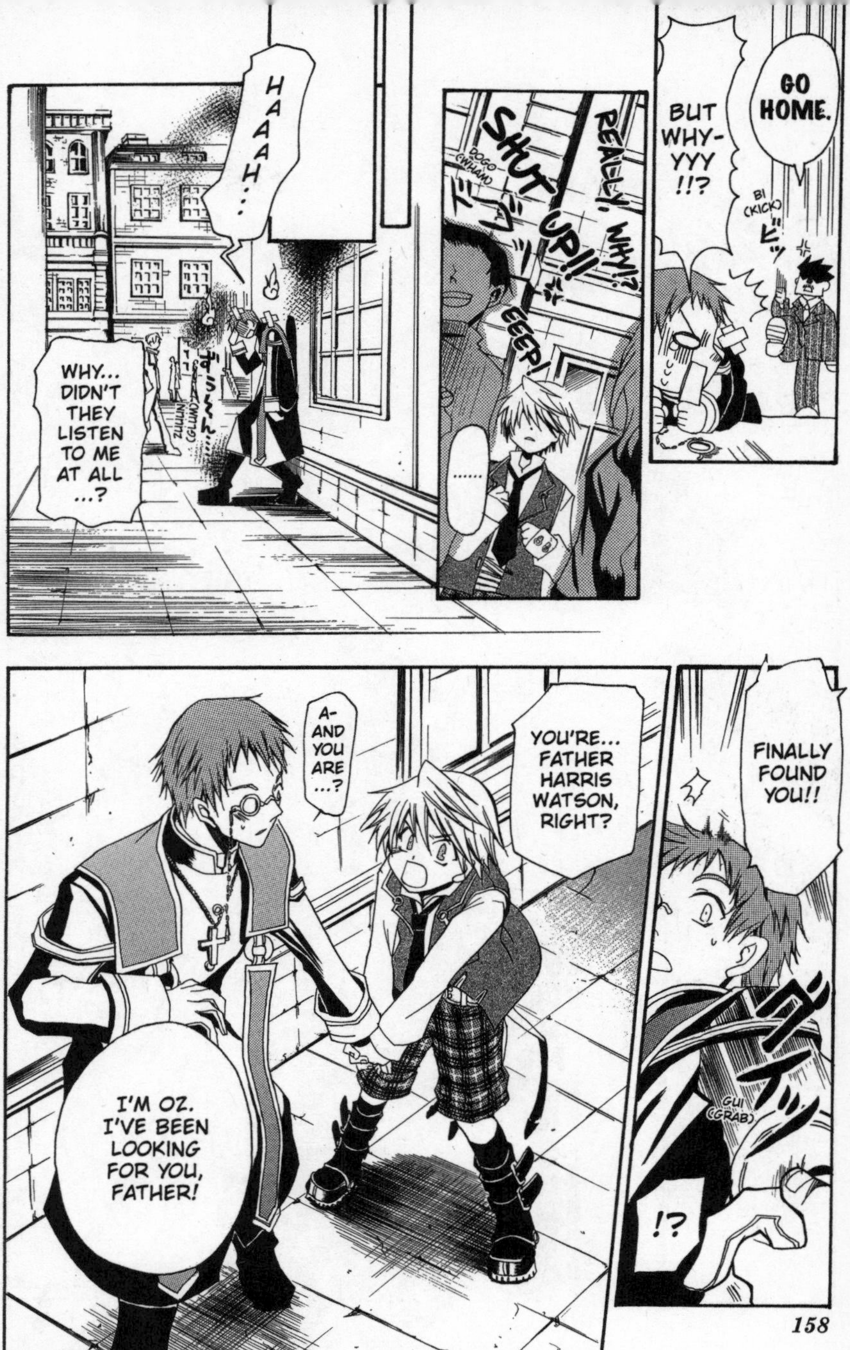
GO HOME.
BUT WHY-YYY!!?
BI (KICK)
REALLY, WHY!!?
SHUT UP!!
DOGO (WHAM)
EEEP!
......
HAAAAH...
WHY... DIDN'T THEY LISTEN TO ME AT ALL ...?
ZULUN (GLUM)
FINALLY FOUND YOU!!
GUI (GRAB)
!?
YOU'RE... FATHER HARRIS WATSON, RIGHT?
A- AND YOU ARE ...?
I'M OZ. I'VE BEEN LOOKING FOR YOU, FATHER!

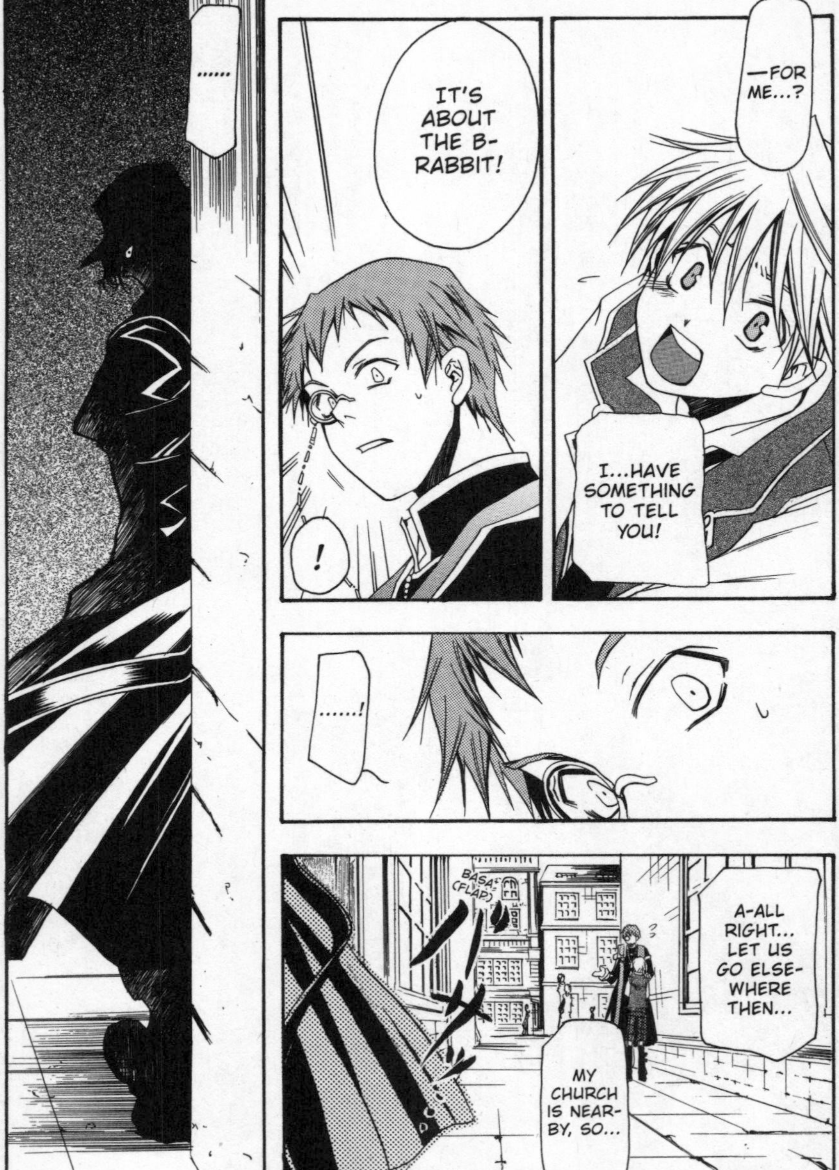

—FOR ME...?
I...HAVE SOMETHING TO TELL YOU!
IT'S ABOUT THE B-RABBIT!
!
......!
A-ALL RIGHT... LET US GO ELSE-WHERE THEN...
BASA (FLAP)
MY CHURCH IS NEAR-BY, SO...
......

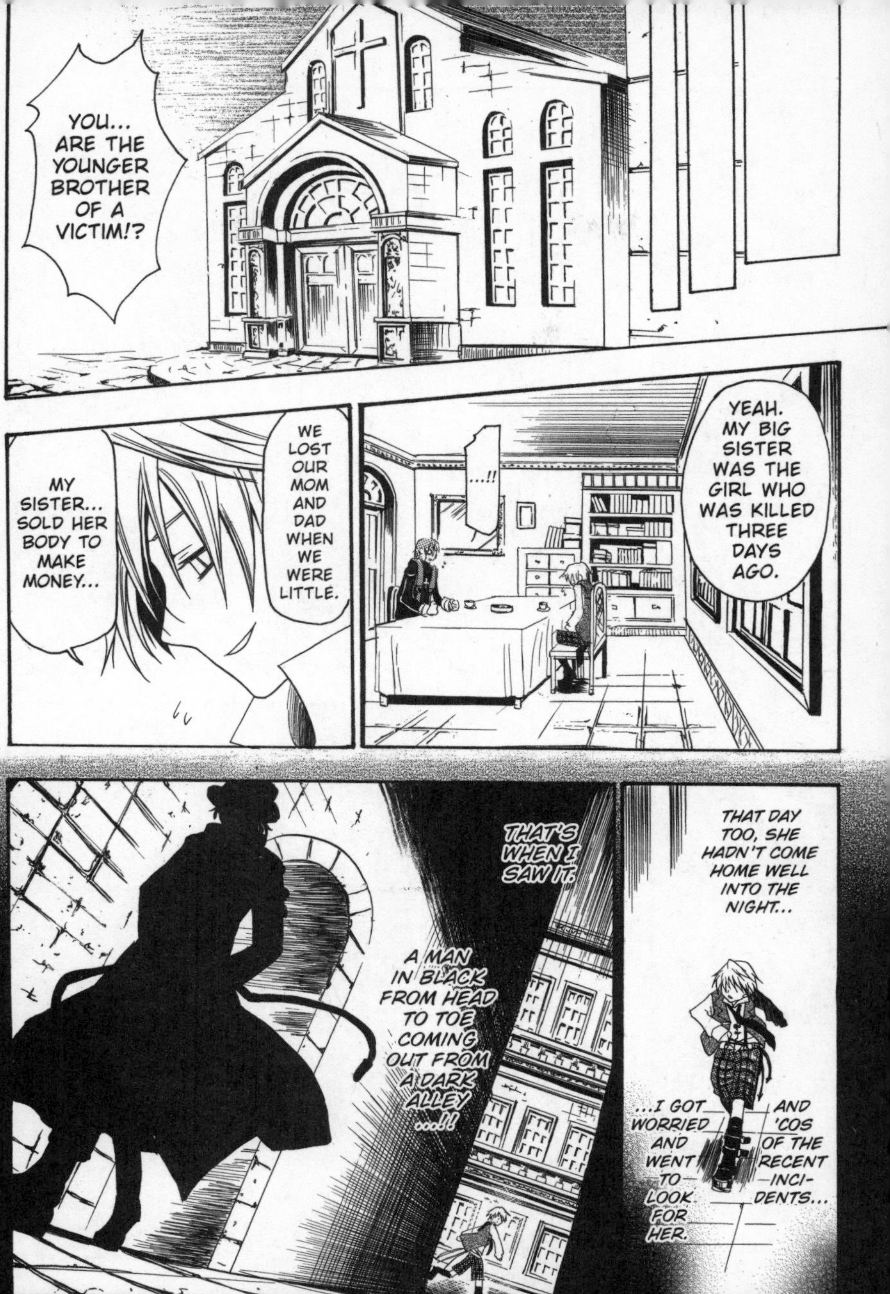
YOU... ARE THE YOUNGER BROTHER OF A VICTIM!?
YEAH. MY BIG SISTER WAS THE GIRL WHO WAS KILLED THREE DAYS AGO.
...!!
WE LOST OUR MOM AND DAD WHEN WE WERE LITTLE.
MY SISTER... SOLD HER BODY TO MAKE MONEY...
THAT DAY TOO, SHE HADN'T COME HOME WELL INTO THE NIGHT...
AND 'COS OF THE RECENT INCIDENTS...
...I GOT WORRIED AND WENT TO LOOK FOR HER.
THAT'S WHEN I SAW IT.
A MAN IN BLACK FROM HEAD TO TOE COMING OUT FROM A DARK ALLEY ...!!

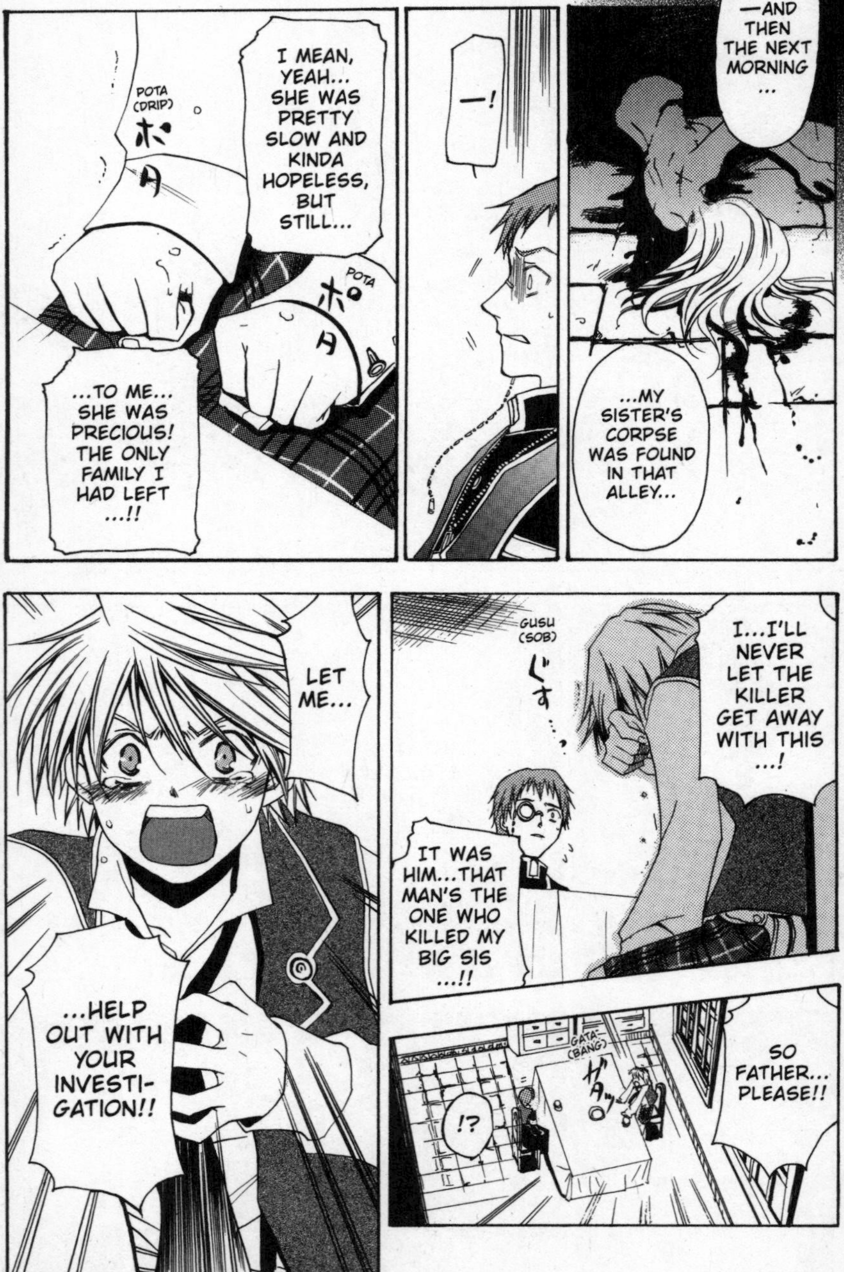
—AND THEN THE NEXT MORNING ...
...MY SISTER'S CORPSE WAS FOUND IN THAT ALLEY...
—!
I MEAN, YEAH... SHE WAS PRETTY SLOW AND KINDA HOPELESS, BUT STILL...
POTA (DRIP)
ポタ
POTA
ポタ
...TO ME... SHE WAS PRECIOUS! THE ONLY FAMILY I HAD LEFT ...!!
I...I'LL NEVER LET THE KILLER GET AWAY WITH THIS ...!
GUSU (SOB)
ぐす...
IT WAS HIM...THAT MAN'S THE ONE WHO KILLED MY BIG SIS ...!!
SO FATHER... PLEASE!!
GATA (BANG)
ガタッ
!?
LET ME...
...HELP OUT WITH YOUR INVESTIGATION!!

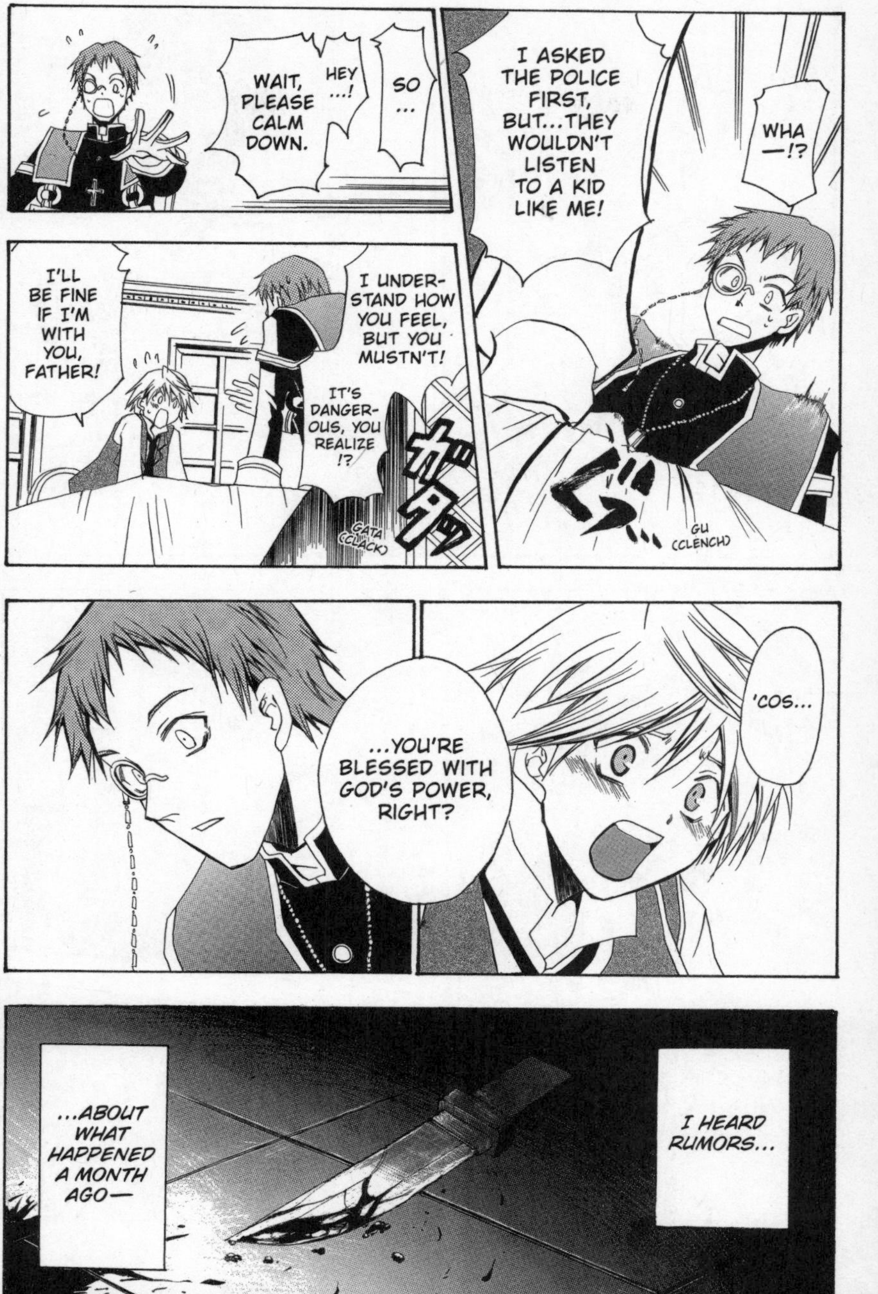
I ASKED THE POLICE FIRST, BUT...THEY WOULDN'T LISTEN TO A KID LIKE ME!
WHA—!?
GU (CLENCH)
SO...
HEY...!
WAIT, PLEASE CALM DOWN.
I UNDERSTAND HOW YOU FEEL, BUT YOU MUSTN'T!
IT'S DANGEROUS, YOU REALIZE!?
GATA (CLACK)
I'LL BE FINE IF I'M WITH YOU, FATHER!
'COS...
...YOU'RE BLESSED WITH GOD'S POWER, RIGHT?
I HEARD RUMORS...
...ABOUT WHAT HAPPENED A MONTH AGO—

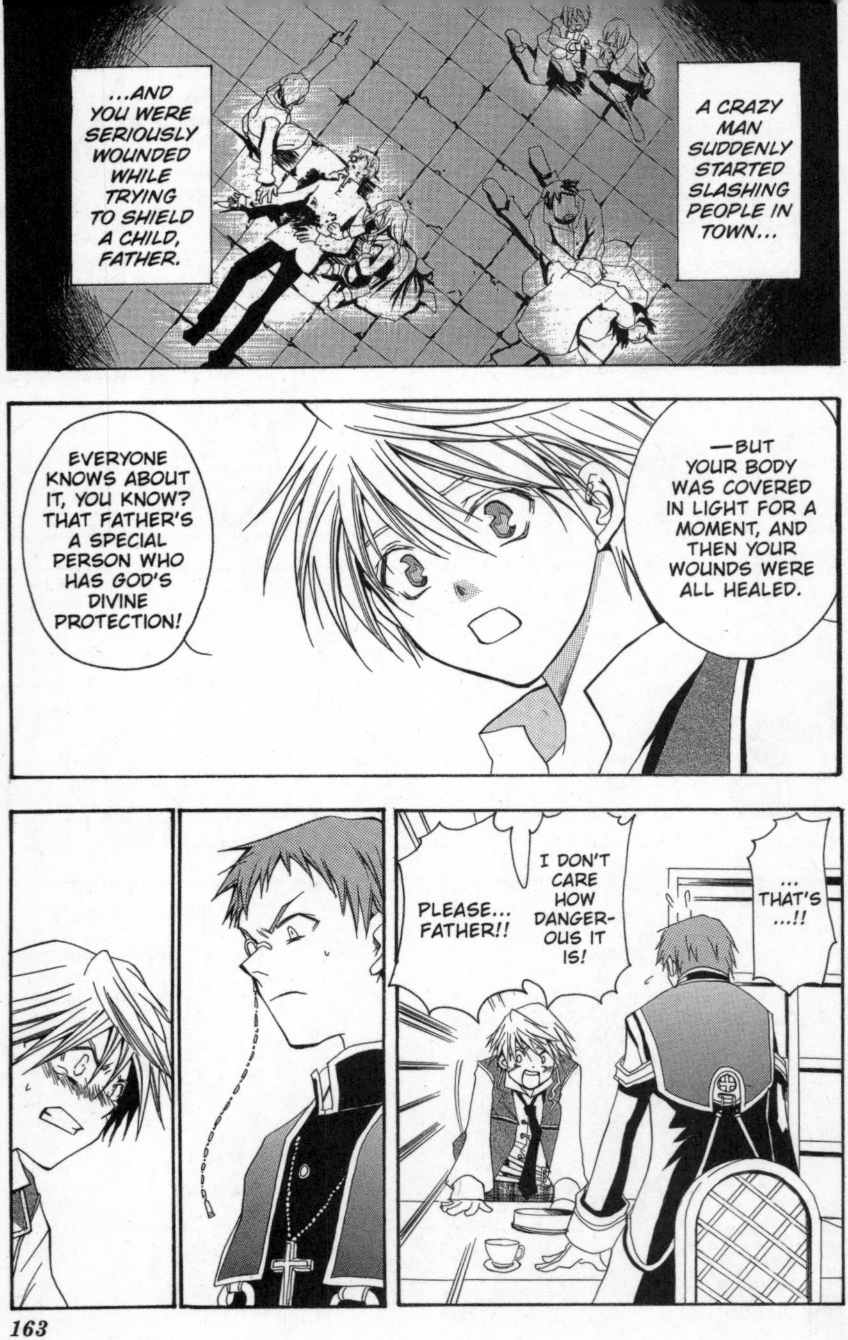
A CRAZY MAN SUDDENLY STARTED SLASHING PEOPLE IN TOWN...
...AND YOU WERE SERIOUSLY WOUNDED WHILE TRYING TO SHIELD A CHILD, FATHER.
—BUT YOUR BODY WAS COVERED IN LIGHT FOR A MOMENT, AND THEN YOUR WOUNDS WERE ALL HEALED.
EVERYONE KNOWS ABOUT IT, YOU KNOW? THAT FATHER'S A SPECIAL PERSON WHO HAS GOD'S DIVINE PROTECTION!
... THAT'S ...!!
I DON'T CARE HOW DANGER-OUS IT IS!
PLEASE... FATHER!!

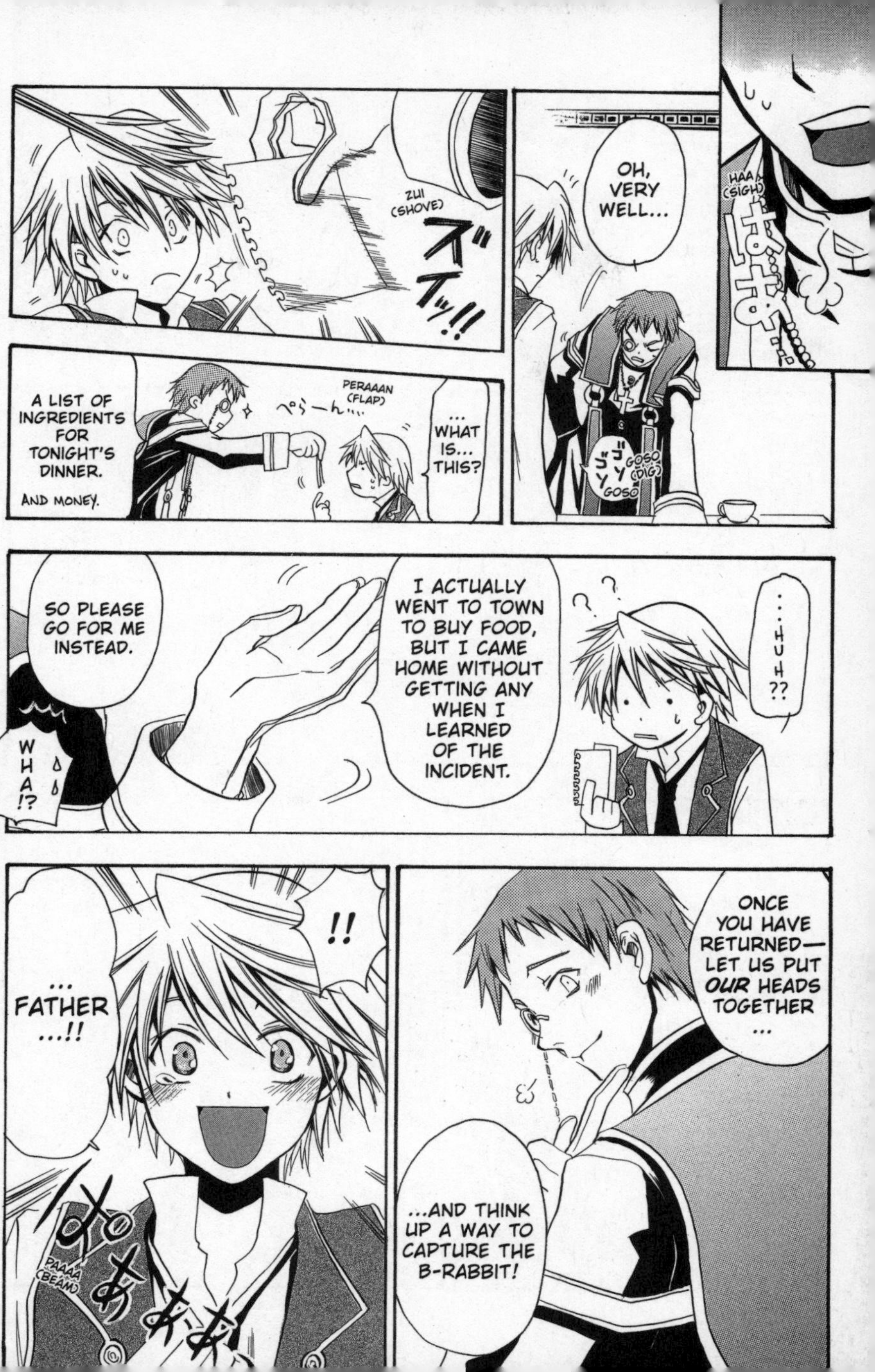
HAA (SIGH)
はぁ…
OH, VERY WELL...
GOSO GOSO (DIG)
ZUI (SHOVE)
ズイッ!!
... WHAT IS... THIS?
PERAAAN (FLAP)
ぺらーん
A LIST OF INGREDIENTS FOR TONIGHT'S DINNER.
AND MONEY.
...HUH??
I ACTUALLY WENT TO TOWN TO BUY FOOD, BUT I CAME HOME WITHOUT GETTING ANY WHEN I LEARNED OF THE INCIDENT.
SO PLEASE GO FOR ME INSTEAD.
WHA!?
ONCE YOU HAVE RETURNED—LET US PUT OUR HEADS TOGETHER ...
...AND THINK UP A WAY TO CAPTURE THE B-RABBIT!
!!
... FATHER ...!!
PAAAA (BEAM)

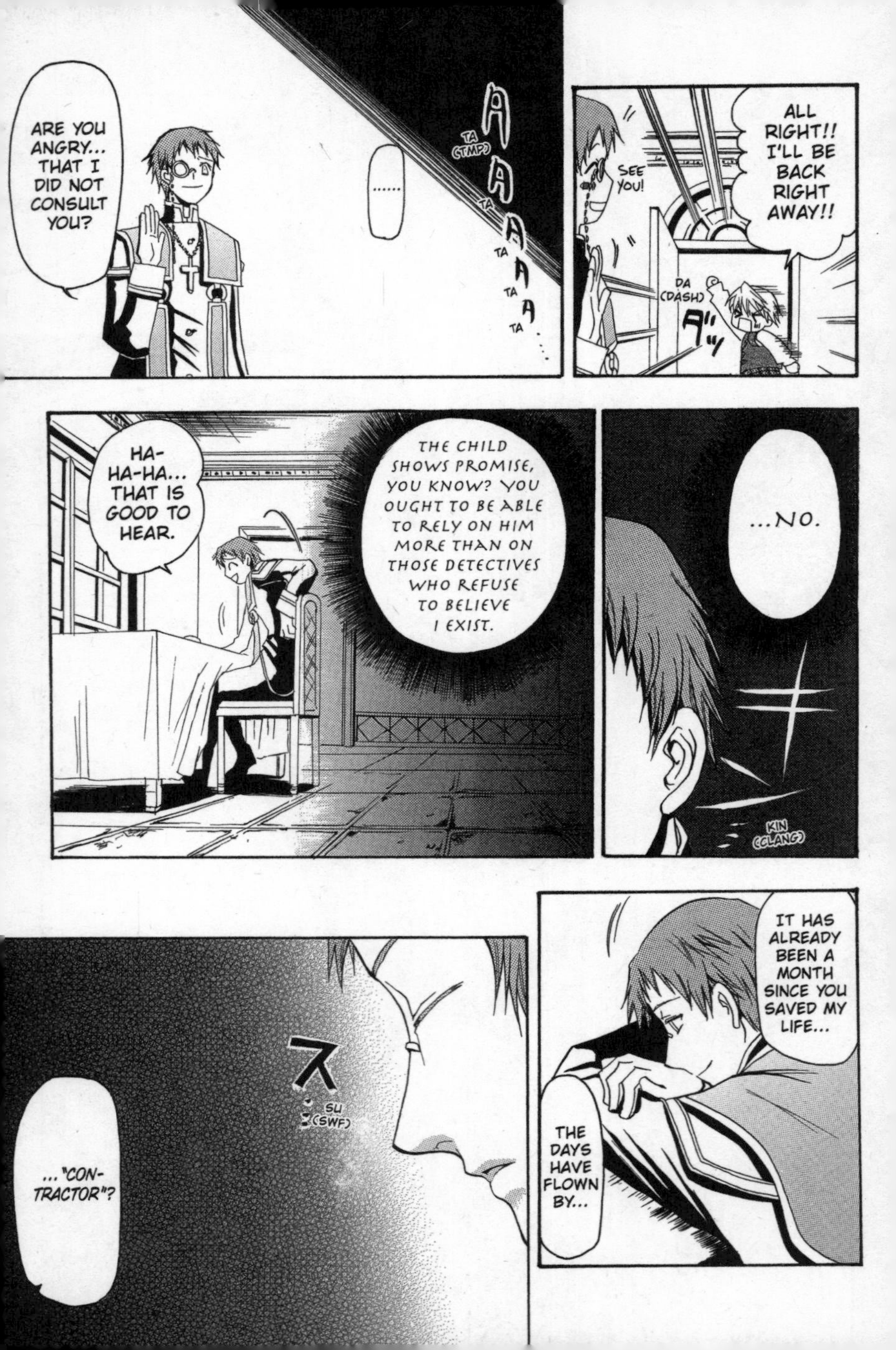
ALL RIGHT!! I'LL BE BACK RIGHT AWAY!!
SEE YOU!
DA (DASH)
TA (TMP)
TA
TA
TA
TA...
......
ARE YOU ANGRY... THAT I DID NOT CONSULT YOU?
...NO.
KIN (CLANG)
THE CHILD SHOWS PROMISE, YOU KNOW? YOU OUGHT TO BE ABLE TO RELY ON HIM MORE THAN ON THOSE DETECTIVES WHO REFUSE TO BELIEVE I EXIST.
HA-HA-HA... THAT IS GOOD TO HEAR.
IT HAS ALREADY BEEN A MONTH SINCE YOU SAVED MY LIFE...
THE DAYS HAVE FLOWN BY...
SU (SWF)
..."CONTRACTOR"?

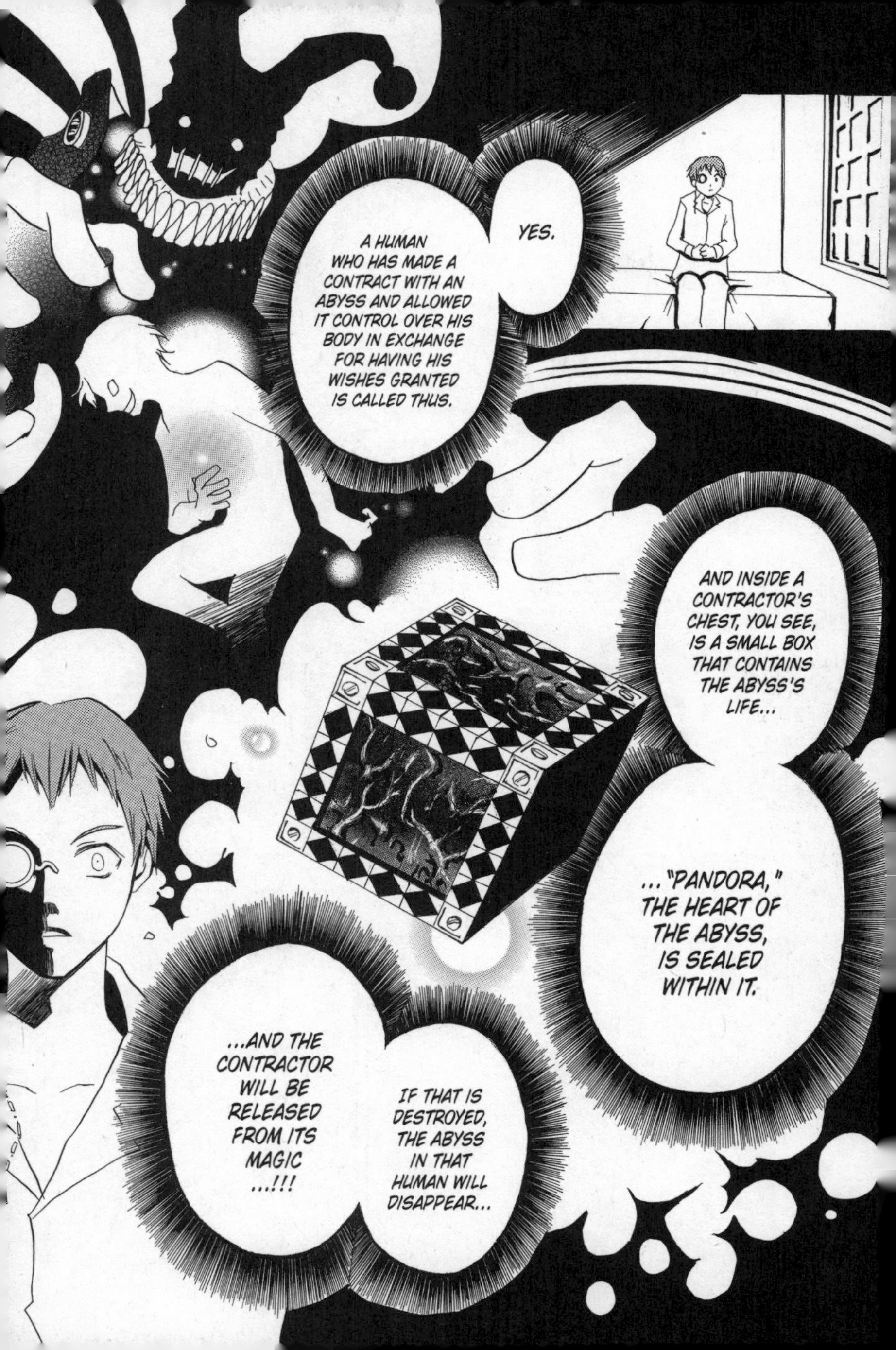
YES.
A HUMAN WHO HAS MADE A CONTRACT WITH AN ABYSS AND ALLOWED IT CONTROL OVER HIS BODY IN EXCHANGE FOR HAVING HIS WISHES GRANTED IS CALLED THUS.
AND INSIDE A CONTRACTOR'S CHEST, YOU SEE, IS A SMALL BOX THAT CONTAINS THE ABYSS'S LIFE...
..."PANDORA," THE HEART OF THE ABYSS, IS SEALED WITHIN IT.
IF THAT IS DESTROYED, THE ABYSS IN THAT HUMAN WILL DISAPPEAR...
...AND THE CONTRACTOR WILL BE RELEASED FROM ITS MAGIC ...!!!

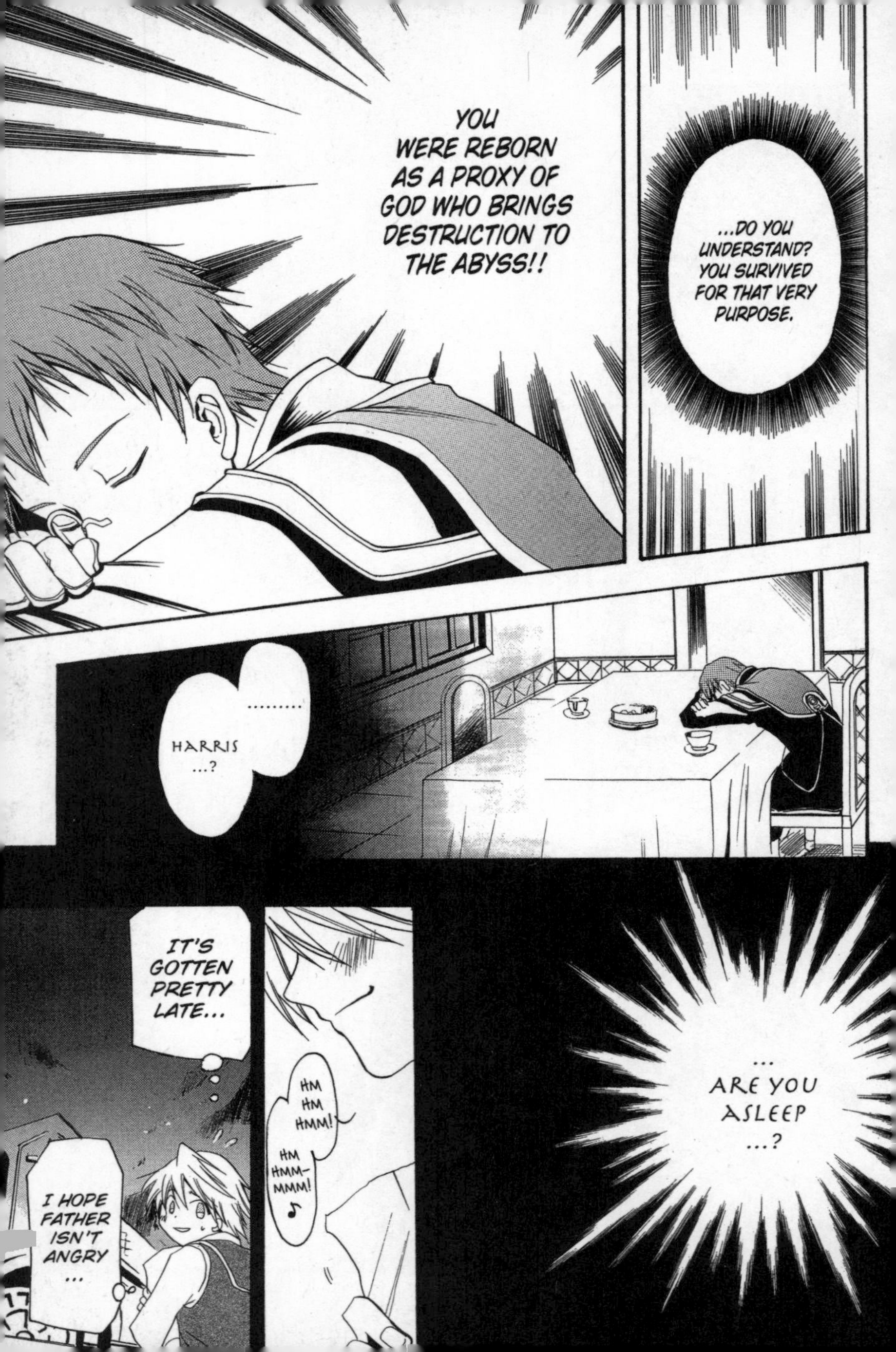
...DO YOU UNDERSTAND? YOU SURVIVED FOR THAT VERY PURPOSE.
YOU WERE REBORN AS A PROXY OF GOD WHO BRINGS DESTRUCTION TO THE ABYSS!!
....
HARRIS ...?
... ARE YOU ASLEEP ...?
HM HM HMM!
HM HMM-MMM! ♪
IT'S GOTTEN PRETTY LATE...
I HOPE FATHER ISN'T ANGRY ...

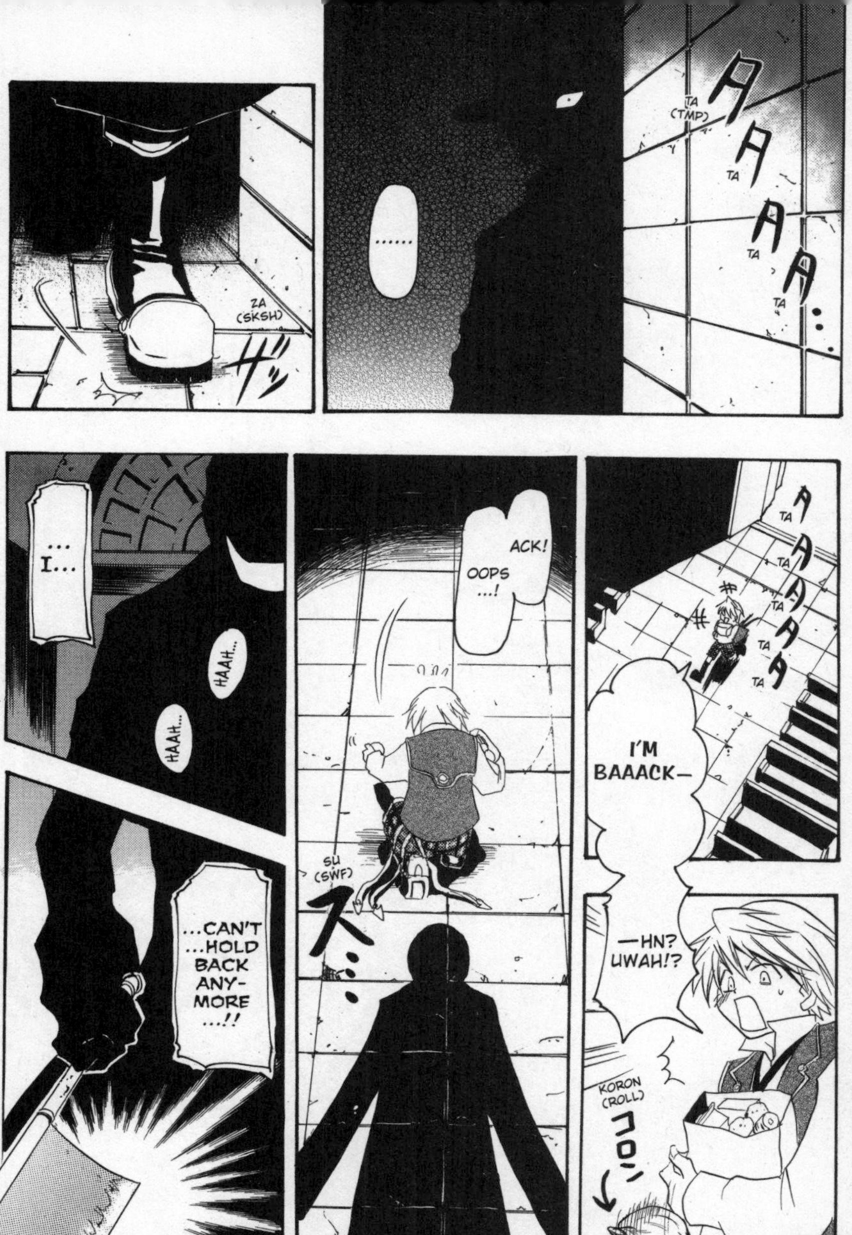

TA (TMP)
TA
TA
TA
......
ZA (SKSH)
TA
TA
TA
TA
TA
I'M BAAACK—
—HN? UWAH!?
KORON (ROLL)
ACK!
OOPS ...!
SU (SWF)
... I...
HAAH...
HAAH...
...CAN'T ...HOLD BACK ANY-MORE ...!!

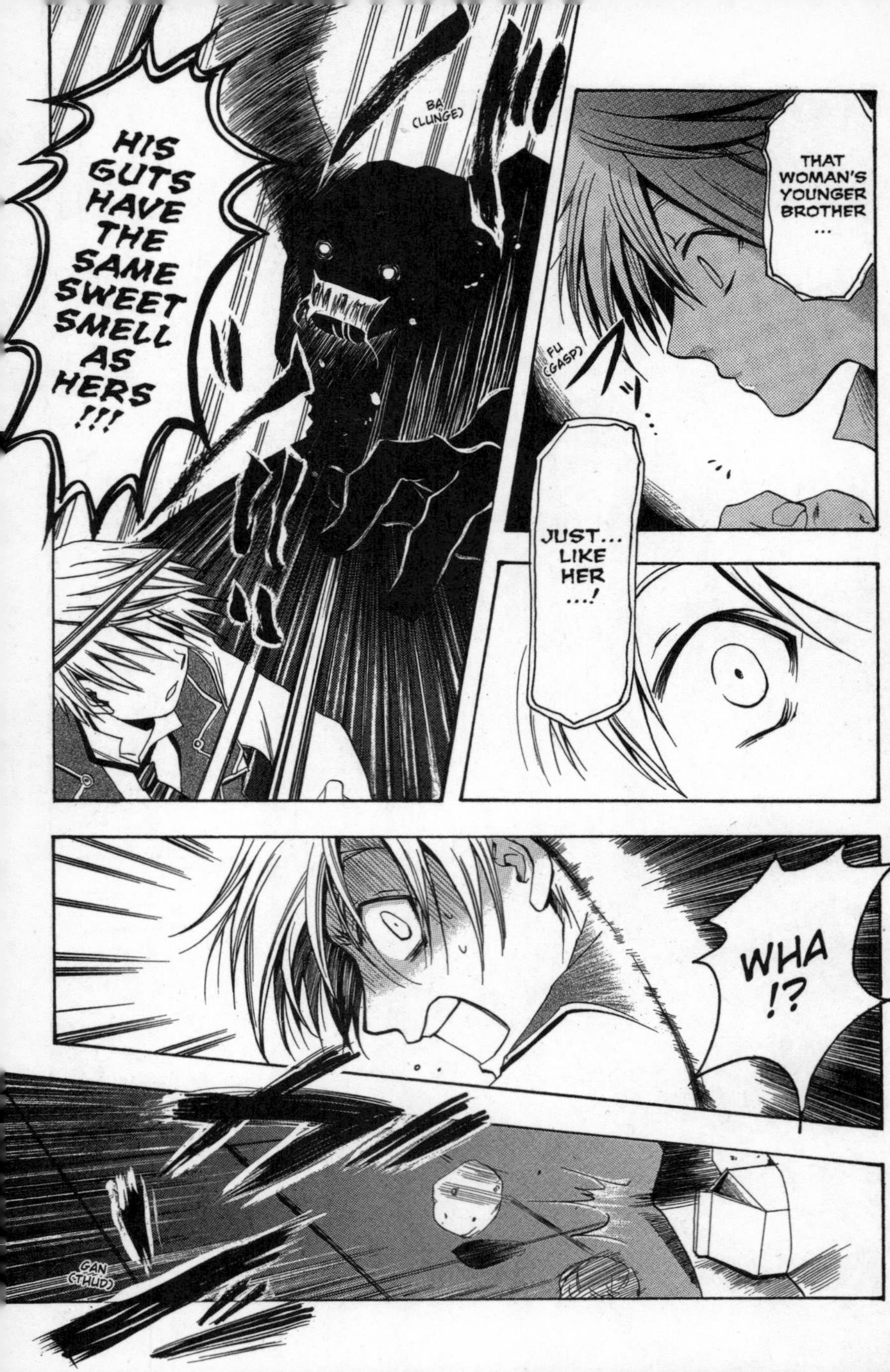
THAT WOMAN'S YOUNGER BROTHER ...
FU (GASP)
JUST... LIKE HER ...!
BA (LUNGE)
HIS GUTS HAVE THE SAME SWEET SMELL AS HERS !!!
WHA !?
GAN (THUD)

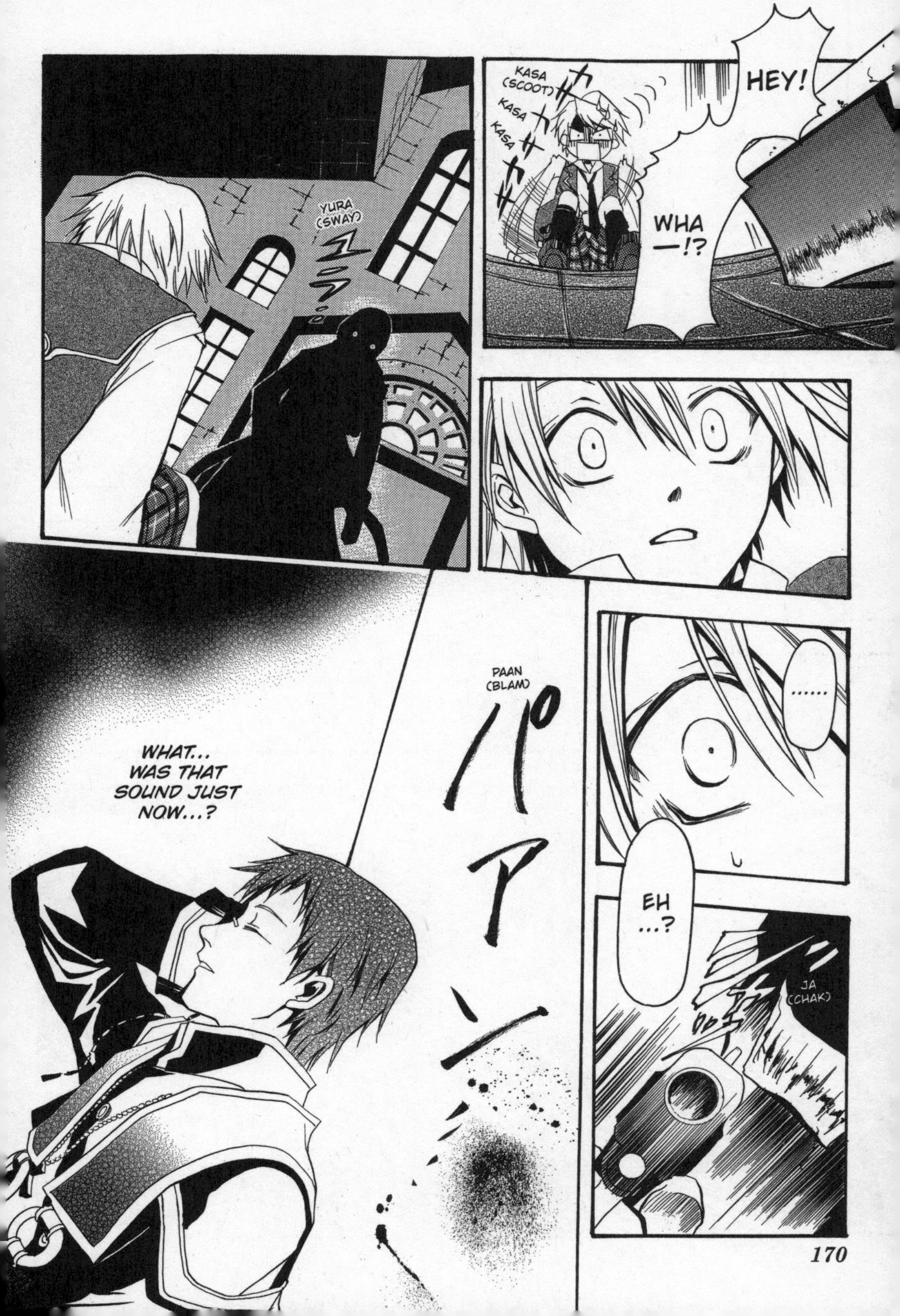
HEY!
KASA (SCOOT) KASA KASA
WHA—!?
YURA (SWAY)
......
EH ...?
JA (CHAK)
PAAN (BLAM)
WHAT... WAS THAT SOUND JUST NOW...?

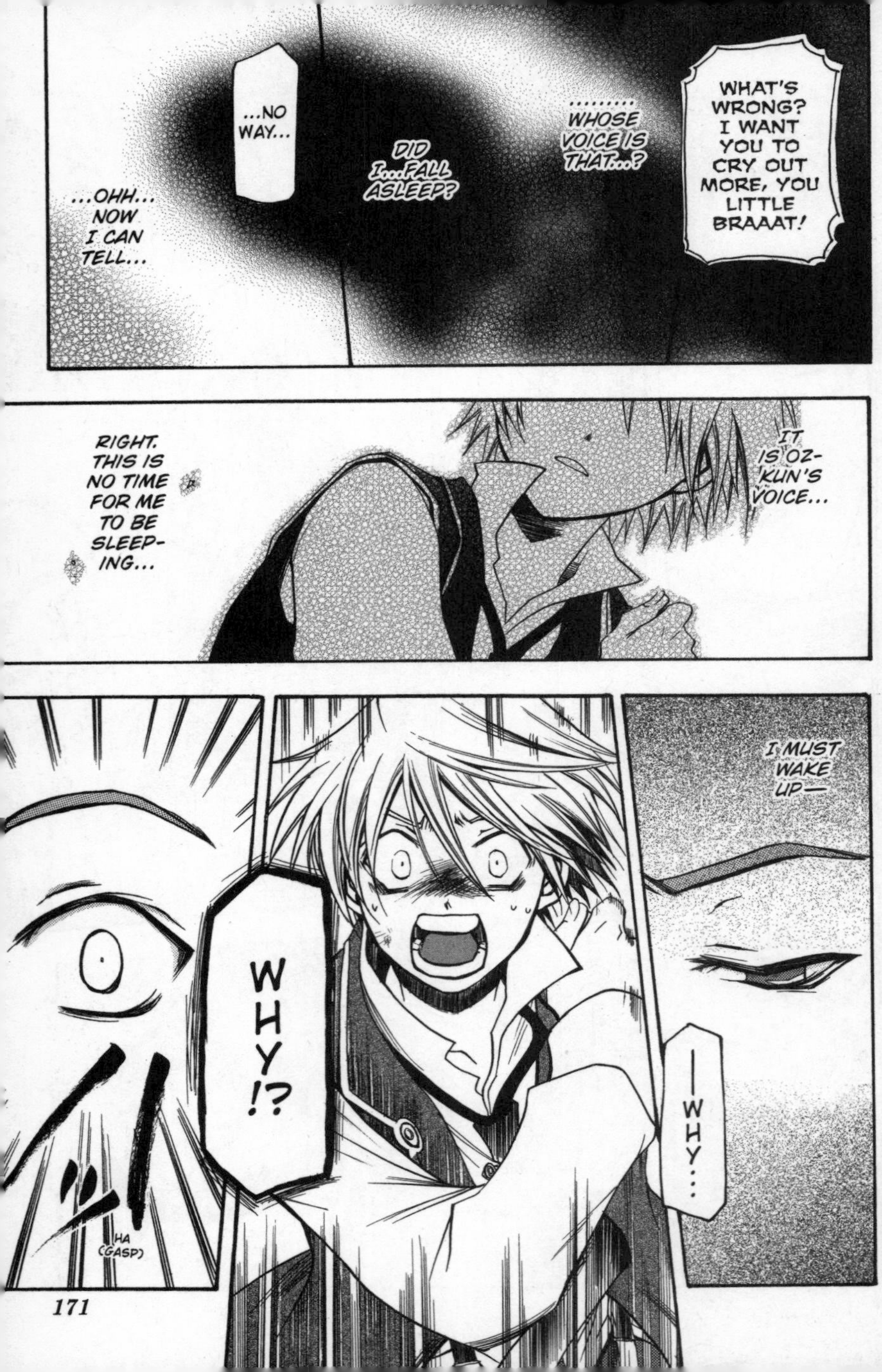
WHAT'S WRONG? I WANT YOU TO CRY OUT MORE, YOU LITTLE BRAAAT!
.........WHOSE VOICE IS THAT...?
DID I...FALL ASLEEP?
...NO WAY...
...OHH... NOW I CAN TELL...
IT IS OZ-KUN'S VOICE...
RIGHT. THIS IS NO TIME FOR ME TO BE SLEEPING...
I MUST WAKE UP—
—WHY...
WHY!?
HA (GASP)

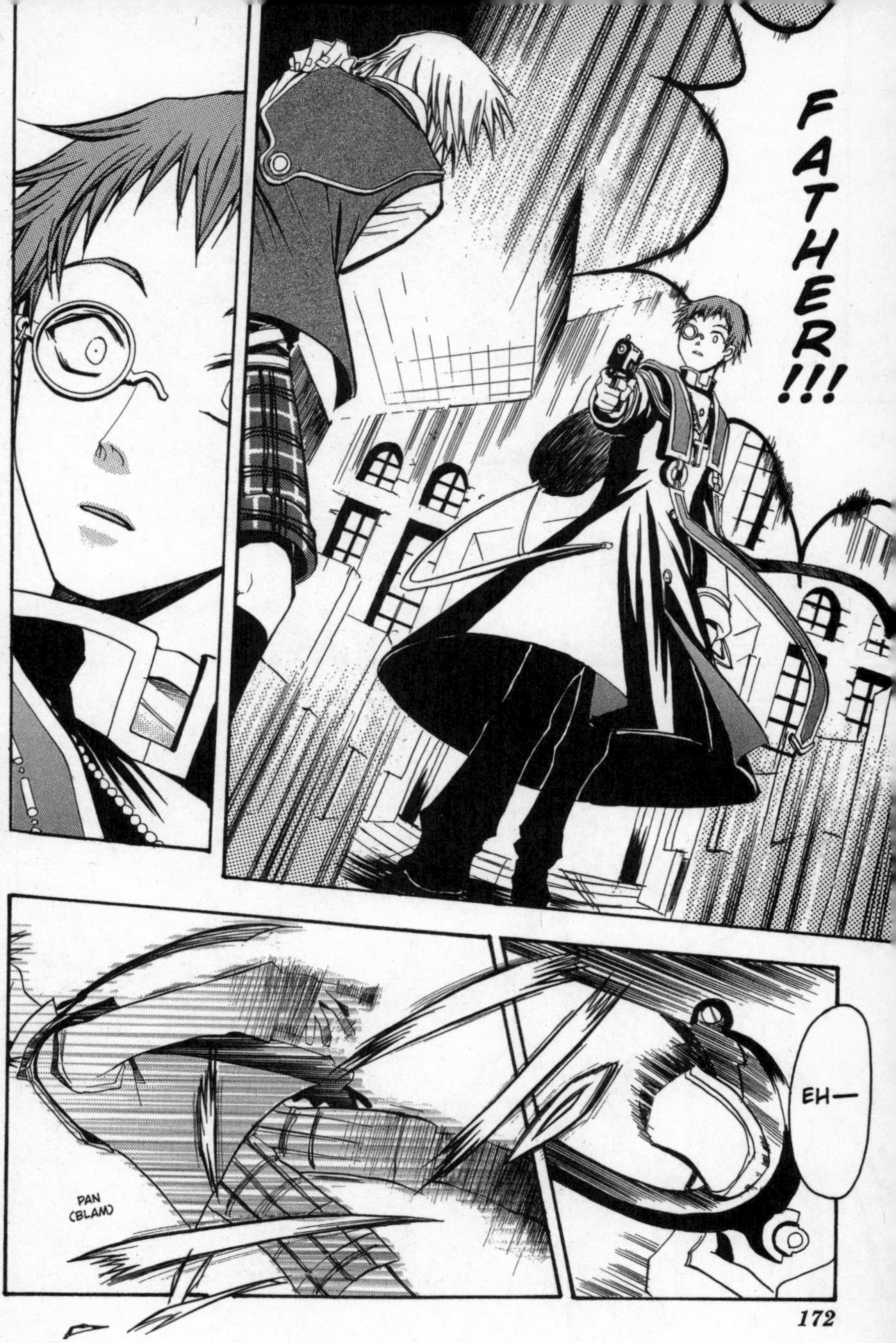
FATHER!!!
EH—
PAN
(BLAM)

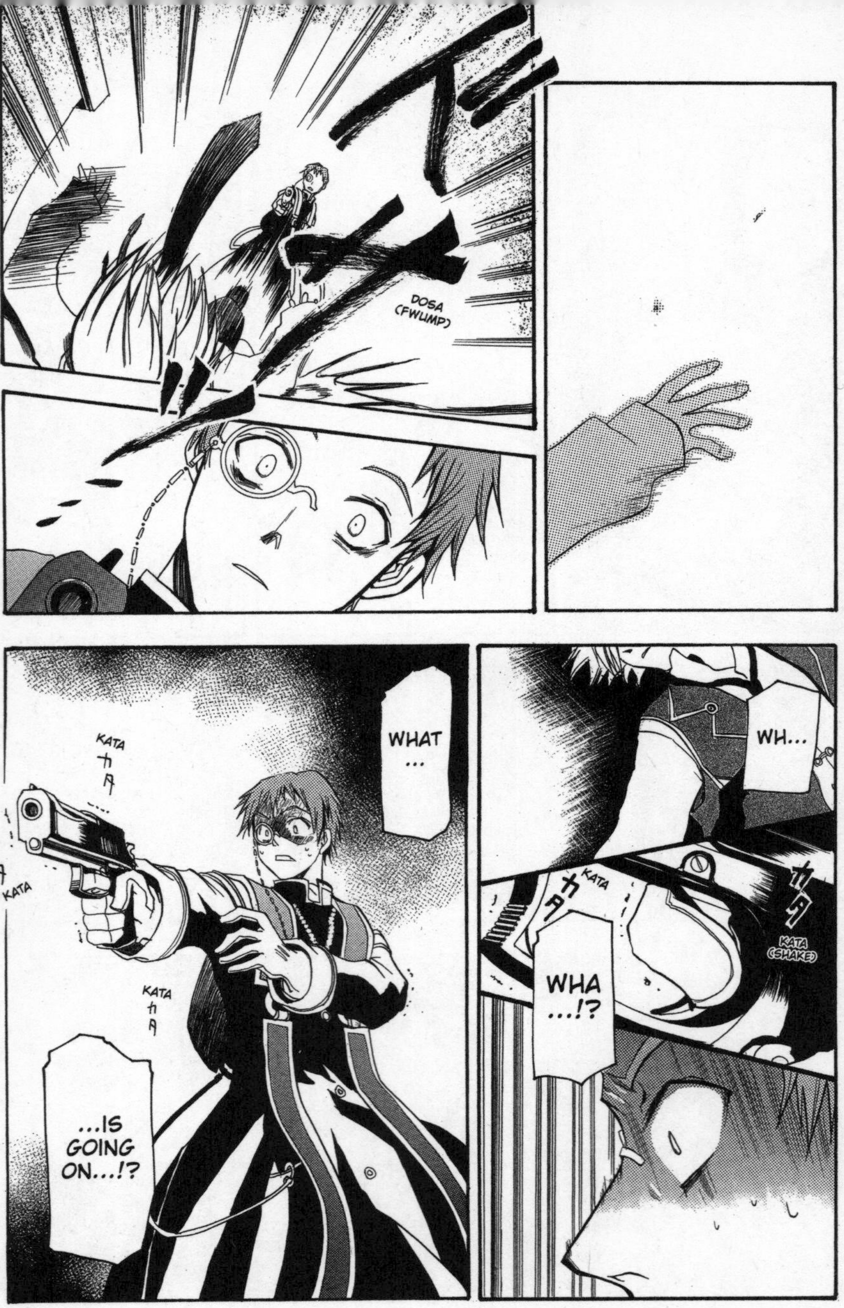
DOSA (FWUMP)
WH...
カタ
KATA
カタ
KATA (SHAKE)
WHA ...!?
WHAT ...
KATA
カタ
カタ
KATA
KATA
カタ
...IS GOING ON...!?

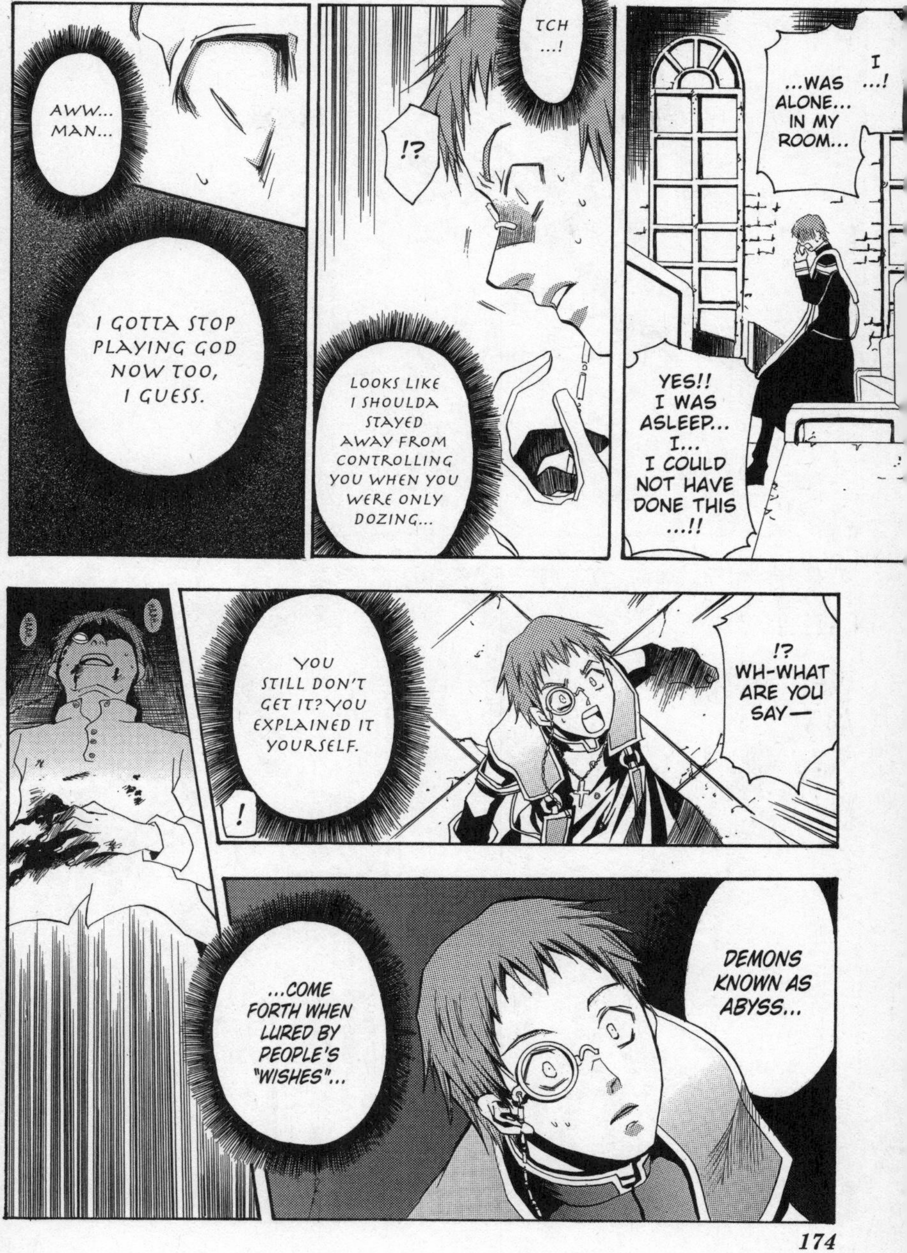

I ...!
...WAS ALONE... IN MY ROOM...
YES!! I WAS ASLEEP... I... I COULD NOT HAVE DONE THIS ...!!
TCH ...!
!?
LOOKS LIKE I SHOULDA STAYED AWAY FROM CONTROLLING YOU WHEN YOU WERE ONLY DOZING...
AWW... MAN...
I GOTTA STOP PLAYING GOD NOW TOO, I GUESS.
!? WH-WHAT ARE YOU SAY—
YOU STILL DON'T GET IT? YOU EXPLAINED IT YOURSELF.
!
DEMONS KNOWN AS ABYSS...
...COME FORTH WHEN LURED BY PEOPLE'S "WISHES"...

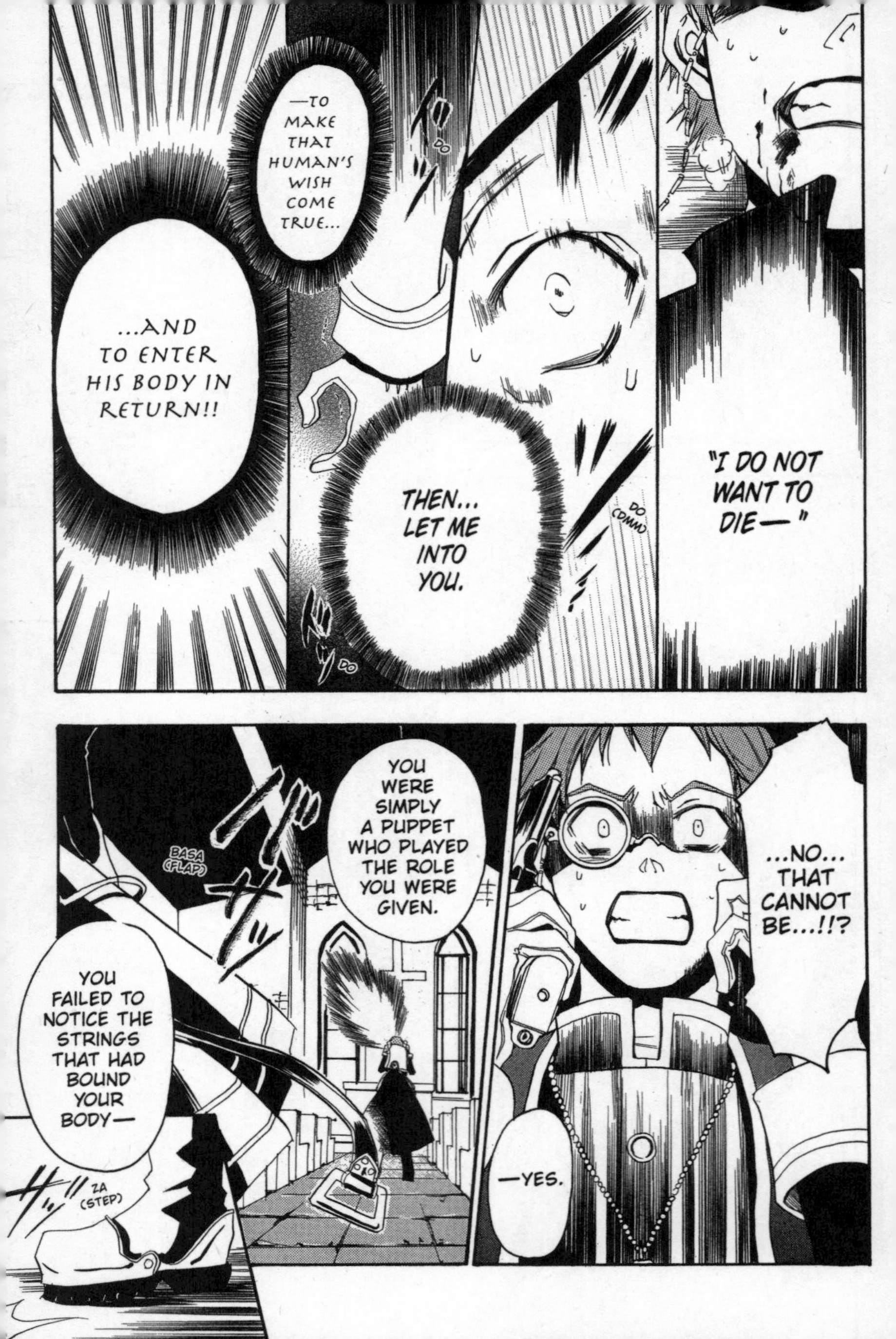
"I DO NOT WANT TO DIE—"
DO
DO (DMM)
THEN... LET ME INTO YOU.
DO
—TO MAKE THAT HUMAN'S WISH COME TRUE...
...AND TO ENTER HIS BODY IN RETURN!!
...NO... THAT CANNOT BE...!!?
—YES.
YOU WERE SIMPLY A PUPPET WHO PLAYED THE ROLE YOU WERE GIVEN.
BASA (FLAP)
YOU FAILED TO NOTICE THE STRINGS THAT HAD BOUND YOUR BODY—
ZA (STEP)

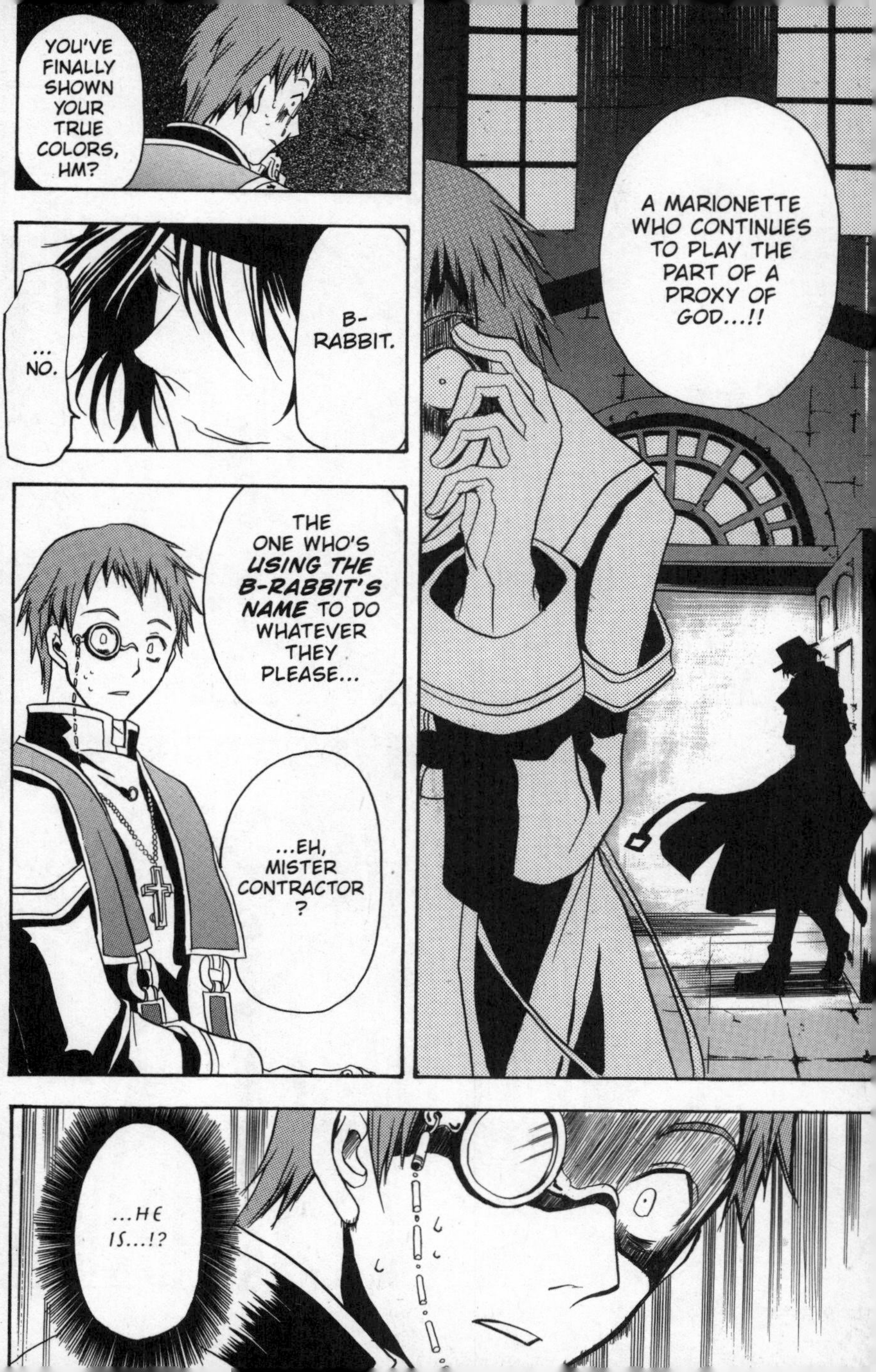
A MARIONETTE WHO CONTINUES TO PLAY THE PART OF A PROXY OF GOD...!!
YOU'VE FINALLY SHOWN YOUR TRUE COLORS, HM?
B-RABBIT.
... NO.
THE ONE WHO'S USING THE B-RABBIT'S NAME TO DO WHATEVER THEY PLEASE...
...EH, MISTER CONTRACTOR?
...HE IS...!?

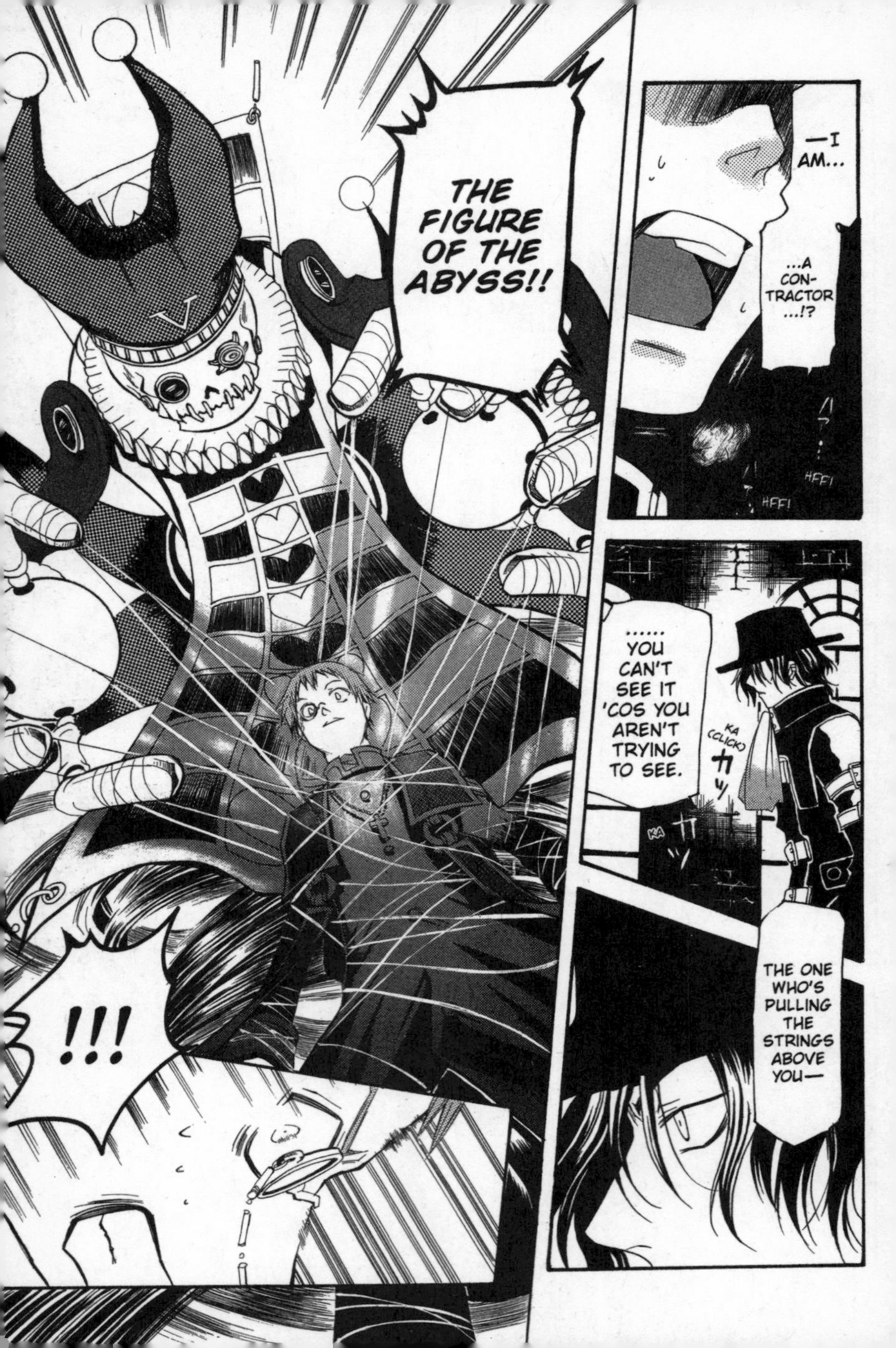
—I AM...
...A CONTRACTOR ...!?
HFF! HFF!
...... YOU CAN'T SEE IT 'COS YOU AREN'T TRYING TO SEE.
KA (CLICK)
KA
THE ONE WHO'S PULLING THE STRINGS ABOVE YOU—
THE FIGURE OF THE ABYSS!!
!!!

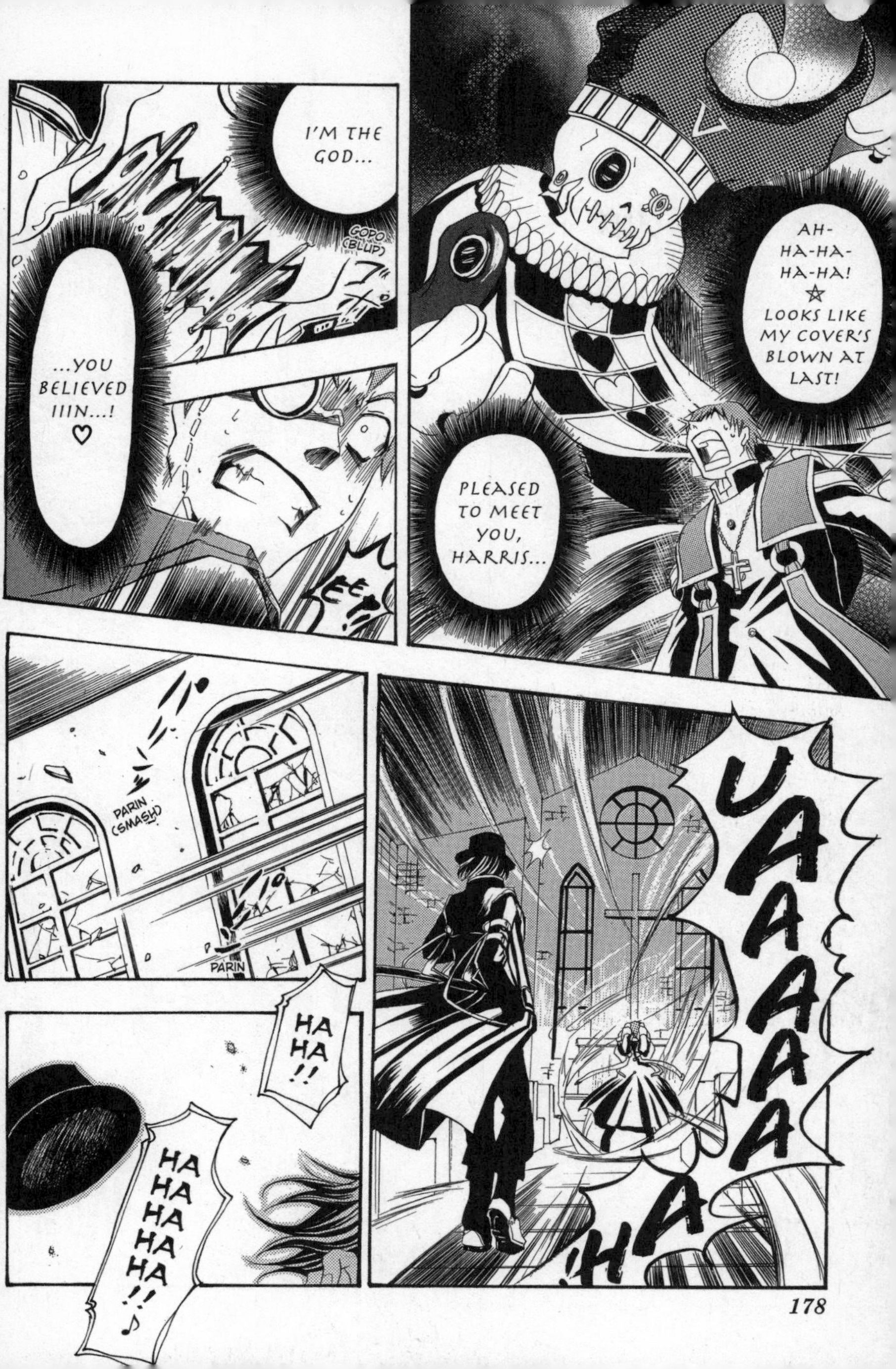
AH-HA-HA-HA-HA! ☆ LOOKS LIKE MY COVER'S BLOWN AT LAST!
PLEASED TO MEET YOU, HARRIS...
I'M THE GOD...
GOPO (BLUP)
...YOU BELIEVED IIIN...! ♡
EE?!
UAAAAAAAAAH!
PARIN (SMASH)
PARIN
HA HA!!
HA HA HA HA HA!!♪

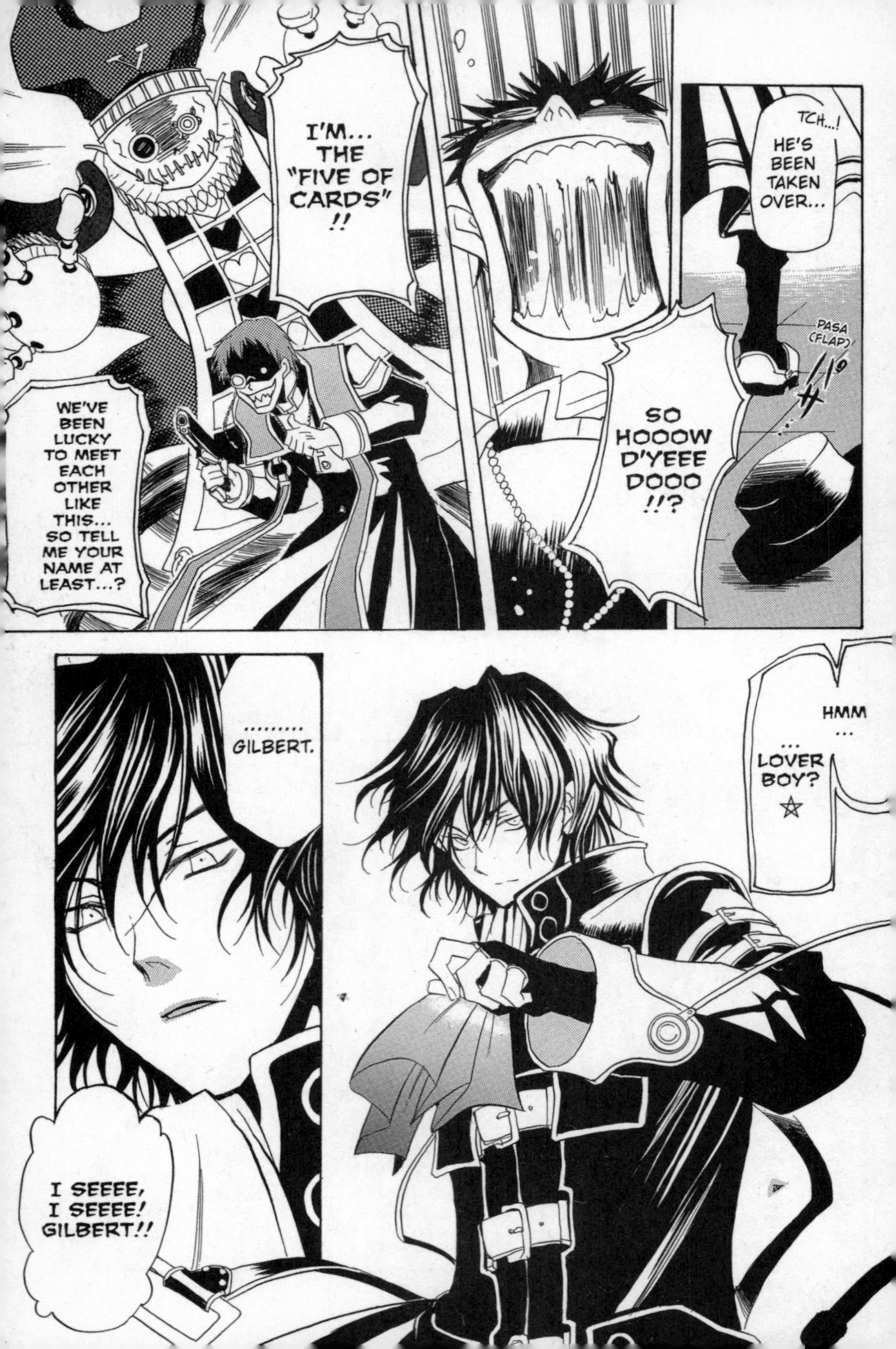

TCH...!
HE'S BEEN TAKEN OVER...
PASA (FLAP)
SO HOOOW D'YEEE DOOO !!?
I'M... THE "FIVE OF CARDS" !!
WE'VE BEEN LUCKY TO MEET EACH OTHER LIKE THIS... SO TELL ME YOUR NAME AT LEAST...?
HMM ... ...LOVER BOY? ☆
.... GILBERT.
I SEEEE, I SEEEE! GILBERT!!

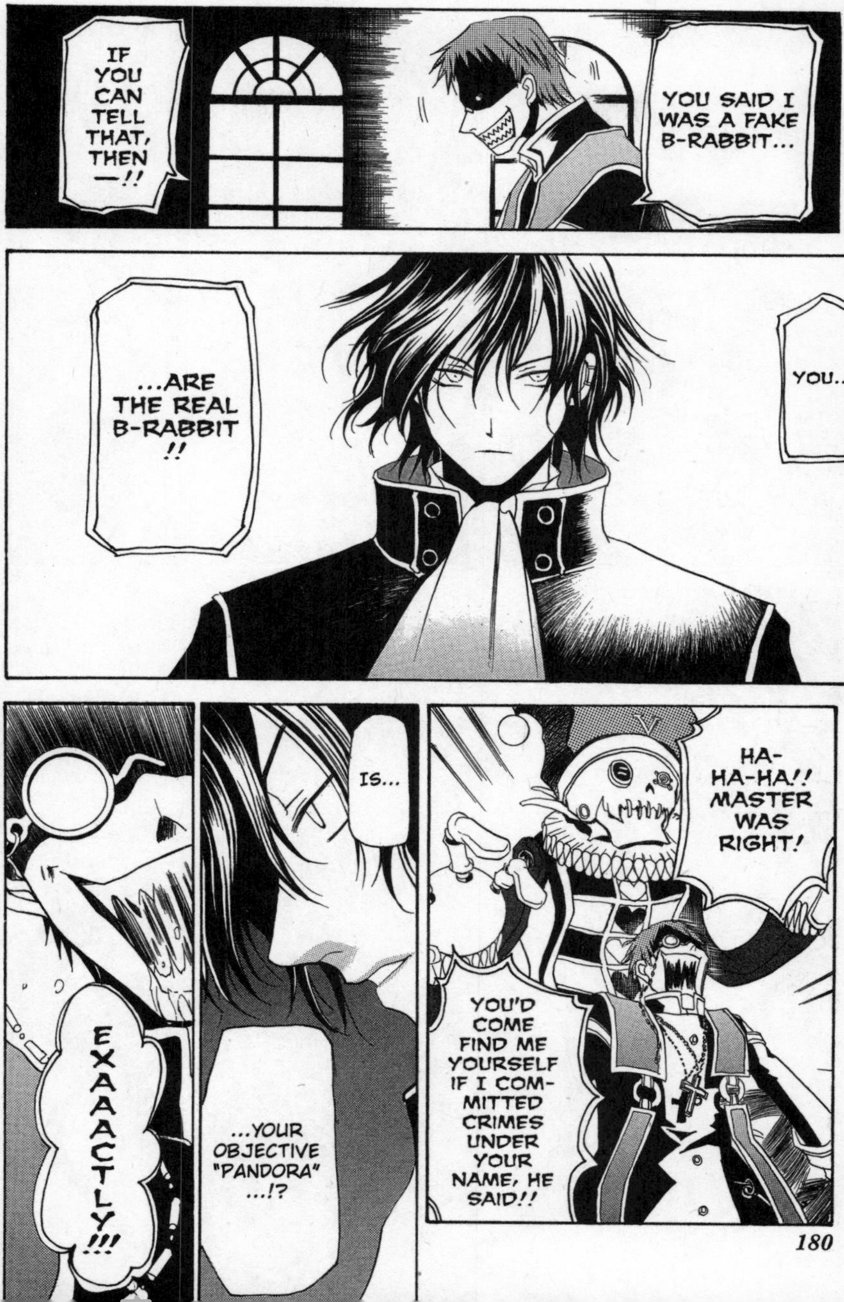
YOU SAID I WAS A FAKE B-RABBIT...
IF YOU CAN TELL THAT, THEN—!!
YOU...
...ARE THE REAL B-RABBIT!!
HA-HA-HA!! MASTER WAS RIGHT!
YOU'D COME FIND ME YOURSELF IF I COM-MITTED CRIMES UNDER YOUR NAME, HE SAID!!
IS...
...YOUR OBJECTIVE "PANDORA" ...!?
EXAAACTLY!!!

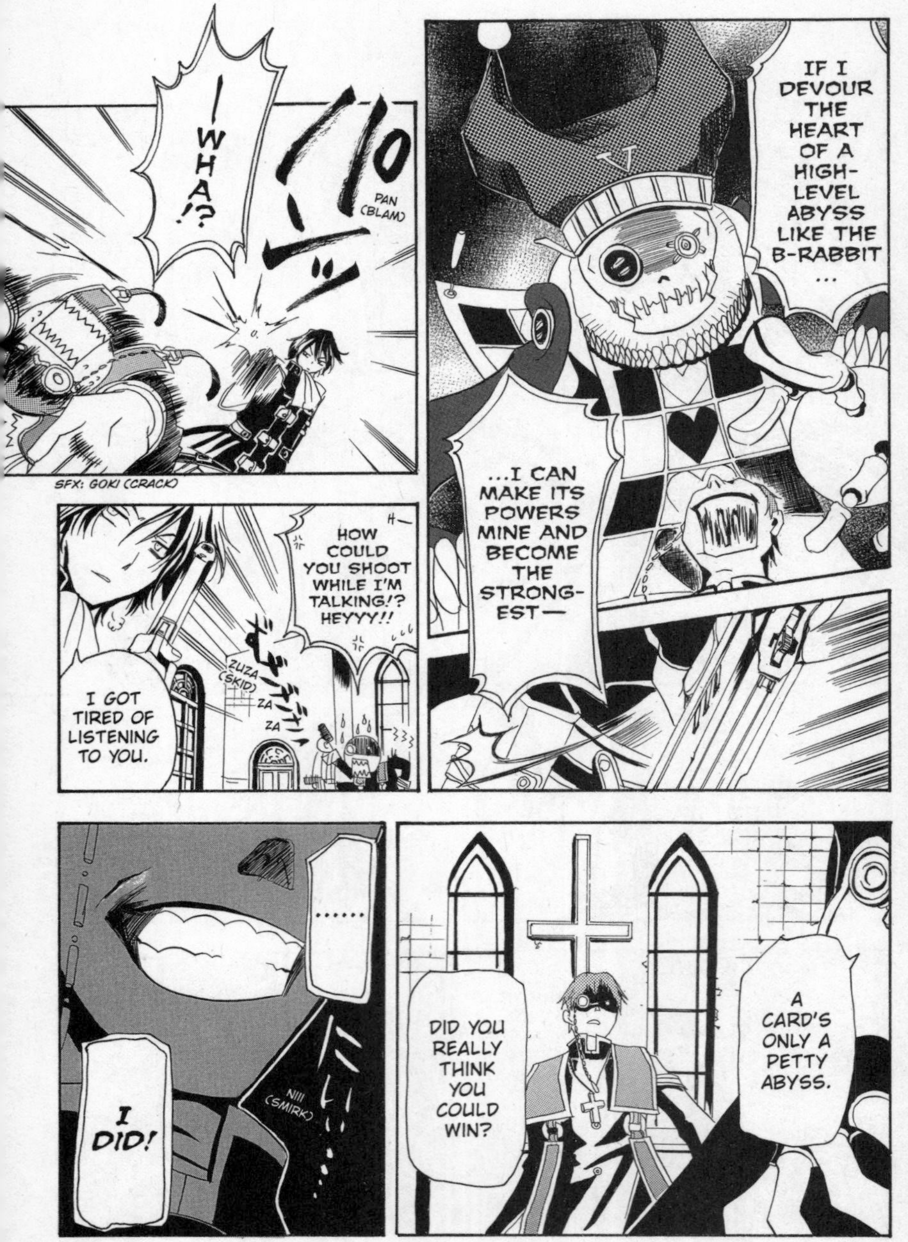
IF I DEVOUR THE HEART OF A HIGH-LEVEL ABYSS LIKE THE B-RABBIT...
...I CAN MAKE ITS POWERS MINE AND BECOME THE STRONG-EST—
WHA!?
PAN (BLAM)
SFX: GOKI (CRACK)
H—
HOW COULD YOU SHOOT WHILE I'M TALKING!? HEYYY!!
ZUZA (SKID)
ZA
ZA
I GOT TIRED OF LISTENING TO YOU.
A CARD'S ONLY A PETTY ABYSS.
DID YOU REALLY THINK YOU COULD WIN?
......
NIII (SMIRK)
I DID!

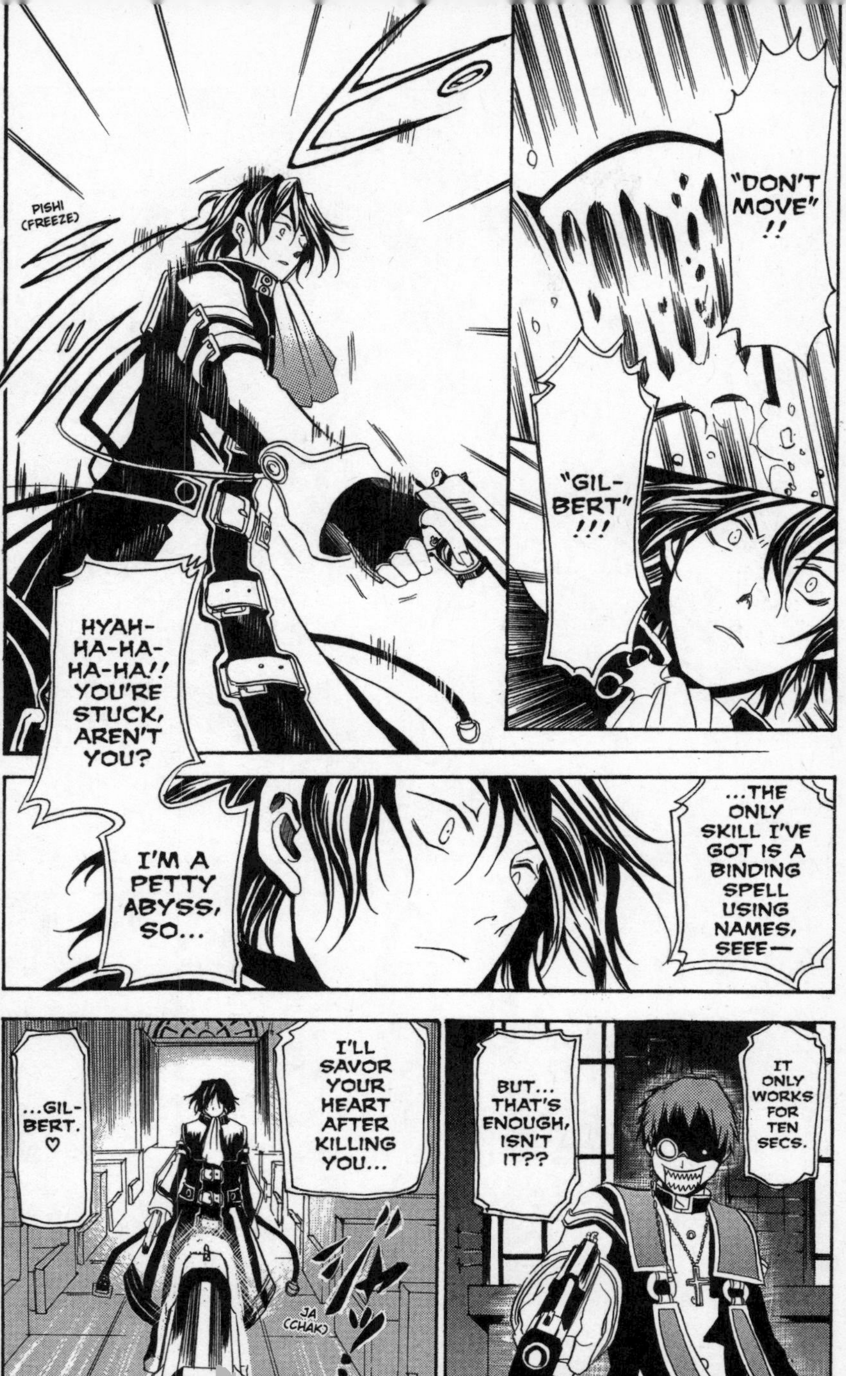
"DON'T MOVE"!!
"GIL-BERT"!!!
PISHI (FREEZE)
HYAH-HA-HA-HA-HA!! YOU'RE STUCK, AREN'T YOU?
...THE ONLY SKILL I'VE GOT IS A BINDING SPELL USING NAMES, SEEE—
I'M A PETTY ABYSS, SO...
IT ONLY WORKS FOR TEN SECS.
BUT... THAT'S ENOUGH, ISN'T IT??
I'LL SAVOR YOUR HEART AFTER KILLING YOU...
JA (CHAK)
...GIL-BERT. ♡

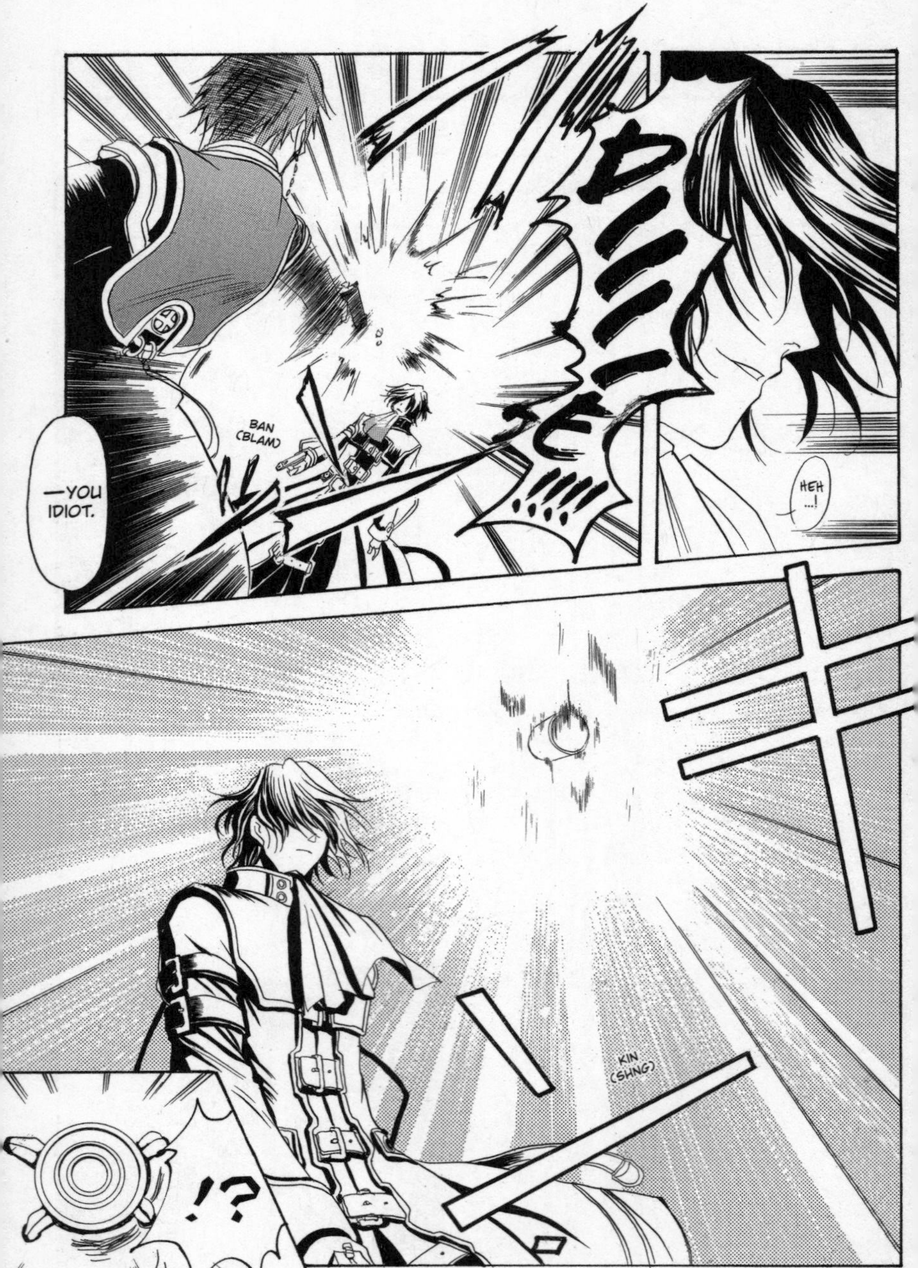
HEH ...!
BAN (BLAM)
—YOU IDIOT.
KIN (SHNG)
!?

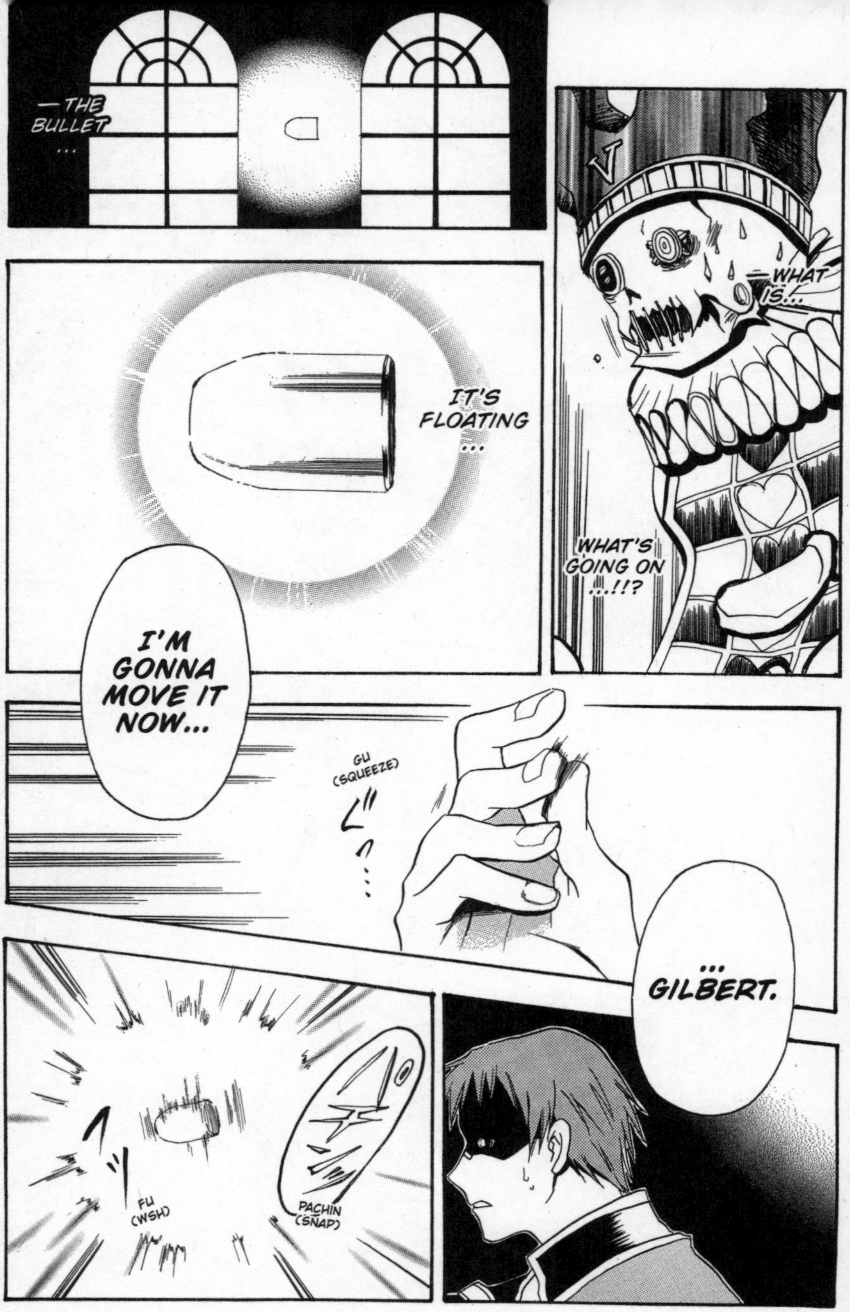
—WHAT IS...
WHAT'S GOING ON ...!!?
—THE BULLET ...
IT'S FLOATING ...
I'M GONNA MOVE IT NOW...
GU (SQUEEZE)
... GILBERT.
PACHIN (SNAP)
FU (WSH)

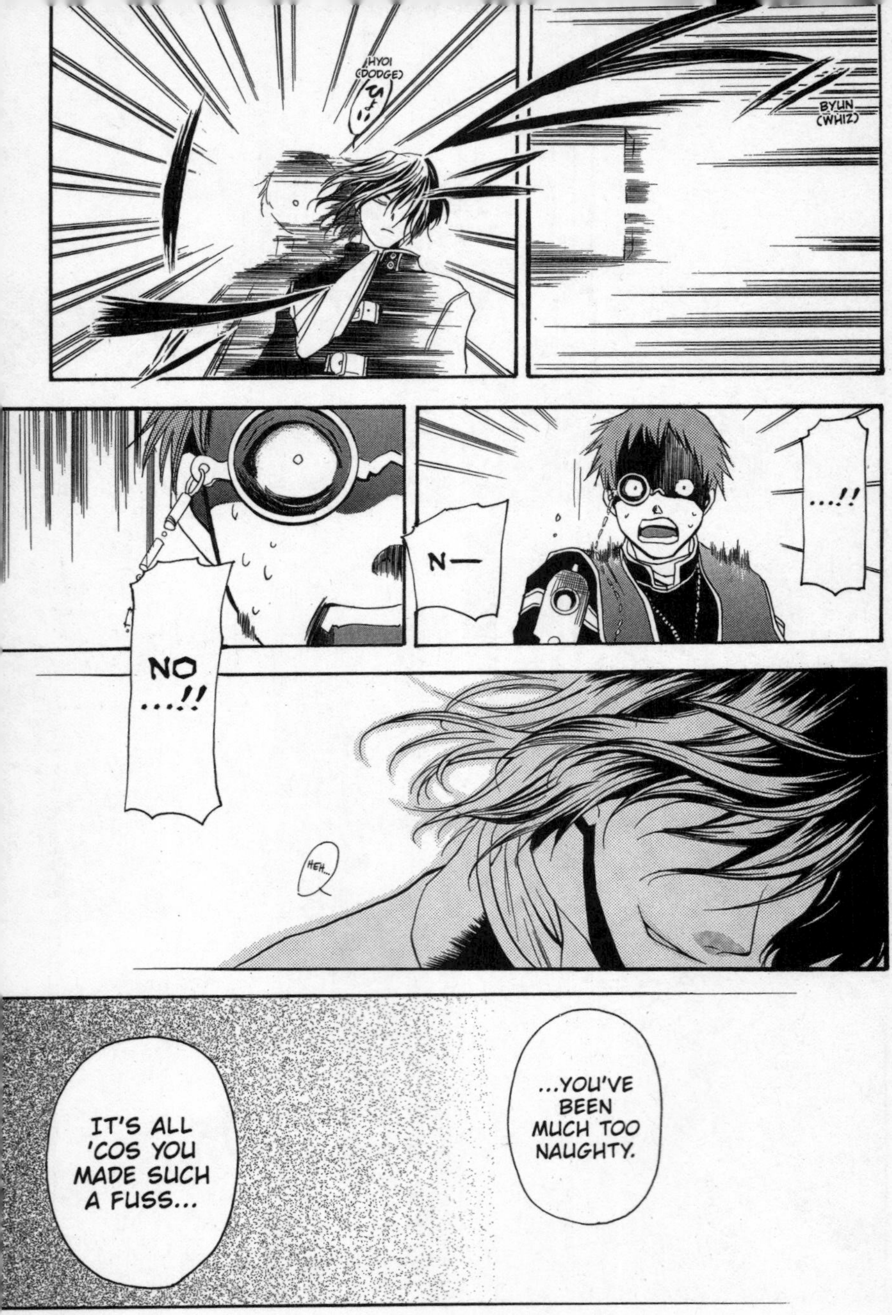
BYUN (WHIZ)
HYOI (DODGE)
...!!
N—
NO ...!!
HEH...
...YOU'VE BEEN MUCH TOO NAUGHTY.
IT'S ALL 'COS YOU MADE SUCH A FUSS...

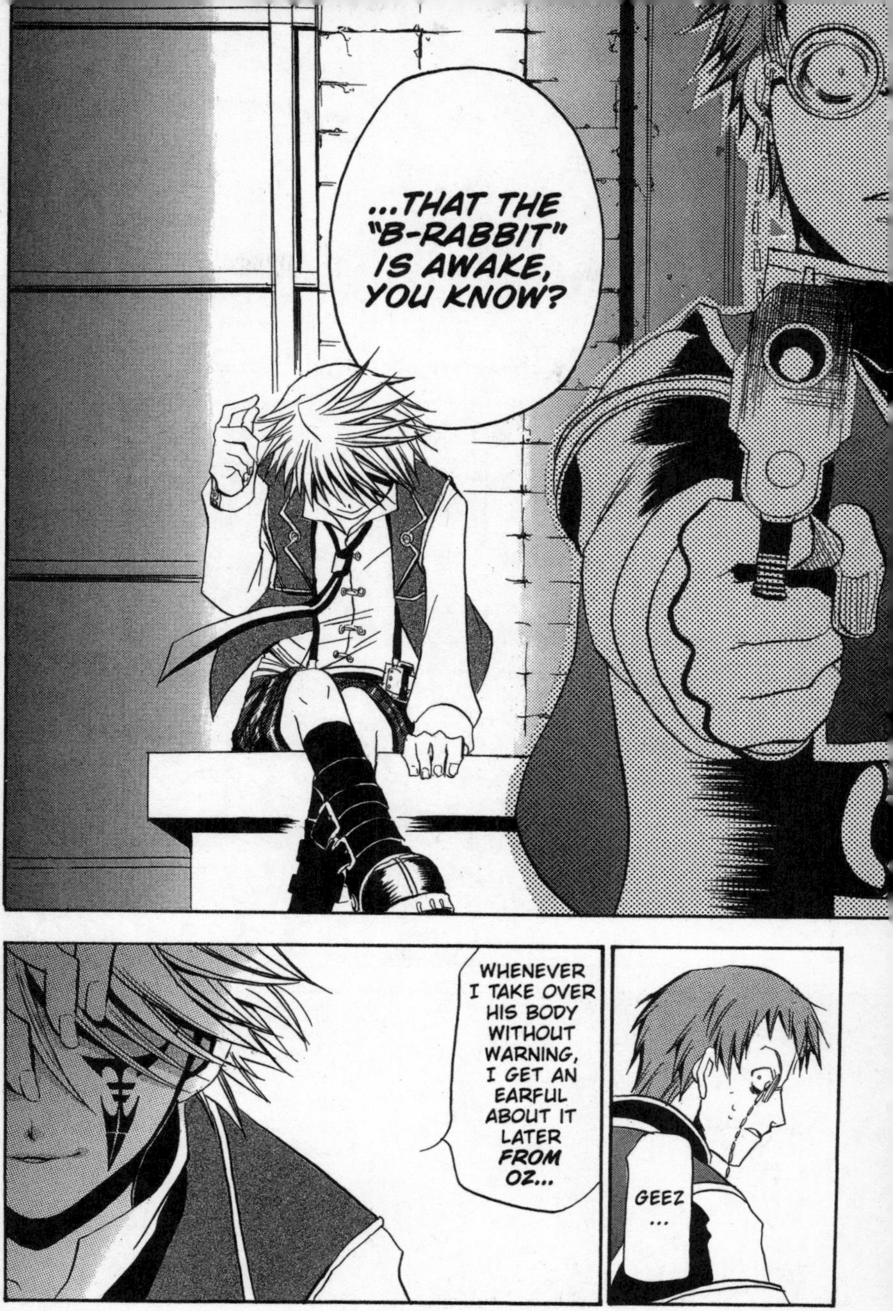
...THAT THE "B-RABBIT" IS AWAKE, YOU KNOW?
GEEZ ...
WHENEVER I TAKE OVER HIS BODY WITHOUT WARNING, I GET AN EARFUL ABOUT IT LATER *FROM* OZ...

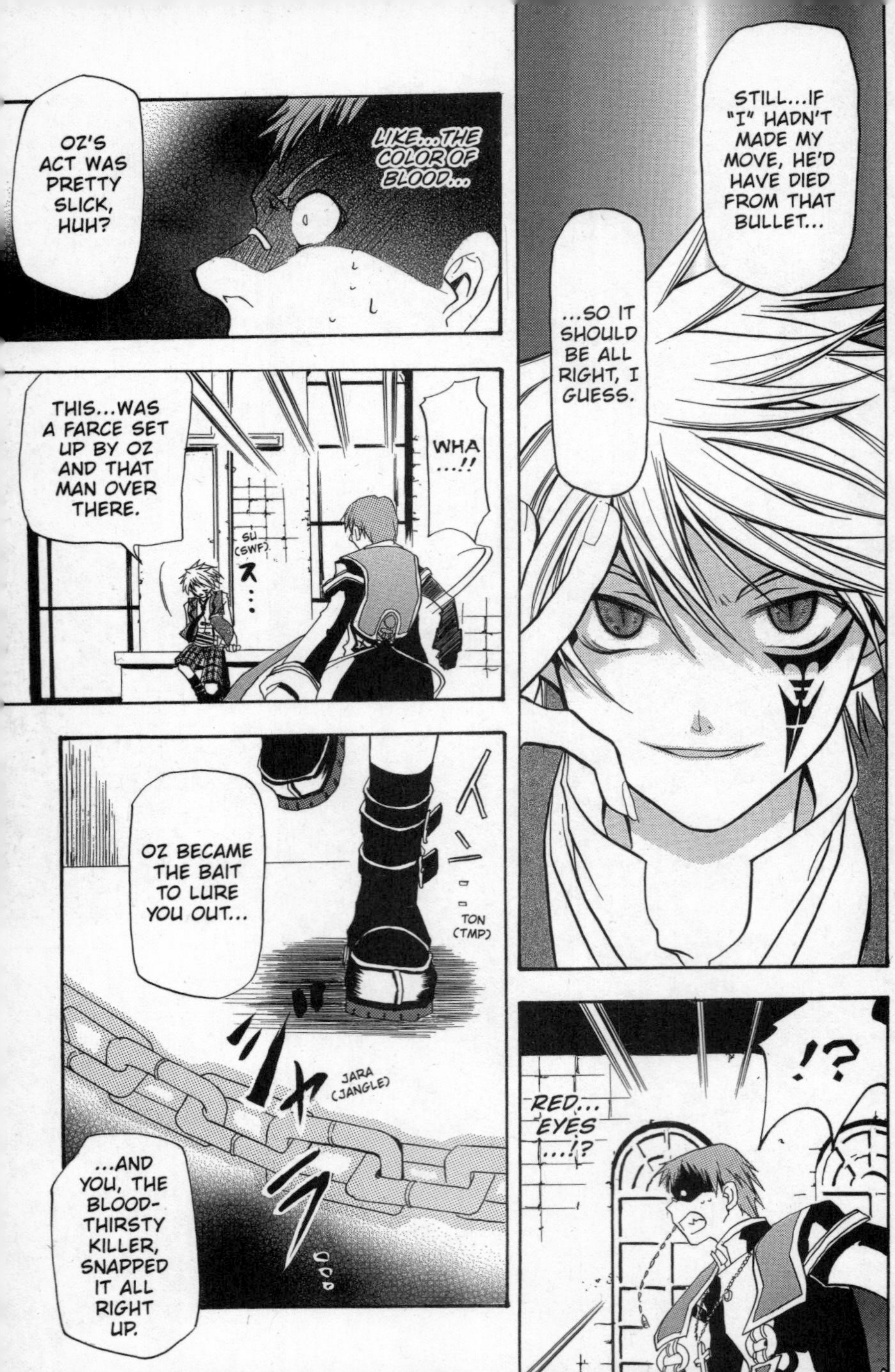
STILL...IF "I" HADN'T MADE MY MOVE, HE'D HAVE DIED FROM THAT BULLET...
...SO IT SHOULD BE ALL RIGHT, I GUESS.
!?
RED... EYES ...!?
LIKE...THE COLOR OF BLOOD...
OZ'S ACT WAS PRETTY SLICK, HUH?
WHA ...!!
THIS...WAS A FARCE SET UP BY OZ AND THAT MAN OVER THERE.
SU (SWF)
ス...
TON (TMP)
OZ BECAME THE BAIT TO LURE YOU OUT...
JARA (JANGLE)
...AND YOU, THE BLOOD-THIRSTY KILLER, SNAPPED IT ALL RIGHT UP.

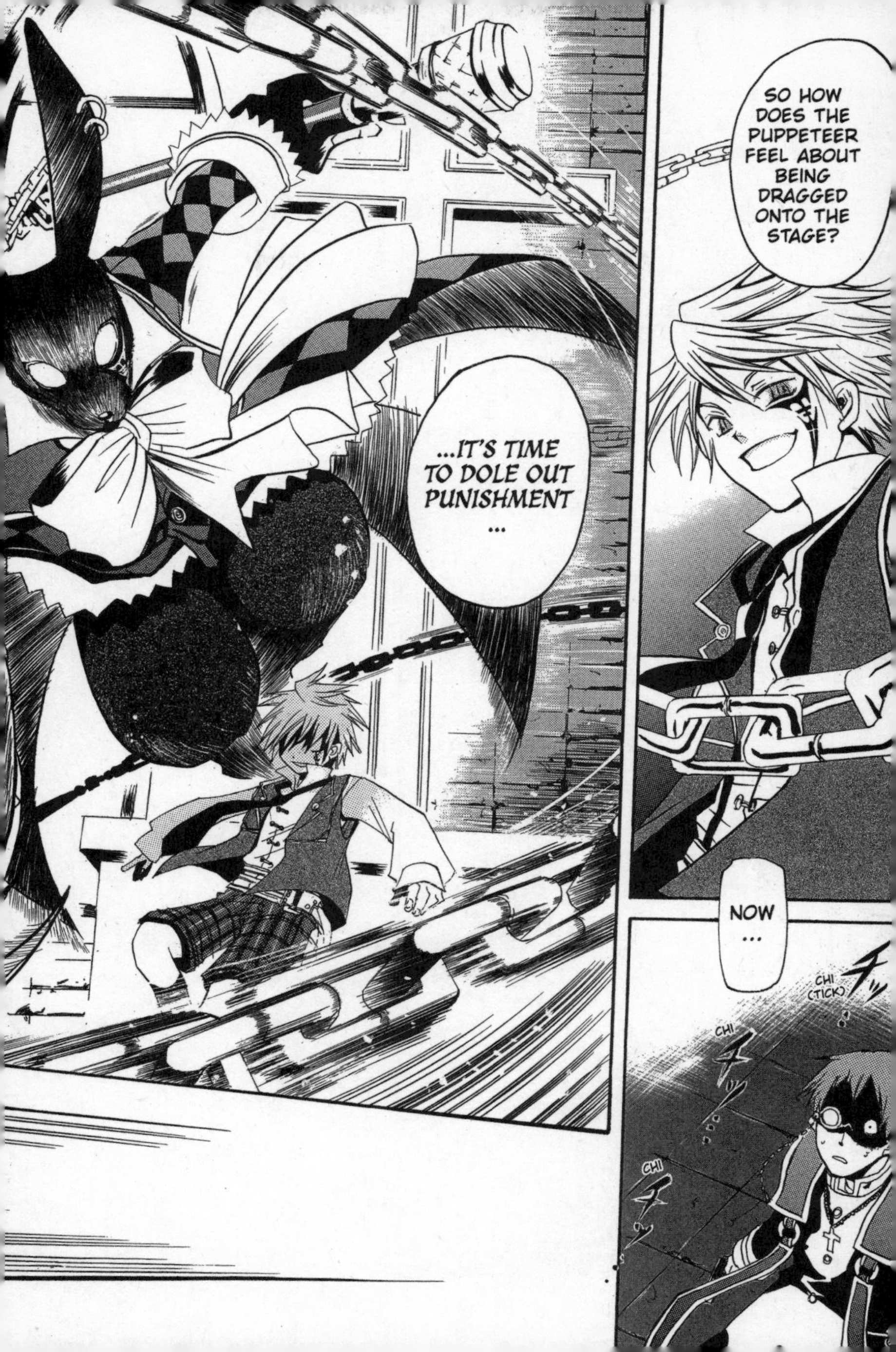
SO HOW DOES THE PUPPETEER FEEL ABOUT BEING DRAGGED ONTO THE STAGE?
...IT'S TIME TO DOLE OUT PUNISHMENT ...
NOW ...
CHI (TICK)
CHI
CHI

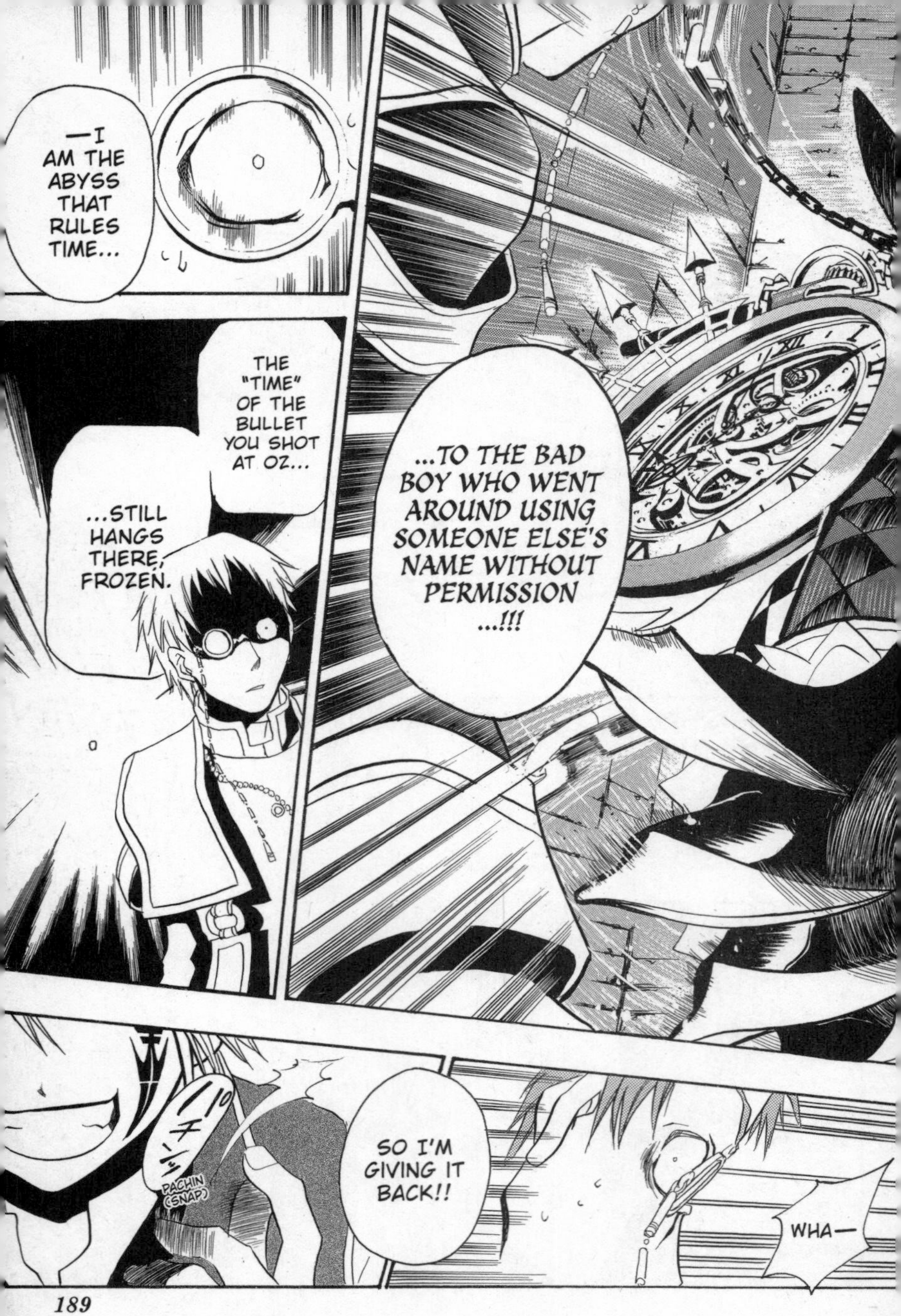
—I AM THE ABYSS THAT RULES TIME...
THE "TIME" OF THE BULLET YOU SHOT AT OZ...
...STILL HANGS THERE, FROZEN.
...TO THE BAD BOY WHO WENT AROUND USING SOMEONE ELSE'S NAME WITHOUT PERMISSION ...!!!
SO I'M GIVING IT BACK!!
WHA—
PACHIN (SNAP)

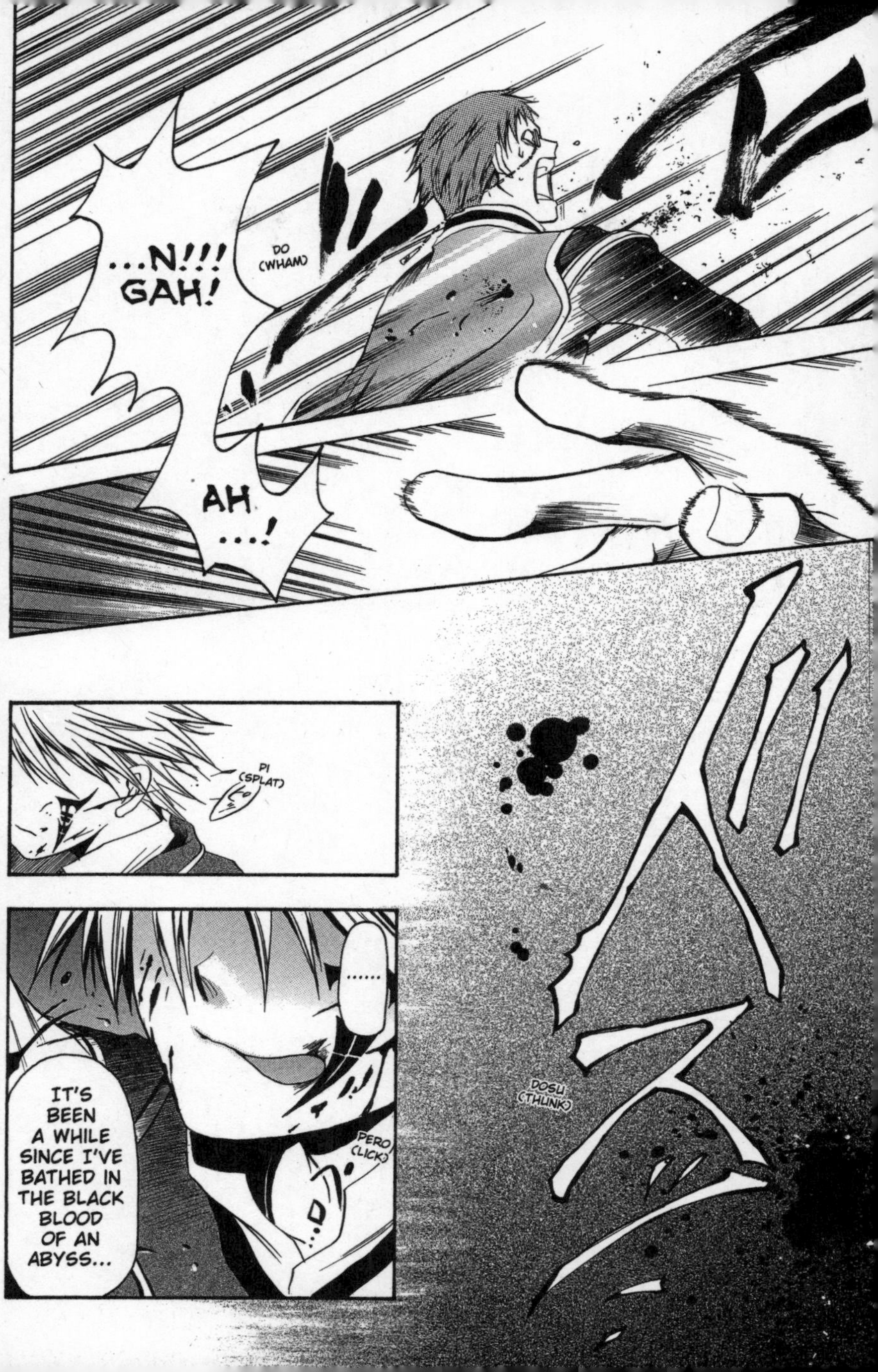
DO (WHAM)
...N!!! GAH!
AH ...!
DOSU (THUNK)
PI (SPLAT)
......
IT'S BEEN A WHILE SINCE I'VE BATHED IN THE BLACK BLOOD OF AN ABYSS...
PERO (LICK)

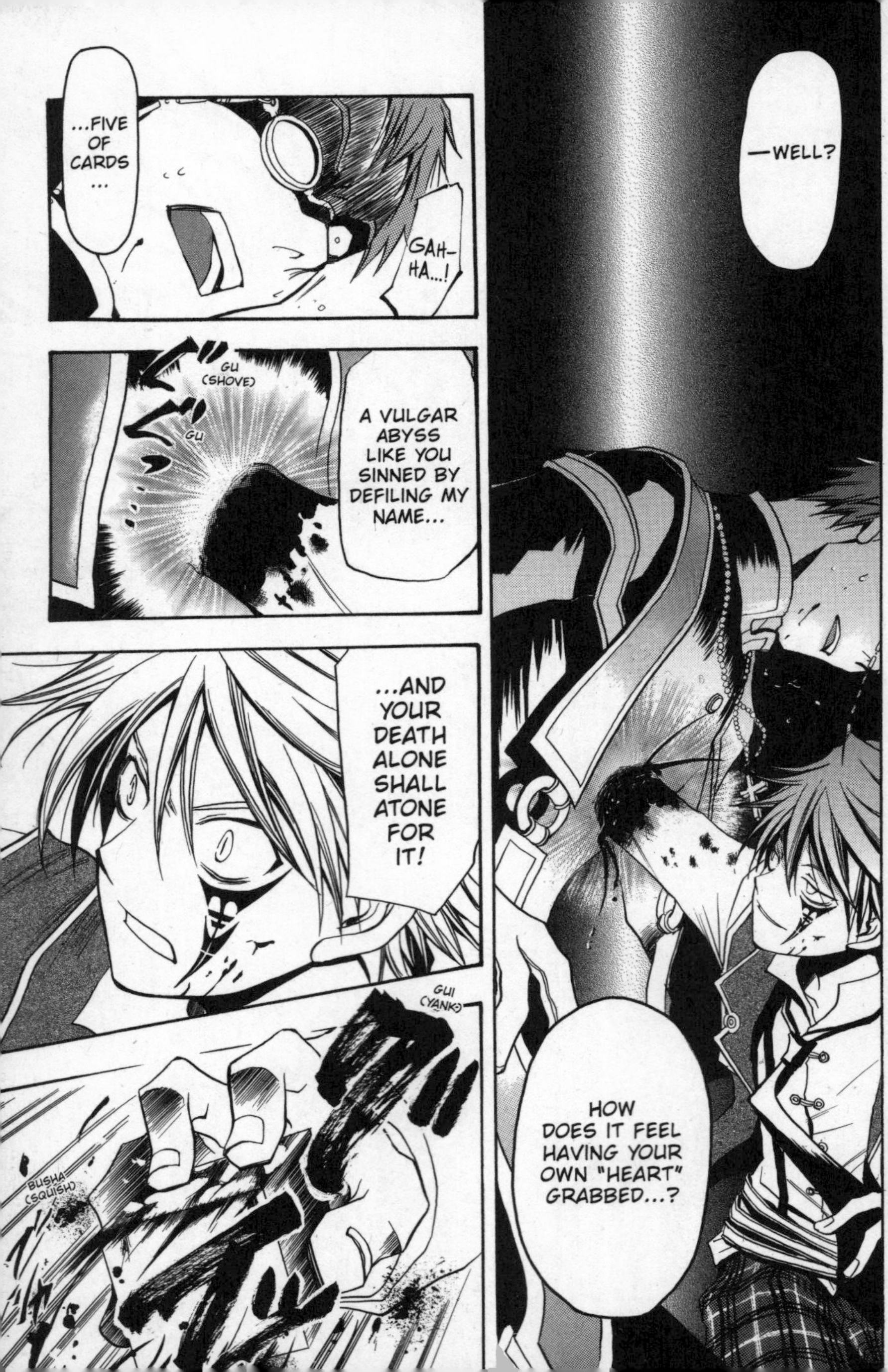
—WELL?
HOW DOES IT FEEL HAVING YOUR OWN "HEART" GRABBED...?
...FIVE OF CARDS ...
GAH-HA...!
A VULGAR ABYSS LIKE YOU SINNED BY DEFILING MY NAME...
GU (SHOVE)
GU
...AND YOUR DEATH ALONE SHALL ATONE FOR IT!
GUI (YANK)
BUSHA (SQUISH)

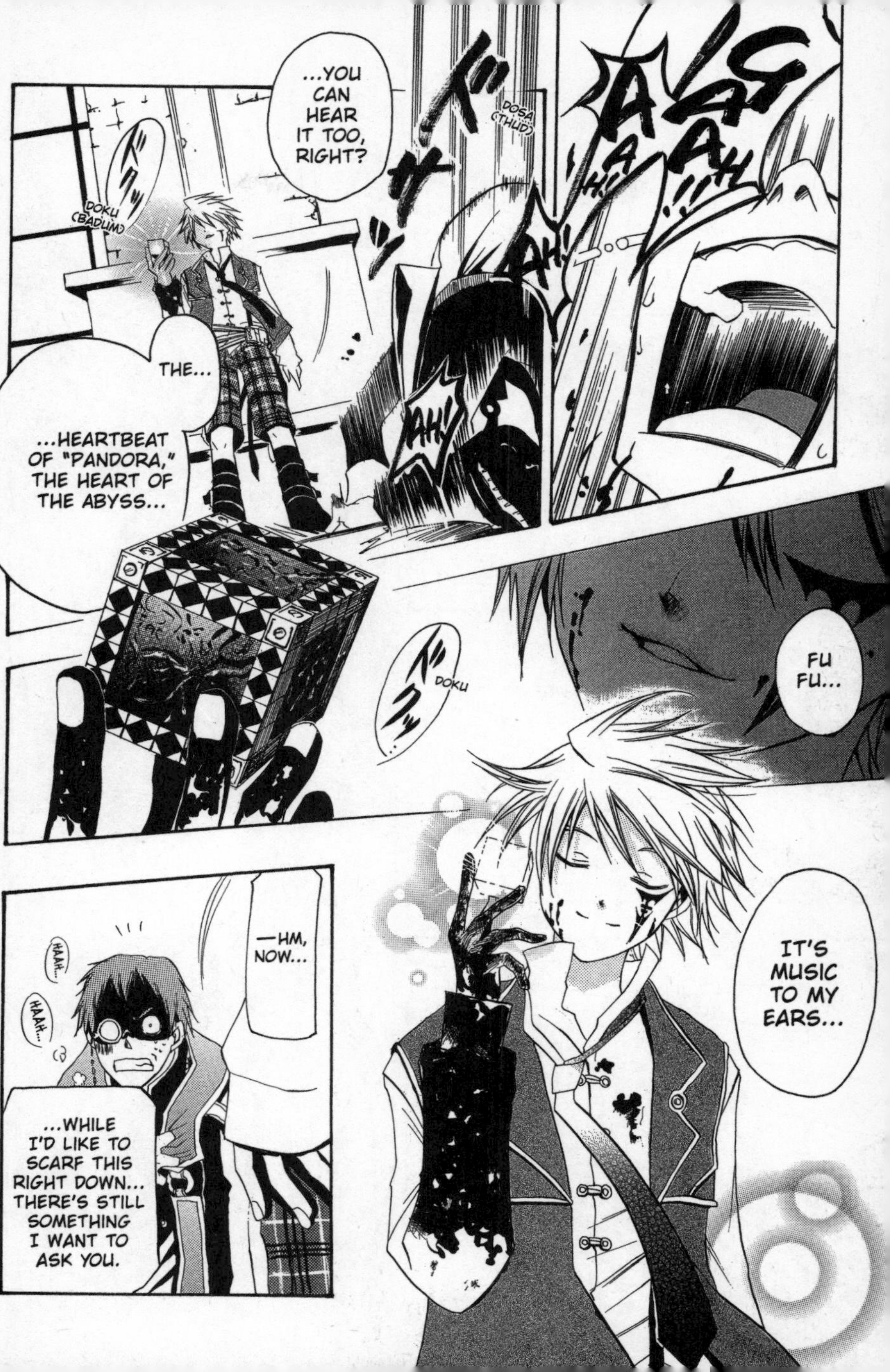

AH!
AH!
DOSA (THUD)
...YOU CAN HEAR IT TOO, RIGHT?
AH!
DOKU (BADUM)
FU FU...
DOKU
THE...
...HEARTBEAT OF "PANDORA," THE HEART OF THE ABYSS...
IT'S MUSIC TO MY EARS...
—HM, NOW...
HAAH...
HAAH...
...WHILE I'D LIKE TO SCARF THIS RIGHT DOWN... THERE'S STILL SOMETHING I WANT TO ASK YOU.

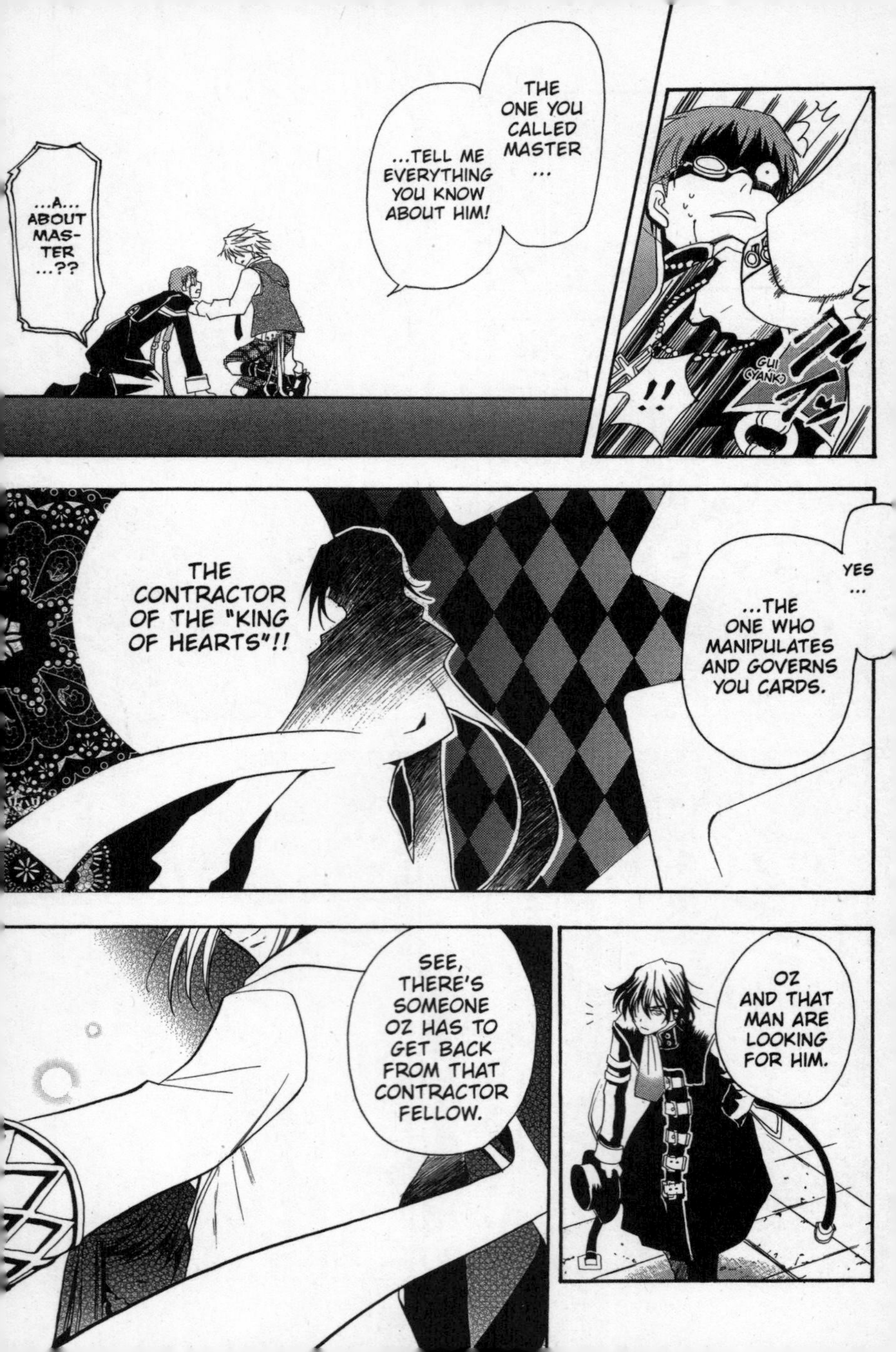
GUI (YANK)
!!
THE ONE YOU CALLED MASTER ...
...TELL ME EVERYTHING YOU KNOW ABOUT HIM!
...A... ABOUT MAS- TER ...??
YES ...
...THE ONE WHO MANIPULATES AND GOVERNS YOU CARDS.
THE CONTRACTOR OF THE "KING OF HEARTS"!!
OZ AND THAT MAN ARE LOOKING FOR HIM.
SEE, THERE'S SOMEONE OZ HAS TO GET BACK FROM THAT CONTRACTOR FELLOW.

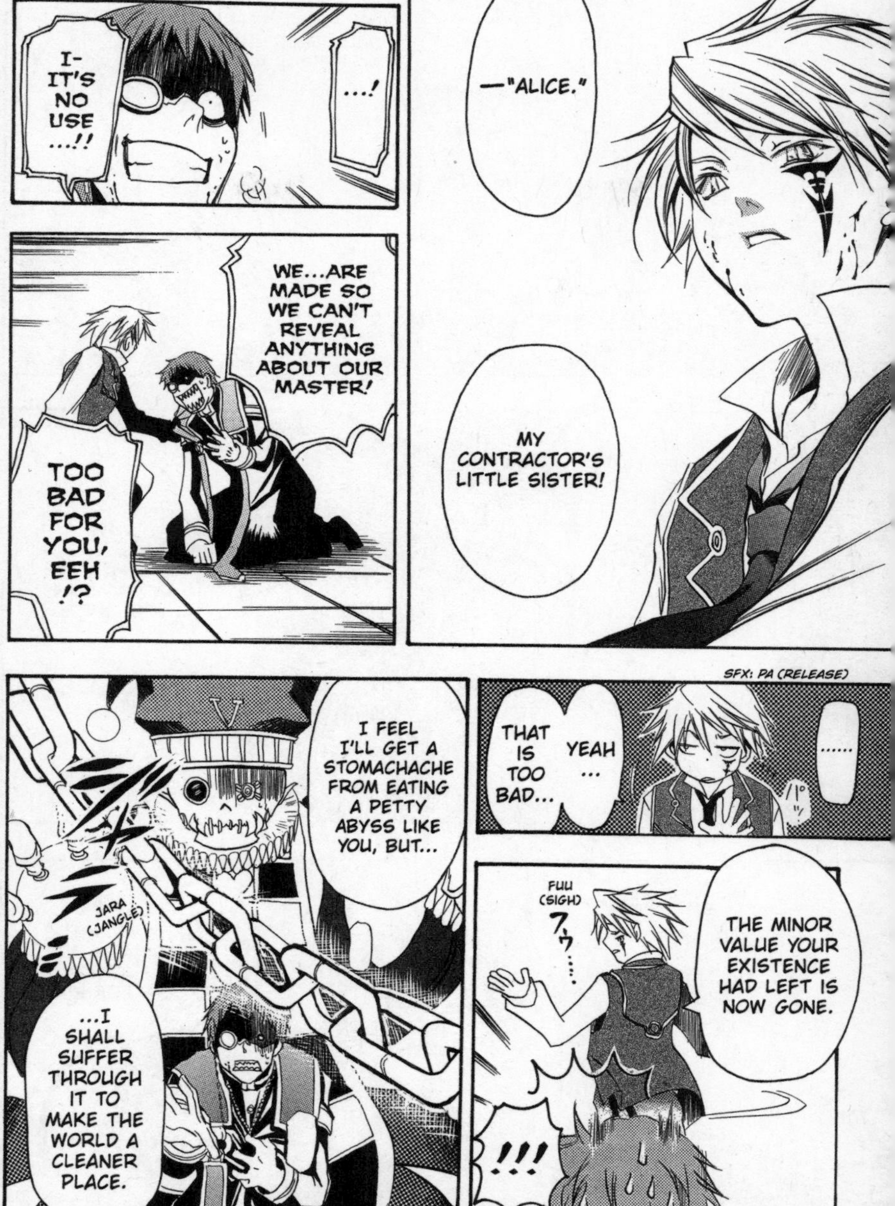

—"ALICE."
MY CONTRACTOR'S LITTLE SISTER!
...!
I- IT'S NO USE...!!
WE...ARE MADE SO WE CAN'T REVEAL ANYTHING ABOUT OUR MASTER!
TOO BAD FOR YOU, EEH!?
SFX: PA (RELEASE)
......
YEAH...
THAT IS TOO BAD...
FUU (SIGH)
THE MINOR VALUE YOUR EXISTENCE HAD LEFT IS NOW GONE.
!!!
I FEEL I'LL GET A STOMACHACHE FROM EATING A PETTY ABYSS LIKE YOU, BUT...
JARA (JANGLE)
...I SHALL SUFFER THROUGH IT TO MAKE THE WORLD A CLEANER PLACE.

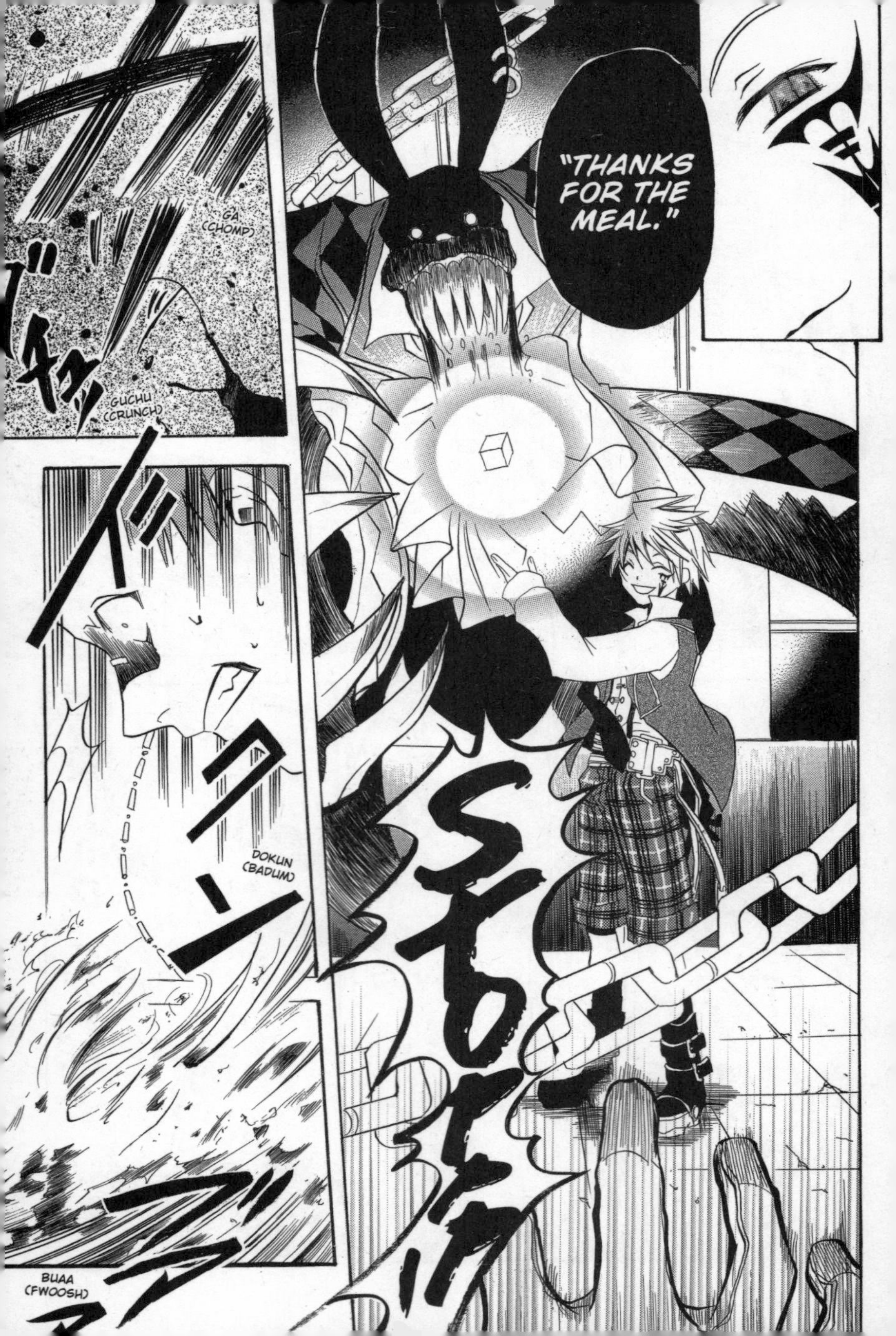
"THANKS FOR THE MEAL."
GA (CHOMP)
GUCHU (CRUNCH)
DOKUN (BADUM)
BUAA (FWOOSH)

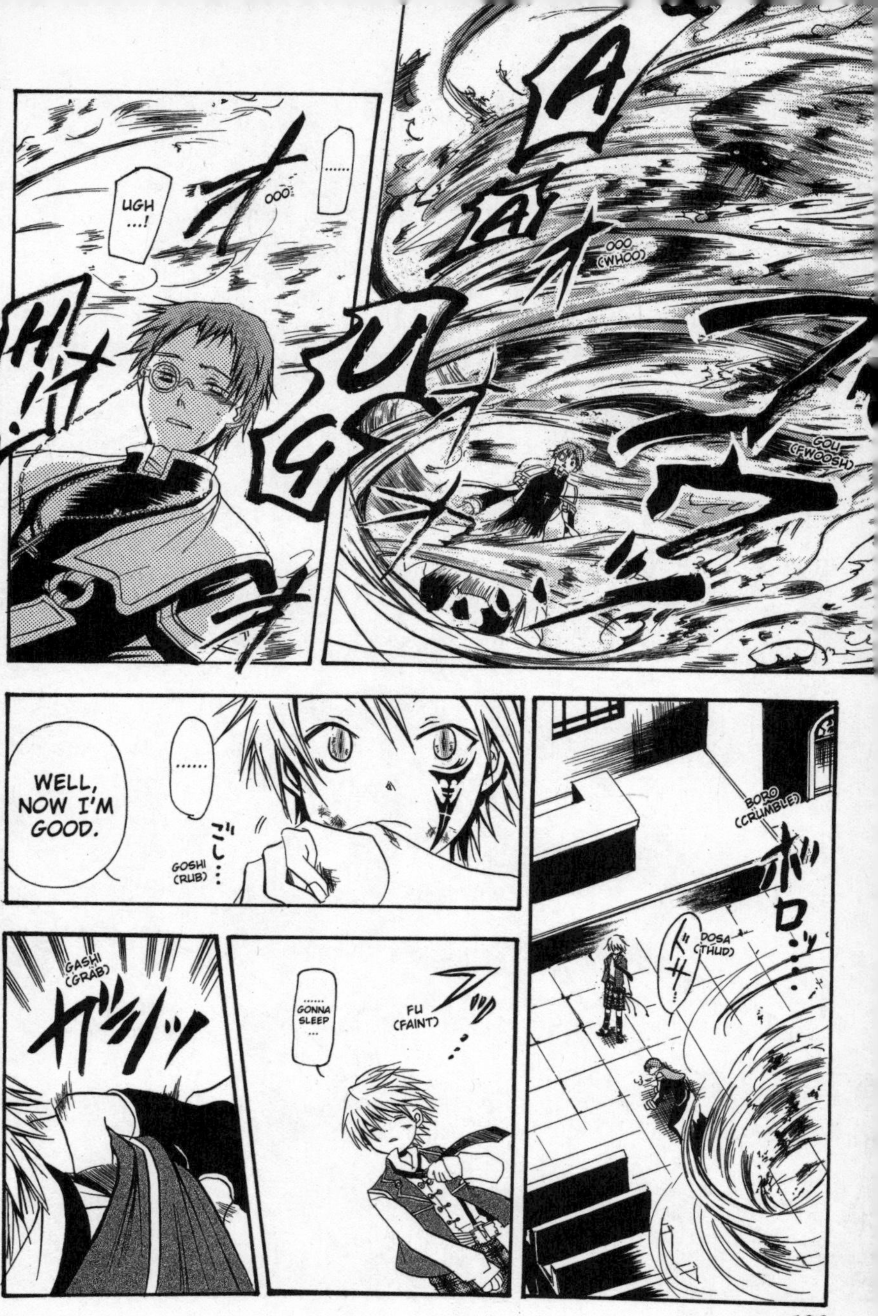
OOO (WHOO)
GOU (FWOOSH)
UG
......
UGH ...!
OOO
H!!
BORO (CRUMBLE)
DOSA (THUD)
......
WELL, NOW I'M GOOD.
GOSHI (RUB)...
...... GONNA SLEEP ...
FU (FAINT)
GASHI (GRAB)

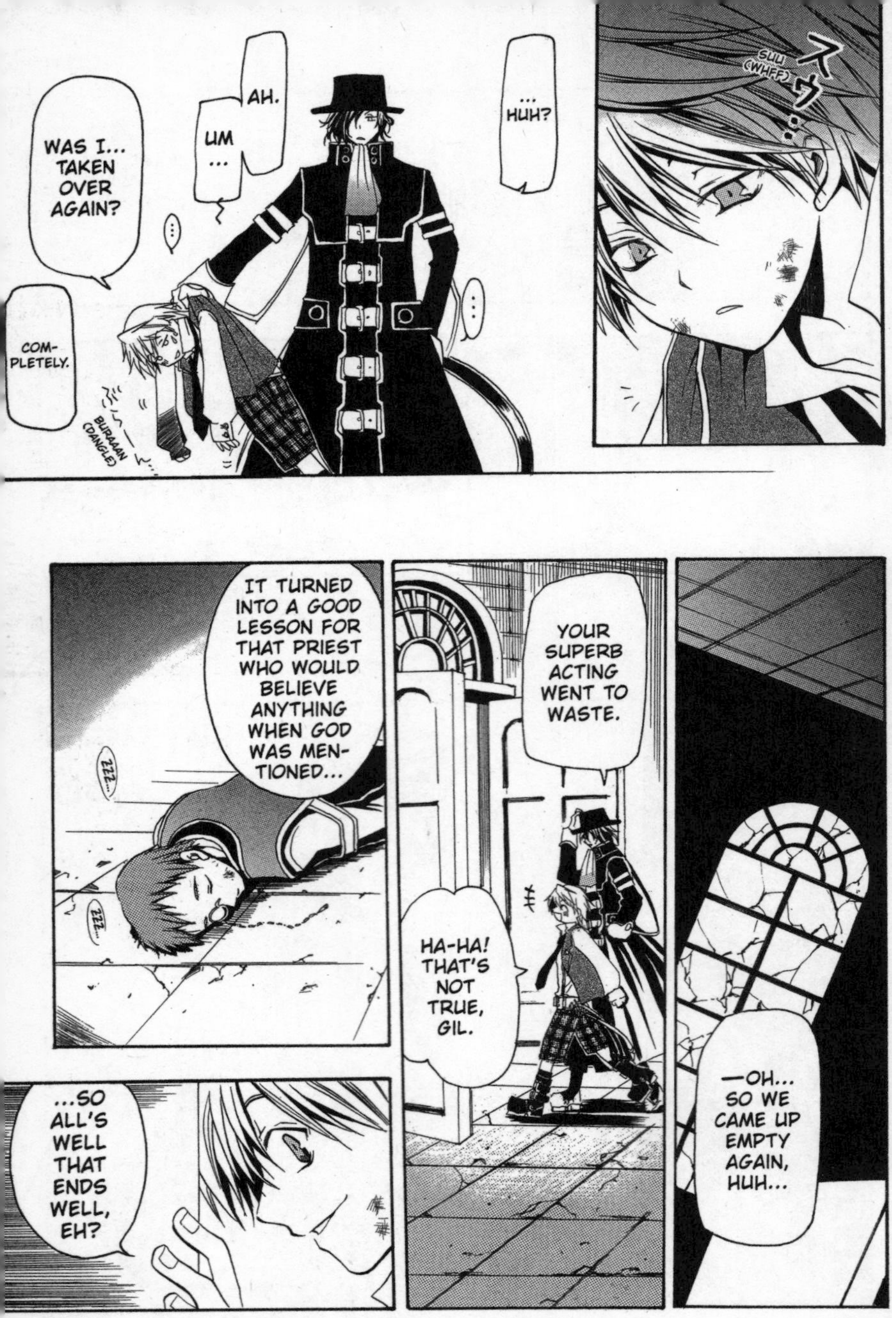
SUU (WHFF)
...HUH?
AH.
UM ...
...
WAS I... TAKEN OVER AGAIN?
...
COM-PLETELY.
BURAAN (DANGLE)
—OH... SO WE CAME UP EMPTY AGAIN, HUH...
YOUR SUPERB ACTING WENT TO WASTE.
HA-HA! THAT'S NOT TRUE, GIL.
IT TURNED INTO A GOOD LESSON FOR THAT PRIEST WHO WOULD BELIEVE ANYTHING WHEN GOD WAS MEN-TIONED...
ZZZ...
ZZZ...
...SO ALL'S WELL THAT ENDS WELL, EH?

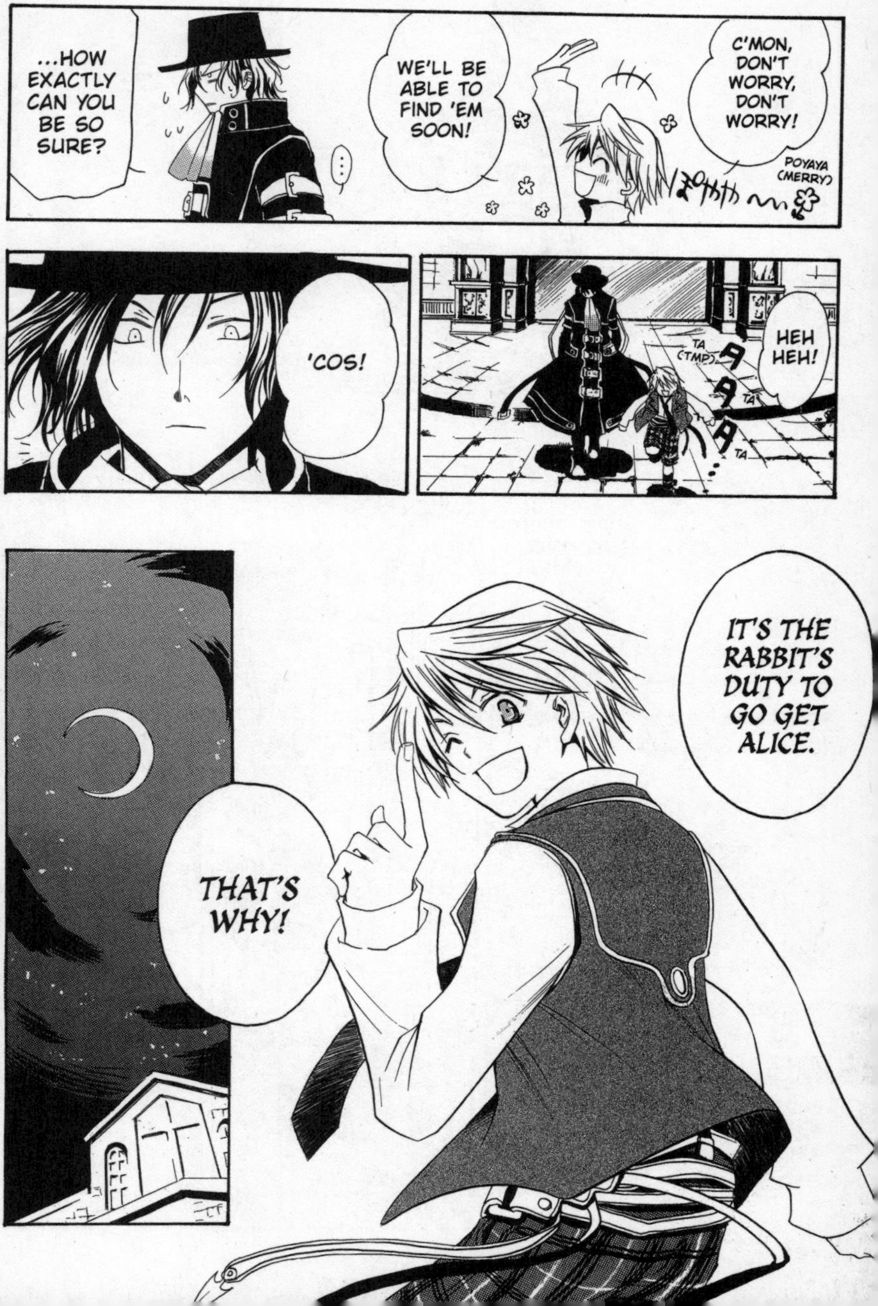
C'MON, DON'T WORRY, DON'T WORRY!
POYAYA (MERRY)
WE'LL BE ABLE TO FIND 'EM SOON!
...
...HOW EXACTLY CAN YOU BE SO SURE?
HEH HEH!
TA (TMP)
TA
TA
'COS!
IT'S THE RABBIT'S DUTY TO GO GET ALICE.
THAT'S WHY!

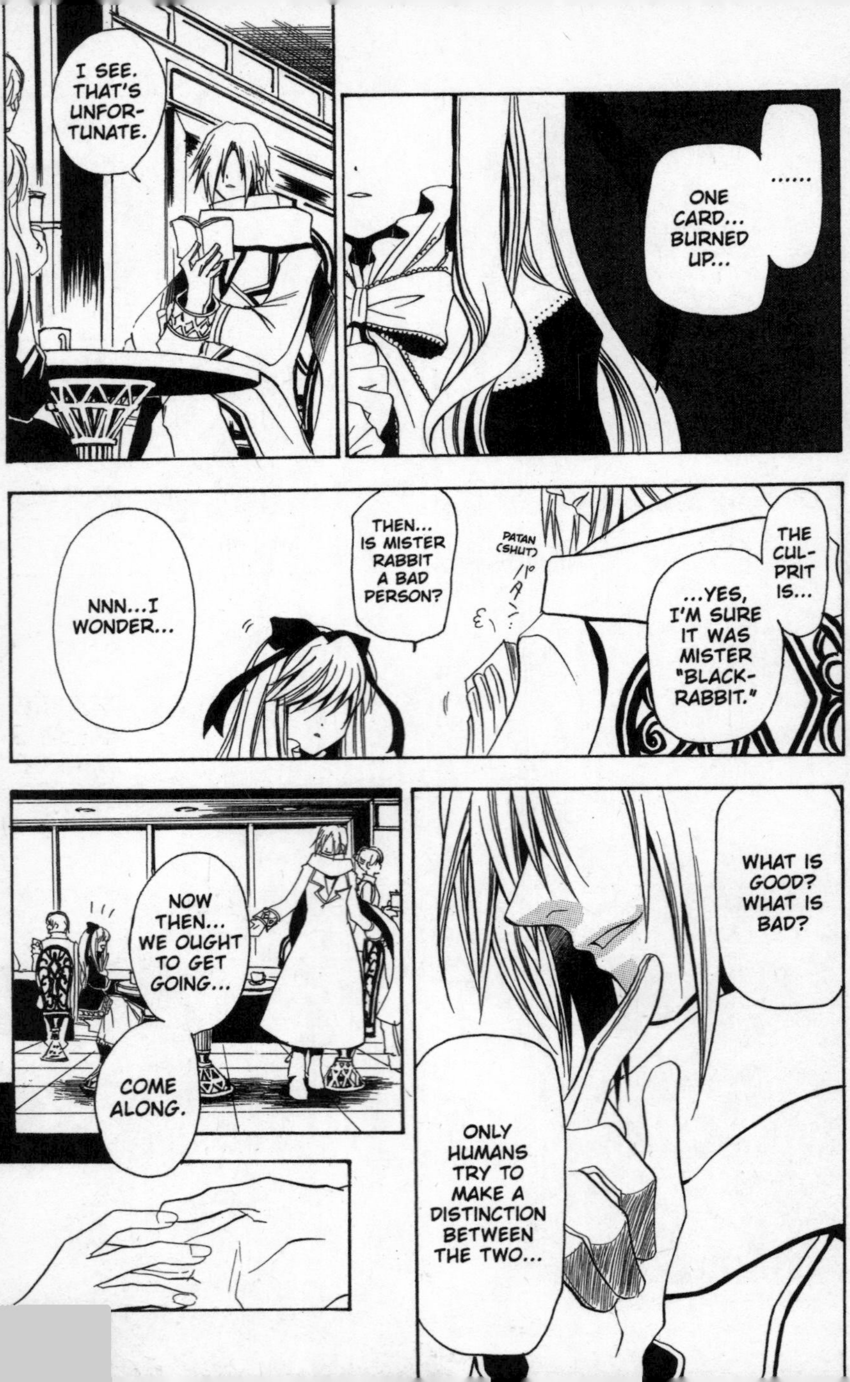
......
ONE CARD... BURNED UP...
I SEE. THAT'S UNFORTUNATE.
THE CULPRIT IS...
...YES, I'M SURE IT WAS MISTER "BLACK-RABBIT."
PATAN (SHUT)
THEN... IS MISTER RABBIT A BAD PERSON?
NNN...I WONDER...
WHAT IS GOOD? WHAT IS BAD?
ONLY HUMANS TRY TO MAKE A DISTINCTION BETWEEN THE TWO...
NOW THEN... WE OUGHT TO GET GOING...
COME ALONG.

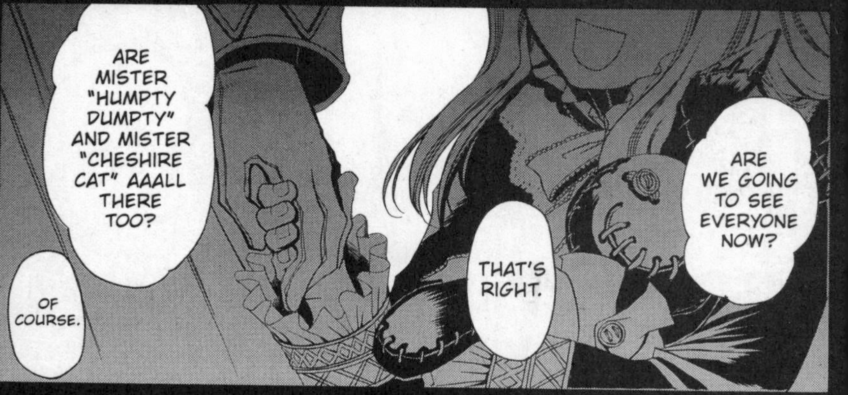
ARE WE GOING TO SEE EVERYONE NOW?
THAT'S RIGHT.
ARE MISTER "HUMPTY DUMPTY" AND MISTER "CHESHIRE CAT" AAALL THERE TOO?
OF COURSE.

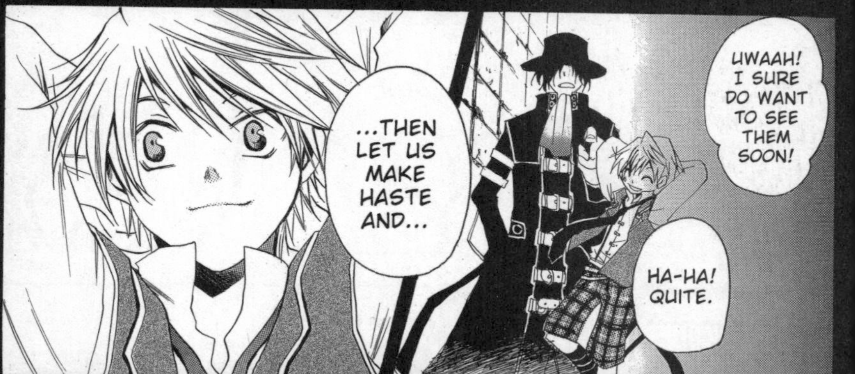
UWAAH! I SURE DO WANT TO SEE THEM SOON!
HA-HA! QUITE.
...THEN LET US MAKE HASTE AND...

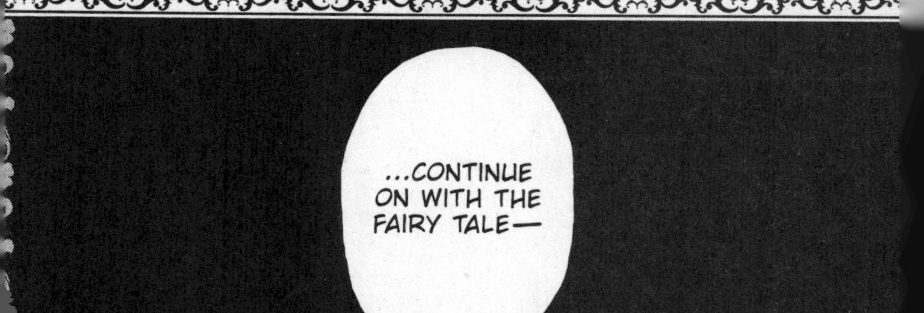
...CONTINUE ON WITH THE FAIRY TALE—

TO BE CONTINUED IN PANDORA HEARTS 9

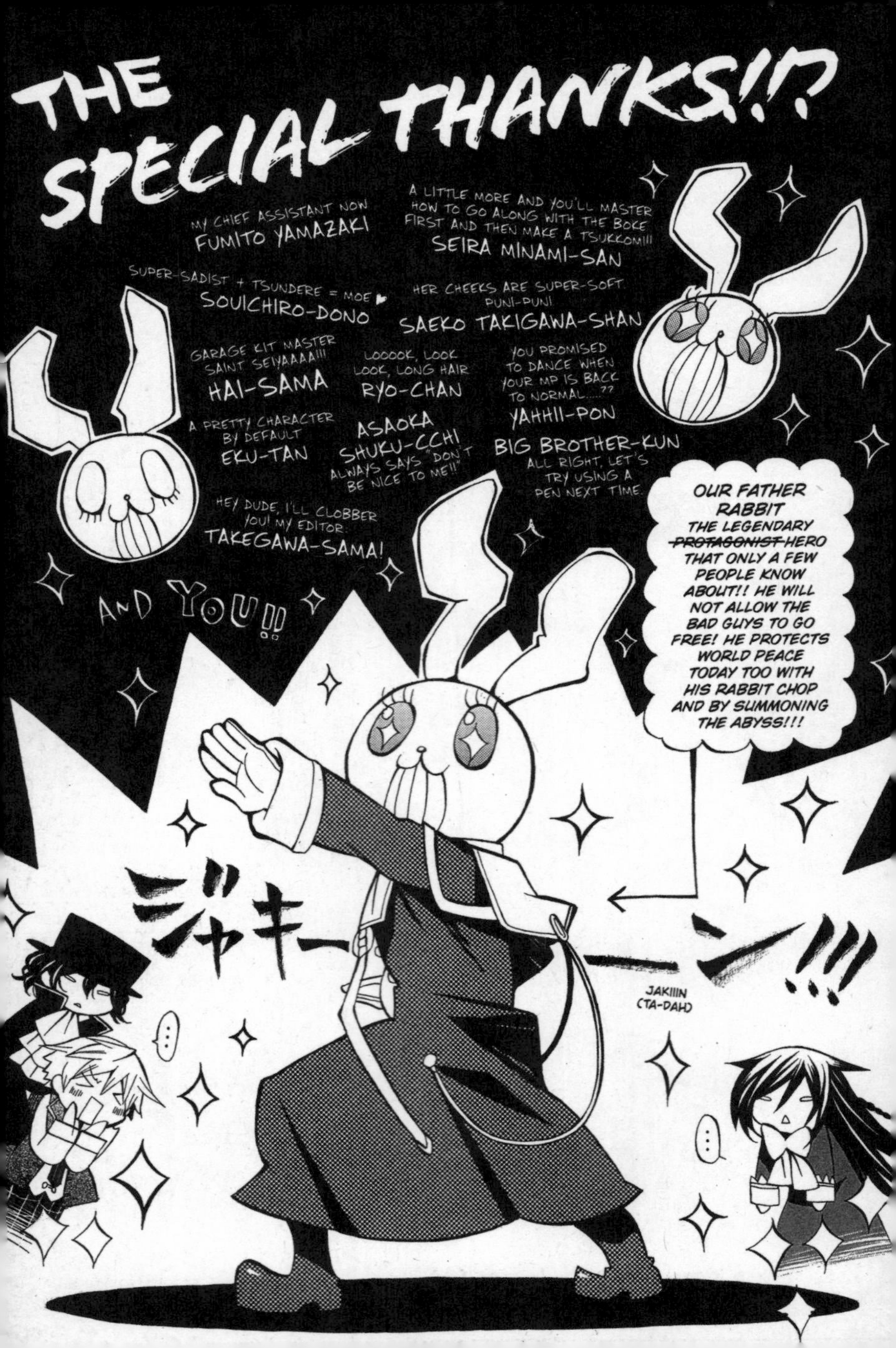
THE SPECIAL THANKS!?
MY CHIEF ASSISTANT NOW
FUMITO YAMAZAKI
A LITTLE MORE AND YOU'LL MASTER HOW TO GO ALONG WITH THE BOKE FIRST AND THEN MAKE A TSUKKOMI!!
SEIRA MINAMI-SAN
SUPER-SADIST + TSUNDERE = MOE ♥
SOUICHIRO-DONO
HER CHEEKS ARE SUPER-SOFT PUNI-PUNI.
SAEKO TAKIGAWA-SHAN
GARAGE KIT MASTER SAINT SEIYAAAA!!!
HAI-SAMA
LOOOOK, LOOK LOOK, LONG HAIR
RYO-CHAN
YOU PROMISED TO DANCE WHEN YOUR MP IS BACK TO NORMAL.....??
YAHHII-PON
A PRETTY CHARACTER BY DEFAULT
EKU-TAN
ASAOKA SHUKU-CCHI
ALWAYS SAYS "DON'T BE NICE TO ME!!"
BIG BROTHER-KUN
ALL RIGHT, LET'S TRY USING A PEN NEXT TIME.
HEY DUDE, I'LL CLOBBER YOU! MY EDITOR:
TAKEGAWA-SAMA!
AND YOU!!
OUR FATHER RABBIT THE LEGENDARY ~~PROTAGONIST~~ HERO THAT ONLY A FEW PEOPLE KNOW ABOUT!! HE WILL NOT ALLOW THE BAD GUYS TO GO FREE! HE PROTECTS WORLD PEACE TODAY TOO WITH HIS RABBIT CHOP AND BY SUMMONING THE ABYSS!!!
ジャキーーン!!!
JAKIIIN (TA-DAH)
...
...

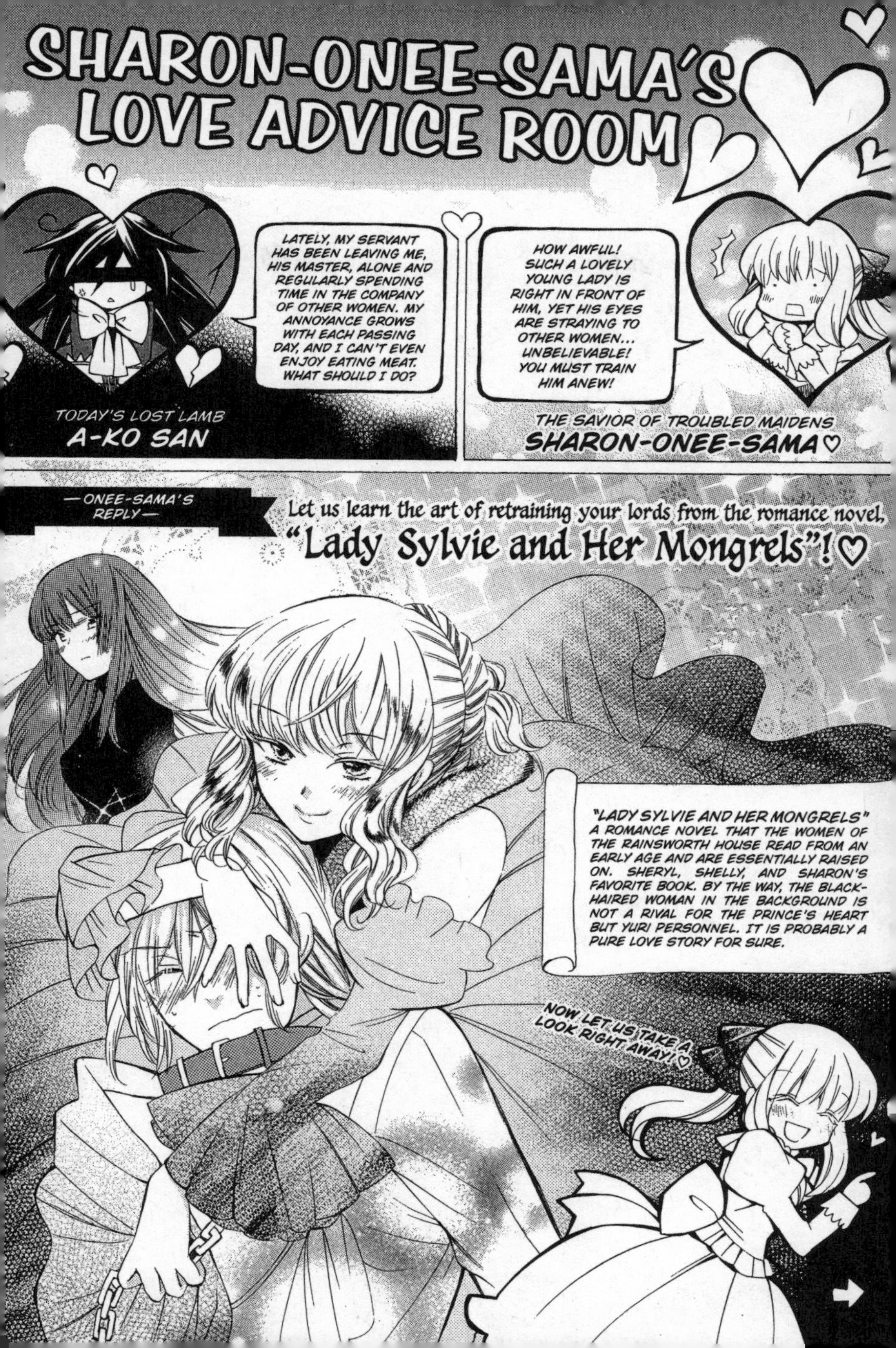
SHARON-ONEE-SAMA'S LOVE ADVICE ROOM
LATELY, MY SERVANT HAS BEEN LEAVING ME, HIS MASTER, ALONE AND REGULARLY SPENDING TIME IN THE COMPANY OF OTHER WOMEN. MY ANNOYANCE GROWS WITH EACH PASSING DAY, AND I CAN'T EVEN ENJOY EATING MEAT. WHAT SHOULD I DO?
TODAY'S LOST LAMB
A-KO SAN
HOW AWFUL! SUCH A LOVELY YOUNG LADY IS RIGHT IN FRONT OF HIM, YET HIS EYES ARE STRAYING TO OTHER WOMEN... UNBELIEVABLE! YOU MUST TRAIN HIM ANEW!
THE SAVIOR OF TROUBLED MAIDENS
SHARON-ONEE-SAMA♡
—ONEE-SAMA'S REPLY—
Let us learn the art of retraining your lords from the romance novel, "Lady Sylvie and Her Mongrels"!♡
"LADY SYLVIE AND HER MONGRELS" A ROMANCE NOVEL THAT THE WOMEN OF THE RAINSWORTH HOUSE READ FROM AN EARLY AGE AND ARE ESSENTIALLY RAISED ON. SHERYL, SHELLY, AND SHARON'S FAVORITE BOOK. BY THE WAY, THE BLACK-HAIRED WOMAN IN THE BACKGROUND IS NOT A RIVAL FOR THE PRINCE'S HEART BUT YURI PERSONNEL. IT IS PROBABLY A PURE LOVE STORY FOR SURE.
NOW LET US TAKE A LOOK RIGHT AWAY!♡

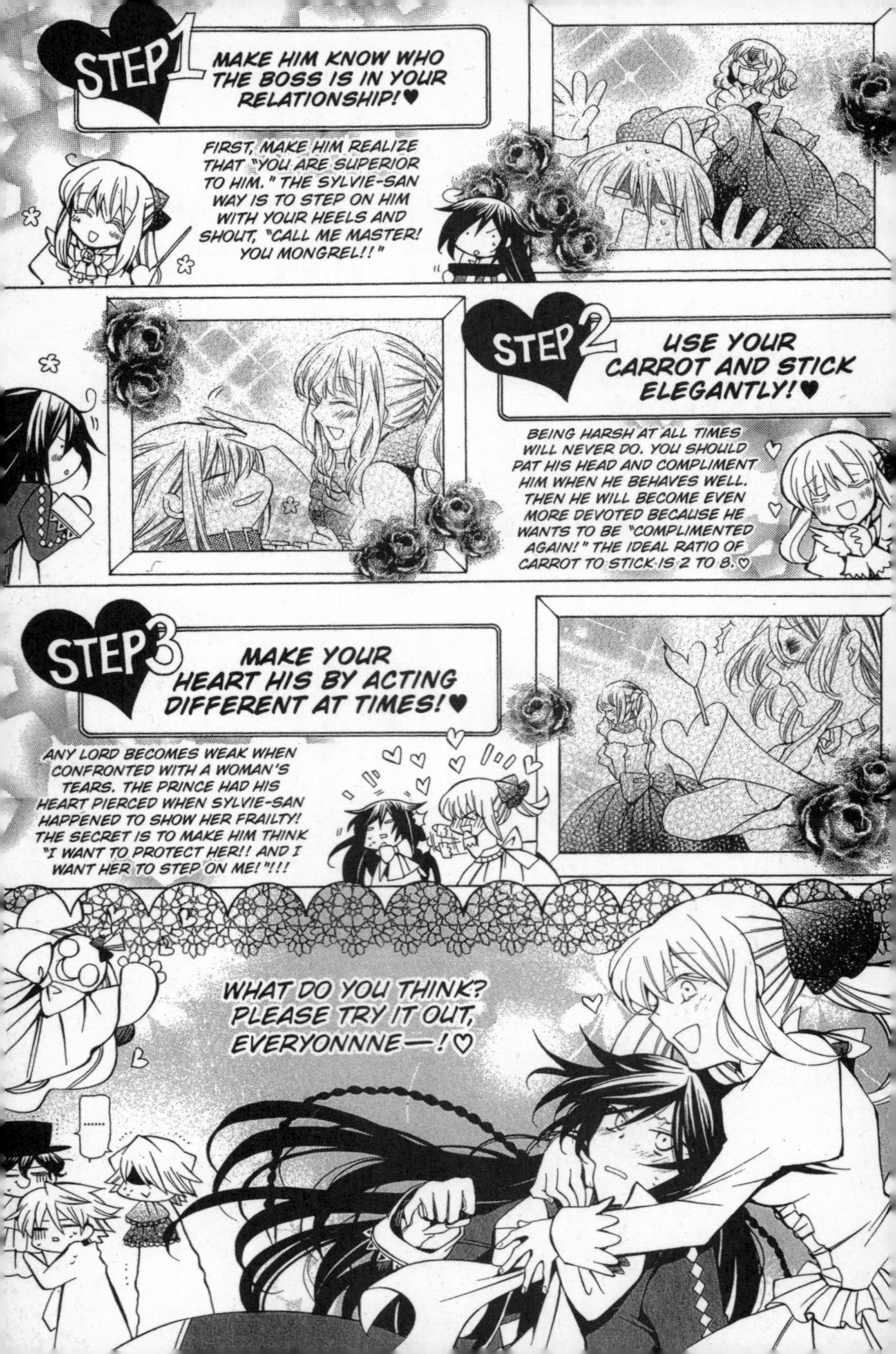
STEP 1
MAKE HIM KNOW WHO THE BOSS IS IN YOUR RELATIONSHIP!♥
FIRST, MAKE HIM REALIZE THAT "YOU ARE SUPERIOR TO HIM." THE SYLVIE-SAN WAY IS TO STEP ON HIM WITH YOUR HEELS AND SHOUT, "CALL ME MASTER! YOU MONGREL!!"
STEP 2
USE YOUR CARROT AND STICK ELEGANTLY!♥
BEING HARSH AT ALL TIMES WILL NEVER DO. YOU SHOULD PAT HIS HEAD AND COMPLIMENT HIM WHEN HE BEHAVES WELL. THEN HE WILL BECOME EVEN MORE DEVOTED BECAUSE HE WANTS TO BE "COMPLIMENTED AGAIN!" THE IDEAL RATIO OF CARROT TO STICK IS 2 TO 8.♡
STEP 3
MAKE YOUR HEART HIS BY ACTING DIFFERENT AT TIMES!♥
ANY LORD BECOMES WEAK WHEN CONFRONTED WITH A WOMAN'S TEARS. THE PRINCE HAD HIS HEART PIERCED WHEN SYLVIE-SAN HAPPENED TO SHOW HER FRAILTY! THE SECRET IS TO MAKE HIM THINK "I WANT TO PROTECT HER!! AND I WANT HER TO STEP ON ME!"!!!
WHAT DO YOU THINK? PLEASE TRY IT OUT, EVERYONNNE—!♡
......

COMMON HONORIFICS

no honorific: Indicates familiarity or closeness; if used without permission or reason, addressing someone in this manner would constitute an insult.

-san: The Japanese equivalent of Mr./Mrs./Miss. If a situation calls for politeness, this is the fail-safe honorific.

-sama: Conveys great respect; may also indicate that the social status of the speaker is lower than that of the addressee.

-kun: Used most often when referring to boys (though it can be applied to girls as well), this indicates affection or familiarity. Occasionally used by older men among their peers, but it may also be used by anyone referring to a person of lower standing.

-chan: An affectionate honorific indicating familiarity used mostly in reference to girls; also used in reference to cute persons or animals of either gender.

Hannya
page 60

The frightening face behind the Duchess is a Hannya mask, a Noh mask with the face of a female demon.

boke
page 201

In Japanese manzai comedy duos, the more simple-minded of the two individuals is known as the *boke*.

PandoraHearts

This year I would really love to go to Great Britain. I'd also like to go all over Europe to Italy, France, Germany and immerse myself in fantasy worlds!! Just imagining it makes me very happy. Hyahhoo!

MOCHIZUKI'S MUSINGS

VOLUME 8

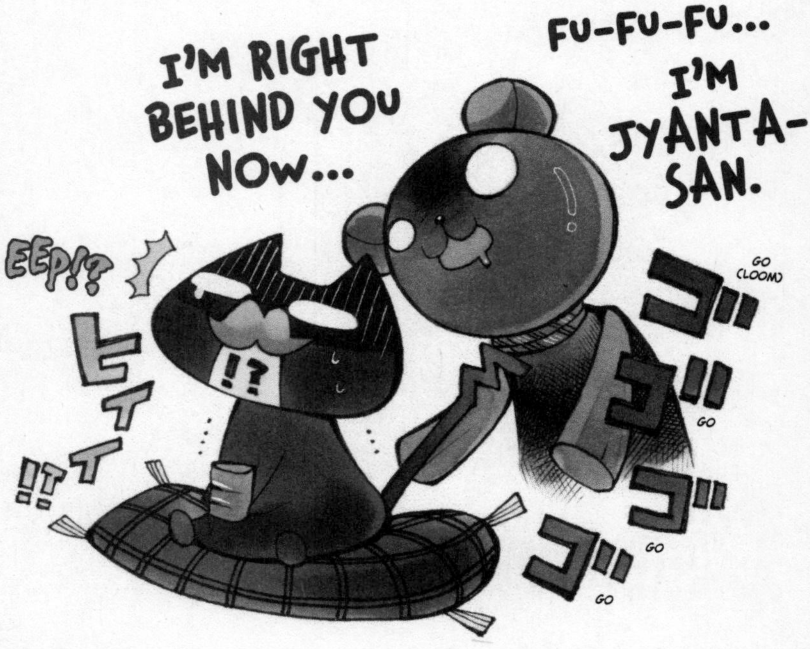
FU-FU-FU... I'M JYANTA-SAN.
I'M RIGHT BEHIND YOU NOW...
GO (LOOM)
GO
GO
GO
EEP!?

PandoraHearts

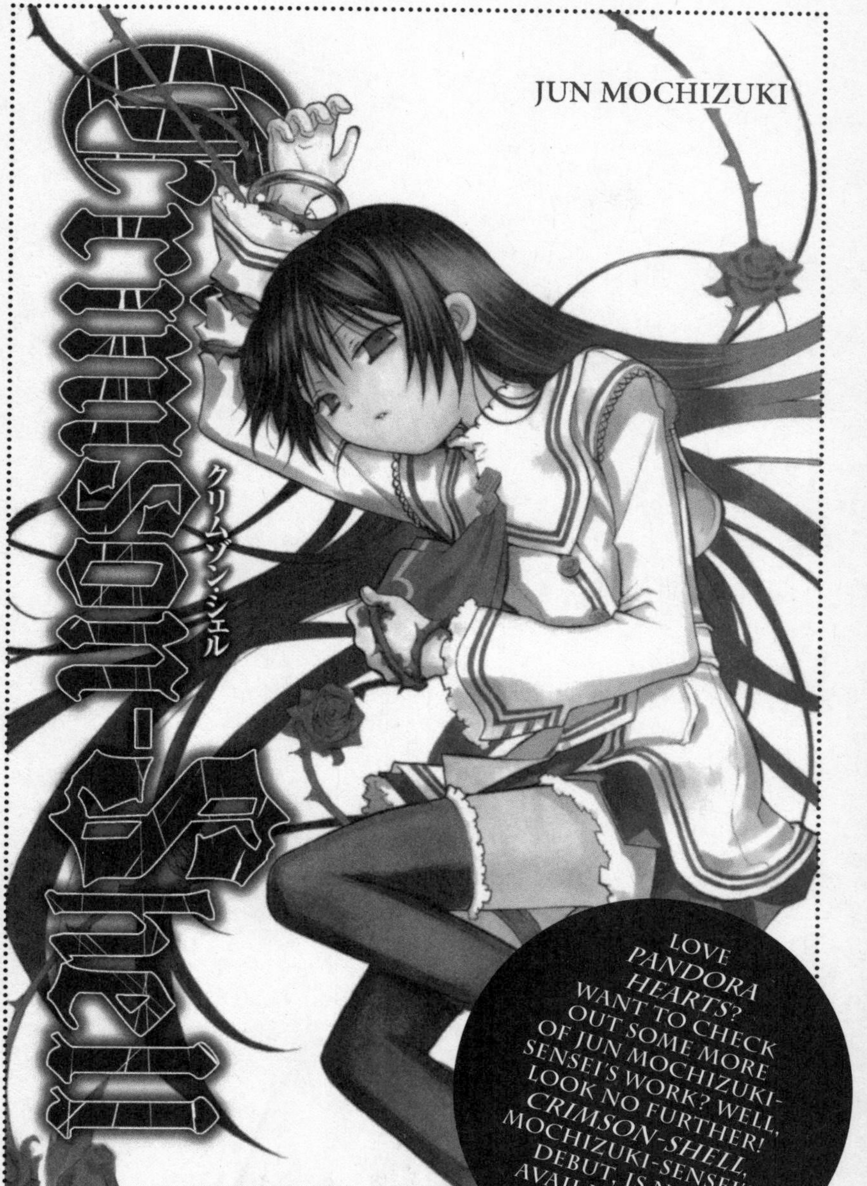
JUN MOCHIZUKI
Crimson-Shell
クリムゾン・シェル
LOVE *PANDORA HEARTS*? WANT TO CHECK OUT SOME MORE OF JUN MOCHIZUKI-SENSEI'S WORK? WELL, LOOK NO FURTHER! *CRIMSON-SHELL*, MOCHIZUKI-SENSEI'S DEBUT, IS NOW AVAILABLE FROM YEN PRESS!

PandoraHearts

PANDORA HEARTS 8

JUN MOCHIZUKI

Translation: Tomo Kimura • Lettering: Alexis Eckerman

PANDORA HEARTS Vol. 8 © 2009 Jun Mochizuki / SQUARE ENIX CO., LTD. All rights reserved. First published in Japan in 2009 by SQUARE ENIX CO., LTD. English translation rights arranged with SQUARE ENIX CO., LTD. and Yen Press, LLC through Tuttle-Mori Agency, Inc.

English translation © 2012 by SQUARE ENIX CO., LTD.

Yen Press
1290 Avenue of the Americas
New York, NY 10104

Visit us at yenpress.com
facebook.com/yenpress
twitter.com/yenpress
yenpress.tumblr.com

First Yen Press Edition: January 2012

Yen Press is an imprint of Yen Press, LLC.
The Yen Press name and logo are trademarks of Yen Press, LLC.

The publisher is not responsible for websites (or their content) that are not owned by the publisher.

ISBN: 978-0-316-19725-0

10 9

BVG

Printed in the United States of America